THE MINERS

IN CRISIS AND WAR

ROBERT SMILLIE

PRESIDENT, MINERS' FEDERATION OF GREAT BRITAIN, 1912–21
(AND FULL-TIME PERMANENT OFFICIAL 1919–21)

From an oil painting by A. MENDOZA (1920)

THE MINERS

IN CRISIS AND WAR

*A History of the Miners' Federation
of Great Britain
(from 1930 onwards)*

BY

R. PAGE ARNOT

GEORGE ALLEN & UNWIN LTD

RUSKIN HOUSE · MUSEUM STREET · LONDON

PRINTED IN GREAT BRITAIN
in 12 point Baskerville type
BY UNWIN BROTHERS LIMITED
WOKING AND LONDON

FOREWORD

THIS volume of the history of the miners is rich with lessons for present-day miners and, in fact, for workers outside the mining industry. It covers the period from 1930 to 1944, during which we were faced with an economic crisis at home and an even deadlier crisis throughout the world.

The economic crisis led to mass unemployment with all the consequent suffering that follows in its train. Our people suffered almost beyond belief. Mining villages were centres of desolation, pits closed, and no alternative occupation anywhere near. If young miners will ask their fathers or grandfathers they will hear stories of hardship and hunger which we must see never descend on our mining communities again.

Throughout this period the Miners' Federation was battling with all the power it possessed, to protect, so far as was humanly possible, our people in this desperate situation.

One issue that is of special interest at the present time was the fight for a National Agreement. Each generation, we are often told, must learn from its own experience, but while there is truth in this, it is also true that each generation can learn much from preceding generations. And this question of a National Agreement, in face of insistence of the mine-owners on separate District Agreements, has an important lesson for us today.

In the international field, the rise of Fascism and Nazism brought to Europe and the world the dread menace of a Second World War. You will see in this volume how strenuously the miners sought to avert that terrible disaster; they must strive with even greater zeal in the new dangerous situation that menaces their lives, their homes and their families.

To tell this story we are fortunate in having as writer one who has not only a grasp of the essential processes of history and of historical struggles, but who can relate the complicated and detailed annals of the colliers to their background in national and international events. Quite apart from his sustained power of writing and his vivid portrayal of the clash of personalities, Mr. Arnot is outstanding amongst trade union historians in that he himself has played a part in the events which he describes, and has been linked with our trade union activities since he was associated with Robert Smillie in the First World War. He worked with us at the time of the Sankey Commission in 1919, writing *Facts from the Coal Commission* and *Further Facts*; and helped in the preparation of our case in many subsequent inquiries.

The reader will also see the arduous and hazardous nature of the miners' occupation. There is still "Blood on the Coal."

We are proud to be the successors of the men and their leaders who battled through such perilous and trying times and to have the opportunity of presenting a further volume of this history of the mine-workers of Great Britain.

W. Ernest Jones   *President*

E. Jones   *Vice-President*

Will Paynter   *Secretary*

National Union of Mineworkers

April 10, 1960

PREFACE

THE original intention for this work was that it should cover a stretch of twenty years from the last months of the Ramsay MacDonald administration of 1929–31 to the end of the Attlee administration which carried through the Coal Industry Nationalisation Act and administered the first five years of its operation. But it proved impossible to set out all the events of that score of years within short compass and the resulting volume would have proved too bulky and too high-priced—especially as I had been asked to add supplementary chapters. It therefore seemed better to leave to a further volume the events of 1945 onwards and to survey in it the history of what was now become a single national trade union under conditions of State ownership. This has the advantage that after a decade and a half it is more easy to get a view of the significance of what has happened than when the events were nearly contemporaneous, and it will therefore be possible in a year or two to see more clearly the effect upon the industry of the changes that followed the ending of coal shortage in 1957 and the irruption of oil into the fuel and power market.

This volume therefore deals with the shorter stretch of years from the end of 1930 to the opening of 1945. These were mainly years of crisis. They began with a crisis of the whole economy, falling with particular severity upon the coal-mining industry, and ended with the crisis of war.

Just as the subsequent change to complete State ownership might seem like a reversion on a millenary scale to the State ownership of the mines in Roman Britain when primitive workings were wrought under licence (as today is the case with the lesser mines under the National Coal Board), so in the much briefer history of trade unionism the formation of the National Union of Mineworkers in 1944 might seem to revert to the Miners' Association of Great Britain and Ireland of 1841 when Chartism was still in the ascendant. But the resemblance in each case is only superficial. In the mediaeval and modern history of the British coal industry since the first pits were being dug about the time of Magna Charta, there are over three centuries where little is known, and perhaps little is knowable. As coal output extended and increased fourteenfold in the century and more between the birth of Francis Bacon and the revolution of 1688, there is an immense amount of historical research still to be tackled following upon the pioneer work of J. U. Nef. There is here a challenge to the National Coal Board to do better than their predecessors by setting up an historical section or in some other way

A*

playing their part as custodians of the past of the great industry for which they are now responsible. Again in the two hundred years since the revolt of the pitmen on the Tyne and Wear there is a trade union field which the newly-formed Society for the Study of Labour History may plough with profit to all.

To all earlier attempts at national organisation the Miners' Federation of Great Britain (1889–1944) was the successor. From the beginning it was federal. It felt itself to be in the position, or to have the potentiality, of linking up over the whole island the county associations which had by that time reached the stage of what Beatrice and Sidney Webb defined in 1894 as "a continuous association of wage-earners for the purpose of maintaining or improving the conditions of their employment." Maintenance was centred upon wages: improvement upon hours of labour underground and safety. Wages were maintained, or very nearly so, in the difficult years of the 'nineties. After twenty years of persistent campaigns the miners gained the nominal Eight Hours Act, which was in operation from 1909 to 1919. But it was not until 1908 that they were able to bring the miners' unions of all the coal-fields within their federal structure. Nor were they then able to achieve the single National Conciliation Board that so many of them had striven for in the early years of this century: this objective, together with the long-desired Ministry of Mines, was to be achieved only under the pressures of world war.

By 1911 there were over a million wage-earners in the coal and shale mines of Great Britain. By 1921 there were a million and a quarter. Out of every 10,000 occupied males aged ten years and upwards in Great Britain, no less than 947 were in the mining industry. The total number of households that this represented is unknown, but with the much larger families of those days, it is clear that the mining community at that time cannot have numbered much less than five million all told, or more than a tenth of the total population of the island. There were more colliers and their families in Great Britain than there were Danes in Denmark.

Just as the mining community was a very large part of the total population so the miners' unions, now all united under the Miners' Federation of Great Britain, comprised a high proportion of the number employed, with a membership that was to reach 945,487 in 1920. The quality of that trade unionism was soon to undergo a change. The miners united became the miners militant. For a period of fifteen years from 1911 there was growing tension between employers and wage-earners. The miners were making a determined effort not only to maintain their conditions, but to gain a marked

improvement in wages and hours, while their old desire for nationalisation became an immediate claim that was put forward in the shape
of a parliamentary Bill. These fifteen years were marked by bitterly
contested industrial struggles. There were two great strikes, in 1912
and 1920; and two great lock-outs, in 1921 and 1926. Royal Commissions and Courts of Inquiry wrought at the problems of the
industry: and the attention of governments and parliaments was
centred on the coal-mining industry for weeks on end.

The years 1927 to 1930 marked a great change alike in the
beginning of the technological transformation of coal-mining and
in the relative position of the two sides of the industry. Trade
unionism was weakened by the crippling effect of the Trade Disputes
and Trade Unions Act of 1927: and the Miners' Federation lost its
cohesion very largely when it was deprived of its function in wage
negotiations. Mass unemployment had become a permanent feature
of the industrial scene, and nowhere more than in the coal-fields.
Wages were low and the nominal Seven Hour Act passed in 1919
had lasted only seven years: the shift was back to eight and a half
hours underground. But though the horizon was dark, the miners
perceived a ray of hope in the existence of the second Labour
Government which they had helped to return in the General Election
of 1929, and through which they had hoped to get rid of the lengthened hours of labour and otherwise retrieve their lost conditions. It
is at this point, at the end of 1930, that this volume begins.

In the compilation of it I have relied mainly on the voluminous
records of the Miners' Federation of Great Britain, with occasional
use of District minutes. In dealing with this mass of material, which
tends to grow greater with successive years (a recent minute of a
monthly meeting of the National Executive Committee of the
National Union of Mineworkers runs, with Annexes, Appendices
and Reports of sub-committees, to seventy-eight closely printed
pages), I have had the difficult task of selection of what seemed
significant for the mainstream of development. I have had to leave
out much that might find place in a fuller chronicle, but need not
here be particularised. Of these necessary omissions from this volume
there is one which I would have preferred to include, namely, the
question of Health and Safety with which at all times in this dark
and dangerous trade the Miners' Federation was very closely
concerned. But the magnitude of this subject has grown to a point
where it was impossible to include it in what was already a sufficiently
large book. I hope to deal with it in another volume and have here
limited myself to dealing with the causes and consequences of
the one great disaster that occurred in these years. Some may be

disappointed not to find a treatment of the capital structure of the industry; or of its techniques and markets, with its product channelled to domestic consumers through some twenty thousand merchants; or the detail of annual festivals or of particular struggles that involved the Districts. But it was never my intention to cope with any of these. Other books have been and will be written on these subjects, and the more histories of the old county associations that are written, the better. This history deals only with the mainstream of the national body representing the British miners. I have tried wherever possible to picture events as mirrored in their own outlook and in their own words either in resolutions, minutes or speeches: content in this to follow Richard Fynes of Blyth. In his history of 1873, *The Miners of Northumberland and Durham*, he wrote: "Wherever such has been possible, I have made the actors in those scenes tell their own tales by quoting largely from the speeches made by them."

I have had the advantage throughout of acquaintance with many of the leading figures in the coal-fields and I have to thank all the past and present members of the Federation or of the National Union for their courtesy and helpfulness. I have also to thank the many friends who have helped, and if I single out the great assistance of the staffs of the Labour Research Department, it is partly because of the excellence of their records, and partly for old time's sake. I hope, however, to put detailed acknowledgements in another volume.

R. PAGE ARNOT.

45 Fitzroy Road, London, N.W.1.
August 1, 1960.

CONTENTS

ACKNOWLEDGEMENTS

To the trustees and staff of the British Museum for their courtesy and help in the matter of books and periodical press.

To the National Coal Board for their courtesy and help in supplying illustrations facing pages 160, 161, 288, 289, 321.

To *Radio Times* Hulton Picture Library for their courtesy in supplying reproductions of the illustrations facing pages 32, 64, 65, 97, 128, 352.

To P.A.–Reuter Photos for permission to use the illustration facing page 320.

To Odhams Press for their courtesy in supplying reproduction of the illustration facing page 257.

ILLUSTRATIONS

CHAPTER I

WORLD ECONOMIC CRISIS

I. FOUL WEATHER

THE third and fourth decades of the twentieth century each began with an economic crisis that enveloped most of the world's population and affected nearly every trade and industry. But the crisis of the early 'thirties was much more serious and in its effects far more shattering than the crisis of 1920–21. In October of 1929 there had been a crash on the Stock Exchange in Wall Street, New York. This financial collapse marked the beginning of an economic crisis which spread from country to country and was interwoven with an agrarian crisis throughout the world. It was the deepest, widest and longest of all such crises. In one country after another, goods could no longer be sold. In the new kind of mechanised till, then coming into vogue, there was a red tab with the words "NO SALE": it became symbolic. The economic mechanism, if mechanism it was, had ceased to work effectively. Output was less everywhere, work diminished, prices fell: but prices did not fall fast enough or far enough to meet the needs of those who were out of work, but who though idle could still hunger and thirst. Moreover the fall in price of food crops and industrial crops brought ruin to the husbandmen. So the peasantry of five continents, making up the majority of mankind, could no longer purchase the tools made in the workshops of Europe and North America. Production in the United States fell by one-third; in Germany also by one-third; in France by a quarter. In Britain where for some ten years industry had been under a depression, production could not fall in the same proportion as in countries that had been enjoying "boom" conditions. Nevertheless it sank to some 14 per cent below this already low level. The crisis in the capitalist world appeared the sharper because of the contrast in the same years with the

Union of Soviet Socialist Republics, where industrial output doubled between 1929 and 1933 through the successful carrying out of the first Five Year Plan.

It was explained at the time by expert economists, many of whom had previously taken the view that there never again would be a crisis of over-production, that it was one of the periodic or cyclical crises which had occurred in frequent succession since the beginning of the nineteenth century and that it was bound to come to an end, after which things would be better than before. Those who in 1927–28 had been maintaining that prosperity in a continuous upward curve was assured by the beneficence of Henry Ford and others of his kind, at any rate in North America and Europe, now explained that progress would be in a curve that undulated up and down. These predictions, though much repeated in the press, brought little comfort to those who were out of work and for whom the chance of re-employment in their own industry appeared to depend upon an abstract argument. Least of all did it bring comfort to those whose lot fell in trades and industries where the future prospects were less rosy in actuality than theoretically they should have been.

Among such industries was the coal-mining industry of Great Britain. That industry, which sixty years earlier had produced more than half of the total coal output of the world and twenty years earlier had still produced a fourth, had now an output of little more than a fifth of the world's total. In the twenty years that had passed since 1910 the world output of coal had risen slowly by an average of hardly 1 per cent per decade. Within that rising global output British production was falling not only relatively but absolutely. The world production of coal was to go on rising for another thirty years, but the share of the United Kingdom was to be less and less. The reasons for this were fairly obvious and had been operating for some time. Other countries had been pulling up. Within Europe, France and Belgium, Holland and Poland had been advancing at a considerable pace, while the coal-mines of the Soviet Union had been going ahead by leaps and bounds after their temporary setback in the years of revolution, foreign intervention and civil war from 1917 to 1922.

Outside Europe and North America in one country after another coal was being found and developed.

Apart from the change in the relative position of the coal industry, there had been a steep fall in its export. In the zenith year of 1913 British output had been 287 million tons, of which 94 million tons had gone for export including foreign bunkers: it was a third part of the output: it was nearly one-tenth of all coal consumed in the world outside Britain. This huge export trade was not recovered after the 1914–18 war. There were many reasons for this, both economic and political. Amongst the political reasons was the decision of Britain and her allies in the Treaty of Versailles that Germany must pay reparations partly in free deliveries of coal. These went into former British markets. For example both in France and Italy the fall in imports of coal from Britain was nearly matched by deliveries of "reparations coal" from Germany. Throughout the 'twenties, Lloyd George and succeeding ministers responsible for this could sadly reflect

'Twas thine own genius gave the final blow.

But in the 'thirties, though reparations had ceased, exports were declining further and were soon to sink to less than a quarter of the diminished total output. Thus the huge coal exports which for a century had helped to maintain Britain's balance of payments became less and less available.

Three other main factors affected the consumption of coal. The first was the development of processes in such industries as iron and steel that enabled each ton of metal to be smelted with far less expenditure of coal; or in other industries where improved methods and improved appliances enabled the same energy or the same heat as measured in therms to be yielded by a less expenditure of coal. Second, in the importing countries of Europe the astonishingly high price charged to them for British coal in the period of 1914–18 and for a couple of years thereafter had hastened the resort to an alternative source of energy in natural or artificial waterfalls which in such countries as Switzerland, Norway and France meant in the long run a much decreased import of British coal. Thirdly, after the 1914–18 war which had enabled British ship-owners and British coal-merchants and coal-owners to thrive and wax fat on the needs of their European allies as well as the neutrals, the cessation of hostilities had compelled the magnates of the giant international oil trusts to look around for new uses and new markets in a situation where the feverish war consumption on land and air had fallen away. The result was an increasing substitution in one sphere after another of coal by oil. It had begun before 1914 with the conversion of a large portion of the British Navy, formerly driven on Welsh steam coal, to oil-burning under boilers. It was soon to be followed by the transatlantic liners. A further development that was well under way by the conclusion of the First World War was the growth of motor ships where diesel engines took the place of steam engines.

For all these reasons the coal industry had declined far from its zenith output of 1913 before the onset of the world economic crisis. In 1913 the output from 3,024 mines had been 287,430,000 tons of coal. A dozen years later the coal-fields were settling down (on the average of 1924, 1925, 1927 and 1928) to some 2,500 mines, of very varied size, producing annually 250 million tons of coal. Actually in 1927 there were just on a million men (998,000) employed in 2,569 mines producing 251 million tons with an annual output per man of 252 tons. With the crisis years there came a further steep fall:

Year	Number of mines at work	Production in million tons
1930	2,091	243·8
1931	1,958	219·4
1932	1,888	208·7
1933	1,782	207·1

Thus the economic crisis hit the coal-mining industry with particular severity. Its consequences form the background to the miners' history in the 'thirties of this century.

2. THE OWNERS OF THE COAL-MINES

The impact of the economic crisis upon the coal-mining industry was particularly severe for another reason than the loss of export or the erosion by other sources of energy and other fuels of coal's one-time unchallenged supremacy. This other reason was found in the peculiar structure of the capitalist ownership of the collieries. In the days of Britain's supremacy on the seven seas and in the markets of the world there had grown up very many hundreds of competing companies. Some had specific markets such as Baltic trade, Navy supplies, blast furnaces with coking coal; but even within these limited and special markets there was quite considerable competition subsisting between the owners. As the days of unchallenged supremacy slipped away into the past, little corresponding change took place in the ownership of the collieries. The Ruhr-Westphalian syndicate grew up in Germany and similar developments in amalgamation of competing interests and concentration of capital took place in other parts of the world, especially in the first quarter of the twentieth century. But in Britain the coal-owners as a whole seemed determined to remain in the mid-nineteenth century, as though they wished to be fossilised at the stage which most nearly corresponded to the abstract idea of a fully competitive commercial society. Hence the colliery owners tended to retain that highly individualistic outlook which, while it resisted common organisation, was also prone to resist direction from without. Yet they found themselves owners of partnerships or of limited liability companies in an industry where for nearly a hundred years there had been more and more intervention by the state and by parliament in the shape both of a growing body of positive legislation and of a whole train of Royal Commissions, parliamentary Select Committees and departmental Inquiries. It must have seemed all the more intolerable to men with this outlook than it would have seemed to a more modern type of capitalist in the newer industries. They complained against it bitterly. From the time when Lord Londonderry had fought to the end in the House of Lords against the first effective Coal Mines Regulation Act of 1842, successive generations of mine-owners had taken hard the Commissions and Bills—to which "interference" by State and Parliament they often ascribed any ill fortune that might befall the coal trade. Under these conditions of a multiplicity of small owners and of both large and small colliery companies (with some hundred and fifty thousand shareholders in all) it may be readily understood that modernisation of the pits was not progressing rapidly. "The individualism of a large number of self-contained units was unlikely to encourage major developments in the science of mining"—so ran the verdict fifteen years later of leading mining engineers,[1] who went on to say: "Concentration upon traditional practices, without analysis of the conditions which gave rise to them, was not conducive to the development of new techniques. It is not, therefore, surprising that progress was slow." In addition modernisation was particularly hampered by the continuing existence of royalties, wayleaves and other prerogatives of those who owned the soil and with it the coal-measures beneath the surface. Besides these troubles they had geological obstacles placed in their way by nature itself on whose bounty they were dependent but who with each decade seemed to become a little more grudging.

Lastly, they had what were colloquially called by themselves "labour troubles." Whether these were caused in the main by agitators as some coal-owners in the fourth decade of the twentieth century were still prone to believe, or whether they were due to the notorious imperfections of human nature, a thought in which some of them took philosophic refuge, the fact remained that from the time of the Chartists, and even before, they had never been wholly free from "labour troubles." In the first quarter of the twentieth century these troubles had mounted, had become cumulative and had resulted in huge conflicts that themselves brought further state and parliamentary interference.

But with the opening of the second quarter of the twentieth century it had seemed that both "labour troubles"

[1] Coal Mining: Report of the Technical Advisory Committee (The Reid Report) of March 1945. Cmd. 6610.

on the scale of earlier years and the perils of public ownership with which they had been more recently threatened had become a thing of the past. For in the year 1926 the colliery owners with the help of the Government had been able to inflict severe defeat upon the members of the mining trade unions from whom their natural allies had fallen away. As a result of that struggle, the greatest in the history of the industry, the owners had been able to get rid of national negotiations on wages and had substituted therefor negotiations and agreements that differed from one another in over a score of Districts. Hours of labour, which had been fixed at seven hours plus winding time in 1919, had been raised in July 1926 for a period of five years to a permissive eight hours plus winding time, with the result that in this too there was great difference in over a score of Districts. The government of that day, often called the Baldwin–Churchill Government, had conceded this extra hour and in other ways, too, had accepted the policy of the coal-owners in the belief that better times and prosperity would thus be brought to the industry.

Actually the coal-owners promising these things had not been able to deliver the goods. Production of coal shrank; many collieries had closed never to open again. Longer hours and lower wages had here and there resulted in lower prices but not in a revival of prosperity.[1]

Thus only four years after their great victory in 1926 the colliery companies in their many hundreds and the coal-owners in their thousands found that they could not resist the crisis effectively and that to meet the difficult conditions of the industry new legislation had to be passed by Parliament. The new law, the Coal Mines Act of 1930, must have seemed to many of them more of an interference with their business than anything that had happened in a hundred years. For while earlier legislation had interfered in conditions of production, the new law interfered with their operations on the market. It made arrangements for the settling of

[1] "What has been the result of our coal policy? Collieries selling coal at a loss, unable to pay in some cases their dividends, in other cases even their interest on debentures, overdrafts piled up, royalties reduced and yet in arrears, anxiety for the owners, misery for the miners, poverty for many small people who have lost their savings or who get no return for them." (Lord Sankey in the House of Lords, April 29, 1930.)

quotas of production District by District and colliery by colliery, for the setting of limits to output and for the control to some extent of the market.

The new law ended the old competitive system of the coal-mining industry. Many owners felt it not as a liberation from outworn conditions but as a new fetter on their activities. No longer did the individual coal-owner or chairman of directors journey to London, down from Doncaster or up from Cardiff, to compete in the Coal Exchange whose peculiar architecture was in historic contrast with Billingsgate Market and the column that commemorated the Great Fire of London.

The new law, however, had been acceptable enough to many of the larger coal-owners. Numerous though the separate undertakings were and widely dispersed amongst over fourteen hundred separate owners, actually three-quarters of the tonnage was produced by less than a hundred big concerns: and of these big concerns nearly half had wide-ranging interests in iron and steel, shipbuilding, engineering and other trades. Some of them, notably in the case of the Five Counties Scheme, had already sought to control output and set up marketing arrangements. The Act of 1930 was essentially an endeavour to universalise such schemes as these, though it contained provisions on hours of labour and for compulsory amalgamation which were not to the liking of the coal-owners as voiced by their representatives in the Mining Association of Great Britain. This national organisation, founded in 1854, was made up of twenty-four district or county colliery-owners' associations, which in turn included the great majority (with some notable big exceptions such as the well-known Cambrian Combine) of coal-owners within each District. The different interests, as between one coal-field and another, not to speak of the competing interests within each coal-field, were ironed out in the Central Committee of the national body. But the coal-owners' public unanimity was sometimes purchased at the cost of concessions to the smaller or less go-ahead undertakings.

This had results both in the operation and, as it was to turn out, in the non-operation of parts of the Act of 1930.

In any case the Act was a defective piece of legislation both administratively and fundamentally. On the one hand the cut-throat competition which it was designed to limit nevertheless continued to an extent within each District and as time went on between Districts. On the other hand the Act placed a premium on the weaker colliery units so that the out-of-date capitalist structure of the industry was frozen instead of being progressively liquidated.

3. CRISIS AND UNEMPLOYMENT

World economic crisis was signalised over five-sixths of the globe by unemployment on a scale never before experienced. In the United Kingdom, where the number out of work from 1921 to 1929 had been far higher than in the days before the First World War, the precipitous fall in employment from 1929 to 1933 almost defies description. A million, never less, out of work in the 'twenties; three times as many by the January of 1933: these are the official figures of unemployment amongst insured persons only. Figures help: but it requires a degree of imagination and insight to grasp such a scale of unemployment in all its implications of destitution, malnutrition and misery.

Out of a total population of forty-six million of whom less than half went down in the decennial census as "gainfully occupied" or potentially so, a little over one-quarter were insured against unemployment. The proportion of those eleven to twelve million insured persons who suffered unemployment was very high indeed in the economic crisis of 1920–21; and remained at a high level thereafter. From over two million in December 1921 the proportion varied year in, year out, until in Autumn 1929 it stood at a million and a quarter (one-tenth of the total number of insured persons), just before the onset of the world economic crisis. Even at its lowest level in the 'twenties, the rate of unemployment was some nine or ten times greater than its usual incidence in the South of England in the nineteen-fifties. But this scheme of compulsory insurance, with its regular weekly contributions from the employer, the employed and the Exchequer was limited in its scope. Not only did it exclude employees not engaged in manual labour if their salaries came to more than £250 a year, but it also left out whole classes of persons whose yearly income mostly fell far short of £250. Agricultural labourers and domestic servants, totalling in the 1931 Census nearly two-and-a-half millions, were excluded: so too were wellnigh a million boys and girls under sixteen years of age; and, after the end of 1927, all persons aged sixty-five and over. A half-million of those employed by the railway companies and local authorities were also excepted. Hence the figure of one-and-a-quarter million out of work in October 1929, before the crisis, and all such figures thereafter relate only to compulsorily insured persons: the total number out of work was always considerably larger than the Ministry of Labour tables show. With the onset of the crisis, as the table shows, there was a rapid change from bad to worse.

NUMBERS AND PERCENTAGES OF INSURED PERSONS
RECORDED AS UNEMPLOYED

(Half-yearly from December 1929 to December 1933)

Date		Number	Percentage
1929	December	1,344,220	11·0
1930	January	1,520,448	12·4
	July	2,070,088	16·7
1931	January	2,662,842	21·1
	July	2,806,475	21·9
1932	January	2,854,790	22·2
	July	2,920,944	22·8
1933	January	2,955,448	23·0
	July	2,507,773	19·5
	December	2,262,896	17·6

When we turn to coal-mining, we find that the overall percentage of unemployment conceals the much higher proportion in this industry for whom over a series of years before the crisis no work had been available, or when available, had been only of short duration. Moreover, the fluctuations in employment were very violent. After the bleak winters of 1921–22 and 1922–23 there had been a whole year that raised hopes, in 1924, when the mean percentage of unemployment fell to under 6 per cent—though that diminished figure still accounted for scores of thousands out of work in the coal-fields. But in the next year the percentage was nearly thrice as high, and in the one month of June 1925 actually leaped up to 25 per cent of all the insured persons in the industry. Again in 1927 the mean annual percentage of unemployment was higher still, rising to over 18 per cent. Within the year 1928 the violence of fluctuation in unemployment is clearly exhibited within four months: in April the number of insured coal-miners out of work was 208,921; in May 245,618; in June 299,477; in July 324,972: after which the number fell by December to the April level. The fluctuations were less in 1929: and although in June there were 204,059 or one in every five miners unemployed (double the high rate of 9·6 per cent for insured workers generally), by October the number had fallen to 166,123, a rate of about 15 per cent.

In the next year came the effect of world economic crisis: and once the unemployment figures in 1930 had reached and passed 200,000, there was no recovery from this depth of unemployment for many years. In the summer months of 1930 there were over a quarter of a million miners out of work; in the winter months it was still over 200,000. In 1931, when this volume begins, the deeper effects of the crisis began to be experienced.

NUMBER AND MONTHLY PERCENTAGES OF UNEMPLOYED
IN COAL-MINING (1931)

Date (Near end of the month)	Number (to nearest thousand)	Percentage of insured miners
January	209,000	19·5
February	240,000	22·5
March	293,000	27·4
April	279,000	26·1
May	289,000	27·0
June	379,000	35·0
July	389,000	36·4
August	330,000	30·9
September	318,000	29·7
October	304,000	29·0
November	284,000	27·1
December	257,000	24·6

The next year was to be worse than 1931, with a maximum in August 1932 of 435,000 unemployed miners or 41·6 per cent.

NUMBER AND MONTHLY PERCENTAGES OF UNEMPLOYED
IN COAL-MINING (1932)

Date (Near end of month)	Number (to nearest thousand)	Percentage of insured miners
January	290,000	27·7
February	295,000	28·2
March	282,000	26·9
April	345,000	32·9
May	338,000	32·3
June	425,000	40·6
July	432,000	41·2
August	435,000	41·6
September	405,000	38·7
October	356,000	34·1
November	357,000	34·1
December	305,000	29·2

So it went on, year after year, and indeed long after economic recovery had set in elsewhere. Not until 1937 (with the exception of a couple of months at the end of 1935 and 1936) did the monthly percentage go below 20 per cent.

Successive governments from 1920 onwards had passed a series of Unemployment Insurance Acts, at an average of nearly two each year with varying provisions for rate of contributions, rate of benefits and limitation of benefit. The earlier outlook of at any rate some members of the British Government was succinctly expressed by the Marquess Curzon's dispatch in which he referred to the many millions spent on health and out-of-work benefits as "our insurance against revolution." But as such fears retreated, successive Cabinets began to be concerned more and more with the amount of borrowing needed to maintain the Unemployment Fund (though the cumulative amount up to the end of 1930 was equivalent to an addition of less than 1 per cent to the National Debt) and so, while the rate of benefits was raised (between 1921 and 1931), contributions were also raised and many stringent Statutory Conditions were laid down in limitation of benefit. Amongst these was the 1924 provision that applicants for benefit "must prove that they are genuinely seeking work," under which in five years no less than 808,513 claimants were disallowed: it had been harshly administered[1] and was abolished early in 1930.

Apart from these Acts and other remedial measures the

---

[1] See *The Miners: Years of Struggle*, Chapter XV.

root problem remained, and no government then or later
found a solution for it. There were five Prime Ministers,
heading ten administrations, in a period of twenty years: all
alike proved impotent in face of what now appears as a
catastrophe that fell upon the people of Britain between the
wars.

If unemployment as above recorded was the immediate
effect of the world economic crisis its other effects were
revealed more slowly. A panic fear of social upheaval
stampeded many ruling classes in Europe and brought
the rapid growth of Fascism and the drive towards war.
It was manifest that after the crisis of 1920–21 Fascism
first developed under Mussolini in Italy: after the longer
and deeper crisis of 1929 onwards that Fascism developed
under Hitler and the Nazis in Germany and spread to other
countries of Europe. But the causes were more complex
and the effects wider than this single argument would
imply. In Britain, where things were different but in certain
respects not entirely dissimilar, all activities, industrial and
political, were conditioned by the crisis. The drive to war
accompanied and followed the crisis throughout the 'thirties.
The first focus of war was presently seen in East Asia where
in 1931 the Japanese militarists seized the north-east region
of China (Manchuria) and in 1932 were bombing Shanghai,
then the fifth largest city of the world. Other incidents and
other hostilities followed till one country after another
appeared to be entering the penumbra of a coming eclipse
of civilisation. Throughout the 'thirties not only the miners
but the peoples of Britain and other countries were over-
shadowed by a growing menace of war and of Fascism.

4. FALLEN ON EVIL DAYS

In the beginning of 1931 the Miners' Federation of Great
Britain, at one time so powerful, had fallen on evil days.
In the forty-two years' existence of the Federation, as well
as in the earlier history of the county associations of miners,
there had been bad spells, bad years, and even a succession
of lean years, notably the seven lean years that preceded

the formation of the Federation in 1889. But there had always been a recovery and, up to the beginning of war in 1914, the recovery had brought almost everything connected with the industry to a greater height than before. The total annual output had risen higher, the number of men employed had grown; and while pithead prices, and with them wages, had varied up and down, profits of colliery companies had been rising. Up to the year 1913, which was the zenith year of output in the coal industry, exports had also risen on each occasion beyond any temporary setback.

Even after the 1914–18 war it seemed that the familiar rhythm of the coal industry might reassert itself. The year 1919 had been the zenith year of effort of the Miners' Federation. In the interests of its members the Federation had demanded a higher standard of living and a six-hour day underground. In the public interest as well as in the interest of their members the demand had been made for nationalisation of coal-mines. By the Sankey Commission[1] they had come nearer than had earlier been thought possible to obtaining these which they considered their just demands: and though the cup that they were about to put to their lips was soon dashed to the ground, leaving behind a feeling of frustration and continuing anger, this summit of their demands as a Federation was never forgotten. Thereafter, they were living in hopes. After the slump of 1920–21 and the accompanying strike and lock-out there had been hard and bitter winters. Then in 1923 the French occupation of the Ruhr coal-field had resulted in a leap upwards of exports and then of production generally, so that in the next year the miners, after the Buckmaster Court of Inquiry[2] set up by the short-lived Labour Government of 1924, gained more favourable conditions in the general wages agreement.

But after the General Strike and seven months' lock-out of 1926 the normal and expected recovery had not taken place. Longer hours, lower wages, mechanisation and rationalisation, overtime and speed-up might produce a higher output per man-shift—as well as a higher accident rate—but they had not brought prosperity to the industry.

[1] Coal Industry Commission, Chairman Mr. Justice Sankey. Interim Report, March 20, 1919, Cmd. 84, 85, 86. Second-stage Reports June 20, 1919, Cmd. 210.
[2] Cmd. 2129 of May 1924.

HERBERT SMITH AND THE RT. HON. THOMAS RICHARDS

EBBY EDWARDS (CENTRE) AT THE
WANSBECK BY-ELECTION, 1918

But neither this nor any other demonstrable proof that their opponents had miscalculated was likely to relieve the anxieties of the miners. The Federation had been doubly weakened. In the first place its power to negotiate on behalf of all the mine-workers had been taken away, and for its national agreement there had been substituted a score of differing District agreements so that there could easily arise strife between one District and another. The owners had nearly succeeded in rending the Federation into a score of separated fragments. In the second place the Federation had to face the rise of "rival yellow unions," stimulated and favoured by the employers. Of these company unions the first was formed at the end of 1926 in Nottinghamshire by George Spencer, M.P. There were branches of the Spencer Union opened up in 1927 and 1928 in Scotland, Durham, Northumberland, Yorkshire, Staffordshire, Derbyshire and South Wales—a national total of 273. As a result of all these causes membership, as stated from the chair at Federation Annual Conferences, had fallen from 957,610 in 1920 to 784,986 in 1927, to 625,576 in 1928 and to 543,822 in 1929. By the end of the year 1930 the figure had fallen to 529,958.

Rent asunder as far as wages negotiations were concerned into a score of Districts, the Miners' Federation from 1927 onwards could no longer speak with one voice. Yet they came together in annual and special Conferences and it was seldom that they would admit in public how severe a wound had been dealt them, or bemoan the evil days on which they had fallen. The Miners' Federation of Great Britain, formed to combine for industrial and legislative purposes, was now largely driven back mainly on to the latter activity, so that for a time its practice resembled the patient lobbying, deputationing and electioneering that marked the later activities of Alexander McDonald and Tom Burt and their Miners' National Union formed in 1863. There was, however, a big difference between these earlier mining Members of Parliament and the mining group in the House of Commons half a century later. The earlier mining M.P.s had accepted the Liberal Whip in Parliament, both in the nineteenth century and in the first decade of the twentieth

century. But now for twenty years since 1909 the Miners'
Federation had been a constituent part of the Labour Party:
and the mining members whom it sustained in Parliament
were bound to accept the Labour Party Whip. These
acceptances worked both ways. The Federation officials
argued strongly for help from the Labour Party in their hour
of need. At a meeting with the Parliamentary Labour
Party officials on March 26, 1929, they had obtained in
the election manifesto a formula that "The disastrous
Act by which the Tory Government [in 1926] added an
hour to the working day of the miners must be at once
repealed."[1]

Ten weeks later the General Election on May 30th made
Labour the largest single party in the House of Commons,[2]
so that Ramsay MacDonald had been able to form his
second administration. Hopes rose high. Moreover, in the
months preceding the General Election it seemed that the long-
expected trade recovery was at length in sight: an increase
in demand and more working days in each week had brought
more employment for the miners and increased earnings.
With the liveliest anticipations, therefore, they had looked
forward to the measures of the Labour Government. At the
Annual Conference that summer a resolution "That we press
for the immediate repeal of the Eight Hours Act" was
passed unanimously. "The said Act," they were convinced,
in its operation "had caused wages to be reduced, aggravated
the causes of unemployment, and increased the number of
accidents in the mining industry." (July 25, 1929.)

Six months after the election pledge had been given, a
meeting with Cabinet members on September 27th made it
clear that the MacDonald administration would not do

[1] See Appendix to this chapter.

[2] THE FOUR GENERAL ELECTIONS OF THE 'TWENTIES

Year	Labour	Conservative	Liberal	Other	Total
1922	142	347	117	9	615
1923	191	258	158	8	615
1924	152	415	42	6	615
1929	289	260	58	8	615

what the Miners' Federation had expected of it.[1] Instead
of a restored seven-hour day they were offered seven-and-
a-half—which meant no change at all for Districts such as
Yorkshire. Moreover, this half-hour reduction was to be
part of legislation to regulate supply and sale of coal which
was being elaborated in discussions with the coal-owners.
The miners' representatives, loath to accept this, had six long
meetings with Cabinet ministers. Then there had followed
the painful and protracted M.F.G.B. Special Conference of
November 5, 1929, when the Yorkshire delegates refused to
accept the Government proposals on hours. It was then that
the dramatic change took place, that the Yorkshire delegates
left the Conference, and that Herbert Smith, President since
1921, left the chair and the Conference. It almost looked like
the break-up of the Federation. Yorkshire, however, disappointed those who hoped for such a break-up and
remained within the Federation but in a minority opposed
to the compromise on hours. The majority of the Federation
reluctantly accepted it[2] and rested on a new-found hope
that within five months there would at any rate be legal
uniformity of hours. But it was nigh six months before the
Coal Mines Bill reached the House of Lords. It was introduced on April 29, 1930, by Lord Chancellor Sankey in a
speech which so pleased the Miners' Federation that they
published it in pamphlet form. Lord Sankey stated that he
had not changed his mind ("I still firmly believe that
nationalisation is the only solution of our difficulties"); but
as a member of a minority Government it was too sweeping
for him to propose: and so he put forward this temporary
measure in the interests of all. "What," he asked, "has been
the effect of the Eight Hours Act?" "Over-production,"
was his answer, "more coal coming into the market than

[1] Philip Snowden, Chancellor of the Exchequer, speaking at Leicester on October 23,
1929, only a short time away from his rapturous reception by the City of London bankers
and merchants after his securing a larger share of war reparations from Germany than
the French had wished, stated:

"The Labour Government were pledged to restore the seven-hour day and that
promise would be redeemed. But they must face facts. An immediate return to the
seven-hour day would inflict grievous disaster on the industry: pits would close and
miners would be thrown out of work." (*The Times*, October 25, 1929.)

[2] "It was not our scheme at all; it was the scheme of the Government which very
reluctantly, and after enormous controversy that almost caused a split in our Federation,
we accepted as a means of meeting our demand for a return to the 7-hour day." (Tom
Richards to the Federation Conference of March 19, 1931.)

there was market for. With what result? Fewer men employed and coal still sold at unremunerative prices." Miners in Britain, once the most advanced country, were now working longer hours than on the continent of Europe.

Their Lordships (many of them deeply interested in coal) gave the Lord Chancellor a patient hearing: but, in committee of the House, Lord Gainford[1] carried an amendment to permit a "spread-over" of ninety hours a fortnight. The Government were aghast. The amendment wrecked their Bill: for it meant that in some Districts the miners would still be on eight hours. Should they now withdraw the Bill? The question was turned over and over. Eventually, with a proviso that the "spread-over" in any District must have the assent both of the Mining Association of Great Britain and of the Miners' Federation of Great Britain, they reluctantly swallowed the amendment: and the Bill became law.

In the latter months of 1930 the miners' leaders were asked by MacDonald not to veto the spread-over, but to agree to it. This set the Federation Districts at sixes and sevens. There were desperate strikes as well as much wrangling, much confusion throughout the early winter of 1930–31. Not only the seven-hour day, but the uniform $7\frac{1}{2}$-hour day that they had reluctantly accepted in its stead was being put off from one quarter to another. Once more their hopes were unfulfilled.

So by January 1931, when this story begins, hope and trust were ebbing away. Unemployment was rising: wages were falling: a common policy on hours was bedevilled by the "spread-over." The new year of 1931 opened with a lock-out of the South Wales miners, who had refused the "spread-over." "It is not fair to let them fight alone" ran a resolution from the Lancashire District to the Federation Executive Committee, meeting on January 15th. The Committee decided "that districts be invited to make a voluntary contribution." Instead of a compulsory levy, as in times past, the sinews were now shrunken. The Miners' Federation had indeed fallen upon evil days.

[1] Lord Gainford (1860–1943), a leading coal-owner, was a Liberal minister from 1905 to 1916. He was Vice-President of the Mining Association of Great Britain.

5. M.F.G.B. ENDS THE "SPREAD-OVER"

It was thus in a mood of disillusion that the Special Conference of the Miners' Federation of Great Britain met in Transport House on March 19, 1931. This was reflected in the speech of the venerable Chairman, the Rt. Hon. Thomas Richards, who had been connected with the mining industry for nearly as long as any one of the delegates could remember. He was born at Beaufort, Ebbw Vale, on June 8, 1859, and was working in a coal-pit at the age of twelve. He had early come to the fore and had been chosen General Secretary of the South Wales Miners' Federation when it was founded in 1898. He had remained Secretary ever since. From 1904 to 1920 he was Member of Parliament for Ebbw Vale. He was an Alderman of the Monmouth County Council, its Chairman since 1924, a County Magistrate for the counties of Breconshire and Monmouthshire, and a Knight of Grace, St. John's Ambulance Association. Through all the stormy times he had helped to guide the fortunes of the South Wales miners. Nobody but had a good word for "old Tom Richards." But it had put a heavy strain on him when, from the more or less honorary position of Vice-President to which he had been elected in 1924, there had been thrust upon him suddenly, in November 1929, the onerous and difficult office of the Presidency.

All the blighted hopes of so many months, all the sad experiences of the ninety-hour spread-over (to decide for or against its extension was the purpose of the Conference) were reflected in the speech of Tom Richards. He recalled that when Ramsay MacDonald had asked the Miners' Federation to extend for three months the "spread-over" of the ninety-hour fortnight, they had agreed. Moreover, he said: "The Prime Minister gave his reasons for asking us to do so; that an opportunity might be afforded the marketing schemes, fixing quotas, regulating quota schemes, fixation of prices, etc., to bring revenue into the industry to make way for a straight $7\frac{1}{2}$-hour day. These were his hopes, and were our hopes." Now, these hopes had not materialised and had such an effect that old Tom Richards even used the phrase: "What a horrible condition we are in as a Federation generally." He said: "The Government have not been able—I will put it as kindly as that—to offer us any protection in the operation of their plan. We urged, urged, urged that if we accepted this plan, then we could reasonably expect not to be subjected to an attack upon our wages."

Despite this, concluded Richards, "it has failed, and miserably failed." He put it bluntly: "Where the spread-over has been imposed upon them the workmen have had to accept it. In most instances where there has been no spread-over, they have had to submit to reduction in wages, so that there has been really no protection of any kind."

Then, in a melancholy retrospect, Richards spoke of how leaders of the Miners' Federation had risked their reputation:

—if we had a shred of reputation—risking it by urging a disgruntled body of men to accept this, accept that, and accept the other, because it was a Labour Government, believing they were trying to assist us, or believing they were sincere in their attempt to reorganise the industry and that ultimately we should have better conditions. Gentlemen: all that has gone. (March 19, 1931.)

Then he raised the question "What can we do?" And himself gave the answer that "we shall have to turn our attention to something else and say to blazes with all these methods of fixing wages, and see if we cannot get Parliament to fix a decent Minimum Wage."

The Special Conference went on all day; but the delegates obviously regarded Tom Richards's speech as the keynote to be followed. At the end votes were taken on a series of proposals. One was that the matter should be relegated to the Committee. This was defeated by 393 votes to 142. Another was that there should be reference back to the Districts. This was defeated by 312 votes to 223. Then came the proposal for the extension of the spread-over, which had the support of Lancashire, Scotland, Nottingham, North Wales, Cumberland, and the smaller Districts of Bristol, Cleveland, Leicester and Somerset. This was overwhelmingly defeated by 401 votes to 134, and the resolution as carried ran:

That the Federation refuse to approve any application under Section 14,[1] Coal Mines Act, 1930, to extend beyond 31st March next any arrangement for a spread-over of working hours made under that section. (March 19, 1931.)

The delegates had rung the knell of the spread-over, which for a twelvemonth had been "a source of very great trouble and irritation." Three months after its burial the Executive Committee had this to say of it:

The "spread-over" was merely a subterfuge to cover the intention of the owners of continuing a working day of eight hours and of robbing the workmen of the shorter working day. It is therefore a negation of the principle of the shorter working day, and it also destroys a principle which the Federation has always regarded as of vital importance, namely, the principle of uniformity in relation to hours. . . . The "spread-over," therefore, is contrary to and destructive of the movement towards closer unity and centralisation, and tends to perpetuate those differences between the districts, the removal of which is a *raison d'être* of the Miners' Federation. It is a most reactionary measure and one which, we trust, will never again be countenanced by the Federation. (*Annual Report*, June 30, 1931.)

Miners could now look forward to July 8, 1931, the date on which the temporary Eight Hours Act of 1926 would expire, and automatically the seven-hour day would come into force. With a seven-hour day thus in sight, they would not, however, disperse until they had dealt with the separate

---

[1] Coal Mines Act, 1930, Part III, Hours of Work, Section 14.

"(1) During the continuance of the Coal Mines Act, 1926, section three of the Coal Mines Regulation Act, 1908, shall have effect as if for the words 'one hour' there were therein substituted the words 'half an hour':

"Provided that, if an application, by agreement between representative organisations of the owners of and the workers employed in or about the coal mines in any district, is made to the Board of Trade in that behalf with the approval of the Mining Association of Great Britain and the Miners' Federation of Great Britain, the Board of Trade shall make an order, which shall become effective forthwith, that the substitution of the words 'half an hour' for the words 'one hour' in section three of the Coal Mines Regulation Act, 1908, shall not apply as respects any mine in such district at which the daily hours below ground on an average taken over the twelve weekdays in any fortnight do not exceed the daily hours permissible under section one of the Coal Mines Regulation Act, 1908, as amended by the Coal Mines Act, 1919, by more than the extension of half an hour made under section three of the Coal Mines Regulation Act, 1908, as amended by the Coal Mines Act, 1926, and this section.

"At any mine where an extension of time is in any week made under the said section three, the workmen, by agreement between representatives of employers and workmen, may, notwithstanding anything in the Coal Mines Regulation Act, 1908, as amended by any subsequent enactment, begin their period of work on the Saturday of that week before twenty-four hours have elapsed since the beginning of their last period of work, so long as at least eight hours have elapsed since the termination thereof.

"(2) This section shall come into operation at the expiration of the period of four months from the passing of this Act."

but equally serious problem of wages. This problem, speakers had urged in the debate, could be solved immediately by amending the Minimum Wage Act of 1912. The Conference unanimously decided on this legislative remedy for their wages grievance: and the delegates, having charged their Executive with the task of seeing it through, departed with hopes renewed.

6. TO AMEND THE MINIMUM WAGE ACT

The Coal Mines (Minimum Wage) Act of 1912, resulting from the first national strike of miners,[1] had an elaborate District machinery of administration. But, having no effective provisions to cope with the rise in the cost of living, it had largely fallen out of use. To meet the miners' needs it only required to be brought up to date and otherwise amended. This was not a new demand. Together with the demand for a weekly in lieu of a daily minimum wage, it had been resolved upon in 1928. Only the previous year the Weston-super-Mare Annual Conference had repeated it briefly:

That the Minimum Wage Act be amended so as to provide for a much higher minimum for all workers in and about a mine. (August 14, 1930.)

The Federation Executive Committee, instructed by the Special Conference "to request the Government to introduce" the necessary Bill, moved fast. Before the end of the month they had met the mining Members of Parliament, with whom by mid-April they had worked out proposals and completed a week later the supporting argumentation, which was published as a pamphlet.[2]

The argument for the claim of the Miners' Federation was that their wages were lower than in most other occupations and were "wholly incompatible with the exhausting and dangerous nature of the miner's work"; that without a barrier to further wage reductions "the industry will never be properly organised"; and that the "reorganisational

---

[1] See *The Miners: Years of Struggle* by R. Page Arnot.
[2] *The Claim for Legal Minimum Wages for Mineworkers.*

measures" that were necessary could "be quickly applied by the coal-owners" so that the industry "could then pay such wages without difficulty." Using official Ministry of Labour figures they showed that wages of miners in December 1930, when the cost-of-living figure stood at 55 points over its base line in Summer 1914, had increased by only 44 per cent. In the same period the wages of railwaymen, road transport workers, printers and others had gone up by 100 per cent, while in nearly every other trade the increase had been considerable. Not only, therefore, was the relative position of the miners much worse than in any other trade, but the actual wages were less than anywhere except in agriculture. They gave the following table:

COAL-MINING INDUSTRY

Earnings per shift worked at December 1930 compared with June 1914

District	June 1914	December 1930	Per cent increase
	s. d.	s. d.	
Scotland	6 8¾	9 2½	36
Northumberland	6 2¼	7 8¼	24
Durham	6 2½	7 11¾	29
South Wales and Monmouth ..	6 9	9 6¼*	41
Lancashire and North Staffordshire	6 0¼	9 2½	52
Yorkshire	6 10	10 2	49
North Wales	5 10	8 3¾	42
North Derbyshire and Nottingham	6 6¾	10 4½	58
South Derby, Leicester, Cannock and Warwick	6 1½	9 9¾	60
Cumberland, South Staffordshire, Shropshire, Bristol, Forest of Dean and Somerset	5 6¾	8 9½	58
Great Britain	6 5¾	9 3¾	44

* October 1930.

The figures shown for December 1930 have been reduced in certain areas by reductions enforced since that time.

The increase in the cost of living at December 1930 was 55 per cent over 1914.

A similar unweighted average of the top six Districts in the table, comprising some four-fifths of the membership of the Federation, would yield an increase of about 39 per cent. Moreover, the number of shifts worked was no longer at the old level of 5½ per week as it had been five or six years earlier. It was well under five per week, so that average money earnings in the third quarter of 1930 had stood at 42s. 8d. per week. In the month that they were compiling these low wage figures, the number of miners unemployed had risen to 279,347 (April 1931). On these facts alone they felt they had good ground for a legal minimum. All the two score mining members agreed "to co-operate with us to the fullest extent in pressing the Government to introduce such a Bill."

To work on the details five members were chosen, Aneurin Bevan, Tom Cape, Duncan Graham, Gordon Macdonald and Tom Williams. These five, together with seven from the Federation Executive Committee, met as a joint committee, and drafted the following outlines of a parliamentary Bill to be put to the Cabinet.

That the Coal Mines (Minimum Wage) Act, 1912, be amended so as to provide:

(a) That the Act (including the provisions hereunder) be made applicable to all workers in and about Coal Mines (including Mines of Stratified Ironstone).

(b) That the wages to be settled under the Act be not less than the wages prevailing in June 1914 plus a percentage thereon equivalent to the percentage increase in the cost of living since that time.

(c) That the percentage so fixed be adjusted in accordance with variations in the cost of living as ascertained and published periodically by the Ministry of Labour.

(d) That the following weekly amounts be guaranteed to every employed adult workman, provided such workman has worked, or is available to work, the full number of shifts available for him during the week, whether such shifts are actually worked or not—

For day wageworkers: £2 per week.
For pieceworkers: £2 10s. per week.

These amounts to be adjusted in accordance with variations in the cost of living.

(e) That the power of the employers to withhold payment of minimum rates of wages for any alleged failure to comply with the Rules be revoked. The onus of proving a contravention of the Rules by the workman to be upon the employer. The minimum wage to be continued unless and until such contravention is proved by the employer under the machinery of the Act.

(f) That payment be made of minimum rates of wages to aged and disabled workmen unless and until a certificate to discontinue payment be given by the District Boards.

(g) That provision be made for the infliction of penalties upon

employers for contravention of the Act; such penalties to be
similar to those provided under the Trade Boards Acts and
the Agricultural Wages Board Act.

April 16, 1931.

The Joint Committee of the Federation and the Mining
M.P.s were not men to hide their light under a bushel. That
there were such proposals was soon known: and even before
their formal adoption, the Miners' Federation received an
invitation from Lloyd George to lay the facts before the
Coal Committee of the Liberal Party. This they did at a
meeting on April 28th: for it seemed important to get the
support of the Liberal Party in Parliament: and Lloyd
George had been one of the four Liberal ministers chiefly
responsible for the original Act of 1912. Meantime, the
proposals had been told to Emanuel Shinwell, Secretary for
Mines; and soon the Executive Committee received an
invitation from the Government to meet the Coal Committee
of the Cabinet. They went, taking with them the five mining
Members of Parliament to this encounter, and heard the
Prime Minister propose "a private, but heart-to-heart talk
over the situation in which you find yourselves and in which
we find ourselves." So the talks began. The deputation had
entered Downing Street, committed by the Special Conference to a clear-cut strategy. They were to ignore the
question of hours and to concentrate on wages legislation.
By July 8th, the legal seven-hour day would automatically
be in operation and there should be no thought of tampering
with the law: nor need there be any discussion on that point.
It was known to them that to offset the legal seven-hour
shift the owners would insist on heavy reductions, and without them would not open the pits to mining labour. This
could mean a national stoppage which the Miners' Federation were not in a position to sustain, fallen upon evil days
as they were, with over a quarter of the miners unemployed.
To avert both the wage-cuts and a stoppage, they had come
armed with their draft Bill. The Coal Mines Act of 1912 to
fix minimum wages had been passed to settle a strike. A
similar Act in 1931 would prevent a lock-out.

But as soon as they had explained their proposals, they
found that the ministers had quite other ideas about how

their wages problem should be solved. The notice to the press, however, was confined to the following:

The Prime Minister, accompanied by the Lord Chancellor, the Secretary of State for Foreign Affairs, the President of the Board of Trade, the Attorney-General, and the Secretary for Mines, received a deputation from the Miners' Federation and the Members of the House of Commons representing mining constituencies, today at 10, Downing Street.
A general exchange of views on the situation in the mining industry took place, and it was agreed that a Committee representative of the Government and the Executive of the Miners' Federation should further examine the position at meetings to be held in the immediate future. (April 30, 1931.)

7. DIALECTICS AT DOWNING STREET

The studiously moderate tone of the public statements at this time and later hardly convey the content of that discussion with the leading members of the Cabinet. The first half of the meeting was taken up (as nearly always happened where those outside the industry were discussing with people inside it) with a series of misunderstandings as to the exact significance of various phrases and figures that were comprehensible to the miners but very puzzling to those outside. A difference emerged when the Prime Minister, Ramsay MacDonald, suggested there would be difficulty in getting the House of Commons "to legislate on a formula," forgetting that something similar had happened nearly twenty years earlier in debates in which he himself had taken part. But S. O. Davies was able to recall the Minimum Wage Act debates of 1912, and after a series of spirited exchanges the Prime Minister did not pursue his point any further.

When, however, it came to a discussion of the proposal in Clause (d) for a guaranteed weekly wage, it was no longer a question of clearing up misunderstandings.

PRIME MINISTER: That, of course, introduces a totally new principle, and you might perhaps like to give some information about it.
Mr. RICHARDS: It is a new principle, admittedly, in so far as

legislating the regulation of wages is concerned, but not new in some industries in this country. Railwaymen, of course, have been referred to with their guaranteed week, which has operated for a number of years.

Mr. SHINWELL: They must work.

Mr. RICHARDS: We do not object to work, but, unlike the railwaymen, in the mining industry the miners are to work just how and when the employer chooses. In my own days as a collier, I have trudged two miles to the top of the pit in the snow very often in winter, and been told when I got there, that there was no work to do because there were no trucks, and I have had to trudge two miles home again. (April 30, 1931.)

For some time that morning MacDonald and Shinwell plied the miners' representatives with questions about the economics of their proposals and there was much to-and-fro discussion. The cross-talk ended with a sapient reminder from the Prime Minister that they must "consider immediate results and the best method of handling a continuing situation." Tom Richards, wary of being drawn into an economic argument by the argute Shinwell or any other of the ministers present, said very simply:

We have not come here to talk the economics of the thing. We have finished, absolutely and entirely finished. The owners have refused all the overtures you have made. We worked the spreadover. There again, as Lord Sankey will appreciate, I am sure, they secured that under false pretences altogether.

It is no use harrying us with the economics of the industry because we are not going to look at them. This industry can be put upon a basis to pay the wages we are asking for in three months. It could be done tomorrow, almost, by an increase in the price of coal for consumption in this country. It is possible with a very little increase in the price of coal which the people in this country are prepared to pay.

Tom Richards then tartly recalled how Lloyd George had made an "airy speech" (on the Second Reading of the 1930 Act) prophesying that coal-owners under its provisions would rush up the price of coal for the hearth: but that they had done nothing of the kind. On the contrary they had carried on as before, competing with each other, "with the result that they had reduced the wages." Therefore, said Richards, since the coal-owners had disregarded the Government's plan and since the miners, perhaps against their own better judgment, had accepted it, the Government were surely bound to meet the request for a minimum wage Bill.

Neither Willie Graham whose business it had been, as President of the Board of Trade, to reach some agreement with the coal-owners, nor Attorney-General Jowitt opened their mouths: but presently Lord Chancellor Sankey made a speech in a summing-up manner which must have seemed to the miners to be favourable to their outlook—all the more when the Prime Minister acidly commented upon it.

Thereupon Tom Richards uttered some conclusions that had been forming in his mind for many months as he wrestled with the owners' side on the Conciliation Board for the Coal Trade of South Wales. There he had been confronted with an ever-polite and courteous but massive and inflexible opposition voiced by Evan Williams, their President. For nearly a score of years Evan Williams had been Chairman of the Monmouth and South Wales Coal Owners' Association; for a dozen years he had been President of the Mining Association of Great Britain. Evan Williams had been the spokesman and also the chief strategist for the coal-owning interests of Great Britain throughout the turbulent days of 1919 to 1921; and again in the lock-out of 1926 when he had out-manœuvred his ally Churchill, then deputy for the Prime Minister, in the later stages of that struggle and bent the Government to his will. From his ancestral home in Carmarthenshire, or in Cardiff, or in London, Evan Williams was always active, calculating how to check possible dangers to the profitability of mining and how to checkmate any government which sought to meddle in the coal trade. For this "interference," he believed, had been the source of nothing but trouble in an industry which would get on very well if left to itself. What was good for the colliery companies was good for Britain: and this narrow outlook, by which his family interests and his fellow owners' interests coincided with the tenets of nineteenth-century political economy learnt at Cambridge, he held with a singular tenacity and unfailingly expressed with precision and in exactly-formulated phrases. He was the head and front of opposition alike to Tom Richards in the Federation and to Cabinet Ministers in Whitehall. Coal-owning capital, personified in Evan Williams, was present in their minds that day in Downing Street: and presently his name was on the lips of Tom Richards, who burst out with these words:

This industry is managed chiefly by men who are not interested in it. They are interested in all other manner of industries of which they are directors and general managers and agents. I should like really to find out where their money is invested, but we shall get hold of it some day. They really cannot be interested in their industry.

I told Evan Williams that, I shall have to tell him again, but you might as well tell the Sphinx of Egypt as say anything to him.

It is no wonder if Evan Williams, "subtle as Sphinx," had maintained an enigmatic silence: for, beyond his family companies, he himself was a director not only of the huge Powell Duffryn Ltd. but also of Lloyds Bank, as well as companies in gas and other industries. In the year the Labour Government took office he held directorships in seventeen concerns and was Chairman of five of them. His personal position thus gave an indication of what had been happening more and more to the coal trade: the ever-increasing grasp upon its operation of the big banks and big monopoly firms, linked together this century in a "finance-oligarchy."

But now Tom Richards made a final statement of the miners' case, saying:

We are satisfied, we are prepared to take all the risks of the derelict village and the stoppage of collieries wherever it may happen, we are prepared for all that, if you will tell the coal-owners, "You must pay a wage somewhere reasonably near the cost of living increase since 1913, and that as a minimum rate of wages, and put your prices up to meet it." They can do it.

According to Richards, pit-head prices were only about 29 per cent higher than in 1913, whereas coal consumers were getting far higher wages. He said:

Mr. RICHARDS: We cannot stand it. Look at the irony of this situation. Every dock labourer in the country is getting a minimum of 12s. a day, and here we are working 50 per cent of our men for nearly half that, 6s. 1od.

PRIME MINISTER: That, of course, is the irony of it.

Mr. RICHARDS: If you cannot come to our salvation there is no salvation anywhere. We want you to take your courage in your hands, and the country will be with you. These coal-owners must pay these wages.

PRIME MINISTER: It is not a question of courage or anything like that. The dockmen have their 12s. on their own power to negotiate.

Then MacDonald put a hypothetical question: if the owners were approached and if they were to reply in the negative, saying to the Government "We cannot do it," what would the miners do then?

PRIME MINISTER: You would not appreciate my saying to you, "Yes, we will do it because we are so sympathetic we know you are right, we will do it," and then we come to you when the answer has been given, and say, "We are awfully sorry, we never visualised this situation. Now, let us see what we have to do." What will you say to me then? You will kick me up hill and down dale and denounce me in every part of the country for leading you into a bog.

Mr. RICHARDS: We should not say that.

PRIME MINISTER: Then you ought to say it.

Mr. RICHARDS: We are not suggesting you should consult them in this case at all. What we are saying to you is that the coal-owners having flouted you—flouted you over and over and over again, refused to operate the machine you have put into their hands—would pay these wages and more. You will tell them you have no other remedy but to compel them to do it. You have created this machinery and it depended upon their goodwill. They have displayed no goodwill, they have opposed you at every turn; now what we say is: disregard them entirely. (April 30, 1931.)

Already angry, Richards now had his teeth set on edge by MacDonald's suggestion: for it was in the course of this trafficking with the owners that the promised seven-hour day had been lost in Autumn 1929. If pressure from the owners had been strong then how much stronger would it now be, in the depth of crisis. Yet as an old parliamentarian Richards could have guessed the outcome: a proposal for bold action might succeed with some Prime Ministers, but not with Ramsay MacDonald.

8.   ARTHUR HENDERSON GETS A JOINT COMMITTEE

The Prime Minister, after having suggested that experts from each side should work out detailed figures, at this stage had to go and it was then left to his colleague Arthur

Henderson to gather what results were possible from the very different standpoints that had been expressed. Arthur Henderson, now Secretary of State for Foreign Affairs, was a very different type from the Prime Minister. Born in Glasgow and serving his apprenticeship as a moulder on Tyneside, he was always firmly attached to the trade union side of the Labour movement. He had been nurtured in Liberalism and indeed may be said to have served his apprenticeship to politics as a Liberal candidate's agent. In 1903 at the age of forty he had stood as a candidate for the newly formed Labour Representation Committee (afterwards the Labour Party) and had won the seat of Barnard Castle in Durham. He was the most experienced member of the Cabinet in all matters relating to the Labour Party of which he had been Secretary from 1910 onwards, Chief Whip in the Commons on more than one occasion, and both before the war, from 1908 to 1910, and again during the war, had been its parliamentary leader. He had also a more extensive experience of the work of government then any of his colleagues, having held a variety of posts in two administrations during the First World War and then in the two Labour Governments afterwards. Henderson had been typical of that Nonconformity and Liberalism that was the hall-mark of trade union leaders in the 'nineties, and, as far as the miners were concerned, for the first decade of the twentieth century. He was a total abstainer and a leading Wesleyan Methodist. Not until he was turned fifty did Arthur Henderson declare himself a Socialist when he joined the Fabian Society. Though he had incurred much odium, especially in the Socialist sections of the Labour Party, by remaining a member of the Asquith Coalition Government that was responsible for the court-martial and execution of the Irish Socialist leader James Connolly after the Easter Rising of 1916, he was well enough liked by the miners' leaders: his relative straightforwardness, absence of self-conceit or of intellectual pretensions, and above all his intimate knowledge and long-lasting connection with the trade unions gave him a reputation for reliability which was not accorded to the more devious and subtle mentality and the aloofness of the Prime Minister.

Arthur Henderson's chairmanship of this meeting began
with an immediate suggestion for a small committee from
both sides of the table. He said that the situation of the
Liberal Government who passed the Minimum Wage Act
in 1912 was "entirely different from our situation." For the
Liberals were "there with a majority," i.e. they could do
just what they wanted. "Unfortunately," said Henderson,
"we have to walk much more cautiously." Then Arthur
Henderson put the Cabinet point of view:

Moreover another aspect of the case has not been discussed this
morning. We are within eight weeks of a very important change
which must have a serious bearing upon your industry. Can we
afford to take no notice of that change? Therefore, if you would
agree, five of you, to meet five of us, sit down and turn the whole
thing over, nobody would be committed until you had reported
to your full Executive and we had reported to the Cabinet.

He suggested that this would be a reasonable and "a very
proper way of carrying on what has been opened this
morning," and, he hoped, would lead to "a very satisfactory
agreement eventually between us." The others did not object
to this. But Tom Richards still wanted to express what he
knew to be the feelings of the miners, especially the feeling of
frustration that had been mounting in their minds for so
many months; he recalled that in every constituency where
miners predominated a supporter of the Government had
been elected, and ended with something of a warning if not
a threat:

Mr. RICHARDS: As my last words to you . . . you may depend
upon it that if the Government fail us it is going to have a very
serious effect.

Mr. HENDERSON: I do not think it should be a case of our discussing this morning a Government failure. The Government, as
has been said, has tried to come to an understanding as to the best
course to be adopted. That is why you were invited to come here.

Mr. RICHARDS: I thought they would have been in as raging a
temper as I am. You are too philosophical.

Arthur Henderson then said that the coal-owners might tell
a different story, and summarised the position thus:

You are here this morning; you have put in a request; the
Secretary for Mines has reported to us; we thought the best thing

we could do would be to get the sanction of the Cabinet that the Coal Committee should be, for this purpose, increased by the addition of the Prime Minister and the Lord Chancellor; all, I think, giving evidence of the importance which we attach to the question, and the first thing we thought we should do was to ask you to come here and have this exchange of views.

Proposals for further procedure by Arthur Henderson were agreed to. But in the final exchanges of opinion it became clear that while the miners wished to keep the question of hours separate from the question of wages, the Government, on the other hand, felt that the two things must be taken into consideration together in view of the situation that would arise when the permissive Eight Hours Act of 1926 came to an end on July 8th.

Mr. BEVAN: You want to broaden the terms of reference of the committee to discuss certain matters. The Government, as you have said, has to make up its mind as to what its attitude is going to be to the reduction of hours in July. Let the Government make up its mind. Our mind is made up quite clearly.

Mr. HENDERSON: Just a minute. Mr. Richards has not put that case before us on behalf of his Executive today. We have put that side of the case, and when we have it out on the committee, if you would care to ignore it, of course we will have to take your ignoring of it into account, but we will be bound to ask you to give some attention to it.

Mr. SHINWELL: Is that weekly minimum wage to be related in any way to the hours of labour? Is it related to a 40-hour week, 30 hours, or 50 hours, or 90 hours a fortnight?

Mr. BEVAN: To whatever is the legal working week.

Mr. SHINWELL: Surely, therefore, it is quite relevant and you cannot exclude it. We are not trying to impose it on you.

Mr. BEVAN: It is relevant in the economic sense, but it is not relevant to our present strategy, that is the whole point.

Mr. HENDERSON: You look after your own strategy. Your strategy would be all right if you were not asking us to introduce legislation. (April 30, 1931.)

So the Downing Street conference ended. The Coal Committee of the Cabinet had not given an answer one way or the other. But the miners went away with a shrewd suspicion that their proposals were not welcomed and that their strategy was not likely to become the legislative plan of the

Cabinet. Eight weeks later, in their Annual Report, they said of the Downing Street conference:

At this meeting, the Government insisted that the proposals for a Minimum Wage Bill could not be separated from the question of hours; that as far as the Government was concerned, it must consider the question of wages in conjunction with the question of hours which would arise in July. The Government maintained this attitude in all the subsequent discussions and has never departed from it. On our part, we insisted that the Minimum Wage question was one which should be considered and dealt with by the Government irrespective of the hours question. (June 30, 1931.)

9. DISCUSSIONS WITH THE OWNERS

The first meeting of the Joint Sub-Committee with the Government had been fixed for May 5th. The Joint Sub-Committee held a number of meetings. At the outset, there was some difficulty in interpreting the proposals in terms of pounds, shillings and pence, and the Federation side of the Committee agreed to investigate and if possible to settle the figures with the officials of the Mines Department. But although they agreed on interpretation in terms of wage-rates in the various Districts, and while application of the proposals for amendment of the Minimum Wage Act of 1912 was being sedulously worked out on the Joint Sub-Committee, it had to be admitted that there was no certainty that legislation would follow. In fact, as the M.F.G.B. Executive Committee ruefully stated two months later:

The Government continued to evade any direct decision on the question of a Minimum Wage Bill. It continued to insist on the interdependence of wages and hours, and at an early stage of the discussions we were informed that it had decided to get in touch with the owners. (June 30, 1931.)

It was not long after the meeting in Downing Street that the Government decided to get into touch with the coal-owners, but their hope was for some sort of agreement between coal-owners and coal-miners. The Government had no intention, as it turned out, of proceeding with an amendment to the Minimum Wage Act. They did, however, hope that the two sides of the industry would reach agreement, since each must be conscious of the rapid approach of July 8, 1931, on which day the temporary Eight Hours Act of July 1926 would lapse and the industry would revert to the nominal seven-hour day as settled by the Act of 1919. So having refused to meet the representatives of the miners for five years the owners now changed their tune. After the Federation officials had thrice met the officials of the Mining Association, the Federation Executive on May 21st received from the owners the proposition that they were "now prepared to discuss with the representatives of the Miners' Federation all the implications of the effect of the Hours legislation on the industry, including the question of the safeguarding of wages." Thereafter discussions took place on June 5th, 11th and 19th between the two sides. What was the purport of the discussions? Would the miners agree to ask the Government to suspend the operation of the nominal seven-hour day? If so, under what conditions? The miners' representatives wanted solid assurances. The coal-owners said the seven-hour day would mean that they "would be compelled to press for reduction in wages in every district." But the Mining Association stated on behalf of most Districts that "existing wages should be maintained for six months providing present hours remained." Bargaining went on. The miners had only one trump card in their hand—the hours factor. In addition according to their own Report:

We also pointed out that the Government had informed us on numerous occasions that, in the event of an agreement not being reached between the parties the Government would do nothing to suspend the seven-hour day. (June 30, 1931.)

The owners treated this as bluff. The Cabinet Committee kept in touch with both parties and the Federation representatives reported each development to the Cabinet Committee. The Federation on June 19th had informed the owners that their proposals were "totally inadequate." They now sat back and the Cabinet Committee met the owners directly.

On behalf of the owners Evan Williams wrote to the Prime Minister on June 26th with proposals, but emphasised that "in no circumstances" could the Mining Association be placed in the position of exercising any power of review of district wages arrangements, and that it is not possible for the owners to give any guarantees of wages except on the basis of a Bill unlimited in respect of the period of its operation apart from the contingency of the ratification of the Geneva Convention.

I feel that even now it is not fully realised how great are the sacrifices and how serious are the risks which the owners have faced in offering guarantees even for six months, and still more in extending them to twelve months, in the existing financial conditions of the industry and in view of the very uncertain future; but I trust that you will be able to appreciate that in assenting to the proposals embodied in the enclosed statement the owners have gone as far as they can reasonably be expected to go in a serious effort to avoid the terrible calamity—both for the industry itself and the country —of a stoppage in the coal mining industry.

After insisting that the "spread-over" must be included in discussions, his letter concluded:

I need only add that, as I am sure you have fully appreciated, the owners have approached this matter in the sincere desire to do all that is reasonably practicable and in no spirit of bargaining and that this is the definite limit to which they can go.

What was "the contingency" to which Williams referred? A draft international convention limiting the hours of labour underground in coal-mines was adopted by the general Conference of the International Labour Organisation of the League of Nations on June 18, 1931. The Miners' Federation and the Miners' International had striven for many years for a convention limiting hours of labour, as set forth in the 1919 Peace Treaty of Versailles. That spring of 1931, the Miners' International Committee decided on what they should propose for the forthcoming I.L.O Conference, composed of governments, employers and workers. By a majority they agreed (on March 4th) to set forth their claim in favour of "seven hours bank to bank." (Under British conditions, where winding time has to be added to the nominal legal limit of hours, this was equivalent to a claim for a six-and-a-half-hour shift.) Their resolution went on:

That if this should fail we fight for a seven-and-a-half [hour] day bank to bank.

That if it be impossible to obtain a seven-and-a-half-hour day, and it becomes necessary to do so to secure a Convention, we agree to a seven-and-three-quarter-hour day bank to bank. (March 5, 1931.)

From May 28th to June 18th the M.F.G.B. officials were attending the I.L.O. Conference at Geneva, which adopted the convention with the proviso for "a seven-and-three-quarter-hour day from bank to bank." If this were ratified by the governments concerned they knew that the British miner, who only a year earlier had been working longer hours than any other in Europe, would henceforth be on the same level. Moreover, not only would it be better than the nominal seven-and-a-half-hour day but, by fifteen minutes, it would be an improvement on the nominal seven-hour day to which the British coal-fields were due to revert on July 8th. These were the prospects opened up by the I.L.O. Conference's adoption of what was called "The Geneva Convention." They were taken very seriously, were assumed by both the trade union and the owners' representatives and were even written into Acts of Parliament. But all these prospects depended on ratification (by a third of the governments of the countries concerned) which was fully expected to follow within a twelvemonth of June 1931 —hence the references to it in the mining negotiations. But ratification was postponed by the governments concerned.[1] In the end there was no ratification: and what had appeared to be on the brink of achievement turned out to be a will o' the wisp.

The outcome of the discussions up to that point and the further discussions in the last week of June 1931 were told to two successive Special Conferences of the Miners' Federation on June 25th and July 2nd. At the first Conference the delegates were dismayed to learn that their proposals to the Cabinet Coal Committee for a Minimum Wage Bill had never been put to the whole Cabinet. Bitter words were uttered. S. O. Davies's remark that the Government's proposals were really "that they shall introduce legislation in the interests of the coal-owners" brought an angry reply from A. J. Cook who for over a year had been defending the policy of Ramsay MacDonald. At the second of those Conferences the delegates (now "mandated with plenary powers") were faced with the "final proposals" of the Government which they had to accept or reject. The Government

[1] It was the British Government that on February 20, 1933, at Geneva refused to ratify.

proposed to introduce a Bill containing provisions to the following effect: firstly, the 7½-hour day would be continued temporarily for a period of twelve months. Secondly, during the twelve months of "the temporary extension of the 7½-hour day" the minimum percentage additions to basic rates and to subsistence allowances in all the 7½-hour Districts would continue in force as minimum rates, that is to say, they would not be reduced.

The Executive Committee had decided to recommend these proposals of the Government. Finally, in the early afternoon of July 2nd they were accepted by the Conference. It was less than a two to one majority, 346 to 186. The Yorkshire Miners' Association was no longer alone amongst the coal-fields in its opposition to the mining policy of the Labour Government; after twenty months it had now been joined by South Wales. Cumberland and Forest of Dean were also in the minority, but the other Districts either retained their confidence in Ramsay MacDonald and his colleagues though with hopes much diminished, or else they voted as they did because they did not see what else they could do.

10. THE COAL MINES BILL

On Monday, July 6, 1931, the Prime Minister, Mr. Ramsay MacDonald, rose in his place in the House of Commons at four o'clock of the afternoon and said: "I beg to move that the Bill now be read a second time." He spoke briefly, saying:

This is not the sort of Bill that one would have liked. It is purely temporary. It does not give the owners what they wanted, it does not give the men what they wanted, but it gives them both enough to go on with; and that is the main concern for the moment from the point of view of this country's position in relation to the state of world trade and industry.

He was followed by the Leader of the Opposition, Mr. Stanley Baldwin, who said:

All possibility of agreement had disappeared by the end of last week. It is not a new situation in that trade, and the Government have been compelled to act at the eleventh hour, and in the circumstances today I am certainly not prepared to oppose the Second Reading of this Bill. There is no alternative to it but trouble, which none of us want to see.

Sir Herbert Samuel, speaking on behalf of the Liberals, agreed that the Bill was "unavoidable in the circumstances," but criticised the Prime Minister "respectfully" for not making clear that fully half an hour has to be added to the figures in common use "in order accurately to describe the length of time that the miner is required to be below ground at work." He pointed out that British miners "as a rule were working about half an hour a day longer than the miners on the Continent." Samuel was also very critical of the coal-owners:

The owners were anxious that the miners should continue to work what is called the $7\frac{1}{2}$-hour day. The miners were anxious that their wages should not be reduced. The miners said to the owners: "Guarantee our wages for a year and we will work your hours for a year." The owners said in reply: "Work our hours indefinitely and we will guarantee your wages for a year."

The position taken up by the mineowners seems to have been an unreasonable one. The agreement should have been a guarantee of wages for a year in return for the longer hours for a year, or else an indefinite guarantee of wages in return for an indefinite continuation of the longer hours.

The fourth speaker in the debate was Mr. Ebby Edwards, the Acting Chairman of the Miners' Federation of Great Britain, who said:

Let me make it quite clear at once that this Measure does not satisfy the miners. There is nothing about the concessions in this Bill calculated to make the miners jubilant. Our claim is for a 7-hour day and a minimum wage, and hon. Members can well understand the dissatisfaction of the miners in regard to a Measure of this kind.

Edwards then said they were "merely asking for existing wages, which I defy any Member of this House to show are too high," and continued:

Let me give a concrete case. Here you have a subsistence wage applying to over 40 per cent of the adult men in one of our northern coalfields, of 6s. $6\frac{1}{2}$d. a day, and the average number of days last year was slightly over five—5·04. If they work the maximum number of days, with no ill-health and so on, that would represent 32s. 8¾d. In no industry are there such heavy deductions from wages as in the mining industry. On a wage of 32s. 8d. they average about 3s. 6d. but, taking them at only 2s. 8d., that means that there is 30s. left for the week.

But the men in that coalfield, like the men in this House, have to live seven days, and not five days, a week, and when you divide that sum by seven it means that the wage for these men is but little over 4s. 3d. a day. Allowing, for the two adults in the house, three meals a day at 6d. a meal, that means 3s., so that there is 1s. 3d. left for all the rest of the family, and, if there are three children, that amounts to less than 2d. a meal. That is not allowing for clothes, there is no question of household utensils, nor of anything for the church collection—there is nothing even to buy newspapers.

It can be understood that the men in the mining areas are not only down physically, but down morally. What must these men feel, looking upon their relatives as the husbands in this House look upon theirs, when they see their wives and children having to live on this pittance? It is no wonder that there are cases where men wish that God would take away the spark of life that He has created, so that the misery may end.

Ebby Edwards concluded by emphasising that the Bill was a temporary measure, a truce under existing conditions for twelve months. He said:

It is merely a truce. The alternative is a stoppage, and speaking for the Miners' Federation of Great Britain, I say that we do not want a stoppage.

We want to utilise from now onwards, and I take this opportunity of making the offer to the employers now—we want to utilise from now onwards the two great national organisations so that we may not only maintain the existing conditions in the industry, but, by joint conscientious and considered action, we may be able to build that industry higher towards the day when it can give to our men a living wage—a real wage on which they can live.

After these opening speeches of the leaders of the parties, and after the sombre utterance with its moving passages of the spokesman of the Miners' Federation, there was no question but that the Bill would pass without difficulty. The next day the Bill went through Committee in a little over one hundred minutes, and then was read a third time and passed. The next day, July 8, 1931, there came a message early in the afternoon from the House of Lords that they had agreed to the Coal Mines Bill.

Before seven o'clock the Commons were invited to attend the House of Lords to hear the Lords Commissioners, and on their return the Speaker reported that the Royal Assent had been given to the Coal Mines Act, 1931.

II. ANNUAL CONFERENCE JULY 20–24, 1931

The events of history in Britain were now moving fast and, as the miners were soon to find, not only within the coal industry. Twelve days after the remarkably expeditious passing of the Coal Mines Act, 1931, the Annual Conference of the M.F.G.B. assembled in Blackpool at the Co-operative Hall. Little time had been given the miners to reflect either on the effect of this legislation which had been rushed through so rapidly, or upon the prospects that now lay before them. The Vice-President, Ebby Edwards, had to give, without much preparation, a Presidential Address.[1] He said that the industrial depression "which for so many years has enveloped our chief industries" was at last affecting the entire economic and financial systems of the world. In this country, the so-called sheltered workers—the railwaymen, the transport workers, the distributive workers, the civil servants, etc., "had all had their wages menaced" during the past year: and they had lived in an atmosphere of "wage cuts." "In fact," said Edwards, "the contradictions of world capitalism will ever seek to readjust themselves on the bodies and souls of those least able to defend themselves; on those with no other means but the power to labour." Then on the recent settlement he said:

Judged in comparison with our demand for a 7-hour day and a legal minimum wage, it is nothing to be jubilant about. Yet, contrasted with the alternative of a national stoppage which with the risks and uncertainties to the men and to the trade would have been a national calamity, our settlement or truce was at least one in respect of which we can declare a certain amount of commonsense satisfaction. (Monday, July 20, 1931.)

[1] Ebby Edwards had not only presided at the M.F.G.B. Special Conferences of the end of June and beginning of July, but had given to the delegates the full report of the negotiations both with the Government and with the owners. Throughout that summer Vice-President Edwards had been acting both for the President, Tom Richards, and for the Secretary, A. J. Cook, each of whom was a very sick man.

Then he went on to speak of the immediate future: what policies were necessary in the interests of the industry and "likewise in the interests of our members." He put forward two essentials:

Firstly, to raise the economic level of the industry, and secondly, to make our own organisation fully representative of the mineworkers of this country: both policies are of vital importance.

In this one sentence lay the programme which Edwards, and the Federation as it came to accept his guidance, was to pursue for many years ahead. After elaborating on these two policies he dealt with rationalisation, first in its application to production ("the Federation favours the fullest possible extension of labour-saving machinery") and then in its social aspect. He gave the following figures:

Year	Total output cut by machinery	Coal-cutting machines in use	Coal conveyors in use
	%	No.	No.
1901	1	445	n.a.
1914	9	3,093	408
1921	14	5,259	818
1930	30	8,000	3,000

After giving these figures of mechanisation, Edwards considered the effect this was bound to have in reducing the numbers employed, saying:

It is not a process adapted to meet the human needs of the workers. The primary motive of rationalisation is an economic weapon to be used in an industrial war of competition. Once monopoly goes and competition becomes general, rationalisation is merely an instrument in the industrial fight for cheapness.

Under a sane system of society rationalisation should reduce the working time and give improved standards to the workers. Instead of this, you rationalise and produce unemployment, and the reduced number work with increased intensity. Such are the conditions as they exist today. Rationalisation should be carried out in conjunction with the workers' organisation, to secure full protection for those displaced and for the safety of those working. (Monday, July 20, 1931.)

Lastly he turned to the application of scientific methods. In this he called attention to the various processes and made some remarks, the full significance of which was perhaps only appreciated many years later both in his references to oil and also the sugar beet industry "which . . . has received in six years a £60,000,000 subsidy."

Why cannot this nation set itself the task of establishing a synthetic oil industry? It is claimed that the hydrogenation process allows for the conversion of coal either into pure petrol, or into petrol, diesel oil and fuel oil in variable proportions. The small plant at Billingham has proved this. If only twice the money we have given to the sugar beet industry was utilised in this way a demand exceeding 20 million tons of coal per annum would be the result. This would materially assist the industry economically and it would also provide employment for a considerable number of persons. On these and similar lines we welcome every advance.

Edwards ended with a call upon the owners and the Government to make the fullest use of the possibilities in this direction. But to this call there was no adequate answer either then or later.

The delegates then passed a series of resolutions, most of which required legislation for their fulfilment. These demands were that tools and explosives should be supplied free by the employer; that workmen should not be required to work in high humidity underground; that part of the Miners' Welfare Fund be used for a pension fund for aged miners; that the Health Insurance Act be amended so that full benefit be given, "irrespective of any previous periods of sickness." Then they turned to the question of checkweighmen. It was in 1860 that the first Act was passed enabling checkweighers to be chosen by the men employed. It is notorious, and indeed widely recorded,[1] how much trouble this gave in the later nineteenth century. There must, however, have been many who thought that no further amendment of the law was necessary after the great legislation of the Coal Mines Act of 1911 and similar smaller measures. But at the beginning of the fourth decade of the twentieth century the delegates from the coal-fields were still discussing how to get a law that would give the needed security to the elected checkweighmen.

[1] See S. and B. Webb, *History of Trade Unions*; and also *The Miners* (1949) and *The Scottish Miners* (1955), both by R. Page Arnot.

Lastly, the Conference considered the following resolution, spoken for by Executive members from nine Districts:

That we press the Government to introduce a Bill for the Nationalisation of Mines and Minerals, and in case of failure to pass such a measure, we urge the Labour Party to make Mines Nationalisation the chief plank in its next election programme. (July 22, 1931.)

It was carried unanimously. As we shall see, events within a few weeks were completely to overturn any possibility of this kind for many years to come. But the second portion of the resolution was carried out nearly a decade and a half later.

12. THE MINERS AND UNEMPLOYMENT

Over the delegates at Blackpool there hung a dark cloud. One-fifth of the miners unemployed in January and then an increase on this figure at a rate of over 30,000 a month —this was indeed cause for alarm. In an industry where depression before the crisis had lasted so long, the Miners' Federation had for years been increasingly concerned with unemployment: but at this Annual Conference their concern was concentrated on the Royal Commission on Unemployment Insurance, set up on December 9, 1930. The General Council of the Trades Union Congress denounced it and especially its terms of reference (to make recommendations on the Unemployment Insurance Scheme, on "the means by which it may be made solvent and self-supporting," and on arrangements "outside the scheme for the unemployed"). They refused at first to give evidence, but a soft answer turneth away wrath: and this was given to them in deputation by Ramsay MacDonald. Therefore the Miners' Federation Executive Committee put its views in a memorandum prepared by S. O. Davies of South Wales and T. Trotter of Durham. These were embodied by the T.U.C. General Council and formed part of their Memorandum of Evidence submitted to the Royal Commission on May 4, 1931. This lengthy memorandum put forward a complete alternative to the unstable system of the Unemployment

Insurance Acts. Its argument may be briefly summarised. At the outset it denounced the discrimination and "splitting the unemployed" implicit in the terms of reference, saying:

We cannot agree for a moment when the mere fact of a man being fairly regularly employed entitles him to benefit as a right when unemployed, that one less fortunate, who really needs more benefit and not less, should be deprived of it altogether or subjected to a prying inquiry into his domestic circumstances as a condition of receiving it.

The attempt to operate unemployment benefit on an insurance basis had proved impossible. As far back as the 1920 Act the contention of the workers' representatives had been for a non-contributory basis. There followed a classic statement of the standpoint, once expressed in Keir Hardie's Right to Work Bill:

Unemployment is a national and international problem resulting from the industrial system under which we live. The workers are not the authors of the system but the victims of it, and unless the community so organises its resources as to provide work for every willing worker, the unemployed, as the reserves of industry, are entitled to maintenance.

However strong, skilful, capable and willing a worker may be, his ability to get a livelihood depends on whether his labour can be turned to profitable account by somebody else.

It is surely obvious that a system so organised against the individual must, if it cannot employ him, provide an income for the unemployed worker, not because he is a beggar or a suppliant for relief, but because he is a member of the community with the same right to live as every other member of it. If he is to obey the community's laws, then the community must safeguard his inherent right to a livelihood. (May 4, 1931.)

It was then argued that the contributory system of the Acts was inequitable in various ways:

The unemployed are not responsible for unemployment, but the contributory system of unemployment insurance implies that they are, for it imposes a poll-tax on them while they are employed to provide against their unemployment.

The contributory system, unfair both to workers and to employers, should be abolished. This would get rid of "the present pretence of insurance" and relieve industry of "an unjust burden." The cost of maintenance should be borne by the Exchequer and met from the proceeds of ordinary taxation. Since unemployment in 1931 was "abnormal" because of the world crisis, the emergency should be met by a special graduated levy on all incomes, whether from earnings or from interest and profit. The suggestion was made (anticipating the present system) that the levy be deducted at source when wages and salaries were paid. Everyone who satisfied the statutory conditions (e.g. that the applicant was capable and available for work) would be entitled to unemployment benefit. This should be for loss of employment only "and there should be no means test of any kind." Alleged abuses of benefit had been over-stressed. On the other hand there were many cases where benefit had been unfairly refused, while there was rigidity in the administration of the Acts. Administration should be a joint affair of the trade unions in co-operation with Employment Exchanges.

The Trade Unions should be asked to take over for their members the administration of State Unemployment Benefit from the Exchanges, including the placing of workers.

The existing benefits were too low and the scale should be 20s. a week for workers of eighteen years and over, 10s. for the wife or other adult dependant and 5s. for each child. More than one scathing reference was made to the views of Sir William Beveridge who had stated that in the past trade union benefits plus "other sources" had been enough to make it unnecessary to apply to the Poor Law or other form of relief and who had described the system of State benefits as "the dole":

"Other resources" in the case of the workers means their furniture and effects which they had to pawn or sell before they could get relief, or else live on relatives as poor as themselves. Happily these conditions have disappeared to a great extent and we are satisfied that the nation would not tolerate a return to them. . . . We resent the term "dole" being applied to what is after all the same in principle as "compensation for loss of office" in the case of more fortunate people. (May 4, 1931.)

Such was the tenor of the extensive T.U.C. document which embodied the views of the mining unions and was hailed with approval by the delegates, who in a resolution urged

JOSEPH JONES, PETER LEE AND EBBY EDWARDS
Outside No. 10 Downing Street (December 11, 1933)

IN PLACE OF PITHEAD BATHS

that it be made the basis of a new law on unemployment. The interim Report of the Royal Commission[1] on June 1st, confined to Fund indebtedness, increasing Exchequer costs and alleged abuses, was of a very different tenor. Its recommendations were as follows: to raise weekly contributions, to cut benefits, to cut down the period of benefits, to bring in "other resources" for certain classes of applicants and to deprive certain other classes of their right to benefit. The M.F.G.B. Executive Committee described it as "an impossible and infamous document"[2]: and at the Annual Conference the delegates also recorded their strongest disapproval. When they returned to their coal-fields they found a frightful increase in the number of families who would be subject to these proposals, if put into effect. For in the last week of July 1931 there were 389,182 out of work or 36·4 per cent of the total number of insured miners.

[1] First (interim) Report, Cmd. 3872. Final Report November 1932, Cmd. 4185.
[2] Councillor W. Asbury and Mrs. C. D. Rackham refused to sign it. Those who signed it were His Honour Judge Holman Gregory, Henry Clay (afterwards Sir Henry), Dr. H. J. W. Hetherington (now Sir Hector), E. C. P. Lascelles and H. M. Trouncer.

LABOUR PARTY ELECTION MANIFESTO

(*Excerpt from M.F.G.B. Minutes*)

MEETING between the Federation Officials and the Officials of the Parliamentary Labour Party, Tuesday, March 26, 1929.

Present: For the Parliamentary Labour Party—J. R. MacDonald, J. H. Thomas, G. Lansbury, Philip Snowden, and T. Shaw. For the Federation—H. Smith, Thomas Richards, W. P. Richardson, and A. J. Cook.

Mr. MacDonald said that the purpose of the meeting was to arrive at a mutual understanding as to what should be included in the (shorter) Labour programme at the election in regard to the mining industry, and as to the work which would be undertaken by the Party in regard to the industry in the event of its forming a Government after the election.

Mr. MacDonald said that in the first session of Parliament the Party would not be able to deal with the question of Nationalisation, but would proceed with the immediate problems confronting the industry and affecting the welfare of the men, as laid down by the Blackpool Conference, 1927, and published in the pamphlet *The Mining Situation*. These were:

(*a*) The repeal of the Eight Hours Act.
(*b*) The regulation of the supply of labour by—

> (i) Raising the school-leaving age to 15 or preferably 16, with the provision of the necessary maintenance allowances and preparatory training for other forms of employment.
> (ii) The suspension of recruitment of adult labour from outside the industry and the transfer of unemployed miners under proper arrangements to areas where there is a demand for mineworkers; and
> (iii) Superannuation allowance for mineworkers of 60 years and upwards to be provided partly by a levy on coal royalties, and partly out of the future proceeds of the industry.

The question of hours in particular was an outstanding question and one on which they desired to know the views of the Federation, as the Party were prepared to carry out its pledge and repeal the Eight Hours Act in the first session of Parliament.

The Federation representatives said that while the Federation stood for the repeal of the present Act, it desired that future legislation should provide for a seven and a half hour day bank to bank. They regarded the bank to bank formula as one which should be included in future legislation so as to avoid the inequalities caused by different winding times in different pits and districts.

Upon further discussion it was agreed to include the question of hours in the (shorter) programme, and to use the words in *Labour and the Nation*, page 27, as follows:

"The disastrous Act by which the Tory Government [in 1926] added an hour to the working day of the miners must be at once repealed."

This would make it quite plain that one of the first acts of the Labour Government would be to repeal the present Act.

It was also agreed that the policy of nationalisation as defined in the programme should include the by-product and coking industry.

Mr. MacDonald said that the larger programme of nationalisation of mines, minerals, and by-products would be proceeded with after the first essentials had been dealt with.

A. J. Cook, Secretary.

April 9, 1929.

CHAPTER II

THE DEBACLE

I. THE GATHERING STORM

ONE month after the Annual Conference of the Miners' Federation had ended at Blackpool, with resolutions asking their Labour Government to introduce legislation, their Labour Government had ceased to exist. Some sixty years earlier on the international field the regime of Louis Bonaparte in France had suffered a sudden unexpected and utter collapse in the Franco-Prussian war: when that summer of 1870 ended with the defeat and humiliation of France and the suspicion that some of its Marshals had played into the enemy's hands, it was commonly described as "The Debacle." Something similar, though on a domestic scale and without the use of material weapons, overtook the Labour Government. In the third week of August 1931 there was a Labour Government: in the fourth week of August there was a Government composed mainly of Conservatives and Liberals, but headed by three leading members of the Labour Cabinet: J. Ramsay MacDonald, Philip Snowden and J. H. Thomas. With them, too, went Lord Sankey who, in the M.F.G.B. Annual Conference, had been publicly referred to as one of the firmest friends of the miner.[1]

What was the background to these surprising events of 1931? The economic background was the world crisis signalled by the crash on Wall Street in October 1929: it was four months after the second Labour Government

[1] Twelve years earlier Lord Sankey, by his pungent and upright conduct in the chair of the Royal Commission on the Coal Industry had earned the hatred of members of his own class and was exposed to ostracism and boycott in his West End clubs and in the other circles in which he moved. Having later joined the Labour Party, he was made Lord Chancellor in the second MacDonald administration of 1929–31. Now he was to be regarded as a turncoat to the party in which he had made his spiritual home; yet it must be said that both at the time and afterwards the only real regret amongst former colleagues for those whose departure nearly destroyed the Parliamentary Labour Party was in the case of John Sankey.

had taken office with 288 seats in the House of Commons, while the Tories had 260 and the Liberals 58. During the next two years the Labour Government was able to maintain itself precariously only by entering into close relations with the Liberal Party headed by Lloyd George. Wherever the Liberals did not agree with any proposed measures the Labour Cabinet found itself in a dilemma: either to push ahead with the proposed measure and risk Liberal opposition votes in Parliament which, added to the Tory vote, would have brought the Government down and a dissolution of Parliament; or to retreat. On the other hand, the Liberal Party were not so willing to face a dissolution until their proposal for a reform of the electoral system by an Alternative Vote had been carried through by the Government. Thus the Liberals were also in a dilemma whenever a difference arose between them and their Labour Government allies. It has to be recorded, however, that on most of the major issues Ramsay MacDonald and his Cabinet retreated. The result of this was that not only the miners but other Labour supporters were increasingly dissatisfied. This mood found its main expression in the General Council of the Trades Union Congress, with whose views, for example, on the Royal Commission on Unemployment Insurance the Miners' Federation Annual Conference were in such full agreement. Meanwhile pressure was being exercised by bankers of the City of London and by other big financial and monopolist interests who sought to bind the Labour Government to their way of thinking and to adopt the solutions that best suited them for the ever-deepening economic crisis.

The world economic crisis had brought problems including increased mass unemployment which the Labour Cabinet proved incapable of solving: and for which they proposed, in the main, well-worn traditionalist measures, including the plans of the Chancellor of the Exchequer, Philip Snowden, whose outlook on finance had become largely that of the orthodox bankers in the City of London. Snowden was a fanatical adherent of the Gold Standard, and also of Free Trade, to which Liberal dogma he held firm even after the bankers in their manifesto had abandoned it in 1930. After many months of worsening conditions and for a mass of the unemployed of increasing destitution, Snowden, faced by a possible budget deficit, accepted early in 1931 a Liberal proposal for an "independent" Committee to suggest cuts.

In the House of Commons a Conservative motion of censure on the Government for its increased expenditure had been countered by this Liberal amendment. Snowden in his speech had startled some members of his own party and had said that to get over "the present temporary crisis" would need an effort:

It will involve some temporary sacrifices from all, and those best able to bear them will have to make the largest sacrifices. In the general sacrifice, the Members of the Cabinet are prepared to make their substantial contribution. (February 11, 1931.)

After the Conservative motion of censure was defeated by 310 votes to 235, the tellers for the Liberal amendment found they were getting the support of the majority of the Labour Party and also, needless to say, of the Tory Party. Their amendment, which was carried by 468 votes to 21, ran as follows:

That this House considers that, having regard to the effect of the present burden of taxation in restricting industry and employment, the Government should at once appoint a small and independent committee to make recommendations to Mr. Chancellor of the Exchequer for effecting forthwith all practical and legitimate reductions in the national expenditure consistent with the efficiency of the services. (February 11, 1931.)

The twenty-one opponents in the No Lobby were mainly made up of the followers of James Maxton as leader of the I.L.P. in the House of Commons. There were also some M.P.s of independent mind or whose position as General Secretaries of trade unions made them more aware than other members of how menacing the resolution was, such as Dr. Somerville Hastings, John Bromley of the Locomotive Engineers and Firemen and also T. E. Naylor of the London Society of Compositors. There were only three of the two score mining M.P.s who seem to have perceived all that it might mean. But amongst these three was Ebby Edwards, who represented the leadership of the Miners' Federation inside the House of Commons, and outside was not only Vice-Chairman but soon to be Acting Chairman and Acting Secretary.

The others were Thomas Cape of Cumberland (always very close to the M.F.G.B. leadership) and Fred Hall of the Normanton division of the West Riding of Yorkshire.

The "small and independent committee," sometimes referred to as the "Economy Committee," but more often as the "May Committee," had terms of reference corresponding to the Commons resolution.

Of its seven members only two had any connection with Labour: one was Arthur Pugh, General Secretary to the Iron and Steel Trades Confederation; the other was Charles Latham (later Lord Latham), an accountant by profession, neither of whom signed the Report. The others were men whose names were constantly to be found on Government Committees and Inquiries; but who, above all, were company directors of the biggest industrial and financial interests, which ranged from banks, insurance, railways and shipping to oil and overseas trading concerns. Their Chairman, Sir George May, was in addition the Secretary of the Prudential Assurance Co., Ltd.

The setting up of the May Committee had tided the Government over a difficulty by this concession to its Liberal allies. But as it turned out the operations of the May Committee, whose sessions were taking place in the spring and early summer of 1931, were to involve the Government, and also the finances and economy of the country, in greater difficulties than before.

2. THE FINANCIAL CRISIS

Other countries of Europe were also deeply involved in the world economic crisis. As the crisis deepened the strain on the financial structure, including the banks, greatly increased. In Austria on May 11, 1931, the Kredit-Anstalt Bank in Vienna failed. In Germany the Darmstadter Bank closed its doors on July 13th. There was a run on the other banks: and on the next day, July 14th, the German Government closed all banks including savings banks. In Hungary, Roumania and other countries banks failed. As one financial failure followed another payments were stopped. In particular

interest on long loans which financial institutions in Britain
had made to Germany could no longer be paid. At this point
President Hoover of the United States announced a mora-
torium on reparations payments. The British banks and
other financial institutions suddenly found themselves in a
cleft stick. The British Government hastily summoned a
financial Conference of seven European Powers on July 20th:
after three days the Conference disbanded having accomplished little. A series of heavy withdrawals of gold from
London began. By July 22nd the Bank of England had lost
£22 million in gold. The next day it raised the bank rate
from 2½ per cent to 3½ per cent. This had little effect and a
week later the rate was raised to 4½ per cent (on July 30th).
Two days later the Bank of England announced that it had
obtained £50 million credit in equal parts from the United
States and from France. At this point, on Friday, July 31st,
the May Committee's Report was published.[1]

This Majority Report (for the two Labour members
refused to sign it) contained a most depressing and, as many
have estimated, a grossly exaggerated picture of the plight
of British economy. It foretold a budget deficit by spring of
1932 of £120 million and made recommendations for cuts
of over £96 million in State expenditures, mainly on social
services; and for £24 million to be met by new taxation.
Unemployment benefit was to be cut by 20 per cent.
It also proposed cuts in pay, including that of teachers
by 20 per cent, of police by 12½ per cent, while the Armed
Forces were to be put back on the 1925 rates of pay. Altogether of the £96 million recommended reductions, two-
thirds (£66,500,000) were to be got out of unemployment
insurance. This Majority Report had two immediate effects:
the first was that it rallied together and combined all the
different pressures of the ruling circles of the City and of the
big financial institutions and industries upon the Labour
Government. The millionaire-owned newspaper press headed
by *The Times* had already been conducting day after day an
unremitting campaign: that campaign was now enormously
intensified. The second effect, perhaps not wholly anticipated,
was the alarm that it caused amongst the financiers of Europe

---

[1] *Committee on National Expenditure Report*, 1931, Cmd. 3920.

and North America. An already difficult position was rapidly worsening. Foreign balances were more and more being withdrawn from London. The temporary credit to the Bank of England of £50 million was rapidly being used up. The belief grew amongst the financiers of Europe and North America that the British economy was entirely unsound, especially because of the condition of the Unemployment Insurance Fund, and a reluctance developed, or at any rate was simulated, towards the grant of any further loan except upon conditions imposed by foreigners. Thus the May Committee, which had been set up to placate the Liberals and Conservatives who were clamouring for cuts in social expenditures, had actually the effect of making the situation very much worse. The forebodings of Ebby Edwards and of the small minority of Labour members who had voted against the May Committee now seemed to be fully justified.

The day before the May Committee Report was published, on July 30th, the Labour Cabinet appointed a sub-committee to examine the Report, by which of course they were not bound in any way, and to submit proposals. The Cabinet Economy Committee, as this sub-committee came to be called, consisted of Messrs. Ramsay MacDonald, Snowden, Henderson, Thomas and Graham. With the extension of the financial crisis they had to meet sooner than expected and had to consider proposals put forward by the Treasury, while at the same time they were to hear increasingly alarming reports from officials of the Bank of England, then a semi-independent body. The bankers, either on their own account, or on the authority of Ramsay MacDonald, summoned the leaders of the Conservative and Liberal Parties, then on holiday in Scotland or elsewhere, to come to London. The Cabinet Economy Committee considered a programme of cuts totalling £78 million at their meetings from August 12th to August 17th. These were submitted to a meeting of the full Labour Cabinet on Wednesday, August 19th, which provisionally accepted cuts totalling over £56 million. Of this amount £22 million was on unemployment insurance, £10·7 million on education, including a 15 per cent cut in teachers' salaries, £9 million on defence, including a reduction in pay of the Forces. It also provided for cuts in

c*

the pay of Cabinet Ministers, civil servants and judges. The saving of £22 million on unemployment insurance included increased contributions, the stoppage of benefit after twenty-six weeks, the imposition of a Means Test on those who thereafter applied for transitional benefit, and finally the removal of "anomalies."[1] The question of a 10 per cent cut in unemployment benefit was discussed and deferred since a minority of Ministers were not willing to agree. Much had been provisionally agreed to on that day of August 19th by the Labour Cabinet.

3. THE DILEMMA—AND ITS OUTCOME

Meanwhile there had been a rapid development of resistance to the cuts amongst the rank-and-file of the trade unions and of all the other organisations of the Labour movement. Apart from those who argued that in capitalist society any talk of "equality of sacrifice" was demagogy or deception of the poor in the interests of the rich, there were others who recalled that when the May Committee had been arranged by Chancellor of the Exchequer Snowden in his February speech, he had stated that "those best able to bear them will have to make the largest sacrifices." It was pointed out that the reverse spectacle was presented by the May Committee's recommendations to cast the burden upon those least able to bear it: and that out of the £96 million proposed savings to the Exchequer over two-thirds would be out of unemployment insurance, and of the remainder the greater part would be at the expense of salaries and wages. Consequently, while the meetings of bankers and Treasury officials, of Cabinet members and Liberal and Conservative statesmen were being convened

---

[1] The saving on anomalies, though included in those figures, had already been decided upon the previous month. The Interim Report of the Holman Gregory Royal Commission on Unemployment Insurance had proposed dealing with "anomalies" and the Anomalies Bill (Unemployment Insurance No. 3) had been hastily passed through Parliament in the latter days of July. This Act prevented an insured married working woman under certain conditions from receiving benefit if her husband was also in receipt of benefit. This bore hard upon families in such districts as Lancashire and seemed to confirm the foreboding of the T.U.C. memorandum that it might "result in penalising women who are perfectly genuine and entitled to benefit." On the Royal Commission Mrs. Rackham had opposed any such discrimination on account of sex or marriage.

and reconvened in the second and third weeks of August, there was mounting opposition and growing indignation against the whole economy programme of cuts initiated by the May Committee and the bankers' offensive. Thus it was now members of the Labour Cabinet who were to find themselves in a dilemma.

If the axe were to fall mainly on the lower incomes, it was openly held and publicly stated that the best way of doing this with the least friction was to get it carried through by a Labour Government. Every possible pressure, including the influence of the monarchy, was to be used for this purpose. But the counter-pressure exerted by the working class was sufficient to set in motion the trade union organisations: and the General Council of the Trades Union Congress now took up a definite standpoint. In the afternoon of Thursday, August 20th, the Cabinet Economy Committee (MacDonald, Snowden, Henderson, Thomas and Graham) attended a joint meeting of the National Executive Committee of the Labour Party and of the General Council of the Trades Union Congress and explained the scheme of economy cuts that had been provisionally agreed to by the Cabinet. That same evening the T.U.C. General Council rose at 8 p.m., having discussed the matter for four hours and having reached the decision that they "must oppose the whole thing." A hundred minutes later their deputation of five met the five of the Cabinet Economy Committee in Downing Street: and, with Bevin and Citrine as the spokesmen, made it clear that they were against all the cuts proposed, while to meet the difficulties they suggested alternatives, such as new taxation upon unearned incomes.

The standpoint of the trade unions was decisive. The sharpened division in the Cabinet, rendered more tense by financial operations against the pound sterling, reached the point on Sunday, August 23rd, when the majority (12) against the minority (9) were for acceptance of a 10 per cent cut in unemployment benefit. This resulted first in deadlock and then in resignation. MacDonald was authorised to offer the resignation of the Labour ministry to the King. George V, who had been conferring with Baldwin and with Samuel (the latter of whom had also given the opinion that "really

adequate" economies carried through by a Labour Cabinet
would be "the best solution" and a National Government
under MacDonald "the best alternative") then persuaded
MacDonald to hold his resignation till there had been a
meeting of the three party leaders with him the next day.
On the morrow (Monday, August 24, 1931) MacDonald
returned from the palace. His Cabinet colleagues were told
first, that His Majesty had accepted their resignation, and
second, that he himself had accepted the royal commission
to form a "National Government" together with Tories and
Liberals in order to keep the pound on the gold standard
and otherwise deal with the financial situation. With him
went Snowden, Thomas and Lord Chancellor Sankey. This
was the switch-over. Beatrice Webb, whose husband was a
Cabinet Minister, wrote that same day in her diary:

A startling sensation it will be for those faithful followers
throughout the country who were unaware of J. R. M. and
Snowden's gradual conversion to the outlook of the city and
"London Society." Thomas has never been a Socialist and will
probably cease, like other *ci-devant* trade union leaders, to be
even formally on the side of the Labour movement.
So ends, ingloriously, the Labour Cabinet of 1929–31. A victory
for the American and British financiers—a dangerous one, because
it is an open declaration, without any disguise, of capitalist
dictatorship; and a brutal defiance of the Labour movement.[1]

Three days later the M.F.G.B. Executive Committee met
and the Committee heard a report from the Secretary of a
meeting[2] between the late Labour Government and the
General Council of the Trades Union Congress respecting
the measures contemplated by the late Government to
meet the financial crisis. The Committee also received a
report of a meeting held between the General Council and
the Labour Party, following the formation of the new
Government. They resolved unanimously:

This Executive Committee having received a full report of the
meetings of the General Council and the Labour Party Executive,
approves of the attitude adopted by these bodies in their determination resolutely to oppose the expedients adopted by the new

[1] *Beatrice Webb's Diaries 1924–32.* Ed. by Margaret Cole.
[2] In the Sixty-Third Report of the Trades Union Congress held at Bristol there is
given a special section setting out an account in considerable detail of this meeting.

Government, particularly respecting Unemployment, and this Executive instructs its Mining Members of Parliament to support, without fail, the policy adopted by the T.U.C. and the Labour Party. (August 27, 1931.)

When it came to parliamentary action this emphatic, and indeed demonstrative, "instruction" was obeyed by the mining Members of Parliament in a body, and they provided the hard core of resistance in the Parliamentary Labour Party.

4. THE GENERAL ELECTION OF 1931

What happened after MacDonald, who was to remain Prime Minister till 1935, had constructed his Cabinet with the help of Baldwin and Samuel?[1] The new "National Government" was to keep the pound on the gold standard: and for this purpose on August 28th received a credit of £80 million from the U.S.A. and France. Before a fortnight was out foreign funds were again being withdrawn. The Forces pay cuts were followed on September 15th by the Invergordon mutiny in the Navy. The financial sluices were burst open. On Wednesday, September 16th, and the two following days £33,000,000 of foreign balances and foreign-held British securities were realised and withdrawn from London—in three days. On September 20th the pound was off the gold standard.

The new Cabinet was to be temporary until the crisis was overcome, when the parties in it would separate and fight a General Election which was to be some way ahead: by October 5th Parliament was dissolved and the "National Government" parties were fighting the election together. The result of the election was an overwhelming defeat of the Labour Party, which got 46 seats against 556 for the "National Government." Out of the serried ranks of the new Government's supporters, a baker's dozen of thirteen were the muster of MacDonald and his direct "National Labour" following. The one ex-Cabinet Minister returned

[1] Lloyd George, who was ill at the time, refused categorically then and later to join the Coalition Government, and Samuel was left to lead the bulk of the surviving Liberals into it.

was George Lansbury, who became leader of the dwindled Labour Party. Other ex-ministers back were Attlee and Cripps.

By the beginning of October the Miners' Executive were considering the list of candidates submitted by Districts for the forthcoming General Election. Polling day was October 27th. In their Report to the Annual Conference of 1932 (completed on June 16, 1932) the Executive Committee stated:

We issued a manifesto[1] to the coalfields urging all our members and all voters in the mining areas to vote for the Labour candidate. Nearly 500,000 of these were sent to the constituencies, and we believe they materially helped to save our mining candidates from the debacle which occurred in other areas.

The results of the voting in the constituencies contested by Federation candidates were as follows:

No. of Federation Candidates	No. of Federation Candidates returned	Votes Cast		
		Federation Candidates	Conservatives	Others
43	23	778,328	536,482	176,286

These results show that more votes were given for the Federation (Labour) candidates than were given for all the candidates of the other parties; indeed, but for the solidarity of the miners in certain areas, the Labour Party would have fared very badly indeed, as the miners' representatives now formed half[2] the total Labour representation in Parliament.

Reflecting on this debacle seven months later the Executive Committee in its Annual Report wrote:

We feel we should say a few words about the Election itself. In our view, Labour never had a stronger case than during the last Election. The financial crisis was the result of the mistaken monetary policy which had been followed for many years by the Bank of England and other financial institutions in this country. That policy, commencing with the return to the Gold Standard in 1925, had the effect of enormously over-valuing the pound sterling in terms of the currencies of other countries.

The result was to make this country an exceedingly good country for other countries to sell in, but a very bad country from which to buy goods. Imports were stimulated, and exports fell away, so that an adverse balance of trade set in causing the inevitable drain

[1] The text of this manifesto, unfortunately, was not preserved in the records.
[2] See Appendix to this chapter.

of gold, which, if unchecked, leads to an unsound financial position. This position had been reached a few months before the Labour Government resigned, and for several months before that time the Gold Reserve was gradually being drained.

The Report noted the part played by the press in preparing public opinion to accept the cuts in unemployment assistance:

The Press then started a tremendous campaign against the Unemployment Insurance Fund. Day after day *The Times* and other papers published scare-mongering articles predicting National insolvency if the Unemployment Fund was not balanced. These articles were published with the object of forcing the Labour Government to take steps to balance the Fund, but they enormously increased the general sense of insecurity caused by the increasing drain of gold, and eventually produced the financial crisis which forced the Labour Government out of office.

The essential point to be grasped here is that the root cause of the trouble was not the Unemployment Insurance Fund, or the existing level of taxation, or any of the other red herrings so assiduously dangled before the public eye, but the over-valuation of the £ which resulted from the policy of our financial authorities.

Our members will readily appreciate that no currency can be indefinitely maintained at an artificial value in terms of other currencies, and that sooner or later it must revert to purchasing power parity. For years our financial authorities had artificially maintained it at a figure which was far above its true value, and disaster was inevitable.

After explaining the effect upon the election results of all these factors, the Report ended on a note of determination:

When the crash came, these people, with their Tory and Liberal allies, endeavoured to place the responsibility for the disaster on the shoulders of the Labour Government, and when the Labour Government refused to accept the responsibility, they were thrown out of Office. In the election which followed, all this was carefully hidden, and the Labour Party was submerged, under a torrent of abuse and misrepresentation.

For those who, in the midst of this avalanche, were firm in their Socialist faith, we have the greatest admiration; they will form the vanguard of the great army which will ultimately ensure the victory of Socialism. (Annual Conference, July 1932.)

The General Election over, Ramsay MacDonald reconstructed his Coalition administration so that instead of the temporary Cabinet of ten (four Conservative, two Liberal and four "National Labour") there were now twenty, made up of eleven Conservatives, three Liberals, two National Liberals, and four National Labour. This Coalition, under the name of "The National Government," was to last for nearly nine years. Already before the dissolution of Parliament on October 7th there had been passed an emergency budget and the National Economy Act, based on the proposals of the Holman Gregory Royal Commission and the May Committee. The general effect was a 10 per cent cut in wages or salaries of all in Government service, an example which employers in private industry were not slow to follow. For those out of work provisions made by Orders in Council under the National Economy Act raised contributions, lowered benefits, reduced the period of benefit, and thereafter handed over applicants to the Public Assistance Committees. The weekly contributions were raised from 8d. from the employer, 7d. from the employed and 7½d. from the Exchequer to 10d. each. Workpeople bore the highest percentage increase in this: it was 43 per cent while the employers paid 25 per cent more, and the Exchequer some 33 per cent. Weekly benefits were cut from 17s. to 15s. 3d. with 8s. (instead of 9s.) for the wife: and 2s. for each child. Six months earlier the T.U.C. memorandum's proposed increase had worked out at 45s. for a family of five, with the argument:

Nobody can conscientiously say that 17s. is more than enough to keep an unemployed man for a week or that 32s. is too much for a man, wife and three children. To any thinking person it is a constant source of wonder as to how the unemployed exist on such amounts. Many of those who urge a reduction of benefit would themselves spend such an amount on a single meal or for a seat at a theatre.

There was to be a limit of 156 days in a benefit year after which there would be no further insurance benefits until ten contributions had been paid. This meant an increase in the number of applicants for "transitional benefit," who would then have to undergo a means test, instituted on November 12, 1931.

This last provision fell with particular severity upon miners, amongst whom so many scores of thousands, long before the crisis years, had exhausted their statutory insurance benefits and who therefore in very large numbers had

now to undergo a means test administered by the Public
Assistance Committees. Wherever any such local authority
proved unwilling to administer the full rigours of a means
test power was taken under the Act to suspend it and to
replace it by an appointee from Whitehall. In most cases,
however, the inquisition into family resources was carried
out and caused widespread resentment. A single example
from Northumberland may make clear the operation of the
Means Test:

> Unemployed man with invalid wife, seven children of school age,
> one girl of 16 years earning 8s. a week, one boy of 14 not working,
> and one in the army sends home 5s. 3d. per week. The son's army
> allowance plus the girl's wages are assessed and claimant's benefit
> under the Means Test is reduced from 37s. 9d. per week to 21s. 9d.
> Therefore, two adults, two adolescents and seven children have to
> live on 35s. a week, out of which rent has to be paid.

This case was not exceptional, but typical of the multitude
of cases reported by the Trades Union Congress, which in
its 1932 memorandum to the Ministry of Labour described
the behaviour of the investigating officials as "harassing and
persecution of the unfortunate unemployed." A later generation may find it hard to believe that in 1931 there was
enacted legislation which brought such moral degradation
to all concerned with it. But a deeper stigma must rest on
those who devised it.

5. NEW OFFICERS

That month after the defeat of Labour was marked by the
death of both the Secretary of the Miners' Federation,
A. J. Cook, and the President, Tom Richards. Cook died
on November 2nd after a long and painful illness. He had
been Secretary since June 1924. In the obituary contributed
by his colleagues it was said:

> The one great desire of our late Secretary's life was to advance
> both the immediate and the ultimate welfare of the men he
> represented, and in his sincerity and wholehearted devotion to
> their cause [he] won the admiration of men in every walk of life.
> The outstanding feature of Mr. Cook's work was his public
> addresses. In this sphere, he did an enormous amount of work

and he never spared himself on these occasions. His speeches were something more than the ordinary Trade Union addresses; they were great physical efforts. In these efforts, such was his devotion to the cause, that it has been well said of him: "He spoke not only with his mouth, but with his arms, his legs, and with the whole of his body."

He was, indeed, a remarkable personality, and his death at a time when his great gifts and energies were being directed and used in the true interests of the miners was a tragic blow to our movement.

Tom Richards died later in that same November. He had been Secretary of the South Wales Miners' Federation for over thirty years, Vice-President of the Miners' Federation from 1925 to 1930, President in 1930 to 1931. The obituary by his colleagues said:

He had all the sagacity and sound common sense of Enoch Edwards; all the great ability and personal charm of Robert Smillie, and when necessary he could fight with all the vigour and determination of Herbert Smith. To these qualities were added a delightful sense of humour, an innate courtesy of manner, and a respect for the feelings of others which marked the true gentleman.

For him, the social conventions which separate man from man did not exist; before his broad and human outlook on life, all artificiality vanished. His very personality typified the classless society of the future, for, as the economic structure changes and as more and more of our people acquire his culture and his qualities, so inevitably must class barriers be broken down. The miners were proud of Tom Richards and they revere his memory. Well may they do so, for of him it may be truly said: "He was a man."

Ebby Edwards had been appointed President of the Federation at the Annual Conference, where the following votes had been given:

President..	..	*E. Edwards	.. 424,082
		H. Smith	.. 100,000
Vice-President	..	*P. Lee ..	.. 196,613
		H. Hicken	.. 164,980
		J. Jones	.. 133,094
		F. Swift	.. 29,395

* Person elected.

From the week of the previous Secretary's death it had been agreed that "the President, Mr. E. Edwards, be appointed to supervise the secretarial work until the vacancy has been filled." (November 6, 1931.) In point of fact

Edwards had been to a large extent filling both the main positions for the previous six months. Nominations for the post of permanent Secretary of the Federation were recorded at the end of January. Candidates were Ebby Edwards (Northumberland), Joseph Jones (Yorkshire), W. H. Mainwaring (South Wales) and Peter Pemberton (Lancashire and Cheshire). Whilst each candidate was nominated by his own District, Ebby Edwards was also nominated by most of the remaining Districts.

The ballot was carried out at the end of February, and by March 10th the Report from the Proportional Representation Society in charge of the counting of the election had been delivered in "a sealed envelope." In accordance with the report it was unanimously agreed that Mr. Ebby Edwards "stands duly elected as Secretary of the Federation." (March 10, 1932). The details given in an Annexe to the Report showed that only two counts had been necessary.

Candidates	First Count No. of Valid Votes	Second Count Transfer of Votes of Mainwaring and Pemberton	Result
Edwards	165,645	+ 29,956	195,601
Jones	98,265	+ 33,801	132,066
Mainwaring	47,239	− 47,239	—
Pemberton	30,186	− 30,186	—
Non-transferable Votes ..	—	+ 13,668	13,668
TOTALS	341,335	—	341,335

Ebby Edwards, who was born in 1884 in Chevington in Northumberland, had been very well known as an ardent advocate of Socialism amongst the Northumbrian miners. His shrewd and pithy speeches (uttered in the strong Northumbrian dialect which he has never wholly lost) had gained attention at miners' Conferences during the 1914–18 war. In that war he contested Wansbeck[1] at a by-election

[1] Ebby Edwards was a hewer at Ashington (by far the largest pit in Northumberland) when he stood as candidate in Spring, 1918, and again at the December General Election of that year. He had joined the I.L.P. in 1906 and soon was carrying on a vigorous Socialist propaganda sometimes in the shape of long letters in the *Morpeth Herald* in which he defended the teachings of Marx against attacks and set forth his tenets accompanied by strong criticism of MacDonald and Snowden. At the same time he was assisting Jack Williams who had been since the 'eighties a close worker with H. M. Hyndman and others of the Social Democratic Federation, to sell copies of *Justice*. For this activity he was in 1909 asked to resign from the I.L.P. In the same year his union, by the decision of the M.F.G.B., had become a constituent of the Labour Party and after this Edwards had no other political affiliation.

on May 28, 1918, and the contest drew the attention of the
whole country.

For over a third of a century the member for the Wansbeck
division of Northumberland had been Charles Fenwick,
born at Cramlington in 1850. Fenwick as a working miner
went straight from the coal-face into Parliament in 1885
where he joined Tom Burt, also of Northumberland, who
at the 1874 General Election, together with the famous
Alexander Macdonald, had been the first working-men
representatives after nearly six centuries' existence of the
British Parliament. Fenwick in the House of Commons was
sustained from the funds of the Northumberland Miners'
Association, but when the Miners' Federation affiliated to
the Labour Party Fenwick refused to sign the Labour Party
constitution, and from the 1910 General Election continued
to accept the Liberal Whip as he had done since his entry.
He had been made a Privy Councillor. When he died on
April 20, 1918, it was clear to everyone that it was "a miners'
seat." So it was decided by the Northumberland miners, and
such too was the decision of the Miners' Federation. But
there was at that moment a Coalition Government and a
party truce. Consequently the Liberal Party could claim
the seat and the Labour Party Executive were against any
candidature. The Wansbeck Labour Representation Committee as a branch of the Labour Party had either to obey
the Labour Party Executive, saying no contest, or the
Miners' Federation insisting on a contest. They obeyed the
latter. They chose Ebby Edwards as their candidate and
as a result on one of the very few occasions in the last three
years of the First World War there was a contested by-
election. The Liberals, with singular absence of tact, had
chosen to oppose a miner with the candidature of a ship-
owner—or at any rate a shipping agent. The shipping interests
already had earned an evil name by the high freights they
charged during the war, which had given rise to the words
"profiteer" and "profiteering."

At the first meeting of the election campaign Ebby Edwards
declared:

I stand here to support the Labour Party war aims programme,
believing that it is the only consistent, the only logical, and the

only correct basis to secure us a lasting and permanent settlement.

When we entered the war in 1914 our lads went for the violation of Belgium and went with the truest spirit of patriotism. We ought to do homage to them, but we have something more to do. What has gone on since then? Secret treaties have been formed. We have treaties to take lads to every part of the globe. Belgium is not now in it.

We have a right to ask—I stand to ask—that all secret treaties that have been formed for the extension of territories be repudiated in the interests of the lads who went to fight for freedom.

I do not stand for peace at any price.

War cannot be an end in itself. If the slaughter is to continue, and if we are out to create an international graveyard then I say life is not worth living. The employing classes have failed, and I say let the working people make a solution of the problem. (May 22, 1918.) (*Morpeth Herald*, May 24, 1918.)

This political attitude expressed with all the bluntness and candour of which he was capable brought down upon the head of Ebby Edwards the vituperation of the daily newspapers both national and local and the same applied to most of the weeklies. But if his forthright attitude forfeited for him any possible support from such papers as H. M. Hyndman's *Justice*, it gained for Ebby Edwards at that time the devoted esteem not only of those who shared his views but of the smaller minority that were opposed to the war.[1]

Soon afterwards Ebby Edwards became Finance and Disputes Secretary of the Northumberland Miners' Mutual Confident Association, and from then forward was usually at Federation Conferences. In 1926 during the General Strike he was the leading figure in the Northumberland-Durham Strike Committee which forced the Government Commissioner, Sir Kingsley Wood (who was later Chancellor of the Exchequer from 1940 to 1943), to enter into negotiations and sue for terms.

In the years that followed, Ebby Edwards rose higher in the councils of the Miners' Federation. The Vice-Presidency was combined with membership of the House of Commons in the 1929–31 Parliament. On him now fell the heavy burden of the secretaryship at what appeared to be almost the lowest ebb of the fortunes of the Federation. It was indeed a heavy task that lay before the miners' organisations.

[1] *Wansbeck By-Election, May 28, 1918.* Alderman Mason, Coalition candidate, 5,814. Ebby Edwards, Miners' candidate, 5,267.

The Districts of the Federation were working under separate agreements which had led to increasing differences in wages, hours and other conditions. The longer these differences lasted, the more difficult would be the task of recreating the unity of the Federation.

6. HOURS BUT NOT WAGES

The question of hours and wages in connection with the soon-to-expire legislation did not come up until three months of 1932 were passed and gone. Then it was a speedy business, speedier than the miners liked. First, the Mining Association of Great Britain invited the Federation to send four representatives "to consider what action should be taken in connection with the expiry of the Coal Mines Act, 1931, on the 8th July next." Accordingly, "the deputation," consisting of J. Jones, H. Twist, J. Gilliland, F. Swift, and the Secretary, went off to the meeting on April 7, 1932. The representatives of the employers were A. Leslie Wright, Evan Williams, W. Benton Jones, Sir Adam Nimmo, and W. A. Lee, their Secretary.

The employers wanted to continue with seven-and-a-half hours. They made a full statement on the economic position, which they said made it impossible to revert to seven hours, studiously avoiding any reference at all to wages. Requested by the miners to declare their intentions on wages ("so that there could not be any misunderstanding"), the owners said they had no intention to discuss wages, that wages being purely a District question was not a matter for them as an association. The Executive decided to "await further negotiations" (April 8, 1932). But no further invitation to discussions arrived. Then on April 20th the full Executive Committee went to meet at the Board of Trade the President of the Board of Trade and the Secretary for Mines. The Federation had only been in touch on minor matters with the Secretary for the Mines Department, Isaac Foot, father of the many Foots who may be described as not so much Gladstonian as Cromwellite Liberals. But to most of the Executive (now that Tom Richards was dead) the new President of the Board of Trade was an unknown quantity. They, therefore, had no reason to take him at other than his face value.

The Rt. Hon. Walter Runciman, son of a very wealthy ship-owner, had once before been President of the Board of Trade, in the days of the Liberal administration of 1905–15. When the whole of the South Wales coal-field was on strike in the late summer of 1915, Runciman was chosen,[1] as a minister with a plausible tongue, to represent the Government in discussions in Cardiff. But now his business was to arrange with the coal-owners for a further meeting between them and the Miners' Federation. This was arranged for April 28th. But there all the owners had to say was that if legislation were passed continuing the seven-and-a-half hours "without limit of time, save such as might result from legislation ratifying an International Convention," and always provided there was no reference to wages in the Act, they "could secure guarantees of wages from the districts for twelve months." The miners' representatives replied that such guarantees could not be accepted unless they were for the same period as the $7\frac{1}{2}$-hour day, or "if limited to twelve months, national machinery were established for regulating district changes of wages thereafter." The same day *The Times* contained the following statement:

It is proposed that the Bill shall not only continue the present $7\frac{1}{2}$-hour day for a further period, or until the ratification of the Geneva Hours Convention, but shall renew Part I of the Coal Mines Act, which deals with the regulation of output, and which expires at the end of this year. (April 29, 1932.)

This made Edwards suspect something was afoot. The more he went into the matter, the stronger became his suspicion, even after the Mines Department had denied the authenticity of the report. Telling the story a month later, he said:

Therefore, on the 30th April (Saturday) this was what I put in writing to the *Daily Herald*:

If the Press indications are true that the Government has already prepared its Bill to introduce before Whitsun—to continue

---

[1] He was chosen then as one who could be relied upon to protect the interests of his own class: and in later years this same Runciman was used for the purpose of persuading the Czechoslovak Government in 1938 to hand over Sudetenland to the German Nazis.

the present 7½-hour day for a further period—then Parliament is being made, along with the miners, the victim of a plot engineered by interested politicians, not over-scrupulous in their method.

The owners seemed to have entered negotiations, informed, however unofficially, that they could rely on the Government to continue a 7½-hour day. In other words, to them would be conceded their full claim by legislation. In these circumstances negotiations are reduced to a farce. It is surely humbug and pretence to ask the Miners' Federation to enter negotiations under such a position. The Government ceases in such circumstances to be a mediator.

This put the fat in the fire. Runciman, then in the North of England, was on the telephone to Whitehall immediately. He desired to reassure the miners' leaders: and asked that a meeting be arranged on May 3rd.

The M.F.G.B. Executive Committee met Runciman, heard what he had to say and then asked him if he would make public his declaration that the press statements were untrue. To this Runciman assented, and the following agreed press report was then issued:

The President of the Board of Trade and the Secretary for Mines met the Executive of the Miners' Federation this evening to hear from them the result of their further meeting with the representatives of the Mining Association last week. In the course of the discussion Mr. Runciman made it clear that the statements which have appeared in the press to the effect that the Government had reached a decision on the hours question, and had its proposed Bill in draft, were both of them unauthorised, incorrect, and without foundation. (May 3, 1932.)

Events were to show what value could be attached to Runciman's statement, and how correct and firmly founded had been the assertions of the miners' Secretary.

Three weeks had elapsed since the second meeting of the Executive Committee with Runciman (following the two meetings of the Sub-Committee, on April 7th and 28th, with the owners) and the Federation was patiently waiting to hear further from the Government about possible steps before their final declaration of policy, when suddenly a letter was handed in to the M.F.G.B. office in the evening of May 25th.

It was a bombshell from the Board of Trade. After referring to his assurance at their meeting that "no overt action would be taken by the Government without the Miners' Federation being informed," Runciman stated that after having "explored all possible avenues to an agreed solution," the Government had taken a decision, "which I now formally communicate to you in advance of its announcement in Parliament." This was worded almost exactly as knowledgeably foreshadowed in *The Times* a month before: a Bill was to be introduced at once to extend the operation of Part 1 of the Coal Mines Act of 1930 for a further period of five years, and the operation of the $7\frac{1}{2}$-hour day until ratification of the Geneva Convention on hours. Only if the Bill were passed for this indefinite period, and omitting "legislative provision in regard to wages," would there be any guarantee by the owners against reductions for twelve months. This was, of course, precisely what the owners had stipulated. Moreover, there was to be no national machinery: Runciman was at pains to stress that on wages the Government had "secured from each of the constituent districts of the Mining Association a specific undertaking, in writing." With somewhat of a flourish Runciman added that the guarantees, "only obtained with the greatest difficulty in view of the very precarious economic position of the industry, represent an extension of security for which it is difficult to find a parallel either in this or in other countries." Such voluntary guarantees he considered to be "preferable to legislative protection, which would have to be forced through Parliament in the face of a strong opposition."

The Executive Committee met early the next morning. In a few minutes they sent a letter "requesting that you should kindly meet a deputation of our full Executive Committee as early as possible prior to making your statement to the House of Commons." For, they stated, it was "very unsatisfactory to intimate to the public the contents of your letter, prior to such interview taking place." (May 26, 1932.) An hour later, at 11 a.m., the Executive Committee were at the Board of Trade.

The President of the Board of Trade, the Executive were now convinced, was an exceedingly wily customer, and so they began by asking for "a shorthand note to be taken of the proceedings." They told Runciman they had understood that he "was going to call for us before any other action was taken" but that "here we find ourselves receiving the terms on the day they are to be put before the House of Commons." Moreover, these terms were identical with the employers' terms four weeks earlier—"no alteration, identical with those terms." They had been prepared to discuss, and, said Edwards, "in no unmistakable language the Executive impressed upon him, even at that late stage, not to go forward with these proposals, but to give us an opportunity to discuss the whole implications that would arise in July." To this Runciman replied that he "was placed in a very peculiar position. He could not make a full statement, and it would therefore be difficult to have a shorthand note, and therefore we have no official agreed report of that meeting. He made no statement *in extenso*, he said, because he was a Cabinet Minister, and it was his duty first to report to the House of Commons. . . ." After this it is not surprising that they felt "most profound disappointment," and decided to call a Special Conference on Tuesday, May 31st, "to consider the whole situation and what action shall be taken in relation thereto."

7. THE COAL MINES ACT, 1932

At the Special Conference meeting in the Kingsway Hall, London, Ebby Edwards gave them a full report of what had happened, or had not happened, in the previous seven weeks. As a prelude he recalled his own significant speech in the House of Commons ten months earlier; the pointed comment on it by the then Secretary of Mines;[1] and, very appositely, the speech in support of the Miners' Federation standpoint of Sir Herbert Samuel as Liberal Party leader who now, in a manner typical of his whole career and especially in relation to the miners, had altered course with a change of wind and as Home Secretary shared responsibility for the Bill.

[1] Emanuel Shinwell had said: "There is no need for a further crisis if the mine-owners will respond to the appeal of my Honourable Friend The Member for Morpeth (Mr. E. Edwards), the acting President of the Miners' Federation. He has pleaded for co-operation and for negotiation; he asks not for strife but for order. Surely the owners cannot resist that appeal. If in the course of the next twelve months, both sides of the industry will engage in discussions and will pursue the course asked for, there is no reason why a crisis should occur, and there is, on the contrary, every reason to suppose that a crisis can be averted." (*Hansard*, July 6, 1931.)

The delegates were anything but pleased with the terms imposed upon them, as was shown by their numerous questions. But what could they do? Had the Executive any proposals? The Executive Committee submitted the following resolution:

This Conference most emphatically protests against the nature of the present Government's legislation introduced in the House of Commons to deal with the mining industry; the legislation makes a reduction in the hours of employment conditional upon the indefinite ratification of an International Convention, does not establish a seven-and-a-half-hour working day, or the co-terminous establishment of wages and hours as laid down by the Coal Mines Act (1931), or provide for the strengthening of National Wages machinery in the industry. The legislation while providing for all the claims of the mine-owners, ignores those of the miners, and the Conference therefore condemns it as being unjust, and inequitable.

Accordingly the Conference instructs the Executive Committee to press for amendments to the legislation which will make it more in accordance with the claims of the miners, and the needs of the industry. In the meantime, this Conference stands adjourned and shall reassemble at 11 o'clock tomorrow morning. (May 31, 1932.)

The South Wales Miners' Federation delegate expressed much dissatisfaction: reference back of the resolution submitted by the Executive was moved by W. Mainwaring and seconded by Jim Griffiths, both of whom made speeches for a militant policy of action. To them Ebby Edwards replied:

You have got to watch you don't lead your men to a position that leads them to a stoppage which will not be successful. There is not a member of our Executive afraid of a stoppage if it can be successful. I suggest to our Welsh friends it may be all right to come to this Conference and make a declaration that is just slightly beyond what you can get, and go back and tell your members that your policy was in advance of the policy which was agreed to. What you cannot do, and you know it, is that you cannot fight this Government and secure what you are entitled to secure in this Bill—wages commensurate with the increased cost of living.

Other speakers supported the Secretary: but, before the Conference ended its first morning's session, Noah Ablett expressed the Welsh standpoint more briefly than in the speeches of the mover or seconder of the reference back— which was ultimately withdrawn:

Are we to take it that because it is suggested this Federation cannot strike that we are finished? That we are dead? Are we finished? Have we to be ridden over rough-shod? Half an hour has been given away for nothing. How can you argue against that? We have no legal obligation. There is nothing in it at all.

Ablett, saying that if it was suggested the miners could not fight "because of our weakness," then they should "go to the T.U.C. and ask them to help us," ended with the words:

We have a moral case in every way. I know we are reduced to arguing our case from the moral point of view, because we have no force or power. If the miners are to be saved there will need to be a oneness throughout the movement which will have to come to our help in this time of trouble.

At 5 p.m. the Executive Committee met Walter Runciman and Isaac Foot, the main anxiety being how far the guarantees the owners had given to the Government would really be implemented; would they approach or equal the legal guarantees embodied in the Bill? The Secretary of the Mines Department, who may be said to have footed the Bill, had that same day in the House of Commons stated: "Our contention is that the guarantee is at least as good as the statutory protection. If that had not been the assumption we should have asked for the statutory protection."

On other matters they did not get much further with Runciman, who had to be in the House for the debate and who "could only give us half an hour." Then the sub-committee met the Parliamentary Labour Party with the Mining Members and worked out amendments, one of which was voted upon and defeated by 273 votes to 53, while two others were on June 1st ruled out of order by the Speaker of the House of Commons.

All this was reported to the Special Conference on its second day. Thereafter there was to be a resolution: but South Wales did not want the matter to be left to the Executive at that stage. They wanted it referred to the Districts. This was moved by Jim Griffiths and seconded by W. Mainwaring: and this time the Welsh standpoint had the support of Yorkshire, Northumberland and Derby.

Their amendment was against leaving action in the hands of the Executive Committee; it proposed "that the whole question be referred back to the districts to enable them to report back to their members, and a further Conference be called as soon as possible." (June 1, 1932.)

After this the Executive's resolution was carried but by a very small majority.[1]

This Conference having heard a report of the interview of the Executive Committee with representatives of the Government on the questions of wages guarantees and the Coal Mines National Industrial Board, instructs the Executive Committee to negotiate with the Government on the question of strengthening the Coal Mines National Board so as to meet the circumstances in the industry at the end of twelve months. It also requests the mining Members of Parliament to press for the necessary amendments to the Bill providing for the claims of the miners, which are possible within the terms of the Bill as presented.

The Conference calls upon the Government to ratify the Geneva Convention on the hours of work underground and to press for international economic agreements on output, prices and markets, and it leaves the question of calling a further conference or other action in the hands of the Executive Committee. (June 1, 1932.)

In Parliament the Mining Members, and the others in that meagre contingent that made up the Parliamentary Labour Party in the four years after the debacle of 1931,

[1] The voting on the resolution was as follows :

District	No. of Members	For	Against
Bristol	1,900	2	—
Cokemen ..	4,200	—	—
Cumberland ..	8,500	9	—
Derbyshire ..	25,000	—	25
Durham	120,000	120	—
Forest of Dean ..	1,000	—	1
Group No. 1 ..	9,700	10	—
Power Group ..	7,494	8	—
Kent	5,100	—	6
Lancashire ..	45,000	45	—
Leicester.. ..	3,000	3	—
Midlands ..	20,400	21	—
Northumberland	25,913	—	26
North Wales ..	8,658	9	—
Nottingham ..	8,000	8	—
Scotland	40,000	40	—
Somerset.. ..	3,000	3	—
South Derbyshire	4,337	—	5
South Wales ..	75,480	—	76
Yorkshire ..	100,000	—	100
Totals ..	516,682	278	239

(June 1, 1932.)

did all that they could to carry out the request of the Miners' Federation. But their effort was not effective in getting any amendment. So the Bill passed unchanged through all its stages between its Second Reading in the Lower House on May 31st to the Royal Assent some two weeks later.

The effect of the Coal Mines Act, 1932, therefore, was that the seven-and-a-half-hour day was to continue until the international convention should come into force. In short, reduction of hours was postponed indefinitely.

8. RETROSPECT AND OUTLOOK IN MID-SUMMER

As the Executive Committee in mid-June drew up their Report to the Annual Conference they looked back on a difficult and troubled year; they summed it all up in a mood of some questioning: "We have been able to ensure the continuation of the existing level of wages in every district for a further twelve months, but we have had to pay a price for these guarantees. Has the price been too heavy?" They had had to give up "hope for an immediate return to the 7-hour day." They now looked back with regret to the Labour Government; for by the Act of 1931 hours and wages terminated at the same time, so that in discussion with the employers, "we could use the hours factor to bargain on wages." But, they wrote, "the present Government have severed hours and wages thus eliminating hours as a bargaining factor." Everything now depended upon whether they were successful in establishing national wages machinery during the ensuing twelve months, and so preventing District attacks on wages when the year was up. In the last resort, bargaining power depended on "the state of organisation" and "on our loyalty and unity of purpose":

We have only the power of organisation to help us; obviously, therefore, we must seek to use the only weapon we have to the fullest advantage, and we can do so only if we act nationally, for if we have to act sectionally, our strength is dissipated.

The coalowners realise this more clearly than anyone, for in insisting on district settlements their whole purpose is to destroy the great power we possess when we speak and act as a national force. This we must never allow them to do, and we must continue to fight the battle of national settlements until the victory is gained.

So their final words were on this theme:

If the men in the coalfield realise that organisation is the *only* power they have, then great things are possible, because the power of the *whole* body of mineworkers, wisely directed, is still one of the greatest forces in the national life.

A month later, a resolution for the setting up of national machinery was moved by the Secretary and seconded by J. McGurk of Lancashire at the Folkestone Annual Conference on the opening day. It argued that District settlement of wages was incompatible with the industry's economic trends, and as in the past would lead to "internecine warfare in the districts." The resolution, which was carried unanimously, ended with these words:

In the event of the owners refusing to so agree, it requests the Government to establish such machinery by Act of Parliament. A special conference to be called in January, 1933, to consider what progress has been made in this direction. (July 12, 1932.)

The Conference of 118 delegates from a diminished total that summer of 511,815 members, then went on with its usual annual business of resolutions and of elections both internal and those for representation upon other bodies. Peter Lee, who had been acting as President since Ebby Edwards had moved from that position to become Secretary, was elected President (receiving 342 votes, and defeating Herbert Smith with 103 and J. McGurk with 70). The new Vice-President was Joseph Jones of Yorkshire, who received 437 votes to 78 cast for Harry Hicken of Derbyshire. The resolutions were on subjects that did not vary very much from one occasion to another during the crisis years and hence were often called "Hardy Annuals," flowers that had to be planted afresh each year. But it was characteristic that one or another of the miners' associations with unflagging persistence on each occasion brought up demands for improvement of conditions. In their aggregate over the years these resolutions constituted a massive programme, to be fulfilled bit by bit as and when opportunity offered. Thus this year at Folkestone they once again pressed "for a revision

of the Checkweigh Act" and once again recorded their
"dissatisfaction with the Workmen's Compensation Act of
1925," in each case listing details of the reforms required.
They registered their protest against the employment of
boys on night-shift and against week-end work and overtime.
On behalf of men underground who worked in

No light; but rather darkness visible

they urged that it be an obligation on each colliery company
to provide "suitable and efficient" lighting. Once again they
asked for pensions at the age of sixty for the older mineworkers, while a majority also wanted pensions for aged
miners to be payable from the Miners' Welfare Fund. The
penny per ton of coal that for ten years had supplied this
fund (and had been renewed for a further five years in April
1931) had come under heavy fire from the Mining Association of Great Britain. The Government had yielded to
this pressure and in 1931 had set up a Committee of Inquiry,
to which the Miners' Federation, on March 16, 1932, had
submitted a detailed Memorandum of Evidence in the hope
that no change in the fund would be recommended as "its
discontinuance or curtailment would be a heavy blow to all
our people." The resolution on Unemployment Insurance
repeated their opinion on the amendment of the Act, strongly
protested against the Means Test by which "families are
being broken up" and "determines to use every means" to
get it withdrawn. Two resolutions dealt with silicosis and
anthracosis, names at that time given to the effect of the
dust underground which killed so many miners. Anthracosis
was not even scheduled as an industrial disease, while payment of compensation for silicosis was not a straightforward
process but was beset by various legal and medico-legal
snares. For example, the Silicosis Order No. 342 of April 1931
caused heavy expense to be incurred by the workman "in
the payment of fees to analysts for the purpose of proving
the presence of silica in the various rocks mentioned in the
Order." Moreover County Court judges still insisted that the
rock must contain 50 per cent of silica before any claim could
be valid—though the Order itself had deliberately omitted
such a provision.

AN AERIAL VIEW OF GRESFORD COLLIERY
After the explosion: September 22, 1934

AFTER THE MARKHAM COLLIERY EXPLOSION, MAY 10, 1938
Children watch as the wheel moves the cage upwards

To some the debacle of the past year might seem a sufficiently severe set-back to all their hopes both on wages and on hours. But, undaunted, the Conference called the attention of the country and Parliament to "the deplorable low wages in this hazardous industry" and urged the Government to pass into law "at an early date" a Bill to amend the Minimum Wage (Coal Mines) Act, 1912.

On the question of hours of labour, the goal of the six-hour day was once again set down in a resolution as follows:

That this Conference reaffirms its demand for a shorter working day in the mining industry; it protests against the delay in introducing legislation to ratify the Geneva Convention and urges the Government to take immediate steps towards such ratification as one step towards a further limitation of working hours as recommended by the Sankey Commission. (July 14, 1932.)

In the debate, the farther goal was stressed by two delegates, on the ground that with so many miners unemployed it would now be "common sense" to reduce the hours to six and so enable some of them to get work. For after ten months of the "National Government" things were worse than ever. Two out of every five miners were out of work. In that month of July 1932 there were 432,000 miners unemployed.

9. REORGANISATION

This year the delegates had before them a Report and proposals on Reorganisation. It was compiled by the Executive Committee on an undertaking given at the 1931 Annual Conference after a debate (which did not go to a vote) on a Kent resolution for a single mine-workers' union. It was not a new subject: and indeed in the M.F.G.B. Proceedings the heading "Reorganisation" recurs for over fifteen years. From 1926 onward, if not earlier, it had become obvious that the structure of the Miners' Federation and of its constituents required to be strengthened either by the advance to a single national body or by intermediate steps towards this goal. A few months after the end of 1926 Durham and Northumberland had raised the question (followed by Nottinghamshire which in April 1927 demanded "one national miners' union"), and the Executive Committee had promptly sought information about the structure and finance of each District. They had then submitted a memorandum on immediate steps to the Llandudno Annual Conference of 1928. This was remitted to the Districts, but by the next Annual Conference nothing whatever had come of it. Now at this 1932 Annual Conference with its programme for national machinery for negotiations, it might seem that steps forward could be taken. The Annual Report, carefully drawn up and at each stage submitted to the Districts (whose comments were embodied in it), gave a picture of mining trade unionism.

At the base was the Lodge with its local elected officials; above the Lodge was every kind of diversity in the twenty constituent Districts. The contributions varied in amount, in the methods of collection and in the allocation of the contribution as between Lodges, branches and central organisations. As to benefits, no two Districts were alike. Benefits differed in character, in extent and in conditions attached thereto, with most unfavourable comparisons when a trade unionist moved from one District of the Federation to another. Moreover, the link between these mining trade unions was slender and consisted in little more than a single chief officer elected by national ballot, to whom neither funds nor elected assistants nor other resources were accorded. The small office in Russell Square was in contrast to the large offices and considerable full-time staffs of the larger constituent bodies. For as was to be confessed by an M.F.G.B. Chairman a few years later, Districts at the Annual Conference "determined the policy of the Federation, not from the wider outlook of the Federation but from the district outlook," while between Conferences "when the Executive meets, our actions are based upon our own district views."

The Reorganisation Memorandum of 1932 ended with tentative proposals that three Districts (South Wales, Scotland and Midlands—each of them Federations) should liquidate their separate union constituents and "consolidate themselves into one centralised organisation in each case."

At the Folkestone debate no one spoke out against reorganisation or centralisation as an ideal: but when it came to the bit, the horses shied away. James Griffiths, then President of the Anthracite Miners' Association, at once voiced his alarm: they could settle things better by themselves in Cardiff than by any recourse to London, and better by themselves in the anthracite area than in closer linkage at Cardiff. He was answered sharply enough from South Wales by Noah Ablett, who said:

We have got the tribal system in operation, with all the little chieftains. We do not desire to continue institutions that are ossified and fossilised. We don't want the little tribes. We want one Union. (July 12, 1932.)

The debate had brought out the differences, but the delegates contented themselves with receiving the Report and deciding that another Conference be called to deal with the matter before the next summer. The result was as it had been four years earlier: the Conference was never called. Nothing happened except that South Wales did carry through a measure of centralisation.

The subsequent history of Reorganisation need not be chronicled each year and can be here briefly summarised. A single Mineworkers' Union was demanded in successive years by one or another District. Each time the matter was discussed the torrent of debate was afterwards canalised into the District channels with very little result. By 1936 the Executive Committee set up a special Reorganisation Sub-committee which continued for many years. At last in 1937 the Kent resolution for a "National Association for all mineworkers" was accepted in principle. Once more a scheme was prepared and once more debated; and once more referred to Districts preliminary to a Special Conference. The date of that Special Conference was fixed for November 23, 1938, but the Conference was suspended when it became clear how little interest was shown by the Districts. It was deferred to January 1939; again it was suspended. But the principle of a national union for all mine-workers had at last gone to a vote. The voting was 325,188 for and 262,498 against, a result which would have meant a union formed out of some Districts, with others left outside. The Reorganisation Sub-committee then set to work on lesser schemes of which nothing falls to be recorded.

GENERAL ELECTION 1931

RESULTS OF THE VOTING IN MINING AREAS

District	No. of Candidates	Name of Candidate	Constituency
South Wales	10	Dagger, G.	Abertillery
		Bevan, A.	Ebbw Vale
		Edwards, C.	Bedwellty
		Grenfell, D. R.	Gower
		Jenkins, W.	Neath
		John, W.	Rhondda W.
		Davies, D. L.	Pontypridd
		Hall, G. H.	Aberdare
		Williams, E.	Ogmore
		Watts Morgan, D.	Rhondda E.
Durham	7	Lawson, J. J.	Chester-le-Street
		Whiteley, W.	*Blaydon*
		Richardson, R.	*Houghton*
		Ritson, J.	*Durham*
		Herriotts, J.	*Sedgefield*
		Batey, J.	Spennymoor
		Lawther, W.	*Barnard Castle*
Lancashire	5	Tinker, J.	Leigh
		Parkinson, J. A.	Wigan
		Rowson, G.	*Farnworth*
		MacDonald, G.	Ince
		Sutton, J. E.	*Clayton*
Yorkshire	9	Lunn, W.	Rothwell
		Smith, T.	*Pontefract*
		Hall, F.	Normanton
		Grundy, T. W.	Rother Valley
		Hirst, G. H.	Wentworth
		Williams, T.	Don Valley
		Paling, W.	*Doncaster*
		Potts, J.	*Barnsley*
		Price, G.	Hemsworth
Scotland	7	*Adamson, W.*	*Western Fife*
		Brown, J.	*South Ayrshire*
		Graham, D.	Hamilton
		Murnin, H.	*Stirling*
		Sullivan, J.	*Bothwell*
		Watson, W.	*Dunfermline Burghs*
		Westwood, J.	*South Midlothian*

District	No. of Candidates	Name of Candidate	Constituency
Northumberland	2	*Shields, G. W.*	*Wansbeck*
		Edwards, E.	*Morpeth*
Derbyshire	1	*Lee, F.*	*N. E. Derby*
Cumberland	1	Cape, T.	Workington
Midlands	1	*Jones, G. H.*	*Lichfield*

NOTE: Names and constituencies in italic show seats that were lost.

CHAPTER III

UNDER THE COALITION GOVERNMENT

1. A LONG CORRESPONDENCE

VERY soon after the special resolution on the setting up of national wages machinery had been carried at the Annual Conference in July of 1932, Ebby Edwards in the beginning of August wrote to the Mining Association asking for a discussion. Apart from acknowledgement there was no reply until October: correspondence continued and a discussion, but on other questions, took place in December. Nothing came of it. Equally illusory were the hopes that had been placed in the possibility of the Coalition Government playing its part in compelling the owners to be "more reasonable." For all the period up to the Annual Conference in the summer of 1933 and thereafter till the next Annual Conference in the summer of 1934, there was to be a history of broken hopes and misplaced trust.

The sad story begins with the lengthy correspondence. To the Federation's request for a discussion "believing that stable and peaceful conditions which are so necessary for the industry depend on certain agreed machinery for co-ordinating wages and conditions in the whole industry" (August 10, 1932), the owners gave a suave answer. While ready to meet the Federation on anything else that was relevant, a meeting on wages and conditions was out of the question since "the Mining Association is not an organisation which has any power to deal with arrangements as to the wages to be paid or the conditions of employment to be observed in the different districts, which are matters for negotiation in the coalfields themselves." (October 5, 1932.)

The next letter of the Federation (October 12th) was to the Prime Minister enclosing the correspondence with the owners, and asking for an early meeting with him to discuss it. His Private Secretary replied that the Prime Minister would have it "at the first opportunity," adding what might be considered a slight reproach in the words: "As you will no doubt understand, his time is very fully occupied today in conversations with M. Herriot."[1] (October 13, 1932.) This came as no surprise to the older members of the Federation Executive who knew from experience that it was always MacDonald's technique to create the impression that he was overburdened by work; one of his phrases, "Ah, my friends, I am so tired," was well known: and women in his audience would sit weeping.

Some two weeks later the Prime Minister was still "very fully occupied," because he passed them on to his new Secretary for Mines, Ernest Brown, who was a more agile Liberal, more so than Isaac Foot, who on September 28, 1932, had followed the Free Traders Snowden and Samuel out of a coalition Government which had swung over to a protectionist policy. They wrote to Ernest Brown, who met them on November 8th. He requested the Federation deputation to have a meeting with the Mining Association, wages and conditions excluded, a suggestion which added nothing to the offer already received from the Mining Association.

A meeting between representatives of the Mining Association and the Federation was eventually held on December 15, 1932, when Evan Williams proposed such topics as recruitment in mines and the question of welfare. The representatives of the Federation retorted that there were questions far more important, ranging from safety in mines and evasions by owners of the 1930 Act to unemployment, production of oil and petrol from coal, exports, royalties, national machinery to prevent labour disputes and the question of what was to happen in July, 1933.

It was left that there should be conversations between the leading officials. As it turned out this was largely because the owners wished the miners to join them in urging the Chancellor of the Exchequer to tax oil imports. However, they evaded any joint consideration of the approaching July situation when the "gentleman's agreement" on not reducing wages would come to an end, on the grounds given by Evan Williams, "that it was quite outside their

[1] The French Premier.

province to discuss the question nationally." (March 1, 1933.)

The Federation Executive Committee after lengthy consideration decided that since the policy suggested in the owners' request had not been endorsed by the members of the Miners' Federation, "we cannot at present agree to join a deputation for the purpose of requesting a tariff." Nevertheless, the Federation was prepared to consider "jointly with the Mining Association, the whole implications of the continuing decline in the consumption of coal and how to arrest it." (February 9, 1933.)

They had got nothing in six months of painstaking correspondence and meetings: but they were in no mood to be deflected from their immediate aim.

2.   HUNGER MARCHES

Meantime, throughout the latter part of 1932 the whole economy of Great Britain, so far from showing any sign of improvement, seemed to be plunging into a greater depth of crisis. Here and there, there was something that might give a flicker of hope, as in some resumption of activity in the building industry. But elsewhere, and particularly in the heavy industries, all hopes had seemed doomed. An economic abyss was yawning: coal-mining, steel, shipbuilding[1] seemed to be on the brink of utter and irremediable disaster. The miners did not need to scan the economic horizon provided by statistical surveys or Board of Trade publications: in every mining village they saw ruin before them, skilled workers thrust into idleness, queues at the Labour Exchange, men trudging for miles to look for work and finding none, families already short of food subjected to the rigours of the Means Test. In every coal-field men and women, desperate at the bleak prospect, sought for some way out: everywhere, those in work knew very well that the meagre wages were guaranteed only up to July 1933 and that for those out of work there would soon be the end of

---

[1] Amongst boilermakers and shipwrights two out of every three in Great Britain were unemployed.

unemployment benefit, after which they would face the mercy of the Public Assistance Committee.

As desperation grew greater, hunger marches of the unemployed began to grow in number. These hunger marches were not new. They had first been seen a quarter of a century earlier in the economic crisis of 1908 at a time when there was nothing but the old Poor Law and the Charity Organisation Society for those in misery and distress through lack of work. But now the scale was far greater. The workers of many industries took part in these marches,[1] and many of the chief towns in England, Scotland and Wales became the gathering-places for marches on London mostly through friendly countrysides. Prominent amongst them were the contingents of unemployed miners.

Against this background of misery on the one hand and growing strong agitation on the other, the Federation Executive had vainly sought to find some way out of the dangers to health and livelihood that encompassed their members. Over half a year of increasing misery had gone by without avail. Soon they would have to call a Special Conference and give it an account of their stewardship of the July Conference resolution: but they must also take some forward step, something that would demonstrate they had the full backing of their members for the cause they were urging, and so far urging in vain. While they were still pondering what policy to recommend, the Federation leaders took the decision on February 9th to call the Conference.

They informed the Government of this. They also informed the Mining Association, telling them that the owners' attitude of "refusing even to discuss the question" of national wages machinery was "quite unwarrantable." To this repeated appeal for negotiation, the owners replied with a politely worded but stony refusal. (February 20, 1933.) When the Delegate Conference met, the Secretary, after giving the Committee's report, moved a long resolution which, after deploring the owners' refusal of discussion which might

---

[1] Organised at this time mainly by the National Unemployed Workers' Movement, which, ably led by Wal Hannington, had a joint committee with the Trades Union Congress General Council from 1921 to 1927. Although the N.U.W.M. was thereafter cold-shouldered by that body, yet it still received the countenance and sometimes the active participation of many Labour Members of Parliament and not a few of the clergy.

D*

"obviate the possibility of a national stoppage in the industry" ended with two operative clauses:

(i) to urge the Government to establish by Act of Parliament, national machinery for the regulation of wages and conditions in the industry,

(ii) to invite the districts to give power to the Executive Committee to call upon all affiliated district organisations to terminate their agreements simultaneously, unless guarantees satisfactory to the National Executive are obtained before July 1933. (March 1, 1933.)

3. EBBY EDWARDS'S PROGRAMMATIC SPEECH

In his speech, one of the frankest ever made by a miners' leader, Ebby Edwards made it clear that he stood for peace in industry (if for no other reason than that the miners' unions were not in a position to fight) and that it was the owners who stood on the platform of class war. Therefore he stressed the pacific nature of their aims, and especially the aim to win national machinery of conciliation. At the same time he sought to arouse in the delegates a consciousness of what very little power was in the hands of the Federation: and why they should put aside for the time being any more far-reaching aims, renounce "the policy of continual conflict," and limit themselves to defence of what little they had within the present system. Having allayed the fears of some District leaders by these arguments, which he put on a high theoretic level, Edwards went on to ask that such powers be given to the Executive Committee as it had never possessed before, powers which would overcome the "divide and conquer" effect of the separate District agreements by making them terminable at the same date.

Voicing their disappointment at having been forced that morning "to give such a gloomy, and more than gloomy, report of our failure" he said that many times the officials had been tempted by the employers' attitude to make a public attack but "we have refused with tolerance and forbearance," as public controversy hampered the coal trade. The Federation during the last two years had tried "to assist as far as possible to put peace in the industry." Yet their tolerant attitude had been construed by both the employers and the Government as weakness. Instead of creating machinery to prevent the industry "from continually being at war," the employers wanted to dominate and to have "the sole right of when and where they desire to attack the already low standards" of the men. "That," added Edwards, "reveals class war as bitter and as naked as has ever occurred in the history of the British mining industry."

So their duty was "to let the public and the Government know, if a struggle takes place in defence of our men, that the responsibility will be on the Mining Association itself."

Edwards went on to anticipate some points of controversy, adding that it was in Conference that principles should be argued and officials and Committee give a record of their stewardship.

"If we do fight, someone may ask: Why fight for mere abstract machinery of wage regulations? Why the mere maintenance of the present wages? A very important question: so important that we must examine it, not in the light of abstract economics and working-class philosophy for the abolition of the system." It must be examined in conjunction with the economic situation of the industry as related to the Miners' Federation; and, in so doing, he would be speaking "for the principles behind a policy which has been adopted for the last two years in this Federation." Then he cited one standpoint:

It may be said that while coal capitalism exists it should not be any concern of ours as to how it functions: we must demand wage increases and coal capitalism should adjust to meet our demands. . . .

It is the policy of continual conflict. I do not say it unkindly, but I believe it was that policy and philosophy that led to the causes by which we have reached our present weakness. I believe it is a policy leading to disaster. On that conception there is no hope. It will lead us from a weak army to greater weakness.

He went on to deal with a contrasting conception, which he described as

an important point of principle that lies at the very base and motive of our objective and the policy which the Committee have pursued for a recent period.

Wage negotiations, power to pay wages, is not determined in

the Board Room in negotiations, but in the policy and conduct of the industry. It is not merely the production of coal, it is organisation of the disposal and sale of coal at an economic price that determines the question of wages. National machinery that will give the workmen an opportunity to raise these issues is not abstract but of vital concern to the workmen in the industry. It is an important principle by which we shall be able to raise the standards of the men. In short, the conduct and policy of this industry precedes the wage policy and determines the capacity of the industry.

These are the reasons why we have supported a definite continuation of the 1930 Act and other suggestions for the organisation of the industry, not that they are satisfactory as they exist now, but because we believed that we were travelling in the right direction. That is the attitude which the Committee adopted and still believe to be correct in spite of the owners' refusal to agree to nothing other than the question of continual conflict. That philosophy lies at the base of this resolution.

The Secretary then dealt with the approach to the Government for legislation to set up national machinery for wages regulation.

Finally he came to the proposal in the resolution giving the Executive Committee power to call on Districts to end agreements.

The committee want the power, if necessary, to be able to control districts: that must be done. We want to be in a position to at least secure uniformity and the maximum of unity when we are approaching the July situation.

Let me say this: while this gives the Executive Committee power, the Executive does not minimise its responsibility. It is a new demand; an important demand; a new measure. We are wanting this power, not for the Executive to send a telegram to districts, "you have all got to stop"; that is not our object. Let us be quite frank. Our object is to get the power to be able to negotiate the maximum for our men.

I am speaking for the Executive when I say, if the worst comes to the worst, districts will be called into consultation before any action takes place. But we want the resolution moved as it is, so that the Executive Committee, in conjunction with its Members of Parliament, viewing the organisation as we do view it, are in a position now (not after July, it is of no use talking about that, now is the most important point, and wrong tactics now may lead us to disaster) to go forward and say to our opponents, we are a united organisation, and our claims are merely asking for even less than justice for the men we represent. (March 1, 1933.)

Some delegates were startled by the proposal. But after long debate, the arguments of their General Secretary for investing the Executive Committee with this extraordinary power won complete success: and the resolution was passed unanimously by the 137 delegates to the Special Conference.

It was just before this Conference that the Executive had decided to issue a pamphlet called *The Position of the Coal Miner*, 36 pages, published at the price of one penny. This publishing of pamphlets had been undertaken some twelve years earlier at the time of the Sankey Commission[1] and at one or two other times. With Ebby Edwards as Secretary, it was for some years a feature of his administration. Thus at the end of 1932 they published *Co-operation or?: A Plea for Unity in the Coal Trade!* (10 pages) and *Memorandum on a National Agreement: The Case for a National Settlement of Wages in the Coal Industry* (16 pages). Again, some eight months later, in November 1933, they were to publish *Coal Problems* (16 pages). This was "a plea for a National Fuel Policy."

4. CORRESPONDENCE WITH RAMSAY MACDONALD

On behalf of the Executive Committee Ebby Edwards then opened up a correspondence with the Prime Minister:

Sir,

At a Special Conference of the Miners' Federation held yesterday, 1st March, which considered the refusal of the Mining Association to discuss the question of national machinery for the co-ordination of wages and conditions in the mining industry, the following resolution was carried unanimously—

> To urge the Government to establish by Act of Parliament, national machinery for the regulation of wages and conditions in the industry.

In view of the fact that the present arrangement on wages between the Government and the Mining Association ends in July, and that serious consequences may arise if no other arrangements are arrived at, I shall be glad to learn that you will meet the

[1] *Facts from the Coal Commission* and *Further Facts from the Coal Commission* published in conjunction with the Labour Research Department by the Miners' Federation of Great Britain.

Executive Committee of the Federation at an early date, so that they may place before you their reasons for asking the Government to implement the resolution as stated above.

I enclose copies of the recent correspondence between the two sides, which show the refusal of the Mining Association to negotiate.

I am, Sir,
Your obedient Servant,

March 2, 1933.   EBBY EDWARDS, Secretary.

The next day there came a personal reply from the Prime Minister, the beginning of a private exchange of views on the matter. This reply, a departure from the frigidity of official correspondence, was friendly and indeed almost ingratiating in tone. But its main purpose was to postpone raising of the issue. It was marked "very private."

> 10, Downing Street,
> Whitehall.
> March 3, 1933.

My dear Ebby,

I have your letter of the 2nd, with the Resolution passed by the Federation. You know that you have approached Government after Government with the same claim, and that, however sympathetic they may be to its idea and purpose, the obstacles in the way have hitherto been insurmountable, because neither the Labour nor the National Government has been able to devise means to settle the industrial result in wages and employment of legislation. Nothing would give me greater pleasure than to meet you again and discuss the Resolution in relation to the terrible conditions which still face us and which seem at the moment to point to further efforts to get a carry-over until the international situation has found some bottom upon which we can build up. You might let the matter lie over, especially as the pressing urgency of certain big world movements in finance and politics are elbowing everything out of my mind for the time being. I shall write you, however, a little later on.

Yours very sincerely,
J. RAMSAY MACDONALD.

The two men knew one another well enough. Edwards when in Parliament had headed the group of forty-three mining members that were a sizeable part of MacDonald's supporters in 1929–31: and in those days had been in many discussions with the Prime Minister. But now Edwards was in no mood to be won over or to respond to the cordial invitation for private talks. His reply, with some verbal concessions in manner, was a skilful restatement of the miners' case, loaded with references to MacDonald's earlier commitments in the matter and to his own pacific stand-point—which he might no longer be able to maintain.

March 4, 1933.

My dear Prime Minister,

I appreciate to the full the very serious and most urgent world problems that must of necessity occupy you and your colleagues of the Cabinet. It is well known to you that for two years, I have tried to keep the mining industry out of politics. Even when you acted for a minority Labour Government, my efforts were then for voluntary machinery to carry on the industry as distinct from legislation.

When legislation was necessary to prevent the Mineowners' attack on wages, I pleaded for an immediate resumption of negotiations so that we might settle our own business. The Mine-owners did not reciprocate.

As a result of last year's legislation, which took away from the mineworkers the power of bargaining, the attitude of the coal-owners has hardened. If nothing is done when the Government's agreement with them ends in July next, they have full power to attack our men. Therefore, does not all the same need for an agreement apply today that applied last year? The owners refuse the necessary machinery to take the industry out of politics. The National Government having taken away from the mineworkers the bargaining power that existed under the Labour Government's legislation surely have some responsibility. The only alternative is to leave us again to fight it out. Remember, the Labour Government's legislation was because of the owners' refusal to negotiate an industrial settlement.

Two of the best brains of the country—the late Willie Graham and Sir William Jowitt—only meant that legislation to be a means to an end. In the Government's letter to the owners on June 26, 1931, the position is made quite clear, viz.:

"If the temporary 12 months period expires before the rati-fication has been accomplished, the Government undertakes to take steps to extend the 12 months period over such further period of time as may be covered by an extended guarantee on the same terms, or on such altered terms as may be agreed between the Mining Association and the Miners' Federation."

Now, had the National Government stood where they were placed with the Labour Government Act of 1931, I am most certain the Mining Association would have negotiated. Last year the National Government changed a legal guarantee to a voluntary offer to maintain wages. During all this time the owners have not moved an inch toward an industrial settlement. We are now within four months of the end of your arrangement. The time factor is important.

I have done all I could to keep coal conflict out of public controversy. I am still willing to do this, but my compromise for the last two years seems to have been interpreted as a weakness.

The time has arrived when Government action must supersede the employers' stupidity. What can you do? Either secure an offer from the employers to renew the guarantee to maintain wages until they are prepared to set up machinery, or if they refuse, you are in common justice entitled to again pass legislation that will meet the same end.

That immediate gesture can now be accepted; failing this and if a four months public controversy on the starvation wages of the miners is launched, no one can say where the mass psychology of the miners will lead.

I am never a pessimist. In negotiations I have confidence to reach a settlement. Denied negotiations, I hope to be able to do that which I do not want to do, lead my men to fight for common justice.

Yours sincerely,
EBBY EDWARDS, Secretary.

When the Prime Minister read this, did there pass through his mind these lines?

> Thrice is he arm'd that hath his quarrel just;
> And he but naked, though lock'd up in steel,
> Whose conscience with injustice is corrupted.

At any rate the significance of the closing sentences was not lost upon him. Edwards, he knew, was now armed with the power given to the Executive to call upon the Districts to act simultaneously: and, unless satisfaction in one way or another were given the miners, their chief officer was here saying he would lead a national strike of the coal-fields. MacDonald did not take this up: but clearly he must go further than the suggestion of his first letter, "to let the matter lie over." So, with no diminution of charm in his manner of writing, he replied after the week-end.

Private & confidential.   March 8, 1933.

My dear Ebby,

I want very much to see you. We are both facing times the like of which nobody in responsible positions has ever had to face.

I must rush off to Geneva, however, not, I am afraid, that I can do very much good, but I must try, and if I fail—well I shall just have to fail. I do not wish to have to accuse myself later on that I left any stone unturned to get an agreement.

I can tell you, however, that although there is no legal power to enforce this, we have got privately a statement that in July there will be no wages crisis [which I think will be observed].[1] The districts are not in a very good frame of mind, but they have been told quite plainly that, although there is no power to interfere with them, they must observe the honour of the position. This is only for your own private ear, so do not let anybody know that that is so, but you can be guided in your own action and advice by the knowledge of the fact.

As soon as I come back, I will let you know and see if we can have a bit of a talk together.

Yours sincerely,
J. RAMSAY MACDONALD.

Ramsay MacDonald's letter, however private and confidential, brought no news to Ebby Edwards, as he was to show in his reply. Nor was he moved to any exchange of courtesies by the flattering invitation to "a fire-side chat": he paid no attention to it. His answer, by return of post, was to drive home the argument about the obduracy of the coal-owners and the responsibility that lay upon the Government.

March 9, 1933.

My dear Prime Minister,

I regret very much your urgent and important call to Geneva. Truly the world is going mad; but its madness must be controlled, even if a cure is far off.

Returning to our private exchange of views on the mining situation, I may say that the position as stated in your letter was known to me as long ago as last August. I made the same statement to our Conference on the 1st March last, namely—"The responsible men in the Mining Association say that districts need not fear an attack on wages in July 1933."

But, if this is true—say my men—why cannot the owners get such a guarantee from the districts and give it to us, or to the Government to pass on to us as was done last year? *A man who has no intention of stealing can easily give a guarantee not to be a thief.* I am certain that the longer the guarantee is withheld, the greater is the danger of the issues widening.

I should like you to note the attitude of the owners and the

---

[1] This insertion was written in ink by Ramsay MacDonald.

progressively worse position the men have been placed in during the past few years, as shewn by the short summary I make below:

July 1931: A legal guarantee given, that wages would not be reduced and that hours would remain until the ratification of the Geneva Convention. In addition the Government informed the Mining Association that they (the Government) undertook to extend the guarantee on the same terms, or on such altered terms as may be agreed upon by the Mining Association, and the Federation.

The change of Government, however, hardened the owners' hearts and they refused to negotiate with the Federation during the 12 months ending July 1932.

July 1932: The new Government gave the owners an indefinite extension of the $7\frac{1}{2}$-hour day, and instead of extending took away the legal guarantee of wages. It accepted instead a gentleman's arrangement with the Mining Association whereby the owners undertook to guarantee wages for twelve months. It also extended Part I for 5 years (an extension with which we agree) and so gave the owners full powers to run the industry and legal authority to control minorities. Despite this the Mining Association still refused to negotiate with the Federation.

1933: After two years conciliatory action and effort on our part, the owners still refuse to negotiate. They refuse to guarantee a starvation wage; our men's wages are the lowest in the country. They want my men blindly to believe that, without arrangement, no reduction will take place when at the same time they want full power to attack wages when and where they like. That is not quite playing the game.

Neither the Government nor the men should be dictated to as they are now by the Mining Association.

Although the Mining Association can act so as to secure from the Government far-reaching legislation for the conduct of the industry; although they can act for the industry in the matter of international quotas, embargoes and agreements, although they can act so as to influence legislation on the number of hours my men shall work, and the conditions under which they shall work, yet they say it is not within their power to act on the question of wages. Their excuses on this question convince no one.

At present it does appear that the Government have a grave national responsibility. The facts since 1931 as here outlined create a mental disturbance, and while I am most anxious to prevent a stoppage I am equally anxious to defend my men.

I feel sorry to trouble you on the mining issue in these times. Yet another stoppage would be more than a national disaster. The last stoppage affected the balance of trade by not less than

£600,000,000 and this stoppage, if it comes, will end the export trade in coal. It may also create an industrial psychology beside which the General Strike situation of 1926 may be insignificant. In these days a fire is easy to kindle, but may be extremely difficult to control.

I appeal to you therefore, in a frank and friendly manner, and as the head of a great majority Government, to do your utmost to move the owners from their present obdurate position, as believe me the situation demands it.

Yours sincerely,
EBBY EDWARDS, Secretary.

There could be no immediate reply. But on his return from Geneva and Rome a few days later, MacDonald showed no disposition to answer this second epistle. There was a sting, if not an implied threat, in its reference to strike action: and a deaf ear had been turned to all the gracious offers. The miners' Secretary had proved to be "even like the deaf adder that stoppeth her ears, which refuseth to hear the voice of the charmer; charm he never so wisely."

So on March 28th Edwards repeated his request of the beginning of the month for the Prime Minister to meet a deputation "comprising my Executive Committee." The reply came a week later.

My dear Ebby,
I have your letter of the 28th March, and trust that your Executive Committee will approach the Secretary for Mines and discuss the subject with him in the first instance. That follows the usual administrative practice and ensures the most efficient handling of the business. Moreover, as I am sure you will understand, my own preoccupations during this very hard time are extremely exacting and are making unusually heavy demands on me, and I do not know what my movements may have to be.

Yours always sincerely,
April 3, 1933. J. RAMSAY MACDONALD.

The private correspondence was at an end: and the miners were recommended to resort once more to official channels. Nor was there any further attempt at "a bit of a talk together." But the Prime Minister was left in no doubt that behind a sweetly reasonable manner of writing, Edwards's arguments had been put forward with a cogency which derived its force from the extraordinary powers now possessed by the miners' leaders.

5. TIME-HONOURED TACTICS

The suggestion in MacDonald's final letter was acted upon immediately: and from the first week of April onwards the renewed tussle with the Mines Department took its course. But at the same time the Federation Executive Committee were insistent in their desire to meet the Prime Minister: and the following letter was written:

My dear Mr. Prime Minister,

On receipt of your letter referring my Executive Committee to approach the Secretary for Mines, I immediately fixed up and an interview took place on the 5th April. I am certain Mr. Brown, the Secretary for Mines will faithfully report to you what arguments we advanced.

In view of the fact that last October, my Committee was referred by you to first follow the usual administrative practice and did so, they thought at this stage of the crisis that they were not being treated fairly by your present refusal to meet them, and passed the following resolution—

> In view of the Prime Minister's knowledge that we had already met the Secretary for Mines concerning our repeated attempts to persuade the Mining Association to negotiate with us to prevent stoppage of work in July next, we protest very strongly at his further refusal to meet the Executive Committee of the Miners' Federation at a time of imminent crisis in the industry.

My Committee believe that the urgency and serious nature of the matters they desire to raise, call for direct intervention by yourself and the Cabinet.

Yours sincerely,

April 6, 1933.   EBBY EDWARDS, Secretary.

After an acknowledgement by the Prime Minister's Private Secretary the next day the reply came a week later, this time from one of the Secretaries at 10 Downing Street, as follows:

April 13, 1933.

Dear Mr. Edwards,

The Prime Minister duly received your letter of the 6th April, and has subsequently been furnished by the Secretary for Mines with a report of his interview with the Executive Committee on the 5th April. He has discussed the question with the Secretary for Mines, who will now be writing to you.

As regards the resolution which is contained in your letter, the

Prime Minister wishes me to explain that it is in accordance with long established practice in every field of administration that representations of this kind should be addressed to the Minister.

Yours very truly,

J. A. BARLOW.

Then on April 22nd Ernest Brown, having that day "duly conveyed to the Government the representations you made to me on behalf of the Miners' Federation at our meeting on 5th April," wrote to Edwards. His reply was that the Government always desired and still did desire some machinery for the discussion of wages; the Mining Association had maintained its refusal to co-operate in setting up such voluntary machinery; but if there were some scheme which the Federation had which would meet the purpose and "though falling short of compulsory arbitration, would afford to the miners the measure of security which they desire," the Government would be interested.

This request to the M.F.G.B. to prepare a scheme for security of wages short of compulsory arbitration was now the theme of replies from the Ministry, combined with repeated statements that it was not thought likely there would be any reductions after July. The Federation wanted something much better than this, and continued to press for national machinery by Act of Parliament and for discussion with the Prime Minister. These aims were doggedly pursued by the Secretary in his letters, and the Federation Executive at its regular meetings throughout the spring, summer and autumn of 1933. The correspondence was voluminous. It was occasionally sharp in tone. But in the end they got very little further, and the feeling began to grow that they were being driven from pillar to post.

At one stage Edwards wrote to Ernest Brown "It appears from your letter, that as far as the Government is concerned, it has no intention of trying to secure, even in face of the employers' persistent refusals to negotiate, any guarantee against further reductions of the very low wages of the men, and is apparently indifferent to the possibility of a struggle between the employers and the men on this issue." (May 11, 1933.) That same month Evan Williams stated that the Mining Association "had always contended that national settlement of wages led inevitably to national difficulties and the danger of national strikes. It was very remarkable," he asserted, "that the Miners' Federation was now using this particular weapon: the threat of a national strike in an attempt to force a national settlement upon the owners of the country."

At another stage, after there had been on May 22nd a brief "interview accorded by the Prime Minister to the President and Secretary of the Miners' Federation" (they asked that the Government should get a renewal of District wage guarantees, due to expire on July 8th) Ernest Brown received instructions "to explore the possibilities in this direction." Five weeks later Ernest Brown wrote that as a result of the enquiries which he had made, he was "satisfied that in no district will the coal-owners, when the guarantees expire, seek an alteration in the rate of wages now being paid under the district wages agreements, and that it is not their intention to do so while the present circumstances obtain." (June 29, 1933.) Four days afterwards the Annual Conference of the Miners' Federation of Great Britain[1] opened at Scarborough. Mr. Brown's claim that private assurances from the owners that there would be no reduction of wages after July 8th (when the public guarantee came to an end) had satisfied him was coldly received. It did not satisfy the delegates from the coal-fields. So their main resolution ran:

This Conference resents the attitude of the owners in persistently refusing to enter into negotiations with the Miners' Federation of Great Britain for the setting up of machinery for the national regulation of wages in the coal industry, which machinery, in its view, is essential to the restoration of peaceful and stable conditions.

Furthermore, the Conference registers an emphatic protest against the attitude adopted by the Government, who, having embodied in legislation the principle of the national regulation of production and prices, refuse to extend the same principle to the regulation of wages, and who refuse to bring pressure upon the coal-owners and keep faith with the miners.

Accordingly, the Conference gives the Executive Committee power to take any action, including the calling of a national

[1] Revision of rules at this Conference included, without debate on the matter, a change of title to Mineworkers' Federation of Great Britain.

stoppage, should wages be attacked in any district in the meantime.
(July 4, 1933.)

This resolution brought a reply that was less suave than
usual from the Mines Department official who wrote that
"Mr. Brown took strong exception to the suggestion that
the Government had refused to bring pressure upon the
coalowners," and added: "As your Federation are aware,
every possible action, short of legislation, has been taken
by the Government to secure the establishment of the
principle of voluntary regulation of wages on a national
basis." (July 26, 1933.) Eight weeks and ten weeks later,
the unvarying polite negative having come from the
immovable owners and a variant of the usual correspondence
having come from Ernest Brown (he did not want to meet
the miners until he had from them a scheme, something in
writing), Edwards could comment: "We were back again
to the original position as previously reported to the Annual
Conference." In the case of the owners, however, they were
back to a much earlier original position: and when in reply
to his July letter Edwards received, in October 1933, the
usual reply, all he could do was to repeat the Federation's
"deep regret" and to say "Your refusal leaves no alternative
to the method of strike action in the event of a dispute."
It ended their attempts with the Mining Association.

Eventually, in December, the Federation Executive had
their meeting with the Prime Minister. What came of it was
told to the M.F.G.B. Special Conference that assembled on
December 28th.

6. A LIVELY CONFERENCE

The Conference was called "to receive a report from the
Executive Committee of the negotiations with the Government in relation to national machinery for the regulation
of wages in the coal mining industry." Ebby Edwards
reported, and after reading aloud the extremely lengthy
correspondence, page after page, came finally to the meeting
on December 11th with the Prime Minister—"the first interview since MacDonald had married the Tory Party. I say

that seriously, because no one was more responsible for the negotiations conducted in 1930–31 than MacDonald himself." Edwards had been through the whole of those negotiations, and was the only one of the deputation who, as miners' official and a Member of Parliament, knew both the industrial and parliamentary negotiations on the 1930–31 legislation. He summarised the interview very briefly saying:

The first principle of national machinery is to try and prevent the playing off of one district against another. In the very early stages of the interview MacDonald was reminded of the situation by the Executive, but the Prime Minister met it by saying he could not be responsible for the work of his colleagues in the Labour Government; but unfortunately for him in this instance in dealing with his colleagues in the Labour Government he was dealing with one who was in the negotiations and knew exactly the promises he himself made, and not his colleagues in the Labour Government.

The deputation quoted from the shorthand record MacDonald's own promises, on the strength of which the Executive had advised their members. These covered not only the 7½ hours, but a legal guarantee for twelve months. Moreover, MacDonald had assured them that if the owners would not give machinery to guarantee wages, the legis-lation should remain on the Statute Book. Only on that basis had they been persuaded to accept the conditions in 1931.

Now we met the same Prime Minister, and our Executive said that he had violated every pledge made to the National Executive and upon which recommendations were made to our people to accept. When we got to that stage he refused to discuss the situation at all and absolutely said he was not prepared to discuss anything that had taken place in the past.

If we had persisted, I think the Deputation would have been at an end. (December 28, 1933.)

At this stage, therefore, they put before the Prime Minister "what we thought was the basis for national machinery," and asked that he might set up a Joint Committee of the Government and the Miners' Federation to explore the possibilities of national machinery, "details in addition to the principles already elaborated in his presence." These details were outlines of legislation for a National Coal Mining Board of seventeen, eight to be nominated by the Mining Association, eight by the Miners' Federation and an independent chairman. Failure to nominate "shall be an offence against this Act." The Board would make recommendations on wages; hours; selling price, production and utilisation of coal; and working conditions. These proposals were submitted to the Prime Minister, who wrote to "My dear Edwards" (no longer "My dear Ebby"), saying they were "ineffective and unworkable in practice" but that he was willing that officials of the Department should meet the miners' representatives to explain why. His letter (December 21, 1933) had ended on a sharp note:

It is, of course, true that we, as well as the Federation, would welcome the co-operation of the Mining Association in a discussion on the subject of the establishment of national wage machinery, but as you know, the Association are not likely to accept an invitation to participate. On the other hand, though the Federation have no responsibility for the Association's attitude, they must take responsibility for their own proposals and see that they are practicable.

The conclusion of the Secretary's exhaustive Report was a brief tale of yesterday. For on December 27th three officials of the Mines Department ("this interview was not with a single representative of the Government") had told the miners' representatives that the owners "will use all the power they can to frustrate national machinery even to the extent of disbanding the Mining Association, and, therefore, our proposal calling for representatives of the Mining Association could not be operated because there would be no Association to call." The Government had made up their minds that there was no midway plan between voluntary machinery and compulsory arbitration; the first was impossible because of the owners' refusal; "if not by compulsion," said Edwards, "then nothing can be done."

After questions had been asked and answered, J. McGurk of Lancashire said that in view of the "doleful report" given by the Secretary, "all we can do now is to damn and blast the government," and therefore he moved "to let us have the recommendations of the Executive." The recommendations, which were given a mixed reception from angry delegates, were as follows:

1. This Conference regrets that despite the sustained opposition of the coalowners, pressure has not been brought to bear upon them

by the Government to participate in a joint examination of the possibilities of establishing national machinery for the regulation of wages in the coalmining industry.

2. It further protests against the action of the present Government in using its power to remove from the Statute Book the only effective safeguard against wage reductions, while at the same time granting the owners' request on hours.

3. It declares that in recent discussions the Government has failed to furnish any evidence of sincerity of its expressed intentions to sympathetically consider the demands of the Miners' Federation for national machinery and calls upon the Government to pass an improved Minimum Wage Bill.

4. Finally, it authorises the Executive Committee to take such action as it considers necessary, including national industrial action, in the event of an attempt to reduce wages in any district.[1] (December 28, 1933.)

Amongst the first to voice opposition was a delegate from South Wales, Aneurin Bevan, M.P., who asked what reasons had led the Executive to put the recommendations in view of the Report? He continued:

You have been meeting the Government for a whole year, and you have had nothing at all from them and were never likely to have anything from the beginning. It appears that in the future they are not prepared to do anything, and yet we are supposed to try and get a Minimum Wage Bill.

That is—I am speaking quite frankly—that is just make-believe.

The sentiment from South Wales was shared by Lancashire. Delegates from Yorkshire, Midlands, Scotland and Cumberland voiced their disappointment with the fourth clause, which more than one of them described as "a policy of despair." They longed for some rousing response to the negative attitude of the owners and the Cabinet. Arthur Horner, who was once more a delegate after some years of absence,[2] made a characteristic speech, dealing with the need "to generate a new spirit of hope in the struggle." The question of national machinery would not mobilise the miners: but "we can acquire strength on the basis of seeking an improvement in wages and working conditions."

[1] In its final form the last paragraph ran:
"Finally, it authorises the Executive Committee to take such action as it considers necessary in the event of a dispute occurring in any district."
[2] See Chapter IV.

As the debate neared its end, Aneurin Bevan returned to the attack. He said with some heat:

We have been asking for a National Wages Board. We have been sending our representatives, the President and Secretary and the Executive to meet these people. They have asked for a National Board, and the Government keep on talking about it indefinitely. It is the Government's job to talk and keep talking when meeting the Miners' Federation. Their object is to bring us into disrepute. The Miners' Federation has fallen so low in the estimation of the Government that you are met only by the Permanent Officials of the Mines Department. We shall be meeting the charwoman and the office boy to take notes. That is where the dignity of the Miners' Federation lies. (December 28, 1933.)

He followed Horner in demanding concrete proposals to improve conditions and rally the spirit of the miners:

You can have a fight on wages or hours, but you cannot have a fight about machinery. The whole thing was unreal from the beginning, because if you are going to get anything from a National Wages Board you have to organise the power in the coalfield.

Ebby Edwards was the last speaker before the midday adjournment. His answer to Bevan was short and polite:

Friend Bevan, with political logic, took the delegates in detail through the resolution. His speech can be easily summarised. He agreed with the first part of the resolution. He agreed with the second part. With half of the third part he agreed: he failed to favour an appeal for new minimum wage legislation. May I remind the Conference that the paragraph re minimum wages was put in the resolution at the special request of South Wales. Knowing he will be loyal to his own district we are only left now with his objection to paragraph four. The fourth paragraph is the same wording as that contained in our Scarborough resolution. If we delete it the principle has already been accepted by the Federation. Why was it put in the resolution? For the same reason that it was carried at Scarborough. It was with the object of preventing attacks on wages in any district. We never put the position higher than that. The fact remains there has been no attack in any district on the general level of wages since 1931. After that explanation I am sure Mr. Bevan is at one with the Executive.

Then Ebby Edwards, briefly enough, gave his answer to the general tone of the debate which had made little impact on his cool judgement of the actual situation. For him, well aware of the past three years and more of disintegration, it had been a step in advance at Scarborough to get adopted a policy of common action if wages were further attacked. The time, in his opinion, was not yet ripe for a further move. Therefore he said:

I note from the speeches a good deal of feeling is being engendered as to the difficulties, and the very bad wages and conditions in the districts. Let me say that the issues we are faced with call for more than mere feeling. It is not emotion that is needed in a situation such as we find ourselves. If it were a mere question of raising emotion, there are members of the Executive who could beat any delegate on the floor of this Conference. What is needed is a question of direction, and much keener and clearer is the direction needed in times of economic difficulties and your members' adversity than it is in times of economic advantage and your members' prosperity.

His answer to Arthur Horner took him rather more time and was more involved. He ended by saying:

It is suggested we should pledge ourselves to assist a district that is making an attempt to improve their conditions. There are two difficulties. The national organisation can only help in two ways. Either by calling a national stoppage, which I have proved is not practicable, or make an appeal for financial help. I want to suggest that we ought not to mislead ourselves nor the men. Neither of these will work. We will admit quite frankly it is not a revolutionary resolution. There was no intention of making the resolution a fighting resolution. If we did ask the men to fight it would be asking them to commit suicide. If a stoppage has to take place we want to choose the time and the circumstances. I want to make a final appeal to the delegates at this stage, as I said at the outset, this is a most critical stage, and a stoppage now would end this Federation. It is better to mark time than march backwards.

This speech of Edwards's had its effect—though it may be remarked that when a forward step came to be taken, some eighteen months later, it embodied the Horner policy. At the moment most delegates accepted their General Secretary's advice, though perhaps they would not go so far as W. Golightly of Northumberland who, in his support of the Executive, said:

Ebby Edwards and the Chairman are leading a defeated army. What we have got to do is to get back our organisation. We have got to realise there is propaganda work to be done.

But some remained unconvinced, such as G. H. Jones of the Midlands who moved this amendment:

In view of the failure of the Government to set up a National Board for the arrangement of wages and conditions in the mining industry, this Conference calls upon the districts to formulate proposals for an increase in wages, and that a further Conference be called at an early date to consider the district proposals and decide upon a policy to carry them into effect. (December 28, 1933.)

There was discussion upon it, and Vice-President Joseph Jones argued vigorously against it and in support of the Executive. Then McGurk of Lancashire said:

If this Conference accepts the recommendation of the Committee, as drafted with the fourth clause, then, in the language of the late Thomas Ashton, we shall have to write over the door of 50, Russell Square, "Ichabod—Thy Glory has departed."

Thereupon Peter Lee rose and made his Chairman's closing speech. He was now in his seventieth year. His had been a hard upbringing. He had wrought in twenty-eight pits; always he had given notice, never waited to take it. Converted to Methodism in his twenties, he had become known to his fellows as "a ranter" (the word is still current in Durham) and both in the trade union and in local government had gained their support and their respect, expressed after his death by his name being given to a new town built in the coal-field. With his tall frame, spare body and commanding presence, the very manner of his utterance, perhaps more than the matter of it, made delegates pay heed to what he said:

Mr. McGurk says that if our resolution carries, then we had better close up Russell Square. As Chairman of this great Federation, I am an optimist. This Federation will not die. This Federation will live.

A few years ago we were almost 800,000 in membership, today we are 500,000. Where are those who were members? They have lapsed. I am not saying any hard things of any district, for, after all, I don't want to think in districts, I want to think nationally, and just as we are weak in one part we will tend to weaken all parts, therefore, I want you to use your energy to keep up your strength in every district.

We have sought a national agreement, and, for the time being, we have failed. Don't get it on your minds that failure will exist for ever.

They must organise, he said, and get ready for the fight that would have to come unless there was a radical change in the Government and mine-owners.

It was not the speech of a defeated leader of a defeated army. His confidence that in the rank and file there was life and hope was strongly shown when he said:

Let us plod on. Let the chaos caused by the coalowners, mismanagement, and indifference of the Government, deepen, as it will deepen, then public opinion will say that the endurance of the miners has been great under great difficulties, and they will recognise that we are seeking that which will be helpful to the nation, because the Government know it, and a lot of the mineowners know it, that without national co-operation on mining matters, things cannot improve in this nation. (December 28, 1933.)

But in order to get national co-operation the mine-owners had to go: and, much later it became clear that to make that national co-operation effective, the character of the governing body would have to be changed. Peter Lee, however, showed he had the heart of the matter in him. It was shortly before his retiral under the age-limit and not so very long before his death. Maybe he was like John of Gaunt, saying

Dying, I have the gift of prophecy.

The delegates adjourned for a quarter of an hour; then on resuming the Chairman took a vote on the Committee's resolution as against the Midlands amendment. The result of the voting was: for the Committee, 361; for the Midland Federation, 141. The minority was made up of the Midlands, Lancashire and South Wales.

7. RUEFUL CONCLUSIONS

Nearly six months later the Executive Committee in its Report dated June 9, 1934, was forced to draw some rueful conclusions. These applied not only to relations with the Government and the trade unions, but to activities in Parliament. On the one hand, the Government had introduced a Bill to reduce the amount of the Welfare Levy from one penny to a half-penny per ton commencing with the year 1932, and to continue the Fund at that rate for a further period of twenty years. This Bill passed its third reading on March 13th, and received the Royal Assent on March 28, 1934.

This Welfare Levy on each ton of coal, instituted after the Sankey Commission of 1919, had been grudged by the owners. Two years earlier, the Chairman of the Powell Duffryn Steam Coal Co. said to his shareholders:

The time has now come when this unfair burden on the industry of the Miners' Welfare Levy should be removed. There is nothing but sympathy for any practical scheme to better the lot of the miner, but to segregate from the profits of the industry a levy of some £1,000,000 per annum in a period of prolonged slump, during which profits have almost entirely disappeared, is indefensible. (March 22, 1932.)

Both the main amendments to the Bill submitted by the mining members had been rejected, but the Government accepted an amendment from a Tory member, which expressly excluded the payment of pensions from the Fund. "Such is the sorry record of the National Government in relation to welfare work for miners," was the comment.

Then again their relations with other unions were not satisfactory. For some years certain craft unions had taken advantage of the economic conditions to poach members, as the Executive Committee stated,

well knowing that in times of stress certain people will always desert their proper place and seek another stall, foolishly hoping that by so doing they will be able to improve their position.

Men have been encouraged to do this by the specious promises made them by the organisations in question, promises which could never be fulfilled, and which, indeed, were made solely to obtain the contributions of these misguided individuals. Far from improving their position, the only effect of leaving the Federation has been to divide the men, to weaken their power of collective action, *and thus to prevent the possibility of improved conditions.*

Moreover, as a result of this relations deteriorated with the Trades Union Congress, in which Ernest Bevin, who since 1926 had never been very friendly towards the Miners' Federation, was now a dominating figure. A year earlier Peter Lee had stated at Scarborough: "The relationship between the T.U.C. and the Miners' Federation is very strained. The treatment they have meted out to us during the last twelve months is not very pleasant."

As a consequence . . . of our failure to obtain proper redress from the T.U.C., our relations with Congress itself, not unnaturally, became somewhat strained during the course of the year.

The generally rueful tone was maintained in their report on "Wages—National Machinery." After recounting the persistent effort to get national machinery set up, the Executive Committee continued:

Why, then, with the Government professing to agree with us, have we not succeeded in obtaining this machinery? The answer, of course, is quite a simple one; the colliery-owners have persistently refused to be a party to National wages machinery and this Government, being of the political complexion it is, would do nothing which was contrary to the desires of the owners.

They recalled the Government's constant reiteration of willingness to consider any "practical scheme" the Federation might offer. To this the answer of the M.F.G.B. Executive was as they stated in their report:

We could only reply that such proposals would be readily forthcoming providing the Government, in its turn, would give an assurance that there would be:

(1) An obligation on the Board of Trade to set up a National Board.
(2) An obligation on the National Associations of Owners and Workmen to attend the Board, and
(3) An obligation on the parties to a dispute to attend the Board.

As you know, when these proposals were put to the Government, it then fell back upon the excuse that while the proposals did not amount to "compulsory arbitration" they were not "practical," because, in their view, to compel the owners was not a practicable policy. By constituting themselves the sole judges of what on the one hand was "practical," and by debarring, on the other hand, the question of "compulsory arbitration," the Government was, therefore, able effectively to checkmate our desires, while, at the same time, appearing to hold the scales evenly between the owners and ourselves.

This was quite a clever move in its way, but it was only a shallow piece of hypocrisy designed to cover up the intention of the

Government not to do anything contrary to the wishes of the owners. As we very frankly told them, their attitude, in fact, amounted to an admission that the owners were more powerful than the State itself.

As a last move in this controversy, they decided at their meeting in April to request the Government to set up a Statutory Committee to hear evidence and report upon ways and means of setting up national machinery in existing circumstances. But the Executive Committee regarded the negative reply which they received as "simply another evasion of the question."

When the rueful conclusions in the Executive Committee's Report were presented to the Annual Conference meeting in mid-July in Edinburgh, there was little debate on them or on any of the seventeen resolutions that were briefly discussed and passed. Some time, however, was taken up with the presentation to Peter Lee, who retired that week, having attained the age of seventy. Joseph Jones,[1] Vice-President since 1932, was unopposed for the Presidency. For the Vice-Presidency, however, there were six contestants. On the first day of the Conference they decided "That where there are more than two nominees for the position of Vice-President voting to be on the alternative system." On the first preference Harry Hicken of Derbyshire came out top and also on the second preference. The third preference resulted in a tie between Hicken and Lawther, 250 votes for each. In a straight vote, the result was Lawther, 253, Hicken, 247. Will Lawther had been prominent both in the trade union and the political field. For the Labour Party he had thrice contested South Shields at successive General Elections, and had sat as M.P. for Barnard Castle from 1929 to 1931. He had been a member of the Labour Party Executive Committee from 1923 to 1936 and sat on the Durham County Council from 1925 to 1929. He had played a considerable

---

[1] Joseph Jones, General Secretary of the Yorkshire Miners' Association and a member of the M.F.G.B. Executive Committee from 1923 onwards, was born in St. Helens in Lancashire, where he had gone through a technical college. From 1926 to 1931 he was a member of the Executive Committee of the Labour Party. From 1930 to 1938 he was H.M. Coal Mines Reorganisation Commissioner, and between 1919 and 1933 he had served on the West Riding County Council and the Barnsley Town Council. He was the first Chairman of the Workers' Temperance League.

On resigning from the M.F.G.B. Presidency on November 30, 1938, he became a member of the Coal Commission and nine years later was also made Adviser on Social Insurance to the National Coal Board. He died on April 1, 1948.

E   *The Miners*

part in the building up of the National Council of Labour Colleges and had been at the Central Labour College in London. More was to be heard of the new Vice-President in the future.

The Conference resolutions, though the treatment of them may have been rather perfunctory, did not echo the somewhat depressed tone of their Executive's Report. Rather, as the list[1] of them shows, they reflected that doggedness and persistence in pursuit of their aims which had been such a characteristic feature of the miners' trade unions for two generations. There was, however, one resolution the need for which was to be tragically exemplified before ten weeks were passed. This, under the heading of "Safety in Mines," instructed the Executive Committee to press for a general revision of the Coal Mines Act of 1911 as being "now out of date." Moving it, Seth Blackledge of Lancashire said there had been no change in the law for twenty-three years and in those years there had been the mechanisation of mines "very largely to the detriment of our people." He added, "where you have got mechanical appliances you get a terrific and almost unbearable noise." "Many of the inquests," he said, "could have been prevented had the coal been got in the ordinary way and the usual indications of danger could have been perceived or heard by the men working under dangerous roofs, but owing to the noise of mechanical appliances, the usual indications of nature by sound are unable to be heard." In the discussion, before the resolution was carried unanimously, the delegate from North Wales ended by emphasising that "we have persons at the present time as Inspectors who know very little about the law and very little about winding engines." This delegate was Edward Jones, attending his first M.F.G.B. Conference: he had been elected miners' agent (and Secretary of the association in North Wales) just three months earlier: he was afterwards to play a prominent part in the national body and to become its Vice-President.

[1] The 1934 Annual Conference resolutions covered the following subjects:

Hours of Work; National Agreement; Workmen's Compensation (two); Safety in Mines; Nationalisation of Mines; Silicosis; Coal and Oil; Wages; Pensions; Overtime; Coal By-Products; Wages Ascertainments; Unemployment Insurance Acts; Check-weighing Acts; Tools, Explosives, etc.; Finance.

8. GRESFORD COLLIERY DISASTER

That autumn of 1934 there occurred the worst colliery disaster for over twenty years. Indeed in the preceding century there had not been on more than half a dozen occasions a greater loss of life than occurred on the morning of Saturday, September 22, 1934, at Gresford Pit in Denbighshire. The total death roll from the explosion was 265 men and boys. The Secretary of Mines, following the precedent of the disaster at Senghenydd in 1913[1] appointed the Chief Inspector of Mines to hold a Court of Inquiry together with two assessors, John Brass and the M.F.G.B. President, Joseph Jones. The Federation Committee, in accordance with its rules, chose as their representatives at the Inquiry Peter Lee of Durham and J. A. Hall of Yorkshire. The North Wales and Border Counties Mineworkers' Association had engaged Sir Stafford Cripps, K.C., Geoffrey Wilson and Arthur Henderson (Junior) to represent it at the Inquiry: it made a request for help to meet the cost. To this the M.F.G.B. Executive agreed with reluctance, stating that the hiring of lawyers on such Inquiries "shall not form a precedent for future cases" (October 18th).[2] The Inquiry opened on October 25, 1934, and went on every working day into the middle of December when it had to be adjourned until the actual workings affected could be examined. The adjournment was to stretch out month after month: and meantime at Conference after Conference of all the parties concerned it was still found impossible to open up the affected area of the pit. It was still too dangerous.

Meantime a Mansion House Fund, that is a fund raised in the name of the Lord Mayor of London, had been opened and had reached £129,000 by mid-October 1934. The report to the 1935 Annual Conference stated that "the traditional generosity" of the British public had been "transcended on this occasion," over £500,000 having been

---

[1] See *The Miners: Years of Struggle*, Chapter II.

[2] It should be here said that some of the most eminent barristers whose names occur in this record (such as Cripps and Pritt) did not take their fee on particular occasions. This was one such occasion: and, as a result, the expenditure of the North Wales Union stood at the low figure of £165. Sir Stafford Cripps claimed nothing at all, while the junior barristers took only travelling and out-of-pocket expenses.

subscribed within a few months, and that "this noble contribution of the British public" was very deeply appreciated by the miners and their families.

The public had been made aware of the horrible conditions at Gresford pit from the facts brought out in the first seven weeks of the Inquiry, particularly the facts elicited from witnesses under cross-examination by Sir Stafford Cripps. Cripps was able to show that there had been "innumerable breaches of the law and regulations laid down for the protection of those who worked in coal mines, and that the behaviour of the Inspectorate had been deplorable"; and also what part had been played by economic factors in causing the disaster. The terrible conditions thus revealed day by day at the Inquiry were summarised in Parliament some two years later in a description of a pit district called "the fourteens":

There is no language in which one can describe the inferno of 14's. There were men working almost stark naked, clogs with holes bored through the bottom to let the sweat run out, a 100 shots a day fired on a face less than 200 yards wide, the air thick with fumes and dust from blasting, the banjack hissing to waft the gas out of the face into the unpacked waste, a space 200 yards long and 100 yards wide above the wind road full of inflammable gas and impenetrable for that reason.

(D. Grenfell in the House of Commons, February 23, 1937.)

These conditions before the explosion having been examined, the adjournment took place and went on throughout 1935, with the Federation repeatedly pressing for a resumption of the Inquiry. Finally the decision was taken not to explore the areas affected by the disaster and the Inquiry, with its scope thus considerably restricted, was reopened in April 1936. In its concluding stage Sir Stafford Cripps analysed the evidence, summed it all up, and drew conclusions from it of very great importance to every mine-worker. "It was a masterly analysis, and in its complete and utter fearlessness was one of the most remarkable utterances of our times"— so wrote Ebby Edwards in a grateful preface to a published summary[1] of the speech, which took over three days to deliver, and ran to nearly 150,000 words. According to this

---

[1] *Gresford Disaster. Report of the Speech by Sir Stafford Cripps, K.C., at the Government Inquiry Into the Causes of the Disaster.* April 15, 16 and 17, 1936.

summary, Cripps showed that the whole atmosphere of the evidence was that of driving for output at all costs; and although no statistics of the Gresford Pit itself had been forthcoming (he deplored that fact), official figures of the mines in Denbighshire showed that between the years 1924 and 1933 the output per man had increased by 35 per cent, or thirty-six tons per man per annum. That illustrated the increased pressure on the men.

But there were other economic factors in his submission that had a very great bearing on the question of safety. The fear of unemployment caused the miner to try and retain his job at all costs. Cripps had said:

In an area like that, where a miner's only hope of employment was at the Gresford pit, it was useless to suggest that the men could make themselves offensive to the management and the firemen by complaining of circumstances which were perfectly well known to the management and the firemen before the complaints were made.

He then quoted the evidence of eleven witnesses to show the fear of victimisation which possessed the men in consequence of the economic conditions under which they worked. Extracts from this evidence (two only) are given below:

1ST WITNESS
Question: Yes; and you were working in the spot where you say the danger was?
Answer: Well; my bread and butter depends on the colliery.
Question: Is that your reply? That is your reason?
Answer: It is my fear of victimisation.
Question: Afraid of victimisation?
Answer: Yes.
Question: From the Colliery Company?
Answer: Yes; from the Colliery Company, by making a complaint as to conditions.

ANOTHER WITNESS
Question: What did you do about it?
Answer: It is a case of your having to keep your mouth closed, or be victimised.
Question: You realised that it was dangerous?
Answer: Yes.
Question: And you thought if you made some report you might lose your job?
Answer: Yes.

Question: Did you think your job was more important than the safety of other men working down the pit there with you?

Answer: I do not say anything about the safety of other men; but I say I was looking after my job for my own family's sake.

Sir Stafford Cripps said that the evidence showed quite conclusively that whatever the theory might be, in practice the miners were not in a position to take any real care of their own safety. They were in a position of getting on or getting out, and if they made any undue complaint it was a question of getting out.

After summing up other evidence which showed that the law had been flagrantly broken and not only had the necessary records not been kept at the place laid down by Parliament, but that "many of those records were never made; others were not kept in the appropriate place; and some were not kept at all," Cripps dealt with the Inspectorate, the inspection of mines being the overriding safeguard upon which the public and the miners were entitled to rely. Here he said that perhaps the most serious aspect of that enquiry had been the demonstration of the failure of the Inspectorate to carry out their job properly at Gresford during the last two years. It was quite true that formal visits had been made, but a large number of them were to the surface only, or in cases where accidents had occurred and the underground inspections had been prepared for beforehand; inspection had been a complete and absolute farce. What, in his submission, had emerged from the evidence was that there were numerous continuing breaches of the regulations of all kinds, of which no notice was taken by the Inspectorate until so many men had been killed at the Gresford Pit. Either the Inspectorate had been quite careless as regards discovering those breaches, or ignorant as regards the regulations themselves, or else they must have, for some reason or other, turned the blind eye upon them in the Gresford Pit.

9.   REPORTS AND DEBATE IN COMMONS

The whole of the Gresford affair was unusual in the long tale of colliery disasters: the causes could be guessed at but could not be found; nor did the Inquiry end till after two years; nor was the Inspectorate free from blame. In addition the formal investigation resulted in not one but three Reports.[1] Commissioner Sir Henry Walker, after an introduction and general information sections, dealt under the heading Ventilation (which amounted to over half his Report) with air measurements. His first paragraph on this was startling enough:

(a) *Air measurements.* The air measurements, said to have been made monthly, as required by Section 29 (2) of the Coal Mines Act, 1911, were entered in the prescribed book, Mines and Quarries Form No. 37, to June 30th; the measurements said to have been made in July and August were found in the note-book of the Assistant Surveyor (William Idris Cuffin), who said he made the measurements. Some 18 months later—in June 1936—Mr. Cuffin, when giving further evidence, said that on the instructions of the Manager he had not in fact made any measurements since June 1934; that the figures in the note-book for July and August were imaginary and that he had concocted them because the Manager had told him to do so a day or two after the disaster (p. 11).

The Commissioner, after this first example of perjury, went on to examine the evidence on another question of ventilation. Here he concluded:

The evidence of these two deputies, on this point, does not ring true and I do not accept it as true. I do not believe that 24's airway —which as I have already said I believe to have been a return and not an intake—was inspected by either of them on September 21 and I do not believe that it was sufficiently open for inspection on that date. (Cmd. 5358, p. 36.)

The system of ventilation by which air is driven through intakes to the coal-face or other workings and thence by return airways is, of course, well known. In every manager's room the plan of the pit shows intakes and returns in different colours. A state of affairs in which there could be dubiety about the kind of airway or where the evidence on it of the deputies could be disbelieved revealed an almost inconceivable negligence in the organisation of safety. On

[1] *Reports on the Causes of and Circumstances attending the Explosion which occurred at Gresford Colliery, Denbigh, on September 22, 1934.* By Sir Henry Walker, C.B.E., LL.D., H.M. Chief Inspector of Mines (Commissioner), and Mr. John Brass, M.Inst.C.E., M.I.Min.E., and Mr. Joseph Jones, C.B.E., J.P. (Assessors). January 1937. Cmd. 5358.

this, as on other points, John Brass, a Yorkshire coal-owner, in his separate Report, accepted this suspect evidence, saying:

There is no reason to doubt the veracity of the Deputies Parry and Edwards, and if their evidence is not clear in places, the effect of the hostile atmosphere of the public in the Court, the cross-examination by one of the most eminent Counsel of the day, and the nervous tension which they and many other witnesses were suffering from must be borne in mind. (Cmd. 5358, p. 118.)

John Brass also stated the mine could not be regarded as a "gassy mine" (p. 116).[1] Mr. Brass did not agree with Sir Henry Walker on a whole number of matters and the general effect of his Report was to shield or exonerate the owners and the management.

Under a section headed Hours of Work Below Ground the Commissioner stated that:

men were allowed to work and did work longer hours than are permitted by the Coal Mines Regulation Act, 1908—generally known as the Eight Hours Act—as amended by later Acts. In fact the provisions of that Act were, to all intents and purposes, ignored.

From the Report by Joseph Jones two points may be quoted. The Inspectorate he described as "both inadequate and ineffective," stating:

As further evidence of the entire absence of effective supervision by the Inspectorate, there is the admission of the Divisional Inspector, Mr. Charlton, who also had not visited the Gresford Mine during the period mentioned, and who relied solely upon the reports (when such reports were made) of the visiting inspectors.

A statement by the Divisional Inspector as to the probable cause of the explosion, made largely as a speculation and under conditions when he could not be subjected to cross-examination, was promptly taken up and put forward by the Counsel for the colliery company. Joseph Jones said of the explosion:

Nor do I think it could have occurred in the neighbourhood of the "Clutch" as suggested by Counsel for the Colliery Company,

[1] The Report of Mr. Joseph Jones made a directly contrary statement, that the main source of the output of coal at the colliery was "of a very gassy nature,"

Hartley Shawcross.[1] Indeed, I regard the suggestion that "the ignition was at the telephone when it was *about to be used for warning those inbye of the influx of gas in the Drift*" as being extremely unlikely, and entirely unsupported by any reliable evidence whatsoever.

Joseph Jones listed over a dozen serious breaches of law of which the Manager, Mr. William Bonsall, was guilty; and stated that the under-manager and the other subordinate officials, deputies and shot-firers had also been "similarly guilty of flagrant and persistent breaches" of the Coal Mines Act and General Regulations, and "all should be dealt with as the law directs." Finally he gave his opinion that a Chief Inspector of Mines should *not* in future be called upon to conduct formal investigations of this kind and added that:

I do not impute incompetency or unfairness to the Commissioner at this Inquiry. I do assert, however, that it imposes upon any person directly associated with the Inspectorate a dual loyalty which must inevitably strain impartiality to the farthest limits.

The Report of the Inquiry was issued early in February 1937 and on Tuesday, February 23rd, a debate upon the explosion of September 22, 1934, lasted six hours in the House of Commons. The debate began on the following motion by Mr. David Grenfell, Member for Gower, who himself had been present throughout the whole Inquiry:

That this House views with deep concern the conditions revealed by the inquiry into the Gresford Colliery explosion in which 265 lives were lost, and is of opinion that grave responsibility rests upon the country and Parliament to prevent such disasters by adopting immediate and effective measures for ensuring that the industry is carried on under conditions of maximum safety.

In his speech David Grenfell was extremely critical of three participants in the Inquiry, the Divisional Inspector, the counsel for the company and the employers' assessor:

The speeches of Mr. Charlton and Mr. Shawcross are reproduced in this report. They indicate how little these gentlemen have profited from the revelations of the inquiry.

In the case of Mr. Shawcross, it does not matter very much,

[1] Afterwards a Labour Member of Parliament for St. Helens from 1945 and appointed Attorney-General in the Labour Government in the same year. Some years after the end of the Labour Government he retired from active politics but took a prominent post in connection with one of the big oil companies.

E*

except that he is quoted in the report. In the case of Mr. Charlton, the position is different. The Commissioner has taken the evidence seriously and quotes it fully in his report.

Mr. Charlton rejects or ignores all the evidence as it seems most convenient to him. He is even now unwilling to believe that gas was present in all the lower parts of the Dennis main area. He rejects the evidence of workmen and officials who admit the entire story of neglect and carelessness. He is impervious to the evidence. One might almost say he is gas-proof. He has produced a theory and falls back on futile and mischievous speculations regarding the cause and place of ignition. There is not a scrap of justification, not a sign or an indication, to confirm his belated explanation.

The inquiry was perfectly open. Mr. Charlton could have put forward his theories during the investigation, but he chose to come later when he could not be cross-examined. He has given a lead which Mr. Shawcross, counsel for the company, adopts, and which Mr. John Brass includes in his report without quoting a word of evidence in support. (February 23, 1937.)

In the course of the debate many quotations were made by members from the Report by Sir Henry Walker, the Chief Inspector of Mines. Amongst these was one from which Sir Stafford Cripps drew the inference:

There must have been constraint put upon the manager by the owners, otherwise his conduct is absolutely inexplicable.

But even more disturbing was a conclusion by Sir Henry Walker that bore upon the Inspectorate of which he was the chief. He stated:

In the sections of this Report dealing with ventilation and with precautions against coal dust, it has been my duty to say that in certain respects, in my judgment, certain inspectors were at fault in their dealings with this colliery over a period of years. (Cmd. 5358, p. 90.)

The fact that Sir Henry Walker who held the Inquiry as Commissioner had also to deal with the Inspectorate of which he was the chief, led many members to suggest that in future such inquiries should be held by one of H.M. Judges—but this was not a standpoint that was normally held by the M.F.G.B. Executive who had been in favour of Sir Henry Walker conducting the Inquiry. There was one other statement which interested both the Members of Parliament and also the miners' leaders who well knew how weak trade union organisation had been in this District at the time of the disaster. Sir Henry Walker wrote:

I hope that I am not exceeding my function in saying now what I have held for many years that miners should be members of some effective trades union. That opinion is based on the grounds of safety, with which alone I am concerned, for I believe that a well organised trades union, wisely directed, can be as potent an influence for promoting greater safety in mines as it is already in matters, for example, of wages and conditions of employment.

Actually of the 265 killed only seventy-eight were paid-up members of the union in North Wales. Many were in arrears with contributions: others, unfortunately, were non-unionists.[1]

There was no amendment by the Government; indeed the Secretary for Mines had taken the sting out of the debate by acceptance of the motion. He defended the Inspectorate and went on to say:

The other problem which comes up is whether the general organisation of the inspection districts is right. The present organisation was the result of the Royal Commission of 1909 and there again, for advice as to the future, we must await the report of the present Royal Commission.

The House will remember that the setting up of that Royal Commission was one of the important points in the Government's programme dealing with coal at the last General Election and one of the first things that we did when this Parliament met was to set up that Commission. (February 23, 1937.)

10. THE PROSECUTIONS

Eight weeks later in Denbighshire, at the Wrexham County Petty Sessions, the prosecutions began against the colliery company owning Gresford and nine of its officials. As the Dennis section of the mine where the explosion occurred two-and-a-half years earlier had not yet been re-entered— it was still too dangerous—no one could say what was the cause of the explosion. Therefore no one could be held in law to be responsible for it. The defendants could only be charged

---

[1] "It struck me as a young man just entering this field that had there been a much stronger Union Branch at Gresford conditions which led to the disaster would not have been so readily tolerated."—*Letter from Edward Jones to author.*

with breaches of the Coal Mines Act of 1911 before September 22, 1934; and no allegation was made that by any of these acts they were responsible for the explosion. Hence it was a case of forty-two summonses on such charges as are usually dealt with in Courts of the lowest jurisdiction. What was unusual was the appearance before this local bench of magistrates of the Solicitor-General, Sir Terence O'Connor, K.C., one of the two Law Officers of the Crown in the Government; and of the appearance for the defence of Sir Patrick Hastings, K.C., a leader of the Bar who had been Attorney-General in the Labour Government of 1924: with him was Hartley Shawcross.

The proceedings lasted for over a week, during which witnesses were examined and cross-examined. Sir Patrick Hastings conducted the defence with such skill that in the course of the hearings several of the charges were withdrawn as being legally inadmissible, while the Solicitor-General agreed to withdraw all summonses against defendants other than the colliery company and the manager. The skilful use made of the Inquiry evidence of thirty months earlier by the defence was exemplified when W. J. Charlton, Divisional Inspector of Mines, was in the witness box. He said that he had not received any complaint of any sort from the Mineworkers' Federation in respect of Gresford pit.

Sir Patrick Hastings: Do you think it credible that no complaints should be received from anyone if the mine were in the condition suggested on behalf of the prosecution?
W. J. Charlton: To me it seems incredible. (April 21, 1937.)

Considerable skill was also shown by the under-manager as witness for the defence, whose statements tending to exonerate the management were maintained under cross-examination by the Solicitor-General who had suggested that the witness was not telling the truth.

In opening for the prosecution, the Solicitor-General had pointed out that the maximum penalty in some of the cases was three months' imprisonment and in others £20 or £5 and added:

It may occur to the Bench and it may be thought at large that those are grossly inadequate penalties if it were established, as I hope to establish in some of these cases, that the safety of human beings was involved through the negligence of people who had responsible duties in this coal mine. (April 20, 1937.)

The magistrates, however, at the conclusion of the case dismissed the ventilation charges as unproved, while they held that the remaining charges (mainly of alleged failure to take measurements, to keep records of various quantities of air in a part of the mine and to show certain requisite data on the ventilation plan) were proved. They therefore imposed fines of £15 each on four charges and £20 each on four other charges. United Westminster and Wrexham Collieries Ltd. and William Bonsall, their manager, had each to pay £140 in fines. There was also an order to pay £350 costs.

The Mineworkers' Federation, who had memories of a not entirely dissimilar prosecution after the loss of 439 lives at Senghenydd a quarter of a century earlier, were ill satisfied with this ending to the long story of the Gresford disaster. It increased their determination to strengthen the law for safety measures in coal-mines.

II. ROYAL COMMISSION ON SAFETY

The horror caused by the Gresford disaster and the widespread dissatisfaction at the slow progress of the formal investigation had one significant result. A month after the General Election of November 14, 1935, by Royal Warrant of George the Fifth, ten Commissioners were appointed to enquire:

Whether the safety and health of mineworkers can be better ensured by extending or modifying the principles or general provisions of the Coal Mines Act, 1911, or the arrangements for its administration, having regard to the changes that have taken place in organisation, methods of work, and equipment since it became law, and the experience gained, and to make recommendations. (Royal Commission on Safety in Coal Mines Report, p. xvii. Cmd. 5890.)

Their appointment was confirmed by a Royal Warrant of Edward the Eighth on February 12, 1936, and yet again by a similar Royal Warrant of George the Sixth on December

21, 1936. On this Royal Commission there sat as Chairman Evelyn Cecil (created Lord Rockley in 1934), a cousin of the Marquess of Salisbury. Ebby Edwards and D. R. Grenfell, M.P., were also members of the Commission, which for the rest consisted of two civil servants and another five who had experience in the mining industry. The Commission thus appointed and constituted took three years to complete its work. During this time they examined fifty-two witnesses representing all the principal interests concerned, and received many written statements. They themselves inspected selected mines in all the coal-fields and altogether covered most fields of necessary investigation. The evidence from the Mineworkers' Federation of Great Britain referred to below was submitted in December 1936 and January 1937 and in its printed form covered twenty pages. It was submitted by the President, the Vice-President and other members of the M.F.G.B. Executive. The scope of the Report is shown by its chapter headings, as follows:

Historical.	Haulage and Travelling.
Changes since 1911.	Explosions and Fires.
Administration of the Law.	Miscellaneous Accidents Underground.
Organisation and Management of the Industry.	Conditions of work on the Surface.
Ventilation.	Safety Organisation and Training.

Support of Workings.
Health, including First Aid and the Prevention of Occupational Diseases.

The Report with final recommendations was published in December 1938. Some reservations were made by members of the Commission. A reservation by Ebby Edwards ran as follows:

While I am in general agreement with the conclusions and recommendations made by the Commission, and have signed the same with a view to expedite an immediate change in the existing mining legislation, I regret that my colleagues on the Commission did not accept, and embody in the recommendations, a number of the suggestions made in the memorandum of evidence submitted by the Mineworkers' Federation.

I do not think sufficient regard has been paid to the economic factor, the speeding up and the intensification of production as one which is responsible for counterbalancing the work that has been done by scientific research.

The piecework system, payment by results, is without doubt the cause of many accidents.

I also believe the entry into mines of boys should be raised to 16 years of age, and the daily working hours of all classes of mine-workers reduced.

EBBY EDWARDS.

Many of the recommendations were such as could be put into force by regulations issued by the Mines Department, but the work of the Commission as a whole formed the basis for the preparation of a new law.[1] This did not come as fast as Edwards had expected. Due to the war of 1939–45 no Bill was brought forward in Parliament. After the war the work of preparation proceeded relatively slowly. It was not until sixteen years after the Report of the Commission—and more than twenty after the Gresford disaster —that the Mines and Quarries Act, 1954, finally became law.

[1] The Commission's Report and the new law based upon it will be examined in another volume.

APPENDIX TO CHAPTER III

PRINCIPAL COLLIERY DISASTERS* FROM ALL CAUSES IN THE YEARS 1914–42†

Year	Date		Name of Colliery	County	Nature of Disaster	No. killed
1914	May	30	Wharncliffe Silkstone	Yorkshire	Explosion	12
1915	Feb.	25	New Hem Heath	Stafford	Underground fire	12
	June	30	Bentinck	Nottingham	Shaft accident	10
	Sept.	21	Exhall	Warwick	Smoke and fumes descending shaft	14
1916	Aug.	13	Woodhorn	Northumberland	Explosion	13
1918	Jan.	12	Podmore Hall, Minnie Pit	Stafford	Explosion	155
	July	9	Stanrigg and Arbuckle	Lanark	Inrush of moss and water	19
1922	July	13	Plean	Stirling	Explosion	12
	Sept.	5	Whitehaven, Haig Pit	Cumberland	Explosion	39
1923	April	20	Caldean	Carmarthen	Runaway trams	10
	July	28	Maltby Main	Yorkshire	Explosion	27
	Sept.	25	Redding, No. 23	Stirling	Inrush of water	40
1925	March	30	Montagu Main	Northumberland	Inrush of water	38
1927	March	1	Marine No. 1	Monmouth	Explosion	52
	March	1	Bilsthorpe	Nottingham	Shaft accident	14
1928	Feb.	12	Whitehaven, Haig Pit	Cumberland	Explosion	13
1930	Feb.	26	Lyme	Lancashire	Explosion	13
	Oct.	1	Grove	Stafford	Explosion	14
1931	Jan.	29	Whitehaven, Haig Pit	Cumberland	Explosion	27
	Oct.	31	Bowhill	Fife	Explosion	10
	Nov.	20	Bentley	Yorkshire	Explosion	45
1932	Jan.	25	Llwynypia, No. 1	Glamorgan	Explosion	11
	Oct.	10	Bickershaw, No. 9	Lancashire	Shaft accident	19
	Nov.	12	Garswood Hall, No. 9	Lancashire	Explosion	27
	Nov.	16	Cardowan	Lanark	Explosion	11
1933	Nov.	19	Grassmoor, No. 8	Derbyshire	Explosion	14
1934	Sept.	22	Gresford	Denbighshire	Explosion	265‡
1935	Aug.	24	South Kirkby	Yorkshire	Explosion	10
	Sept.	12	North Gawber	Yorkshire	Explosion	19
1936	Aug.	6	Wharncliffe, Woodmoor, Nos. 1, 2 and 3	Yorkshire	Explosion	58
1937	July	2	Holditch	Stafford	Explosion	30
1938	May	10	Markham, No. 1, Blackshale	Derbyshire	Explosion	79
1939	Oct.	28	Valleyfield	Fife	Explosion	35
1940	March	21	Mossfield	Stafford	Explosion	11
	June	4	Upton	Yorkshire	Explosion	10
1941	June	3	William	Cumberland	Explosion	12
	July	10	Rhigos, No. 4	Glamorgan	Explosion	16
	July	29	Crigglestone	Yorkshire	Explosion	22
1942	Jan.	1	Sneyd	Stafford	Explosion	57
	Feb.	17	Barnsley Main	Yorkshire	Explosion	12
	June	26	Murton	Durham	Explosion	13

* Accidents involving the loss of ten lives or more.

† There were no principal disasters recorded in the years 1943, 1944 or 1945.

‡ Including three persons who were killed during rescue operations and a further life which was lost on the surface three days later when the sealing blew off the downcast shaft.

CHAPTER IV

THE WAGES CAMPAIGN

I. BEFORE THE CAMPAIGN

THROUGHOUT 1933 and 1934 the world economic crisis that had lasted since Autumn 1929 was coming to an end. There had begun a revival in many fields of industry. Production of pig-iron, then sometimes taken as a single indicator of the state of heavy industry, was moving upward. In Britain it was not, however, as had happened in the past with these cyclical crises, a rapid recovery up to and beyond previous levels. The economic crisis in Britain passed into a special kind of depression, as shown by the continuing high figure of unemployment. This was particularly true of the coal trade. While consumption of coal within Britain gradually rose to its old level from the year 1933, which marked the lowest point both in production and consumption, export of coal made but a poor recovery, nor did it ever again reach the level of the 'twenties. The effect on coal output is seen in the following ten-year table:

Year	Production (in million tons)	Number of wage-earners on colliery books
1929	258	932,000
1930	244	917,000
1931	219	850,000
1932	209	803,000
1933	207	772,000
1934	221	774,000
1935	222	759,000
1936	228	756,000
1937	240	778,000
1938	227	782,000

So much for the economic situation. The political situation was also changing. With all its huge majority in Lords and Commons, the Coalition Government was encountering a growing stiff resistance to its policies. In the summer of 1935 its foreign policy was to receive a shock in the returns of the

Peace Ballot, organised by the League of Nations Association, in which eleven million of the population participated. In home affairs, its policy for the unemployed suffered a serious defeat. On June 28, 1934, some thirty months after the imposition by Orders in Council of the Means Test, a new Unemployment Insurance Act became law. This Act took the administration out of the hands of the Public Assistance Committees and centralised it under a new Unemployment Assistance Board, of which the former Minister of Labour, at a greatly enhanced salary, became the Chairman. The new Act with its Board was ill-received by the Labour movement, and throughout the last six months of 1934 there was a growing apprehension of what might come out of it. On December 11, 1934, when the new scales and regulations for assessment of the resources of families to be subjected to the Means Test were made public, these fears seemed to be more than justified by the number of cases in which there would be heavy reductions. The Government for its part may well have expected widespread protest on the part of the million-and-a-half workers who would come within the scope of the new scales on January 7, 1935; but the consequence was far beyond anyone's expectation. A storm of protest burst on the astonished legislators (the House of Commons had discussed the new scales and passed them on December 19, 1934) and took a form that was not limited to the expected complaints from the Opposition and the General Council of the Trades Union Congress—which in fact deprecated the forceful action taken, especially in distressed areas. The South Wales Miners' Federation called an All-Wales Conference on January 26, 1935: it was attended by 1,600 delegates: while the next month a Conference on the Act was called by the Durham Miners' Association. On Sunday, February 3rd, in South Wales alone nearly 300,000 people (according to the *Manchester Guardian*) marched in demonstrations. It was the same in other depressed areas and cities. Local hunger marches were received by local authorities, who now readily forwarded the demands of the unemployed to the Government. As the agitation grew, in spite of baton charges by the police and numerous arrests, the Government faltered: and finally on February 5th succumbed to the storm of protest. The new scales were withdrawn and the deductions made in the previous four weeks were handed back.

Not only were the miners part of this general stir of activity with so many of the unemployment demonstrations originating in the coal-fields; but in addition there was in the early months of 1935 a coming together of all sections of the Federation in a national demand for a general increase in wages.

The year before at the Edinburgh Annual Conference the resolutions were still concerned mainly with national machinery and with the sort of wage that was considered desirable. It had resolved "to take immediate steps to organise the mineworkers in every coalfield, with a view to enforcing a National Wages Agreement" and demanded

That a national minimum wage be fixed at 20 per cent above the present average rate; with a 7-hour day, including winding time; and the abolition of all overtime. (July 19, 1934.)

After months and years of hope deferred, now resolutions were coming in from the Districts. Therefore the Executive Committee at its first meeting of the new year (January 17, 1935) decided to call a Special Conference "to consider the establishment of a National Agreement." At the Special Conference (February 14th) in the Kingsway Hall, London, there were 136 delegates present representing 499,269 members. W. Hogg of Northumberland opened the discussion saying that "the outstanding lesson we must have learned is that it is quite impossible for any one district to be fighting a lone battle to regain even a tithe of the reductions in wages that have been sustained over a period of years." He said that the Federation had been inactive. Special Conferences were a sign of activity: but there had been only one of them in 1934. "We should have had several Conferences," said Hogg, who went on to demand that agitation ought not to be "spasmodic," but "continuous." He argued for a return to "the original ideas and opinions of the pioneers and those who did so much to make us a power with the powers that be, even the Government." Jack McGurk of Lancashire, after referring to the seven months' stoppage of 1926, said:

The economic circumstances have revived that spirit today, and all that spirit requires now is a lead from the head, from the top. I am hoping that, as a result of this Conference today, that lead will be given so that the public will know that at last the Miners' Federation of Great Britain, as has been recently stated, is back to life.

Next day the Executive circulated a draft resolution. This was carried unanimously. It reaffirmed the necessity for a national settlement to secure "just and reasonable conditions," and resolved that the coal-owners should now once more be approached:

to devise with the Federation suitable wages machinery providing for an improved standard of life for the mine workers. (February 15, 1935.)

If this failed, the Government should be asked to implement the demands by legislation; and a report should be made to a further Conference.

The situation was difficult, it was stalemate. Efforts of certain Districts to improve wages and conditions had been unsuccessful—because their economic position so closely depended upon that of other Districts. It had become apparent that only a general movement, embracing all the coal-fields, had any chance of success. On the other hand, any national movement would have grave difficulties to overcome. Not only was it a question of the owners' persistent refusal to meet with the Federation on wages questions. The leaders were haunted by a fear that had never afflicted their fathers, namely,

a national movement would be exposed to the organisational weakness which had resulted from the emergence of the industrial unions in Nottingham and elsewhere, and so bring the strong links of the chain down to the level of the weaker ones. (Annual Report, 1935–36.)

The Government also were fully aware of this situation. Moreover, they knew that, quite apart from the debilitating effect of the Spencer unions upon the vigour of the M.F.G.B. constituent bodies, there was the possible sapping effect of the large number of miners still out of work. For in March 1935 there were 243,000 out of work. By June the figure had risen to 300,000, nearly 31 per cent of those insured. This being so there seemed no reason for Walter Runciman in the Board of Trade or for his Secretary of the Mines

Department to feel undue anxiety about any steps that might be taken by the Federation. In April 1935 the Federation (not being able to get contact with the employers) put to the Government a definite request for higher wages: nothing was heard in answer until nearly three months later, when a reply came from a Mines Department official that

H.M. Government regret that . . . there is at present no effective course of action open to them.

On the request for a raising of wages, presumably by a Minimum Wage Bill, it stated

the attitude of H.M. Government towards proposals of this nature has already been made clear. (July 9, 1935.)

It was an attitude of flat refusal. Whatever might have been done by the Asquith administration a score and more of years earlier in their Minimum Wage Act was not to be a precedent. On this the Cabinet were adamant. After all, in 1912 it had been a measure to end a strike: no such compulsion from the mine-workers was visible in summer 1935. So, after some general expressions of benevolence, the civil servant invited "the workmen" to base their hope of a higher standard of living upon the Cabinet's policy, which was for "stimulating the revival of trade." As this did not differ materially from the policy of any Cabinet at any time in the past two centuries, it was cold comfort. The Executive Committee noted the nebulous character of that belated reply. It was, they felt, symptomatic of an attitude towards the Federation. Joseph Jones, M.F.G.B. President since 1934, expressed their feelings in the Annual Conference held at Rhyl Town Hall, North Wales (Monday, July 15, 1935, and following days), about the "way in which the Miners' Federation, as an organisation, is being regarded by the Government, by the general public, and, in particular, by the Mines Department." His presidential address had a marked effect in the coal-fields: it was a stimulus to action.

The Conference delegates, too, felt that they must record their protest and embodied it in the remarkably brief but, as it turned out, momentous resolution on the question of wages. This resolution, put forward on the Tuesday, had actually been drawn up by the Executive at Rhyl on the previous day when they considered the letter from the Mines Department. It therefore took the delegates by surprise and though there was an inkling of what had been in the minds of their President and Secretary in a press report of a speech by Joseph Jones in which he named two shillings a shift as the needed increase, quite a few of them had assumed that this was the statement of an aspiration rather than a definite demand. But here on the morning of July 16th they had in their hands the following resolution to be debated in closed session that afternoon:

That this Conference of the M.F.G.B., having carefully considered the reply of the Government on the wages question, strongly protests against the direct refusal of the Government to consider the scandalous wages in the mining industry. We, therefore, endorse the demand for a flat rate advance of 2s. per day, and that following an intensive campaign in support of this claim a Special Conference be convened to decide what action should be taken to enforce the demand. (July 16, 1935.)

There were many anxious questions raised. For example, how would this affect District agreements? Should those Districts already claiming or about to claim changes in their agreements with the District coal-owners, hold their hand for the time being? Were not the Executive and in particular Joseph Jones and Ebby Edwards being rather precipitate now, having been blamed in the past for being tardy and too cautious? Fred Swift of Somerset immediately voiced his anxiety at "a fresh national policy" being "sprung upon us"; but A. Jenkins of South Wales took a different attitude, saying, "we are delighted with the new life which the Miners' Federation is beginning to show, and which we hope is going to continue to exist." He added: "Trouble has arisen this afternoon, not because the Miners' Federation has shown new life, but because of our attachment to our districts—our district machinery." Vice-President William Lawther of Durham moved the resolution, opening with the words:

I am sure nobody could accuse the Committee, or the Officials, of this Federation of having rushed headlong with a proposal, or with a policy, without giving that proposal, or that policy, the most serious consideration.

It was seconded by Jim Griffiths of South Wales. Delegates from every District supported. Amongst them a delegate coming straight from the coal-face, R. Jones of South Wales, said:

I would like to say I feel, being my first National Conference, pleased to be identified with the resurrection of the Miners' Federation of Great Britain.

The debate was wound up by General Secretary Ebby Edwards:

I have been making a desperate effort for the last three years for peace in the coalfields. I have made appeals up and down the country. Nay, I go further. I believe that the toleration that my Executive has shown has been exploited as weakness on the part of the Organisation, and we say that situation cannot continue. In the appeals I have made I have emphasised the Federation should secure a voice in the conduct and policy of the industry in regard to the disposal of the coal that our men sacrifice their lives to produce. We believe if we were to apply ourselves to the conduct and policy of the industry the economic status of the industry could be raised with satisfaction to the men without any question of a stoppage; and, therefore, we are prepared to make our concrete contribution towards placing the industry on a satisfactory basis.

Ebby Edwards drove his argument home by a comparison of the effect on two coal-fields of the chaotic conditions of the industry in prices, output and wages. The 1934 prices of the sale of coal in Lancashire had been 15s. 8d. per ton, in Scotland 11s. 8d. or 4s. less: earnings per man-shift in Lancashire were 9s. 2·46d., in Scotland 8s. 9·18d. And the reason for this difference?

For every man shift in Scotland they are producing 5·6 cwts. more, and the cost for every ton of coal that is produced in Lancashire, compared with Scotland, exceeds 4s. a ton. Our Scottish friends do not want to sell coal at a less market value than other areas, but they have no say. They are in the hands of the coal capitalists—each district for itself. (July 17, 1935.)

But while Edwards thus stressed both his pacific outlook and the final aim of national control of production, distribution and prices, he made clear his full support of the claim for a national wages advance. But it was not to be as in the past. It had to go step by step, beginning with an intensive campaign, a matter on which he had brooded long and often. The chief officer of the Federation had a strategic plan for a national struggle: and now at last, in his judgement, the time was ripe.

2. THE CAMPAIGN

On July 25th the preliminary arrangements were made for the campaign, and renewed efforts made to get the claims considered by the employers. Direct application to the owners had always brought a blunt refusal, while the Government (as their letter of July 9th showed) would do nothing to move the employers. The first thing to do, then, was to ventilate the matter in the House of Commons. At the beginning of August, therefore, a parliamentary question was asked, to which Captain Crookshank, now Secretary for Mines, made reply that though he had learned the owners' attitude was unchanged he would invite them to meet the Mineworkers' Federation to discuss wages and "if such a meeting were to be arranged, I should be glad, if desired, to preside over it."

The Association said that there was no prospect of it "being authorised by the District Coalowners' Associations to undertake the discussion on the questions relating to wages." On receipt of this the Federation Executive resolved:

This stubborn refusal of the Mining Association, in spite of the increasing unrest in the coalfields due to the appalling low wage rates, increases the danger of the impending crisis unless the Government are prepared to take action. (August 15, 1935.)

They called on the Government "to take appropriate steps." But the Government refused to take the movement seriously, as was shown by the reply from the Ministry (August 21, 1935) to the effect that it would serve no useful purpose "merely to discuss generalisations" to which Ebby Edwards sharply retorted that "The Mining Association, surely, are not in a position to dictate to the Government what they will do. Is the Government prepared to leave the position at the point of the Mining Association's refusal to enter into negotiations?"

All preliminary arrangements for the campaign had been made at the Executive Committee following. Districts were asked not to enter into any commitments with their District employers; and also to make a levy of 2d. per member for the purpose of a special campaign fund (July 25, 1935). The next day, Ebby Edwards sent out a long and detailed circular setting out the results of the Executive Committee's "preliminary survey for an organised campaign" in support of the Miners' Two Bob, as the demand for the 2s. per shift increase came to be called. The circular explained that the "primary object of the campaign is to make the citizens of this country conscious of the serious plight of the mine-workers and their families as a result of low wages." The next step was to ask Districts for information about "special district features" and to appoint someone responsible for propaganda. Plans for public meetings, leaflets, publicity and advertising in the local press, speakers from outside bodies (such as the churches of all denominations) were also suggested. The co-operation of Trades Union Congress and the Labour Party was to be sought.

In their Report submitted to the Annual Conference a year later, the Executive Committee of the Mineworkers' Federation gave a very full account[1] of the whole campaign, with a certain amount of justification for their own actions and policy and a number of comments as follows:

The districts responded to this appeal with enthusiasm, and the campaign was rapidly got under way. A large number of meetings were held in every district, both among the colliers and among the non-mining populations of the larger towns and villages. After an intensive effort lasting some six weeks, the country was made thoroughly familiar with the miners' position. Outstanding events of the platform campaign were the speeches of Federation representatives at the Trades Union Congress and the Labour Party Annual Conference. (*Narrative*.)

Concurrently with platform work there was a large-scale distribution of Federation literature, and frequent statements and manifestoes in the press. This form of publicity,

[1] Hereafter in this chapter referred to as "*Narrative*."

indeed, began immediately after the Annual Conference and continued to the end of the negotiations. The first thing done was to send a copy of the speech delivered by the President at Rhyl to every Member of Parliament and "to nearly every influential person and organisation in the country." This was followed by the issue of posters and by the periodical distribution of the *Miners' Campaign Special*, which dealt with various aspects of their case as they arose from time to time. Nearly 8 million copies were distributed, a number which obviously must have had a considerable influence on public opinion. The interest thus created in the miners' cause may be seen from the mere fact that 60,000 copies were disposed of at Headquarters to casual callers who volunteered to undertake their distribution in and around London. The *Narrative* summed it up in these words:

We think it may be sincerely claimed that from a propagandist point of view the campaign was an outstanding success and that its result was to create a public opinion in this country more favourable to the miners' cause than has existed at any previous time. Indeed, so well was this work done, that towards the end of the campaign there was little need for further efforts on our part.

3.   "ACTION TO ENFORCE OUR DEMAND"

The Special Conference "to decide what action should be taken to enforce our demand" was convened for October 17th, a few weeks before the holding of a General Election. The time was ripe for it. Two months had gone by since the Federation Executive had asked (on August 16th) to meet the Secretary for Mines, only to be told that a meeting would be of no value unless the miners would first of all send to Captain Crookshank other proposals for "overcoming the deadlock." Once more an approach was made: and once more the Secretary for Mines stone-walled, repeating in his letter of October 15th the same formula as before. To this the Federation from their corner replied that if it was the Government's view that wages should be discussed nationally, then "it was surely their responsibility to bring pressure on the recalcitrant party in order to achieve that result." By now, in the opinion of the M.F.G.B. Executive, if there was to be any progress at all, it was necessary to make "some manifestation of our resolve to fight for our claims."

The first day of the Conference was taken up by reports on the campaign from each District. Some of them stated they had achieved smaller meetings and lesser results otherwise than they had expected, and seemed rather apprehensive about the future. This, however, was not the standpoint of the Executive which welcomed the progress made and put forward a resolution for action:

That a Ballot Vote be taken of the men in the coalfields to enforce the claim for a flat rate advance in wages; in the meantime, the Executive Committee to be empowered to conduct any negotiations on the present wages demand. (October 18, 1935.)

At once a division appeared amongst the Districts, some arguing strongly that any such step would alienate the Government and lose the sympathy so far gained from the other trade unions and the general public. Others, though in favour of the resolution, said that they must not hold a strike ballot during the General Election, as this would be ill-received. Quite a number of speakers on both sides of the question gloomily enough recalled the great struggle nine years earlier, saying "No one wants another 1926." But, as a later speaker pointed out, this applied equally (and perhaps even with more force) to the coal-owners and to the Baldwin administration. One District leader rather pessimistically put the view that if the ballot were held and it went against a strike for the Miners' Two Bob they would all be in a much worse position. Here a closely argued speech from the Northumbrian Jim Bowman had a heartening effect: and relieved the President and Secretary from answering all the objections in detail.

It was clear, however, that as in July, the Executive were now driving ahead, having thought out their moves, and were on this occasion in advance of the delegates. But quite a number remained unpersuaded. Eventually it went to the vote, when the Executive's recommendation was accepted by the Conference by a large majority.[1] It was a big decision, first by the Executive Committee and then by the Special Conference—how big can be judged from the fact that the last strike ballot had been taken fifteen years earlier. The decision affected the attitude of the Government to the miners' claim. Thenceforward, they could not afford to treat that claim lightly.

4. THE COMMENCEMENT OF NEGOTIATIONS

The first intimation of this change was at a meeting held with the Secretary for Mines on Monday, October 21st. Captain Crookshank, being told definitely that unless steps were taken to deal with the claim a stoppage of work was inevitable, at once promised to inform the Cabinet. On October 24th he indicated to them, for the first time, that steps would be taken to improve wages in the industry. By July 1, 1936, according to the Secretary for Mines, the Government hoped that central selling organisations would be established in each District and that these would be co-ordinated by a Central Committee. "This was certainly

[1] The voting was as follows:

District	For the Committee's Resolution	Against
Bristol	3	—
Cumberland	8	—
Derbyshire	—	25
Durham	—	113
Forest of Dean	1	—
Group I	(Did not vote, 12)	
Kent	8	—
Lancashire	45	—
Leicester	—	3
Midlands	—	20
Northumberland	27	—
North Wales	—	7
Notts	8	—
Scotland	33	—
Somerset	3	—
South Derby	—	4
South Wales	76	—
Yorkshire	100	—
Power Group	8	—
TOTALS	320	172

(M.F.G.B. Special Conference, Thursday, October 17, 1935.)

a start and a very welcome one, for our propaganda had very strongly emphasised the necessity of securing higher wages through better pit-head prices and a reorganisation of the selling side of the industry," wrote the Executive in retrospect.

What had happened? An official statement, in its opening sentence, revealed the immediate effect upon the Government of the strike ballot resolution:

Since meeting the Executive of the Mineworkers' Federation of Great Britain last Monday, the Secretary for Mines has had three meetings with representatives of the coalowners, and to-night again met the Mineworkers' Federation of Great Britain.

They learned from Crookshank that the Government, having given "careful consideration to all the matters put before them by the Committee on Monday last," had reached the conclusion that the only practical way of attempting to meet "the present difficult situation in the mining industry was to attack the underlying cause of the present unrest," namely, that the proceeds secured by the sale of coal were "not sufficient to enable better wages to be paid to the miners."

The Secretary for Mines stated (October 24th) in the House of Commons that the Government had repeatedly pressed on the coal-owners the view that only by a reorganisation of the selling side could a reasonable price be obtained by the sale of coal and the industry put on such a financial basis as would permit better wages to be paid. This was a point upon which the Federation Executive had laid great stress in their interviews with Captain Crookshank. Furthermore, they were told for some time past "a feeling among coal-owners has been steadily moving in the same direction," and so it was expected that "the selling organisation asked for will be established by July 1."

These steps taken, however, were accompanied by a threefold negative answer to the Federation's suggestions. The Government would not set up an impartial tribunal since the colliery owners held it would be in breach of District agreements: nor would there be any undertaking to legislate for such a purpose; nor would the Government give a grant in aid. It was stated:

The third suggestion by your Committee, that the Government should promise a subsidy to be used to increase wages until such time as the new selling organisation produced increased proceeds, is one which the Government cannot entertain. (October 25, 1935.)

Having obtained the authority of the Special Conference to defer taking the ballot if proposals were received which, in their view, would justify that course, the leaders of the mine-workers had now to decide whether this letter offered such a justification. "But we had little difficulty in making our decision." For obviously these proposals provided no satisfaction on the main issue—an immediate increase in wages; moreover, "while the undertaking to set up selling agencies with central control was a step in the right direction, we had no assurance that the men would obtain any benefits therefrom." Their view was that if the deficiencies which had been accumulated under the terms of the District Agreements were to stand, and if the owners' share of surplus profits were to remain, then the first effect of improved pit-head revenues would be to increase the profits of the owners and to provide nothing for wages in the most sorely pressed of the Districts. Consequently, they stated, "we could not for a moment contemplate a postponement of the ballot in consideration of proposals such as these, and we quickly made our decision known."

The decision, sent to the Government on Friday, October 25th, was also given to the press as part of the publicity campaign. From Monday to Friday in that one week of October the claim had become a public issue and was so to continue. The decision stated: "What the Government offers is merely a hope that at some remote time the proceeds of the industry may be improved and an opportunity afforded of obtaining better wages in the future."

In it there was an appeal for public support:

The miners ask the British public if they consider it fair that they, the victims of bad organisation, should have their wages claim deferred to some future time, while those who are responsible for that organisation are to receive the first benefits of any improvement?

In the same campaigning style the announcement ended with the words:

The miners are prepared to submit their case to an Independent Tribunal and to abide by its judgement. This offer has been refused both by the coal-owners and by the Government.

In these circumstances, therefore, the Executive Committee feels that the suggestions of the Government offer no justification for postponing the ballot vote and accordingly the Federation will continue its fight to obtain elementary justice for the men in the coal-fields. (October 25, 1935.)

Everything was now ready for taking the ballot vote. But before the vote was taken two incidents occurred which must have a place in our narrative, because both had a bearing on the final result. The first was a letter from the Mining Association in which the owners reiterated their refusal to discuss wages nationally, and advanced a number of arguments in support of their refusal. Their first argument was the oft-repeated one that, because of economic and geological differences between the Districts, a National Agreement was impracticable; the second was that the experience of the industry under the National Agreements of 1921 and 1924 had been disastrous; and finally that the tendering of notices would be a breach of the District Agreements which they would not countenance by any discussion of wages on a national footing.

This letter, which was a reply to a further request from us for a meeting, was the first attempt of the owners to make any reasoned defence of their repeated refusals to meet us. Up to that point, although an enormous amount of literature had been circulated on their behalf by the Economic League and other bodies, they had made no official attempt to justify their attitude, and they hoped, no doubt, that this statement would turn the tide of public opinion, which was then flowing strongly in our favour. But this hope was in vain. Our counter-arguments, which we issued immediately, and which on this question are indeed irresistible, not merely restored the balance, but further established the justice of our cause in the public mind. (*Narrative.*)

Obviously feeling that they must try a new tactic, the Mining Association then sought another meeting to explain the new selling schemes. When they met the miners' officials on November 6th, the owners admitted that there had been a certain amount of what they described as:

unnecessary competition in the industry, which they hoped would now be eliminated with satisfactory results to all concerned. They also said that the experience which they had had of central selling agencies in Lancashire and the Lothians showed that the benefits of that form of organisation were quickly felt, and that the improved results which might be expected from central selling agencies would find their way into the wages Ascertainments.[1]

This meeting on November 6 with the owners, though it did not give any immediate results, was not unimportant, for it enabled our officials to have a heart to heart talk with them and was probably the means of encouraging a better spirit among the owners and a more enlightened view upon our claims. It may be, of course, that in asking us to meet them at this time, they desired to help the "National" Government in the General Election, for there was no doubt that the attitude of the owners, and the state of public feeling which that attitude had engendered was highly prejudicial to the Government; but whatever their motives were, we think that the outcome was good. At last we had got contact with the owners, there was at least *a commencement* of national discussions. (*Narrative.*)

But as the owners still refused to discuss wages, the Federation's propaganda campaign and preparations for the ballot had to continue without relaxation.

5. THE GENERAL ELECTION

From the last week of October the General Election was now in full swing, and the miners' leaders were determined to spare no effort to use it to the best advantage. In their manifesto to the nation, of which more than a million copies were distributed, they called attention to their claim amid other argument. The General Election had, of course, involved many more issues than those so much stressed by the M.F.G.B. Executive in their Election Manifesto. It had followed on a summer when there had been inner changes in the Coalition Cabinet. Ramsay MacDonald, on June 7th, was succeeded by Stanley Baldwin as Prime Minister. Sir John Simon, whose attitude towards Japan's seizure of Manchuria had diminished Britain's reputation in the League of Nations, was succeeded by Sir Samuel Hoare. In September at Geneva, when Mussolini's unprovoked aggression on Ethiopia was under discussion, Sir Samuel Hoare had endeavoured to restore the British Government's reputation—only to drag it down a few months afterwards by his "Hoare-Laval Pact" which roused a storm that

[1] See *The Miners: Years of Struggle*, Chapters X and XI.

LONGWALL COAL CUTTER, ROSSINGTON COLLIERY, YORKSHIRE

LYNEMOUTH COLLIERY, NORTHUMBERLAND—MINERS DESCENDING

ejected him from office. The same series of international disturbances had brought about George Lansbury's retirement on October 8th from the post of Leader of the Labour Party, largely as a result of an unrestrained attack by Ernest Bevin. The final upshot was that against the other possible candidatures of Arthur Greenwood and Herbert Morrison, the successor chosen to lead the Labour Party was Clement Attlee.

The M.F.G.B. election manifesto ran as follows:

Why an Election?

It is important that mineworkers should understand the motives of the Government in deciding upon a General Election at the present time. This Election is being fought because the Government hope to turn the international situation to its own advantage. It believes that there will be a disinclination to a change of Government at a time of international crisis, and it hopes to take advantage of this to win votes for itself. It hopes also, that the international situation will afford it an opportunity of obtaining a mandate for the Tory policy of big armaments. Therefore, we are to have a snap election. These are political manœuvres which deserve the contempt of all fair-minded people, but they are exceedingly dangerous for, if successful, they would mean a policy of big armaments at the expense of the social services. To mineworkers, bigger armaments should make no appeal; history teaches us that bigger armaments are not the way to prevent war. On the other hand, the social services are of the highest importance to mineworkers. Better provision for the unemployed, for old age, and for workmen's compensation, are matters which affect them vitally, and these things must inevitably be sacrificed if a policy of bigger armaments is endorsed. Mineworkers, therefore, should vote for the Labour Party and a policy of social reform.

The Present Position in the Coalfields

There are further and special reasons why the miners should vote for Labour. We are now in the midst of a wage crisis, which has been caused by the failure of the coalowners to organise their industry efficiently, and so to lighten the appalling poverty in the coalfields. This failure has occurred, despite the fact that the last Labour Government, by the passage of the Coal Mines Act, 1930, gave the owners an instrument whereby a rapid improvement could have been effected. The Act has been shamefully neglected and abused, and only *now* under the pressure of our claim for better wages, does the Government make an attempt to deal with reorganisation. Even so, our wage claim has not been dealt with and the Government gives no sign of any intention of compelling the owners to give proper consideration to that claim. You should

F   *The Miners*

give your vote, therefore, to candidates who will give a pledge to uphold your wages claim and who will insist on something being done immediately to improve conditions in the coalfields.

THE GOVERNMENT'S RECORD

Shorter hours and a higher school-leaving age with adequate maintenance grants to parents are measures which would also materially lighten your present burdens, but here again the record of the Government is most unsatisfactory. By passing the Coal Mines Act, 1932, the Government robbed the miners of their only bargaining power against the coalowners. Before the passage of that Act, the period during which the working day could operate was strictly limited, and this gave the Federation a weapon with which they could bargain nationally with the employers for improved wages and conditions. Because of this limitation, which was imposed by the last Labour Government, the employers were compelled to enter into national negotiations in 1930, but at the request of the coalowners the present Government took away the limitation, and so robbed the miners of their chief bargaining weapon. The legislation was passed entirely in the interests of the coalowners, and the miners should remember that at this Election. Since that time the Government has persistently refused to compel the employers to undertake national wage negotiations, notwithstanding the fact that it professes to be in favour of such negotiations and that a Royal Commission has unanimously reported in favour of national settlements. Clearly, the present Government will do nothing to offend the colliery owners.

THE DISTRESSED AREAS

The Government will claim that the Trade Agreements concluded with Scandinavia and other countries have been the means of putting large numbers of our people into employment. The hollowness of this claim is exposed by the fact that in 1931—before the agreements came into operation—42·7 million tons of coal were exported, whereas last year only 39·6 million tons were exported. To ask for the miners' support on these grounds is but to mock their misery; for nearly 300,000 miners are unemployed today. Only a few months ago the Prime Minister himself candidly confessed that the Government had failed to deal with the problems of the distressed areas, and the only policy they now offer is a policy of transferring our mining families to other parts of the country, a policy which was tried, without success, by the last Tory Government. Such a policy can never adequately deal with the tremendous unemployment problem in the mining areas, and quite clearly, therefore, a vote for the Government is a vote for a policy of drift, a vote for allowing the present plight of our unemployed families to continue indefinitely.

THE FUTURE COAL INDUSTRY

On the other hand, a vote for the Labour Party would be a vote, not only for an immediate amelioration of your conditions, but for a definite policy of dealing adequately and effectively with all our mining problems. We must all realise that the employment of our people and a permanent improvement in their standards of living depends upon the planned development of an entirely new conception of our industry. The coal industry of the future should be a big complex organisation which would combine the work of coal production with the work of treating and utilising coal to the largest possible extent. It must manufacture gas and electrical power, make oil and petrol, and exploit all the primary and latent by-products of coal. As yet these things are in their infancy, but they are going to develop, and it is for the miners to take every possible means of ensuring that their development is undertaken *rapidly*, and in such a way as the miners themselves will obtain the greatest possible benefits therefrom. The obvious way of doing this is to vote LABOUR and to persuade all their friends to vote LABOUR, for if these processes are developed by private Capitalists outside the mining industry then the miners will never get their proper share of the benefits to be derived therefrom. On the contrary, their wages will continue to be dependent upon the price of a raw product which everyone wants to buy as cheaply as possible. A planned and rapid development of coal treatment and utilisation by the coal industry itself, under a unified public ownership, offers the greatest possible hope of ensuring the future welfare of our people. Only the Labour Party could bring such an industry into being, and even now it is perfecting its plans for doing so. In their own interests, therefore, it is absolutely imperative that all mineworkers, whether employed or unemployed, should vote solidly for the Labour candidates, and so do their utmost to return a Labour Government.

On behalf of the Mineworkers' Federation of Great Britain,

JOSEPH JONES, President.
W. LAWTHER, Vice-President.
EBBY EDWARDS, Secretary.

Polling day was November 14, 1935. The Federation candidates contested 40 seats. Of these they won 35, which included 10 of the seats lost in 1931.[1] The Executive's comment ran as follows:

Of the five unsuccessful candidates, four contested constituencies in which the mining vote did not predominate, while in West Fife, where the Communists were successful by a narrow majority, the result was in no sense a victory for the anti-socialist forces. As far

[1] See Appendix A to this chapter.

as the miners were concerned, therefore, the General Election of 1935 demonstrated once again how deeply our people believe in the principles of Socialism, and how steadfastly they hold to their faith.

The Federation had reason to feel some satisfaction with the election, during which they had seen to it that their campaign for the Miners' Two Bob had not been overlooked by the public.

6. THE STRIKE BALLOT AND ITS RESULT

General Election activity did not, moreover, cause neglect of an even more important work—the organisation of the ballot vote. The winning of public opinion was "not in itself sufficient" to move the owners or the Government. It was necessary that "we should obtain from the men a demonstration of their utmost confidence and support and that they should show their determination to fight for their claims if that course should be necessary." So at the Special Conference of the Federation held on October 17th and 18th, the Chairman had made a strong appeal to the Districts to put in their utmost efforts. He stressed that the Federation was in honour bound to keep to the offensive on the wages issue; that the Districts were the nerve centre from which zeal and confidence should be imparted to the men; that confidence begat confidence; and that every official and active worker in the Federation should do all he could to secure an affirmative answer from the men.

The dates of the ballot, provisionally fixed for November 11th, 12th and 13th, were the last three days before the polls and, says the Executive, "were deliberately chosen by us for the purpose of using the election to further publicise the miners' case." Some thought that to fix a strike ballot during a General Election would bring a revulsion of public sentiment. The Federation Executive did not share that view. "Public opinion had been moving steadily in our direction, and was now definitely on our side." It seemed to them that a General Election offered a great opportunity of directing attention to the miners' case and of consolidating the growing public feeling in their favour.

BALLOT PAPER

Are you in favour of authorising the Executive Committee to press the claim for an advance of wages of 2s. per shift for adults over 18 years, and 1s. per shift for youths and boys under 18 years, even to the extent of tendering your notice to enforce the claim if necessary?

Put your X in the appropriate column according to your desire

YES   NO

A leaflet, given below, was distributed from October 28th throughout the coal-fields.

To the Members of the Mineworkers' Federation of Great Britain. Fellow Members,

Your Executive Committee call upon you to vote in favour of the proposal submitted to you on the Ballot Paper. The low wages paid to mineworkers is admitted by all to be one of the greatest scandals of the present time. For years your representatives have been trying to negotiate with the coalowners in order to improve these wages, but when the workmen in one district have tried to negotiate a wage advance, the employers have told them that an advance could not be granted because of the competition of other districts. To meet this objection your Committee have tried to secure national negotiations, but time after time the employers have refused to discuss wages on a national basis.

The Press, particularly that which is favourable to the owners, insists that the claim for national negotiations has not the backing of the men. In this ballot, we ask you to assert not only that your Committee speaks for you in claiming national negotiations, but that you are determined to use the full power of your organisation to secure an improvement of your present inadequate wages, and to use that power even to the extent of tendering notice to terminate your employment, if that is the only course which is left to you.

Your Executive Committee is still open to negotiate nationally for a settlement of your claims, and we have offered to submit your case to arbitration but at the moment not a single suggestion which we have made, either to the owners or to the Government, has been accepted. By giving to the Committee the power for which they ask you will substantially strengthen their hands in their fight to obtain justice for the mineworkers and their families.

On behalf of the Executive Committee,

JOSEPH JONES, President.
W. LAWTHER, Vice-President.
EBBY EDWARDS, Secretary.

These efforts were reflected in the results of the ballot which, the Federation Committee said, "by the largest majority in our history, gave us the verdict we sought."

NATIONAL WAGES CAMPAIGN—RESULT OF BALLOT VOTE

District						Yes	No	Majority
Bristol	..	..	..	..	..	651	37	614
Cumberland	..	..	..	..	..	2,175	211	1,964
Derbyshire	..	..	..	..	..	15,292	1,059	14,233
Durham ..	..	..	..	..	..	73,765	7,120	66,645
Forest of Dean ..	..	..	..	..	..	3,219	379	2,840
Group No. 1	..	..	..	..	..	5,931	1,614	4,317
Kent	..	..	..	..	..	4,938	384	4,554
Lancashire	..	..	..	..	..	34,146	1,905	32,241
Leicester ..	..	..	..	..	..	1,641	104	1,537
Midlands	..	..	..	..	..	16,018	700	15,318
Northumberland	..	..	..	..	..	23,132	3,105	20,027
North Wales	..	..	..	..	..	5,305	600	4,705
Nottingham	..	..	..	..	..	6,360	185	6,175
Scotland ..	..	..	..	..	..	39,858	3,007	36,851
Somerset ..	..	..	..	..	..	2,102	268	1,834
South Derby	..	..	..	..	..	2,698	264	2,434
South Wales	..	..	..	..	..	85,372	3,843	81,529
Yorkshire	..	..	..	..	..	82,733	4,169	78,564
Power Group	..	..	..	..	..	4,015	261	3,754
TOTALS	..	..	..	..	..	409,351	29,215	380,136

A week later, the Federation Executive met at Barnsley, the old capital city of Britain's coal-fields forty years earlier. There they considered the figures of the ballot vote to be "most gratifying for they showed that we held the confidence of the great majority of our men." With a nearly fourteen to one majority in their favour they might have been pardoned a more jubilant adjective, or even an exultant phrase at the expense of the October pessimists. But they were in a sober mood that quelled any exultation. What were they to do next? Should they call a Conference immediately or should they give time for more meetings and further opportunities of negotiating their claims? Their anxiety that day at Barnsley and the justification of the step they decided upon in the end were vividly enough set down six months later:

We were now approaching the crucial stages of our campaign; while never shirking the possibility that in the last resort we might have no alternative to industrial action, we were determined that on this occasion we were not going to plunge our men into a stoppage if we could possibly avoid it. Our men most ardently desired an improvement in their conditions, *but*, if humanly possible, they desired to obtain this through the process of discussion and negotiation and only if all other methods failed were they prepared to cease work. (*Narrative.*)

They knew that such was the feeling of the great majority of the miners; and every step taken had been with this in mind.

That was why we endured rebuff after rebuff from the coal owners; that was why we took such immense pains to win and retain public opinion, and that was why, at every stage of our campaign we had pursued a policy of prudence and forbearance.

Nothing was to be gained by a departure from this policy; it had in fact already achieved much; we had already got an undertaking to set up selling agencies, and on the wages question the seed we had sown was just beginning to germinate, for already reports had begun to appear of the willingness of certain classes of consumers to pay more for their coal in order that the miners might get better wages. (*Narrative.*)

They decided, therefore, "to give opportunities for further discussion and negotiation" before calling another Conference and resolved that:

The Prime Minister be informed of the result of the ballot and be asked to meet the Executive Committee. (November 20, 1935.)

Prime Minister Baldwin soon replied he would prefer they should see the Secretary for Mines with whom he would be in close touch. On November 27th, Captain Crookshank had little to tell them as he was meeting the coal-owners in the afternoon of that day. The Executive Committee stayed in London to see if anything would come of it. But on Friday, November 29th, they received a message from the Government saying that after protracted discussion with the owners they had failed to extract from them any proposals which they thought justified in passing on and that it had been decided that the owners should go back and consult their Districts and have a further meeting with the Government on Thursday, December 5th.

7. MEETINGS WITH THE OWNERS

The representative coal-owners, having had meetings of their District coal-field associations (in their democratic or even ultra-democratic way) and having concerted with them plans for the immediate future, now met the Government's representatives on December 5th, with whom they remained closeted for several days. Simultaneously, in the main coal-fields, the District owners discreetly approached the District miners' association and offered to put proposals before them. "To the credit of the affiliated districts," commented Vice-President Lawther some ten days later, "no district accepted the bait": and this, he said, explained why proposals were "shelved up as long as ever possible" by the owners while they were meeting in London "in order to break up the unity"of the Federation. One December day followed another and still the negotiations hung fire. Although it may have seemed to the owners, the election being over and the coalition Government confirmed in office, that there was less urgency in the matter, the colliers' wages were still a burning issue before the public.

The Mining Association officials met those of the Mine-workers' Federation on December 6th only to reiterate their refusal to discuss the wages issue. The previous day there was sent out to the press the owners' side of the case. A refutation by the M.F.G.B. Secretary went out on December 9th. The gloves were off. The refutation showed Ebby Edwards in his most controversial style, hitting hard with argument after argument built up on the basis of hard facts.[1]

Meantime, having received no proposals from either the Government or the owners, the officials called the Special Conference which they had held up to see if anything would come out of the negotiations. But nothing had come and, unless something satisfactory emerged, the Conference could be certain to put into effect the strike ballot decision. Then on December 12th Edwards received a letter from the Mining Association Secretary saying: "A small body of owners will be very glad to meet a number of representatives of the Mineworkers' Federation to discuss the general situation": and could this take place on December 17th? This letter seemed to show that either the owners had given way to pressure from the Baldwin Government, which this time wanted to avoid a strike; or they had learned that the

---

[1] See Appendix B to this chapter.

colliery owners' "bait" had in each District been rejected; or possibly both. However that may be, at this meeting the Federation representatives were informed that "as a result of our campaign" some of the large consumers might be willing to pay more for their coal and that the owners, therefore, were trying to get a revision of current contracts on the basis of higher prices so that better wages could be paid. The owners pointed out that about 75 per cent of the total sales were on contract and that over a considerable field and particularly in the export Districts, it would not be possible to revise these contracts or to obtain higher prices for the current and forward sales. The most they could say was that, as and from January 1, 1936, a definite increase of wages should be paid in each District. On this meeting of December 17th, the Executive Committee could feel that after nearly eight months of hard and persistent endeavour, the Federation had now the first intimation that their primary claim—an increase of wages—would be recognised.

But the position was still "most unsatisfactory"; the owners would not put down a figure of any sort; all they would say was that if application were made to the owners in their respective Districts, advances would be given as and from January 1st. They would not discuss the amount of such advances or their method of application, nor would they recognise any right of the Federation to discuss wages on a national basis. Indeed, as the campaign narrative says: "The owners did not meet us as representatives of the Mining Association, which, they were careful to point out, still had no authority to discuss wages." They were merely "a small body of owners" which transmitted the views of the District owners' associations. But the fact that their spokesman, and the only spokesman, had been Evan Williams, President of the Mining Association of Great Britain, suggested some casuistry in their contention.

The next day the Federation leaders told the Secretary for Mines how unsatisfactory they found the proposals of the owners. They again laid great stress on the responsibility of the Government, which, by its long neglect of this question of reorganisation, must share, in their opinion, the responsibility of the mine-owners for the present state of

F*

affairs. Therefore, until such time as the selling schemes were in full operation, the Government itself should make some contribution towards meeting the miners' claims. But they did not find the Government at all responsive. The Secretary for Mines thought that they had made very considerable progress and particularly stressed the advance made in securing from the employers a definite undertaking to increase wages immediately and the further benefits which were "likely to accrue from the selling schemes." He refused to entertain any suggestion of a subsidy in any form whatsoever.

That evening the Government issued a statement[1] of its views, ending with a warning about the "very grave responsibility" of the Delegate Conference then in session. This was repeated in the House of Commons. The Special Conference of December 18th opened, after the Secretary had given his usual full report, with a complaint from Lancashire that the Conference should have been called much earlier and that strike notices could have been given in by December 1st. But the main concern voiced by Lancashire and strongly expressed by the three export Districts, Durham, Northumberland and South Wales, was that the Executive Committee's recommendation did not stress that any outcome must be "national and uniform." The Executive Committee, however, had worded their recommendation after much thought. The long agitation—and the strike ballot—had brought something, but not enough. In their view "some further stimulus was now needed before the Government or the owners could be induced to make us some offer which we might feel justified in placing before the men. . . ." Hence the terms of their recommendation "gave a further month in which to continue our efforts to secure a satisfactory offer and to permit of the fuller development of certain factors which even then were moving steadily in our favour."

The resolution submitted by them to the Conference, and accepted by 478 votes to 28 (Derby and Somerset in the minority), was as follows:

That this Conference regards the suggestions so far made as being entirely unsatisfactory, and as by no means reflecting the

[1] See Appendix C to this chapter.

pronounced opinion throughout the country in support of the miners' wages claim. It resolves, therefore, that notices be tendered on January 13 and 20 respectively, unless wage proposals satisfactory to the Executive Committee are obtained in the meantime. (December 18, 1935.)

This meant that, some Districts being on a seven-day and others a fourteen-day notice, a stoppage would begin on Monday, January 27, 1936.

8. HIGHER PRICES FOR COAL

The resolution fixing the date for a nation-wide coal strike, authorised by a fourteen to one majority in the ballot, had an immediate effect. Rueful memories of the seven-month struggle of 1926 came back with a rush. Whatever might be the outcome inside the coal trade, no one outside it—and least of all the chiefs of the big industries consuming coal—could look with equanimity on the prospect of a repetition of that experience. For them it would be a calamity. To avert any such happening they would go far. In the event, they certainly went farther than anyone would have deemed possible at the time of the General Election. The details of preliminary discussion between the big consumers on the one hand and the Government and the coal-owners on the other were not revealed. But presently the miners were made aware of the development of what they rightly called a "remarkable phenomenon": a voluntary agreement by many of the big consumers of coal to revise their current contracts by paying higher prices for coal on condition that the revenue derived from the higher prices was to go exclusively to the wages of the miners.

One of the first in the field was Imperial Chemical Industries which, in a letter to the Mines Department, expressed its willingness "to agree to an advance over 1935 prices of one shilling per ton under all the forward contracts of the companies under its control in the United Kingdom" as a step towards "bettering the wages of workers in the coalmining industry." The example of Imperial Chemical Industries was followed by a large number of other industrial concerns. The gas and electricity companies were at first reluctant: but latterly they, as well as the iron and steel trades, also expressed their willingness to pay a further 1s. per ton on their current contracts. Soon letters began to come into the Federation office at Russell Square expressing the willingness of particular concerns to pay more for their coal. The movement extended to the public utility concerns and to the domestic coal market: soon all the retail merchants and Co-operative Societies were paying and charging more for their coal, "thus enabling members of the public actively to associate themselves with the movement for getting better wages for the miners."

In practically every case the higher prices were agreed to on the strict understanding that the increase should be devoted exclusively to wages. So the movement spread, and early in 1936 it became evident that, whatever the current financial position of the industry might be, these voluntary increases would assure the establishment of a fund from which an increase could be paid. Recording these facts a few months later, the Executive Committee made the following comment:

All this was thoroughly in accord with our own ideas as to the source from which our claims could be met.

While we had never failed to stress the importance of reorganising the selling side of the coal industry on a permanent basis so as to obtain the most economical distribution of coal and the maximum revenue for the coal industry—a revenue which should not be hidden but fully and freely shared by the miners—yet we never lost sight of the fact that unless the Government granted a subsidy, an *immediate* increase of wages must necessarily come from higher prices; and particularly we had laid great emphasis on the necessity of the gas industry, the electrical industry, the railways and the public utility concerns paying more for their coal, it having been obvious for a very long time that all these concerns were getting their coal too cheaply and could well afford to pay more for it. As we pointed out in our campaign, these industries were making quite substantial profits on the basis of cheap coal; they had already cut their fuel costs enormously by improved technical practices and to pay more for their coal would not hurt them in the least.

But the Federation leaders, when the struggle was over, did not wish to lay over much stress on these material considerations. They preferred to dwell on the degree of "social compunction" which they felt must have induced the big consumers to offer to pay more for coal. So, in their final summing up, they gave both sides of the medal when they said:

This development then was entirely the result of our campaign and the owners themselves freely admitted that but for that campaign these higher prices could not have been realised. Nevertheless, we pay our tribute to all those industries and concerns which in the end came freely and willingly to our assistance, because their action showed that they were not unmindful of the sufferings of the miners and that to some extent they were willing to subordinate their own interests to the higher interests of justice and consideration for those less fortunately placed than themselves.

They could utter this with all the pacific benignity of Pandulph in *The Life and Death of King John*, saying

It was my breath that blew this tempest up, . . .
But since you are a gentle convertite,
My tongue shall hush again this storm of war.

Besides, like Pandulph, they were to find it not so easy to assuage the stormy feelings roused amongst their members, at any rate in some of the Districts, by the unexpectedly overwhelming success of the campaign for the strike ballot.

9. THE FINAL PHASE

The final phase of the campaign was now about to begin. At the meeting with the owners on December 17, 1935, the door to further discussion had not been quite closed. A further meeting would be held early in the new year at which the owners would make another report on the progress made in obtaining a revision of prices under current contracts. At this meeting on January 8th the Federation sub-committee were given a list of the increases in wages which the owners in the different Districts were prepared to make as and from January 1, 1936.

For Lancashire, North Wales, South Derbyshire, Leicester, North Staffs, Cannock Chase, South Staffs, Warwick and Shropshire, the offer consisted of an increase of 1s. per shift; for Yorkshire, Scotland and the Forest of Dean of

9d. per shift, for Somerset of 8d. and 6d. per shifts; for Durham, Northumberland and Cumberland of 6d. per shift and for Kent of 5d. per shift, with a correspondingly lower advance for youths and boys in each case. In South Wales the offer consisted of an advance of $2\frac{1}{2}$ per cent in the minimum percentage and an increase of 5d. per shift in the subsistence wages, while for North Derbyshire and Bristol no advances were tabled.

In many Districts these offers meant a very considerable advance, a bigger single increase than anything secured since the days of coal control in 1916–20. But the inequality of the offers as between the various Districts was a sore point, and took away much of the satisfaction felt at securing "the fairly substantial increase" of 1s. per shift elsewhere.

The next problem for the Federation leaders was how to bring these offers up to a uniform level if that were possible. Their first effort was with the employers. Could they obtain the employers' consent to apply the increased revenue uniformly to wages in every District? In South Wales, Northumberland and Durham and other exporting areas the proportion of coal on which the increase of price would apply was very much less than in those Districts supplying the home market. Therefore the uniform application of the increase of revenue would have meant some form of pooling between the different employers and Districts. Though it appeared from press reports that certain of the employers would not be adverse to this, officially they were adamant in their refusal to consider any such proceeding. The Federation Executive in their narrative said:

We found that the owners in certain districts regarded the owners in other districts with great suspicion: and quite clearly the owners as a whole were neither in the mood nor in possession of the necessary machinery to make any pooling of the increased revenue a practical proposition: to insist upon it would have meant breaking off the discussions. (*Narrative.*)

The alternative was to try the Government again and to get them, either directly or indirectly, to give some assistance to the export Districts so that a uniform advance could be obtained pending the time when the employers could bring their co-ordinating machinery into effective operation.

Accordingly, that same evening of January 8th, the sub-committee went again to the Government and put this request to them "with all the force at their command." "Again and again," runs the record of that discussion, "we pressed upon the Government its responsibility for the situation which existed in the industry and the utter unreason-ableness of expecting the miners in the export Districts to bear alone the full force of the competition of other coal-producing countries." They pointed out that this was not done in the countries of "our greatest competitors," that both in Germany and Poland assistance was given to the export trade. None of their arguments, however, would persuade the Government to make any concession on this matter.

On the next day, January 9th, the sub-committee met the owners again and made further efforts to induce them to improve the offers. After protracted discussions the owners, while holding out no hope whatever of a uniform advance, did agree to ask the District owners to reconsider their offers and to report results in two weeks' time. The full Executive Committee meeting that evening of January 9th had to decide whether the notices should be handed in on the dates fixed or whether they should be postponed. After long dis-cussion they resolved:

That in view of the further joint meeting of the representatives of the owners and men to be held on January 23, the Committee agrees to postpone the handing in of notices and that a National Conference be held on January 24 to hear a report and arrive at a decision. (January 9, 1936.)

The meeting with the owners on January 23rd duly took place; but, as the miners found, little revision had been made of the actual wage offers. The owners insisted that in the export Districts they had gone to the absolute limit of economic possibility and that in Districts like South Wales, Durham, and Northumberland, where the offers were low, it was quite impossible to make better offers; they insisted also that any question of a uniform advance must be ruled out. The Yorkshire owners, however, had agreed to raise their previous offer by 3d. to 1s. per shift for adults. In Scotland a slight modification had been made; they had deleted the word "able-bodied." North Derbyshire was now included in the list with an offer of 9d. per shift.

But though little change had been made in the wage offers, "the owners *did* make an important concession" on the question of national negotiations. Since 1926, the owners had consistently refused to enter into any discussion of wages on a national basis; they would not even consent to discuss the principles of wage application, and had always insisted that wages were a matter for the Districts alone. For years the miners had been endeavouring to change this attitude; and, of course, the sub-committee had urged it at every meeting with the owners. At the meeting of January 8th the owners had at last agreed to ask their District organisations to modify to some extent the view of wages as exclusively a District question. This recommendation had been accepted by the District owners. Hence the following statement:

> The owners' representatives informed the representatives of the Mineworkers' Federation that the coalowners in all of the districts had accepted the recommendation which they had made with regard to future relationships. They were therefore authorised to say that if there is a full continuity of work and no notices given, the coalowners will be prepared to co-operate with the Mineworkers' Federation in setting up a Joint Standing Consultative Committee for the consideration of all questions of common interest and of general application to the industry, not excluding general principles applicable to the determination of wages by district agreements.
> The coalowners make this proposal in the earnest hope and belief that it will conduce to the maintenance of good relationship in the industry and to the benefit of all those engaged in it. (January 23, 1936.)

The Federation Executive were sure that they had now reached the limit of concession from the owners and, as matters stood, nothing further was to be expected from the Government; they were, therefore, now faced with the crucial issue—to hand in notices "relying on the support of public opinion to ensure" that some further concession was made to their cause, or to accept the offers which had been made. They chose the second alternative.

The chain of reasoning which led them to make this choice, as reported six months later to the Annual Conference, stressed the hazards a strike would run in forfeiting the offers, admittedly unsatisfactory, that had already been made, and the loss of public support, and then went on:

There was a further vital reason why we should avoid a stoppage; and that was the disastrous effect it would have had on our unity. Painfully, year after year, we had struggled to achieve national unity and recognition; we had now, in a measure, achieved these objects. But could we have retained that unity in the situation which faced us, a situation in which, if a stoppage had occurred, more than half the men in the coalfield would have been striking against a substantial increase of wages? The owners had always played most cleverly upon our district mentality and if a stoppage had occurred their efforts in that direction would have been redoubled.

Could we possibly have preserved our unity in such circumstances, bearing in mind also that we had always the industrial union to contend with and that some of our districts had already been extremely embarrassed by that organisation? (*Narrative*.)

It ended with the words: "*but in the circumstances*, was it worth our while to run the very great risk of a stoppage? We thought not, and so after prolonged and anxious thought we decided to make the following recommendation to the Special Conference":

The Executive Committee of the Mineworkers' Federation cannot regard the offers made by the coalowners as satisfactory as they are unfair in their incidence and do not afford the miners the standard of living to which they are justly entitled. But in view of the undertaking which has been given by a representative body of coalowners that a National Joint Standing Consultative Committee shall be set up for the consideration of all questions of common interest and general application to the industry, not excluding general principles applicable to the determination of wages by district agreements, it recommends that the present offers be accepted as an instalment of the further improvement which will be rendered possible by the proposed selling schemes.

In making this recommendation the Executive Committee are strongly influenced by the desirability of avoiding industrial disturbance in the present circumstances of the nation and by the keenest possible desire to prevent loss and injury to the public who have so loyally supported the miners' claim. (January 24, 1936.)

That week on the Monday King George V died: and the Conference opened on the Friday with the delegates standing for a few moments at the Chairman's request to pass "*sub-silentio* a vote of sympathy with the Queen and the Royal Family in their bereavement." Thereafter the

Executive's recommendation was moved in a closely argued speech by the Secretary. This was seconded by the Vice-President, after which the Chairman refused an amendment from Cumberland to instruct the Executive Committee that "the advance must be national and uniform in character; if not, notices be handed in at once." The Chairman said that would be in order only if the recommendation were defeated: and he also refused a motion from a member of the Federation Executive, Jim Griffiths of South Wales, that the matter now go to a ballot vote of the men. In the end the recommendation was accepted by the Conference by a big majority, by 360 votes to 112, the minority being made up of South Wales, Northumberland and Cumberland, with Scotland neutral. So ended one of the most remarkable periods in the history of the Federation.

Four months later, in drawing up their report for the July Annual Conference, the Executive Committee looked back with considerable pride on the campaign they had led for the "Miners' Two Bob," even though its final results had not been up to the expectations roused amongst many in the coal-fields. They expressed their gratitude "to the members, to the district officials, and to all who co-operated with us in the campaign."[1] They set out "several important lessons" to be learned from the campaign on its publicity side, as follows:

The first is that truth is the best propaganda. Statements should never be made which are exaggerated or distorted in any way and the greatest care should be taken to ensure the accuracy of figures and quotations.

The second is that mere declamation is always a poor substitute for reasoned argument. It has been said that, even if a statement is untrue, people will believe it to be true if only it is repeated often enough. This is not so with the British people. In this country today, with its freedom of thought and expression, and with its high standard of popular education, people think for themselves more than they ever did before, and therefore an appeal to reason and intellect must necessarily be much stronger than any catchwords or slogans.

[1] Four months earlier a more specific reference "to the Communist section and their service in delivering our literature" had been made by Ebby Edwards in his Conference speech where he said: "I do pay tribute to the work they did on behalf of the campaign of the miners." (January 24, 1936.) In so saying Ebby trod on the corns of the Scottish officials then in deep feud with Abe Moffat and others.

Again, we think that the necessity has been proved, both in writing and in speech, of using language as simple, as pleasing, and as moderate and correct as we can possibly make it. That does not mean that our language should lack force; on the contrary, our case gains in strength by the moderation of our language. In the past we have used an excess of adjectives and blunderbuss methods which are incompatible with the temperament of the British people, and our case has suffered accordingly.

It should be another guiding principle not to stake our claims too high as this may lead to a reaction against a reasonable compromise in the final settlement. (May 22, 1936.)

At the conclusion of this report, the Executive Committee came back again to the question: "What lessons may we learn from it?" Their answer to this was:

We think that we may at least learn one lesson, a lesson which should now be transparently clear to every man and woman in the coal-fields. *Only national action can be really effective in raising the standards of our men.*

Really effective national action, however, can come only when the Federation can speak as an authoritative national body and not merely as the mouthpiece of a number of autonomous districts. These are truths which we have long realised, but they have never been more strikingly manifested than in this campaign. (*Narrative.*)

Many years, however, lay ahead before these truths were to attain a measure of their logical fulfilment.

10.   SCARBOROUGH ANNUAL CONFERENCE, 1936

The delegates at Scarborough came from District unions that had carried on a great wages campaign: and however mingled might be their feelings about the outcome of it, their common endeavour had brought them closer together and induced a militant mood. This was reflected in the tone of the debates and in the resolutions passed. Some of these were on their usual common interests[1] but there were others which went along new paths, such as a demand for

[1] The 1936 Annual Conference resolutions were under the following titles:

Unemployment Insurance and Means Test; District Wages Agreement (Somerset); Welfare Fund; Affiliation to Labour Party; Hours of Work; Week-end Work and Overtime; Holidays with Pay; Coal Mines (Minimum Wage) Act; Abolition of Piece-Work; Damages from Workmen; School-Leaving Age; Workmen's Compensation; Wages; Membership; Conveyor Faces; Pensions; Representation on the Executive Committee; National Wages Agreement.

an educational Bill to raise the school-leaving age to fifteen, and support for the Communist Party to be affiliated to the Labour Party. On this last, as well as on other resolutions before the Conference, the chief speech was made by Arthur Horner, the newly-elected President of the South Wales Federation. To understand the significance of this emergence, or rather re-emergence of A. L. Horner in the M.F.G.B. leadership, which was welcomed even by his opponents, the strongest of whom said: "We need Mr. Horner to plead our case in innumerable ways," it is necessary to give something of the background of one who was to play such a prominent part at this time and in the future.

Arthur Lewis Horner, born on April 5, 1894, in Merthyr Tydfil, had early become an active revolutionary Socialist. As such he was opposed to the war of 1914–18 which the old International Socialist Congress had foreseen and warned against: and was in the constituency where Keir Hardie had stood his ground in opposition to the war and the Liberal Government at a time when so many leaders had abruptly swung over to support Asquith and Sir Edward Grey. As an active revolutionary Socialist Horner hailed the Russian Revolution, as eighteen months earlier he had sympathised with those who sought to form an Irish Republic in the Easter Rising of 1916.

In the Rhondda Valley, which at that time and for ten years earlier had the reputation of containing the most advanced grouping of the South Wales miners, Horner soon was known as an outstanding agitator both in speech and in writing. He joined the Communist Party when this was formed from a fusion of the British Socialist Party with a minority of the Socialist Labour Party and of the I.L.P. Gifted with a quick, penetrating mind and exceptional lucidity and force as a speaker, Horner rapidly came to the fore as an active Communist. When militant branches and sections of trade unions were gathered into the Minority Movement with Harry Pollitt as Secretary, Horner took an active part. The Minority Movement in each industry was the successor of the many reform movements of the previous forty years within trade unionism. These before the 1914–18 war had culminated in the campaigns within each industry for industrial unionism headed by Tom Mann—which had had varying expression within the coal-fields from the propaganda of George Harvey of Durham and the reform movements in Scotland to the Welsh Miners' activities that followed on the strike struggles of 1910 to 1912. These earlier reform movements within trade unions had mostly stemmed from Socialist sources and often had the backing of either the British Socialist Party or the I.L.P. This time, however, the main backing came from the Communist Party. When the Miners' Minority Movement took on this distinctive form and name in the latter part of 1923 with Nat Watkins as Secretary, Horner was prominent in it. In the election of General Secretary of the Miners' Federation in the spring of 1924 the Miners' Minority Movement campaigned for A. J. Cook and he was duly elected. Horner had a very considerable influence on Cook. Indeed, Cook, although not himself a member of the Communist Party, depended considerably on the advice of leading members of that party and particularly upon Arthur Horner. Cook, however, occasionally did not follow the advice of his colleague who was nearly ten years younger and then more than once found that Horner had more correctly estimated the mood of the miners than himself. An outstanding example occurred in the middle of the 1926 lock-out when a standpoint put forward by Cook, accepted by the Executive and then accepted by a Special Conference, was challenged at that Conference by Arthur Horner whose policy on a ballot vote overturned the decisions of Cook, Executive Committee and Special Conference. Before the seven-month 1926 struggle throughout the winter of 1925–26 Tom Mann as Chairman and Horner as Acting Secretary of the Minority Movement were campaigning for preparedness and solidarity with the miners in the struggle that lay ahead.

Thus up to his early thirties Horner had been a rising luminary of the miners' struggle, but that luminary was to suffer an eclipse. In the ebb of the movement that followed the high tide of 1926 Horner maintained his struggle for an advanced policy at a time when one after another the younger leaders inside the Federation were adopting the cautious attitude from which their seniors had scarcely ever departed. Horner persisted in advocating advanced policies expounded by him in books and pamphlets,[1] and stubbornly defended them even when those who supported them were dwindling in number. He did so to the point where the most bitter and exacerbated internal struggles developed: and in the course of these struggles (which belong particularly to the history of the South Wales miners) Horner and the lodge of which he was Chairman were expelled from the Federation. It was a measure of the bitterness of the struggle that while Keir Hardie and other earlier reformers had been cold-shouldered and denounced by official union leaders, it was only in the late 'twenties that the quarrel between Left and Right reached the point of expulsion from the ranks of trade unionism. Though expelled, Horner continued his advocacy of a militant policy: and in November 1933 the miners in the Anthracite District of South Wales welcomed him back into the ranks of trade unionism, by electing him as agent. In the middle 'thirties the agitation carried on by Arthur Horner began to bear fruit. The South Wales Miners' Federation was transformed from a loose federal body into one that was more tightly knit in its structure and on a presidential vacancy occurring in 1936 Arthur Horner was, on May 23rd, elected President of the South Wales Federation: and once more sat on the Executive of the Mineworkers' Federation of Great Britain. From that time onwards he was regularly, or at any rate repeatedly, chosen as spokesman for the Executive Committee. It was the first time in the Federation's history that such a tribute had been paid to the oratorical powers of a colleague who as yet held none of the official posts of President, Vice-President or Secretary.

11.   THE WAGES PROBLEM, 1936-39

When it came to the Annual Conference of 1937, after more than a year had elapsed since the wages campaign, there was a Lancashire resolution on the agenda for a wage increase as follows:

---

[1] Such as *The Bureaucracy in the Miners' Federation*; *One Mineworkers' Union – Why?*; and (jointly with G. A. Hutt) *Communism and Coal*, 316 pp. 1928.

That in view of the rising increase in the cost of living, and having regard to the unsatisfactory nature of the settlement of the flat rate advance in 1936 with the lack of uniformity in the different districts, and also having regard to the fact that the Joint Consultative Committee, which was established as part of the settlement, has failed to fulfil our expectations, we make an immediate application for a uniform flat rate advance of 2s. 6d. per day for all members of the Mineworkers' Federation of Great Britain of 18 years of age and over and 1s. 3d. per day for members below 18 years of age. (Blackpool, July 20, 1937.)

It was decided to refer this and a similar one from Kent to the Executive Committee. Its policy, foreshadowed at the 1936 Annual Conference, when Ebby Edwards made a successful plea for the withdrawal of resolutions demanding a wages increase, was clearly enough stated in the course of the Annual Report of the Executive Committee, dated June 7, 1937. In this it was said that in the course of the year they had reviewed the wages policy of the Federation and had carefully considered "whether we should make some *new* claim" for an increase of wages. They came to the conclusion that "the interests of the members would best be served by continuing our work on the National Joint Consultative Committee, and so endeavouring, *inside the industry*, to create the conditions whereby the wages could be improved without the necessity of embarking upon another spectacular campaign from the outside."

What was their reason for this decision? The reason was plainly enough set out in the next paragraph.

"Our decision in this matter was greatly influenced by the operation of the Selling Schemes. In certain districts the Selling Schemes had already been instrumental in improving in some degree the revenues of the trade, but they were as yet only in the embryo stage." They felt, therefore, that, "for the time being at any rate, we should best serve the interests of the members, and also more surely retain the sympathy of the public, if we gave the Selling Schemes the fullest opportunity of proving their worth, and so automatically bring an improvement of wages in their train." (June 7, 1937.)

A year later the Annual Report dated May 30, 1938, told what had happened in the next twelve months. The

July 1937 resolutions in the names of Lancashire and Kent for an increased wages demand, referred by the decision of the Conference to the Executive Committee, were given very careful consideration at a meeting two months later. The following is the minute as recorded under the heading "Wages":

This question, as remitted from the Annual Conference, was considered. It was agreed to allow the wages question to lie in abeyance as a national issue in view of the demand we were pressing upon the Government for a substantial reduction in both the daily and weekly limit of miners' hours. (September 23, 1937.)

On December 17, 1937, the Secretary reported to the Executive Committee a letter from the South Wales Miners' Federation on the wages question, requesting:

That the M.F.G.B. press forward a demand for an all round increase of wages by 10 per cent to meet the steady and continuous increase in the cost of living.

In view of the importance of this wages demand, related as it must be to previous flat rate advances, and certain wages negotiations which were proceeding (some completed) in the different Districts, the Secretary prepared a memorandum for the use of members of the Committee. The memorandum, packed with facts and figures, ended with the words:

A case for improved wages for the mineworker in relation to the nature of his toil, and the dangers of his calling, still stands.

The question of improving wages is and must be, one of great concern to the Committee.

Is the present the time to seek a national wages advance? If so, what method should we adopt to secure it? Or, should we continue with our national and district wage machinery to achieve results by using the Selling Agencies to improve proceeds as a means to improve wages?

Which will be of the most permanent benefit to the members?

EBBY EDWARDS, Secretary.

December 14, 1937.

They again considered the question of seeking 10 per cent advance in wages "as per the request of the South Wales Miners' Federation," at the meeting on January 13,

1938. After a lengthy discussion the following resolution was passed:

In view of the meeting with the Government and the meeting arranged with the employers, we proceed with the question of seeking for a reduction in hours, and that the question of a 10 per cent advance in wages be deferred. (National Executive Committee, January 13, 1938.)

Yet another year elapsed. There was no general increase in wages, but at the Annual Conference in 1939 there was a discussion on a resolution put forward by one of the smallest districts, Somerset. It was spoken to by Fred Swift. Before the discussion on it could well begin, Ebby Edwards threw cold water on any proposal for a national uniform wage. The resolution was then immediately remitted to the Executive. Thus from the spring of 1936 up till the summer of 1939 there was no wages campaign though some Districts had wanted it: the Federation had concentrated its energies on other questions. Some of these were familiar objects, such as hours of labour, but there were other matters of a nature unprecedented on the agenda of the miners' Committees and Conferences, that now very nearly took first place in their attention. Amongst these were international questions, and to these we must now turn.

Appendix A

GENERAL ELECTION 1935

RESULTS OF THE VOTING IN MINING AREAS

District	No. of Candidates	Name of Candidate	Constituency
South Wales	12	Daggar, G.	Abertillery
		Bevan, A.	Ebbw Vale
		Edwards, C.	Bedwellty
		Grenfell, D.	Gower
		Jenkins, W.	Neath
		John, W.	Rhondda W.
		Mainwaring, W. H.	Rhondda E.
		Davies, D. L.	Pontypridd
		Hall, G. H.	Aberdare
		Williams, E.	Ogmore
		Davies, S. O.	Merthyr
		Jenkins, A.	Pontypool
Durham	5	Stewart, W. J.	Houghton-le-Spring
		Ritson, J.	Durham
		Whiteley, W.	Blaydon
		Lawson, J. J.	Chester-le-Street
		Batey, J.	Spennymoor
Yorkshire	7	Lunn, W.	Rothwell
		Smith, T.	Normanton
		Dunn, E.	Rother Valley
		Williams, T.	Don Valley
		Paling, W.	Wentworth
		Potts, J.	Barnsley
		Griffiths, G. A.	Hemsworth
Lancashire	4	Tinker, J.	Leigh
		Macdonald, G.	Ince
		Parkinson, J.	Wigan
		Rowson, G.	Farnworth
Scotland	7	*Adamson, W.*	*W. Fife*
		Watson, W. M.	Dunfermline
		Graham, D.	Hamilton
		Pryde, D. L.	*Mid and East Lothian*
		Fraser, J. J.	*Berwick and Haddington*
		Welsh, J. C.	Bothwell
		Brown, J.	S. Ayrshire

	No. of	*Name of*	
District	*Candidates*	*Candidate*	*Constituency*
Northumberland	2	Taylor, R. J.	Morpeth
		Dowling, E.	*Wansbeck*
Midlands	1	*Jones, G. H.*	*Lichfield*
Derbyshire	1	Lee, F.	N.E. Derby
Cumberland	1	Cape, T.	Workington

NOTE: Names and constituencies in italic show seats that were lost.

Appendix B

M.F.G.B. STATEMENT TO THE PRESS

(By Ebby Edwards, December 9, 1935)

From whatever angle the case of the miners' wage claim, and the dangers of a national coal stoppage are examined, the coal-owners stand condemned. A meeting between the officials of the Mineworkers' Federation and the officials of the Mining Association was fixed for Friday morning, December 6. A day prior to the agreed meeting, the owners issued nationally their side of the case to the press. What other body of employers in this or any other country would have adopted such a tactic in face of a critical situation in their industry?

The meeting took place on December 6 as arranged. The owners reiterated to the miners' representatives their refusal to discuss the wages issue. The wages issue, the miners' representatives were told, was outside the province of the Mining Association. Nationally the coalowners can consider their coal production, the distribution of coal and its price; they can consider with the Government their trade agreements and seek from the Government assistance for international trade; they can consider any question of legislation as it affects the industry from taxation to mineworkers' hours—even if wages are related to legislation it comes within the province of the coalowners nationally. They can conduct nationally a great public campaign on wages issues. All these things they can and do consider nationally, but the wages of the employees—No. Let me use mild language—the position of the owners is untenable.

The motive of the employers is clear. They desire to depress wages to the lowest district level. It is a policy that defeats the whole principles of the co-ordination of the industry. We have abundant evidence that district wage applications have been refused by the district owners because of the low wages in other districts as a competitive factor.

Wage Rates

The owners say that "if five and a half shifts per week be taken as what a man might reasonably be expected to work in times of normal trade, the average weekly earnings of workers at the coal-face would be 62s., excluding allowances." Surely the owners are misjudging the intelligence of the public by assuming they will accept conclusions of statements preceded by "if." What are the facts in regard to miners' wages? I have never disguised the difficulty of giving to the public, out of the complexity of miners' wages regulations, an accurate picture of details, scales, and rates. One can take the total wages paid, and divide it by the total number of employees, and secure by this method the wages paid on an average over the whole industry. Happily the public can examine the statistical statements issued by the Government on this, and are not dependent on the parties themselves. For the six months ending June 30 of this year, the total wages bill was £42,329,063, covering a total number of working shifts of 91,727,893, or an average wage of 9s. 2¾d. per shift. The average days per week worked, including overtime and week-end work, was 4·84 shifts per week for the same period, making an average weekly wage of £2 4s. 8d. The Government figures give emoluments to wages equalling about 4½d. per shift worked, but they ignore all actual deductions for cost of oil, tools, explosives, and other necessary expenses that must be met by the workmen in the actual getting of coal, these vary according to the class or grade of the miners' work. These expenses rightly offset any addition to the gross average wage here stated.

The owners further declare that the average wage as stated includes the youths. True, but it also includes the earnings of all salaried officials right down from the under-managers. The effect of youths' wages being cancelled out by officials' salaries is evident when the returns show that over 92 per cent of the employees are over 18 years of age. The average wage naturally includes the combination of variations in wage rates. Yet it is evident that an average rate is no good to the miner who receives less than the average. One lives on the actual money received and not on averages. The owners, in their statement, assume an average week of five and a half shifts for coal-face workers, and then calculate from such assumption that a coal-face worker earns 62s. per week— in other words, the coal-face worker earns 11s. 3¼d. per shift. The actual shifts worked on the average for the first six months ending June 30 of this year were 4·84 shifts per week, over 34 shifts or seven working weeks a year less than the owners' assumption.

Let us accept the owners' figure of 11s. 3¼d. per shift as the wage paid to the coal-face workers, and relate it to the actual statistics of the industry for the six months ending June 30 of this year. The total shifts worked during this period were 91,727,893, of which 35,594,753 were shifts worked at the coal-face. The gross wages paid for the total shifts worked was £42,329,063. The coal-face workers, on the coalowners' own wage figure, took £20,057,643 for 38·8 per cent of the workers. This only leaves £22,271,419 to cover 61·2 per cent of the workers, or a wage of 7s. 11¼d. per shift for all classes other than coal-face workers. As the average days worked for the period was 4·84 per week, this means that 61·2 per cent of the miners earn on the average a gross wage of 38s. 5d. per week. Even on the owners' own showing, is this a civilised wage? Relate that wage to the miners' calling and to say it is a scandalous wage is using very moderate language.

I have no desire that the public should found its opinion on rare or exceptional cases of low wages, but when one can take a district like Durham, employing nearly 102,000 miners, and accurately state that *one in three* of the adults are working for a wage of 6s. 6½d. per shift, the success of our wages campaign is easily understood. Examine that wage more clearly. The average days worked per week last year in the Durham coalfield was 4·79. That means that one adult mineworker in every three had an *average weekly wage of 31s. 3d. per week.*

The miners in Durham have to live seven days. Thus the amount to live on is only 4s. 5½d. a day before colliery deductions are made. Take a man, his wife, and three children; the two parents have three meals a day at a cost of 6d. per meal, that is 3s. If the three children each have three meals at 2d. per meal, that is 1s. 6d. or 4s. 6d. per day for the family, while the total gross wage is only 4s. 5½d. per day.

The free house and coals cannot be served up at the meal table. What of clothes and other necessities of life? Will the owners defend those rates of wages? It should also be noted that when we speak of the average days per week it is the average number of days on which the collieries were open for work. We have made no allowances in those calculations for lost time through sickness or other unavoidable circumstances. It is obvious these must further depress the income of the household.

Earnings of Other Workers

The coalowners, by the use of a fictitious figure of working time which has no relation to the facts, attempt some clever multiplication manœuvres by using a special sectional rate, and then proceed to make some comparisons with the wages of other workers. I have proved from the owners' figures that over 61 per cent of the mineworkers have an average wage of less than £2 per week.

The owners quote the weekly wage of other trades. These, they admit, are time rates, but still the figures range from 62s. 8d. to 51s. 7d. per week, the lowest quoted being the average rates per week for labourers in non-trading services. The public can draw their own conclusions from the comparisons we have already made. I note that the mineowners make no comparison of the work and dangers of the miner's life. On this issue their silence is noteworthy.

National Agreements

The owners' comment on the issue of National Agreements deliberately evades the merits of the miners' case. Whoever said that a meeting between the representatives of the Mining Association and the representatives of the Mineworkers' Federation would persuade French or Brazilian consumers to pay more for their coal, or that it would effect the substitution of oil for coal? To allege this as our claim is a pure figment of the owners' imagination, certainly an unworthy product from a body of people responsible for running a great industry. The claim primarily for a national wages agreement rests upon the necessity of properly co-ordinating the wages of the various districts. A central co-ordination of district wages by a National Wages Agreement is as vital a necessity as the central co-ordination of district prices, for if wages are settled in particular districts without reference to the position of other districts, the result must inevitably be to undermine the position of all concerned. It is no answer to say that this point is met by a central co-ordination of prices. Wages form nearly 70 per cent of pithead prices, and to co-ordinate prices, while at the same time leaving wages open to attack by particular district owners, is at once illogical and absurd. District wage settlement without being related to the trade as a whole is inconsistent with every necessary development of the industry.

Selling Agencies and Wages

On the question of selling agencies we are told by the Government that their insistence on the unwilling coalowners to establish schemes to raise prices as a means to raise revenue is their contribution to the present claim of the miners for an increase of wages. The coalowners, on the contrary, are telling the public that they are carrying through on their own "spontaneous initiative" the necessary selling organisation. The miners are not concerned with who is responsible for the proposed schemes if the work is expedited. One thing we are certain of, that nothing of a voluntary nature will work satisfactorily. Selling schemes must have the necessary legal backing for enforcement; unless this is done they will be useless. It should not be forgotten that the Mineworkers' Federation made every proposal that is now being made for selling agencies to the National Government in December, 1931. A printed copy of our proposals to continue and strengthen Part I of the 1930 Act was issued in the early part of 1932. At that time the owners were so divided that they could not give the Government a reply to the issues raised.

Had our advice been accepted, then nearly four years of experience would have been gained. Any lack of industrial and financial capacity to meet the miners' immediate demands must be laid at the door of the owners and the Government. Why should the miners continue to suffer low wages because the owners have failed to apply and improve Part I of the Coal Mines Act of 1930? The miners' claim to an immediate increase of wages is unanswerable. It is useless for the owners to boast to the public of the large sums of money they have spent to improve productive efficiency if the benefits thereof are all wasted by inefficient organisation on the selling side of the industry. The miners have no intention to bear the whole brunt of the owners' inefficiency or the Government's complacency by the acceptance of wages inadequate to maintain an existence called for by a civilised community. It is the duty of the mineowners and the Government to face the immediate necessity of giving satisfactory assurances on the claim for increased wages.

Foreign Markets

Today 76 per cent of the total production of saleable coal is consumed at home. Thus 76 per cent of our coal problem is a home problem. No one can deny that this coal should be disposed of at an economic price: the economic price being that which will give a living wage to the employees, and a fair return on invested capital. Now the miners have never minimised the difficulties of the price factor in foreign markets, but here again we could quote instances where, because of lack of national control of coal exports, this country has not secured the best possible price. Further, we are not unmindful that in January 1932, the British coalowners refused to send representatives to Geneva to consider the possibility of a European Coal Agreement. Because Britain had gone off gold the owners expected to secure unlimited foreign trade. They refused to calculate on repercussions from other national coal trade claims. In the competition and reduced prices Great Britain bargained with the wages of the men. Other countries were assisted by subsidies and rebates of every description. The miners have continually protested against British owners competing on the stomachs of the British miners against foreign subsidies to coal, equalling in some cases 6s. per ton. The miner who works in a mine which supplies coal for export has as much right to a living wage as a miner who works in a mine which supplies coal for the inland trade. The industry must be so organised that exporting coal is an integral part of a national coal policy.

Wages Ascertainments

The very last Wages Award made by Mr. Bridgeman in the case of South Wales cast a doubt on the method of the joint wages ascertainments giving a complete picture of the facts of the industry. When one considers that last year eight companies, controlling between them more than 80 per cent of the total production of the South Wales coalfield, made an aggregate profit of £1,500,000, whereas the joint ascertainment result for the same period showed a loss of £188,000, one can appreciate the need for inquiry. The accountants admitted in the Coal Commission's evidence referred to by the owners that in regard to the quality of the coal that is transferred, they have to rely on the description in the books, and upon the information given by the colliery officials. This is important because no accountant can check the correct price charged to an associated undertaking unless he knows the quality that determines its actual value. To put the matter of transfer prices above suspicion perhaps it would be better to bring into the wages ascertainment the costs and revenues of the excluded activities. This is certainly a necessity where the transactions of the selling agencies and merchanting depots owned and controlled by the colliery companies are excluded from the wages ascertainments.

Now, while the transfer prices to associated undertakings may be open to abuse, and in North Derbyshire coalfield 60 per cent of the output is so transferred, the miners have never lost sight of associated undertakings getting cheap coal because of the low market price. If the selling agencies are to improve proceeds and be immediately reflected in wages, then the ratios in the present wages agreement must be revised. Let me give but two concrete illustrations to prove my point. In South Wales prices could rise 1s. 10½d. per ton and not a single penny would go in wages. In Durham, prices could rise 1s. 4½d. per ton and not a single penny would go in wages. This takes no account of recouping accumulated deficiencies, only the plain application of the terms of the existing agreements. Taking the country as a whole and assuming that prices advanced by 10 per cent, not a single penny would go in wages, while the owners would receive on the average nearly 1s. 6½d. per ton profit. The national issues involved in the miners' wage claim can only be settled nationally.

Appendix C

STATEMENT BY THE GOVERNMENT

DECEMBER 18, 1935

The Government is not prepared to adopt the suggestion made by the Executive of the M.F.G.B. that a subsidy should be granted from public funds temporarily to augment wages in the mining industry, nor the alternative suggestions of a similar kind which have been made, namely, a direct loan from public funds or a Government guarantee for a loan raised from other sources.

The Government is pleased to note that a meeting has been held between representative coalowners and representatives of the M.F.G.B.; it hopes that this method of discussion will be continued and widened; and that it will not again be necessary for the Secretary for Mines to act as intermediary between the parties.

Nevertheless, the Government does not propose to disassociate itself from the subsequent developments, with which the Secretary for Mines will remain constantly and closely in touch, and the Government will use its good offices to assist the coalowners in their endeavours to secure voluntarily from big consumers increases in price for the specific purpose of increasing wages.

It may be pointed out that very substantial advance has been made recently in three matters of the greatest importance to the mineworkers. These are :

(a) The organisation of the selling of coal on lines acceptable to the Government, and in such a way as to improve the proceeds of the industry with advantage to the wage position has been promised by the end of June.

(b) Actual contact between representative employers and the M.F.G.B. has been secured.

(c) An increase in wages in every district with effect from January 1 next has been promised.

The Government hopes that the Executive Committee of the M.F.G.B. will draw the attention of the Delegate Conference to the very grave responsibility which it will assume, both in relation to the workers in the minefields and to the country as a whole, if it should fail to allow the full investigation of the offer made by the owners yesterday.

CHAPTER V

THE CAMPAIGN
AGAINST COMPANY UNIONS

1. THE FASCIST DANGER

WHEN the fifty-two British delegates arrived in the first week-
end of August 1934, at the Town Hall of Lille in the north of
France, there to hold the 31st Miners' International Congress,
they saw prominent on its agenda the item headed "Struggle
Against Fascism and War." It was just twenty years since
the outbreak of war in 1914 had disrupted the Miners'
International Federation, disrupted, indeed, the whole of
Europe. Now their organisation, knit up again, was faced
once more by the danger of war and also with another, new
menace—the danger of Fascism. There were less than a
dozen national miners' organisations represented at Lille,
and these entirely from Europe. The division in the international working-class and trade union movement caused at
the outbreak of war in 1914 and the revolutionary events of
that First World War had sundered the Soviet miners' trade
unions from the other European trade unions. The trade
unions of Asia and Africa had never been included. Though
there were affiliated bodies in the United States of America
and in Australia, they sent no delegates on this occasion.
Internal repressive conditions in Hungary, Spain, Portugal
and Yugoslavia prevented the attendance of miners' representatives from these countries.

The most startling feature, however, of the Credentials
Report was the absence from its list of miners' delegations
from Germany and Austria. Germany had an affiliated
membership of 188,000 miners in August 1932. A year
later they had been dissolved. The German Fascists under
Hitler had seized power in March 1933. At the news of
"the triumph of Hitlerism and the arrest of the militant
workers," Achille Delattre of Belgium (who for seven years

from 1927 was International Secretary) issued a protest on behalf of the Miners' International, beginning:

The arrest of the German Socialist Deputy, F. Husemann, is confirmed. Our friend has been in prison for two weeks.

Husemann is the President of the International Miners' Federation, and, as such, his fate interests all miners affiliated to our International who protest against the arrest of their President by a dictatorship which no longer respects liberty.[1]

Meeting again at Saarbruecken in midsummer 1933, the Executive Committee learned that on May 29th there had been "received the resignations of Comrades Husemann, Berger and Schmidt." The answer was a manifesto:

TO THE MINERS OF THE WORLD

Dear Comrades,

The German Nazi Party, having seized power by the shameless misuse of an electoral victory obtained by terrorist methods, is subjecting the whole of Germany to a regime of unprecedented violence.

The Trade Union, Co-operative and political organisations of the working class, built up by the persevering effort of generations and at the cost of considerable sacrifice, have been dissolved and absorbed in a so-called united front, which is simply a vast organisation at the beck-and-call of Hitler, Goebbels and other Nazi chiefs, in which the workers have no right whatever, except that of paying and keeping silent. The leaders and the rank and file of the workers are persecuted, imprisoned and tortured by their tens of thousands.

Not content with the destruction of the working-class organisations of every kind, the Nazis have outlawed all those who are suspected of non-aryan descent, as well as all intellectuals whose conscience prevents them from accepting the Hitlerite ideas, and who refuse to think at a word of command like a vulgar herd.

In a word, Nazi rule has extended over all Germany social war against the working class as well as a race and caste war which has thrown back the country into a state of mediaeval barbarism.

This attitude has aroused the indignation of the whole world, and specially of the working class. That indignation must remain unabated. But this is not enough. The working class of the whole world must unite, determined to fight Nazi rule, which, with its

[1] A somewhat surprising letter was received from two officials of the German Mineworkers' Federation deprecating this protest: "We appreciate your anxiety about the lot of the German Miners' Federation but we do not believe, however, that this fate can be improved by incorrect protests. Therefore, we ask you to await in any case our information, or to ask for information from our central organisation." (March 24, 1933.) But the International Committee at its meeting on April 26th approved the action of the Secretary.

elder brother, Italian Fascism, constitutes a most serious menace to the working classes and to civilisation in general.

Comrades, stand up resolutely against Nazi rule; fight it with vigour. Everywhere the slogan must resound:

DOWN WITH FASCISM—LONG LIVE THE ORGANISED WORKING CLASS.

> For the International Miners' Federation,
> PETER LEE, President.
> A. DELATTRE, Secretary.
> E. EDWARDS, Treasurer.

June 1933.

There was more to follow. A little over half a year later a second event of the same nature occurred in Austria. But in that country "the workers defended themselves with a desperation which was the admiration of the workers of the world." Meeting in Brussels, the Committee resolved:

The Executive Committee of the Miners' International Federation, after being informed of the heroic struggle of the Austrian workers for the maintenance of their liberties, salutes with emotion and respect the glorious dead in the great struggle, and sends its fraternal greetings to the Austrian workers who have given the world an impressive example in their tremendous struggle against the oppressive forces of fascism. (February 14, 1934.)

These international events of an exceptionally grave character were well known to the delegates at Lille: but, presented afresh to them in their Executive's Report, as we have recorded, they provided a sombre background for the opening of this 31st International Congress. In his opening address as Chairman, Peter Lee sought to hearten their proceedings. He recalled the beginnings of the Miners' International: how in 1889 two Conferences were held in Paris, at one of which Thomas Burt and Charles Fenwick attended from Northumberland; and how "these gentlemen sent a note to all miners' representatives who were attending at either Conference, inviting them to a meeting which was held in a coffee house in a back street in Paris, and at this meeting our Miners' International was born." At that period, apart from mines inspection, there was "little notice taken of mineworkers by the legislature of any nation." Coming to more recent days, Peter Lee spoke of the new kind of rulers, who for a time at least had "destroyed the liberty of the common people," and then referred directly to Ramsay MacDonald: "In my own nation we have a Prime Minister who once stood firm for justice and right, a man of the people. He now associates with those who wear fine raiment, live in castles and have always been the enemies of the people; and as we look round the nations of Europe we find others with similar or worse experience of trust and eventual betrayal. Yet," he said, "all leaders have not proved false," and the workers when united, "will be so strong and powerful that success is sure."

A German miner from the Saar district (at that time by the Treaty of Versailles temporarily outside the borders of the German Reich) was chosen as a particularly suitable person to introduce the resolution on "Fascism and War."

The resolution dealt with "the new danger of fascism, which threatens peace and understanding between the nations"—a danger also to "the liberty, rights and weal of the working classes within the nations." It demanded "disarmament and agreement in favour of universal peace" as asked for by "the working class all over the world and by the Miners' International at all congresses." It was the duty of the national organisations of miners "to take measures calculated to combat the danger of fascism and war."

Speaking to the resolution on behalf of Great Britain, Will Lawther said that there seemed to be a tendency to regard Fascism as a simple development of the last war.

We, on the other hand, want to point out, that where we have seen fascism developing in any country we regard it as the climax in the development of capitalism and imperialism, which is the enemy of all progress and all liberty. We are resolved, so far as the British delegation is concerned, to help and support in every possible way to defeat this danger. (August 7, 1934.)

At the end of this Lille Congress Ebby Edwards, at the insistence of the continental miners, took on the position of International Secretary in addition to his other commitments. The task, therefore, now fell upon him of preparing the biennial Report of the activities of the Executive Committee of the Miners' International Federation, and of undertaking such duties and obligations as must fall on the leading official of an international body. His first duty was a very sad one.

In April 1935 the sections of the Miners' International Federation received from him a letter beginning: "With deep feelings of grief and sorrow, and with bitter and intense anger against his enemies, I write to inform you that our German comrade, Fritz Husemann, has been brutally murdered." Edwards described the circumstances.

Husemann had been sent from one concentration camp to another. Then came temporary release during which he had made known secret methods of terrorism in the concentration camps, and continued to attempt to get compensation for miners who had been dismissed for their opposition to the Nazis.

For this spirit of sturdy independence he was called to answer before the "Gestapo." During cross examination he said openly that he would permit none to usurp his right of opinion. The night following his examination before the "Gestapo," a number of Nazis penetrated into the apartment occupied by our Comrade Husemann and beat him until he lost consciousness. The family, on arrival the next day, were denied the right to see him. They were sent away, being told that Husemann had made his will, and that he did not wish to see his family any more. It is supposed that in the middle of the night Comrade Husemann was beaten to death, and that in order to veil the brutal murder, his body was transported to the Boerdermoor concentration camp. A few days later the family was informed that Husemann had been "shot while endeavouring to escape."

Edwards continued by saying that this "cold-blooded, brutal murder, must breed in the hearts of every loyal miner a strong desire for revenge. The bond of human affinity between fighters of the working-class will be deepened and strengthened by the sacrifice of our comrade." It should be a clarion call to the Miners' International to redouble their efforts to retain free institutions. They were under no illusions about "democracy in the abstract."

Perhaps no section of the working-class movement has fought the Dictatorship phase of capitalism more gallantly than the miners of Germany, Austria and Spain. Comrade Husemann adds to the already large list of casualties. He has paid the supreme sacrifice. No man can do more than lay down his life. The Miners' International sends to his bereaved family and his many German friends its sympathy and condolence. That he died a martyr in the workers' cause should be no small consolation to them. Comrade

Husemann, the workers give salutations to your brave soul! The spirit of your work lives on!

For the Miners' International Federation,

April 22, 1935.   EBBY EDWARDS, Secretary.

When Edwards came to write the Report a year and more later, he quoted the last letter which the sixty-one-year-old German miners' leader had written to his wife from the prison at Bochum:

April 11, 1935.

Dear Mathilda,

Thank you for fulfilling my wish not to come here any more. It is better so, for we have both so heavy a burden to bear. Tomorrow I shall go with my wonted equanimity to Esterwege—that is to say, I shall be taken there. I shall also try to accommodate myself to the order of things there.

Having been a soldier and otherwise accustomed to order, I dare say I shall succeed in this. I think they will not demand anything inhuman of me, and will have regard to my age. You must look at things with the utmost calm. We will both bear what Fate has laid upon us. We have gone through much in the thirty-seven years, as it will soon be, which we have spent together. Why then should we not be able to bear this?

Go about your work, for, in my absence, you will have plenty to do. Go on occupying yourself with our grand-children; they have always shown great affection for you, and this will fill up your time adequately.

I hope that in the not too distant future we shall see each other again. My love to you, the children and grandchildren.

Your Fritz.

Amongst the British miners the shock of such murders and the news of systematic destruction of the trade unions by the Nazis and their replacement by "yellow organisations of social peace" gave rise to growing anger. It also led them to look sharply around them in fear lest it should spread to their own country.

2.   THE STRUGGLE AGAINST SPENCERISM

In their wages campaign of 1935 up to the spring of 1936, the M.F.G.B. Executive had been hampered all the time by the knowledge of the existence of "non-political unions" or Spencer unions in several of the coal-fields. George Spencer had been President at first of the Nottingham "non-political union," when it was set up with the help of thousands of pounds from J. Havelock Wilson, President of the National Union of Seamen—which union on account of his action was in 1928 expelled from the T.U.C. George Spencer was also President of the National Federation of Industrial Unions, which was the title given to the employer-favoured organisation set up at the end of 1926 or soon thereafter. There was an additional reason for opposition to this type of organisation. As the international campaign of the miners against Fascism developed, and against all such manifestations such as the "corporative unions" in Italy or Falangist "sindicatos" in Spain or "labour fronts" in Germany with the Krupps and the Nazis behind them, the M.F.G.B. leaders found it increasingly irksome to acknowledge defeat in this matter. For of course it had to be reckoned as a defeat if the employer-favoured bodies which the miners' leaders considered to be of the same nature as the corresponding bodies developed under Fascism, were to secure a firm and lasting lodgement in the British coal-fields. Indeed, in a Special Conference at a moment of particularly intense struggle against Fascism on the Continent, the idea that it was the same kind of struggle against Spencerism in Britain was voiced by Joseph Hall of the Yorkshire Miners' Association, speaking on behalf of the Executive Committee:

When we get back to our own districts we will instil into our rank and file the idea that what is happening at Harworth[1] and what is happening in the Nottinghamshire coal-field is on a par with and not dissimilar at all from the position that exists in Spain at the present time, and exists in some other countries besides Spain also. (January 20, 1937.)

But before the story is related of the climax of the struggle against Spencerism and the outcome of it all in the year 1937, it is necessary to recall something of the developments of that struggle of over ten years since George Spencer, M.P., was publicly denounced as a blackleg and (on the motion of the M.F.G.B. General Secretary and on the order of the delegates acting unanimously) was expelled from the Federation Conference and from the ranks of trade unions.

[1] See Sections 3 and 4 of this chapter.

A few weeks after the end of the great struggle of 1926 at the first M.F.G.B. Executive meeting of the new year 1927, a letter was read from the Nottinghamshire Miners' Association asking the assistance of the Committee in the campaign it was waging in the coal-field "against the activities of the new industrial union of Mr. G. A. Spencer." Frank Varley[1] amplified the letter by a report of the position in the county. He said that despite all the assistance given by the employers, the Spencer union was not making headway, but on the contrary was losing ground: it had about 4,000 to 5,000 members. The Nottinghamshire Miners' Association on the other hand was regaining its influence and strength. They had increased their membership "from 7,000 to 12,000 during the past fortnight." This, said Varley, had been done in face of the bitterest opposition on the part of the owners, "who by intimidating and victimising the men had done everything possible to help Spencer and break the Nottinghamshire Miners' Association." Upon this the Federation Executive decided to render every possible support and to bear the expenses of speakers sent into the area. At the first Special Conference of 1927 W. Carter of Nottingham said that their membership, 27,500 a year earlier, was now about 13,500, but that:

Although we have suffered a reduction of 50 per cent in membership we are making progress, and I believe we shall emerge finally victorious. (Friday, June 2, 1927.)

At first, and for over a twelvemonth, progress was recorded. But then as days, weeks and months rolled by, the position worsened in Nottinghamshire.

3. PAST HISTORY OF THE NOTTINGHAMSHIRE DISPUTE

Eight years later (January 17, 1935) the M.F.G.B. Executive Committee considered a letter from the Nottinghamshire Miners' Association calling attention to the "unsatisfactory

[1] Frank Bradley Varley, born in Riddings, Alfreton, 1885, was Financial Secretary to the Nottinghamshire Miners' Association; he held the parliamentary seat for Mansfield from 1923 until his sudden death on March 17, 1929. Varley and Spencer had hardly been on speaking terms either in the House of Commons or within the county miners' office for years before 1926: and in that year when it was Spencer whom the owners approached, Varley was bound to take the other side.

G*

conditions" in their coal-field and inviting the officials of the Federation to come and discuss this.

What had happened in these eight years? The answer can be found in the Report of the three national officials (Joseph Jones, Will Lawther and Ebby Edwards) who journeyed on Saturday, February 2, 1935, to attend the full delegate council of the Nottinghamshire Miners' Association. On their return, at the mid-February meeting of the M.F.G.B. Executive Committee, they recalled a sad history and told how the coal-owners generally "only allowed men to secure and maintain employment at a colliery who were willing to sign a form agreeing to deductions being made from their wages (at the colliery office) as a contribution to the Spencer Union." As a result of discussions between the Miners' Federation and the Trades Union Congress in 1927 on this position, an intensive campaign had been conducted in the coal-field early in 1928. Following this campaign representatives of the Miners' Federation and the Trades Union Congress met representatives of the coal-owners to put forward the claims for the recognition of the Nottinghamshire Miners' Association. Thereafter a declaration appeared in the press that "The Nottinghamshire Owners' Association make no inquiry or discrimination in regard to a man's Trade Union." In March 1928, the Miners' Federation and the T.U.C., with the consent and approval of the Nottinghamshire Miners' Association, agreed to ballot the men in the coal-field, to ascertain their views regarding the two unions. The ballot was conducted by impartial people, the result of which was:

> For the Nottinghamshire Miners' Association   32,277
> For the "Non-Political Union"   2,533

There followed an intensive campaign in the Nottinghamshire coal-field to impress "upon the minds of the workmen the necessity of honouring the ballot by joining the N.M.A." But in spite of the press declaration and the result of the ballot vote, the owners persisted in their assistance to the Spencer union. Later the question was once more raised by the T.U.C. with the owners—from whom they got no change. Pharaoh had hardened his heart.

The three officials in their Report then emphasised "the seriousness of the present position" as they had found it in the Nottinghamshire coal-field. They were convinced that "unless perfect freedom can be given to the miner to organise within the Trade Union Movement, suffering will continue." The problem to be overcome was that the employers would not in any way recognise the N.M.A., whether on wages, conditions, or any other grievance. They put it categorically that there was "not a solitary colliery office" that an official of the Association could get into since 1926.

Moreover, in most places collectors of union contributions were "not permitted to approach the colliery premises, even though we had erected collecting stations at most of the pits." They quoted examples of the conditions:

BARBER WALKERS: In November 1934, we received advice that a reduction in the basis rate of wages paid to certain men was reduced [sic] from 7s. 2d. to 6s. 9d.—5d. off the basis. We have written the colliery company several times to which we get no reply. Now it may seem easy to suggest that we have got redress, either in the county agreement or in the Minimum Wage Act, but invariably the miners are so apprehensive of being dismissed that rather than make their claim known, they suffer silently as an alternative.

For example, we were pressed into Court quite recently with two cases of compensation—both of which we won. Neither of these men are now working.

Another example came under the heading of Pit Inspectors:

Another case as late as September 1934. Inspectors were appointed. In order to defeat these men making an inspection, one of them is given notice. They make an application to the management to make an inspection. They are refused, and one of them was called into the office and he was given the option of either giving up the the position of workmen's inspector or leaving the colliery. Force of economic circumstances pressed him to what he believed to be the lesser of two evils. He retained the job.

After giving these and half a dozen other examples, Ebby Edwards said he did not think it necessary to continue the sad recital which was "all too painful to relate." Nor from the speeches at the N.M.A. Council meeting was there much prospect of regaining ground. The spirit was low.

The Council, composed of 35 delegates—"20 of whom are working while 15 are unemployed," were told that the

M.F.G.B. would not resume responsibility unless given full power to negotiate with the owners and with Spencer for a settlement. Thereupon "after a very lengthy discussion" a resolution was carried by 32 votes to 3:

That this Council meeting of the Nottingham Miners' Association agrees to the Mineworkers' Federation of Great Britain being given full power to take what action it desires to complete and restore the organisation in its full capacity to negotiate for and on behalf of the miners in the Nottinghamshire coalfield. (February 2, 1935.)

On the last day of February, Edwards reported that he had written to the Secretary of the Nottinghamshire Coal-owners' Association requesting that the workmen in the Nottinghamshire coal-field be granted freedom in their choice of a trade union, and that the Nottinghamshire owners should meet the officials of the Federation to discuss this matter. A month later, the coal-owners replied coolly refusing to meet the Federation, stating that "the regulation of wages under the present agreement was working satis-factorily and that they regarded it as impracticable to undertake negotiations with any other body."

The Federation wrote again, pointing out that the issue was the freedom of the workmen to join the union of their choice and asking that their request for a meeting be reconsidered by the Nottinghamshire owners. When the officials had to report to the Executive that by March 28th no more than a bare acknowledgement had been received, they were instructed to make every effort "to secure an interview."

Three months later the matter had gone no further. But now the General Council of the Trades Union Congress wrote to ask if they could do anything to help. After once more discussing the matter at length the miners' Executive resolved to: "Ask the Trades Union Congress to use its influence in securing recognition for the Nottingham Miners' Association." (July 4, 1935.)

It was clear that the M.F.G.B. Executive Committee, assuming responsibility in February, had not advanced very far half a year later: and this indeed was all they could report to the Federation Annual Conference. Why? One reason was given by Ebby Edwards in private session of the

Rhyl Annual Conference on July 16th: it was the alarming fall in membership of their own Nottinghamshire Miners' Association. In 1925 it had 32,500 members. The membership in 1928, following the 1926 stoppage, was 15,740; in 1930, 13,475; in 1931, 13,315; in 1932, 12,295; in 1933, 9,985; in January 1935, 8,500; at which date 43,600 were employed in this area. "I think the delegates will appreciate the seriousness of the situation," said Ebby, who added, with his usual disdain of rhetoric, a blunt statement of their ill-success in a single sentence: "Our representations to the owners have not brought the object which we are after."

Thus, the Mineworkers' Federation of Great Britain, having taken full charge, found itself completely at a standstill despite its greater authority and a prestige higher than any possessed by the remnant of the one-time powerful Nottinghamshire Miners' Association. A mere mine manager could refuse to answer letters from the Nottinghamshire Miners' Association; the county coal-owners equally could refuse to answer letters from the Mineworkers' Federation of Great Britain. Nor did the Trades Union Congress itself get any better result. The next move was to come on the initiative of some of the miners in one of the bigger pits in this rapidly developing coal-field. Messrs. Barber, Walker & Co. Ltd. owned half a dozen pits in Nottinghamshire. Of these the most important was Harworth Colliery, where Michael Kane, a member of the Worksop Rural District Council, was President of the Harworth branch of the Nottinghamshire Miners' Association.

4. THE DISPUTE AT HARWORTH COLLIERY

Harworth Colliery is remote from the rest of the coal-field. It lies in a sort of peninsula of Nottinghamshire county pushed up into Yorkshire. The dispute which was to have such momentous consequences for all concerned, began in the middle of August 1936, when an assault was committed by a colliery official upon two boys who were employed at the colliery. The men at Harworth (a majority of whom were

members of the N.M.A.) bitterly resented this. In consequence, the officials of the Nottinghamshire Miners' Association endeavoured to interview the manager, and put to him
the workmen's point of view. The manager, however, refused
to meet them, contending that he would discuss the matter
only with the company union. A further dispute arose a
fortnight later. Two men employed on one of the conveyor
units were dismissed for taking "snap" time without authority
from the management: in sympathy, a majority of the men
stopped work on September 3rd. In this matter also, the
N.M.A. officials made an effort to interview the manager.
No discussion, they were informed, could take place unless
the men first returned to work. On the advice of the
N.M.A. officials the men agreed to do this.

The manager, however, now wanted to punish those
whom, he alleged, had been the ringleaders in the stoppage:
for this purpose he drew up certain conditions which, he
said, they must sign before he would reinstate them. They
refused to do this and, therefore, were not re-employed.
This further inflamed the feelings of the miners who contended that the workmen concerned had been victimised,
and took a ballot for a strike if the men were not reinstated.

At this point the Federation Committee, requested to intervene by the Nottinghamshire Miners' Association, decided:

That we request the Nottinghamshire Miners' Association to
authorise us to take over responsibility for the dispute at Harworth
Colliery, and that we endeavour to arrange a meeting with the
owners of the colliery as soon as possible.

Further, that we take steps to ascertain by ballot vote of the
workmen the Union by which they desire to be represented, and
that, if thought advisable, following the ballot, we take steps to
hand in the notices of the men failing a satisfactory settlement of
the dispute. In the meantime we render every possible assistance to
the Nottinghamshire Miners' Association. (September 24, 1936.)

The Federation were determined to prosecute this matter,
as the Annual Report stated, "not only with the object of
securing justice for the men at Harworth, but for the even
bigger and wider purpose of winning back freedom of
organisation and recognition of our Association in Nottingham generally." The men at Harworth were now

keen to hand in their notices and come out in sympathy with the men who had been victimised. In this, however, they were restrained by the Secretary of the Federation, who advised them not to do this before the Federation itself had had an opportunity of trying "to settle the dispute amicably with the management." Ebby Edwards wrote to Messrs. Barber, Walker & Co., stating that he and the Chairman of the Federation would be willing to meet them. To this he got the curt answer from the colliery company that "my Directors have complete confidence in the management, and therefore no good purpose would be served by a personal interview." (September 29, 1936.) His reply, mildly phrased, was that the question of confidence of the directors in the management had not been raised by him and that:

my letter only requests that you should meet Mr. Jones and myself to discuss the issues. Can you agree for your Manager at the colliery to meet Mr. Jones and myself? As my Committee are most anxious to maintain peace at the colliery, I hope you will reciprocate in the same spirit. (September 30, 1937.)

To this the owners did not trouble to reply, not even with an acknowledgement. Thereupon Ebby Edwards wrote to Sir Alfred Faulkner, of the Mines Department of the Board of Trade, enclosing the correspondence which, he said, "shows a clear indication of industrial trouble at Harworth Colliery," and asking that he should instruct his industrial adviser, Mr. Cook, "to look into the situation and relationship between the men and the Manager at the Colliery."

Upon this the Mines Department approached the owners of Harworth Colliery "to see whether they would welcome the idea of our mediation in the present dispute." They were warned off: and were told that the owners did not consider "that the trouble is of such a nature as to lend itself to arbitration by an outside body." There was nothing more the Department could do, "at any rate at present," as Sir Alfred Faulkner explained in his October 23rd letter to Edwards. In the meantime, matters had been developing at Harworth. By now "the men were very eager to put in their notices, and they were restrained from this course only with great difficulty by our President, Mr. Jones, who was now in constant touch with the situation and visiting Harworth nearly every week-end." (E.C. Report, June 7, 1937.)

There was no doubt in the minds of the Federation Executive members that the Harworth situation was crucial in the long, ten years' struggle against the yellow union. If they won this battle they might win the whole war. Harworth won, it might be the Waterloo of Spencerism. So, on October 22, 1936, they took a number of decisions. At that time, Harworth men on unemployment benefit might be offered work by the Labour Exchange, as it was then called; if they refused to go to other collieries, they would lose their benefit. In such cases, ran the first decision, they would be paid by the union, and "that the Federation re-imburse the Nottinghamshire Miners' Association any sums they may expend in this way." Next, they authorised the President, Joseph Jones, to advise the men to continue to withhold their notices for the time being. Next, they would hold a ballot of the men "with a view to expediting the opening of negotiations." Lastly, they conferred plenary powers upon the Federation officials "to obtain suitable facilities at Harworth for organising the resistance of the men." (October 22, 1936.) The aim of the ballot, the Annual Conference was told later, was "to appease the men, and in order to give a further opportunity to the Company to settle the dispute peaceably, while at the same time letting the management know beyond any doubt that the workmen desired to be represented by the Federation." This ballot, supervised by "a neutral person" who was a Justice of the Peace for Notts County, gave the following result:

For the Nottinghamshire Miners' Association and the Mineworkers' Federation ..	1,175
For the "Industrial Union"	145
Majority ..	1,030

As far as the M.F.G.B. Chairman could calculate, 88 per cent of the men employed took part in the ballot which, however, brought no gesture of any kind from the management, and so, according to the same Annual Report: "The men could no longer be restrained, and we decided that unless in the meantime negotiations were opened up the men should hand in their notices on November 23." Then the Executive of the Federation, in expectation of a long drawn-out struggle and "in view of the importance of the principle in issue," agreed to "ask the districts to pay a levy of 3d. per member." (November 19, 1936.)

On a quite separate issue the colliery had stopped on a checkweigh dispute and was actually standing idle on November 17th: the M.F.G.B. Executive therefore told the colliers to go back in order to keep themselves technically within the law. According to the Annual Report:

We told them that when this had been done we could then resume the fight for recognition and freedom to organise. The men accepted this advice and were returning to work, when the management stepped in again and clarified the whole position. They refused to take the men back unless they would belong to the "Industrial Union." The men, of course, refused, and the colliery then became idle on the straight issue of the refusal of the management to permit the men to join the Federation and to recognise the Federation as the negotiating body on their behalf.

The next meeting of the Miners' Executive was transferred from London to the scene of the struggle, and there at the Miners' Offices in Old Basford, Nottinghamshire, the Committee received two of the Nottinghamshire officials, the delegate from Harworth Colliery, and seven Executive members of the Nottinghamshire Miners' Association. They discussed the general trade union position in the coal-field and the special position at the colliery. They decided to carry on. They took account of the fact that throughout Britain there was a growing interest amongst the miners, evidenced at that meeting in Old Basford on December 11th by a letter from the South Wales Miners' Federation asking for a Special Conference so as to make "some concentrated effort" in the Nottinghamshire coal-field situation. This request they left over to their adjourned session at which they decided unanimously:

That a Special Conference be convened on January 20, 1937, with a view to directing the attention of the Trades Union and Labour Movement, and of the country generally, to the vital issue involved in the stoppage at the Harworth Colliery, namely the principle of the freedom of the individual to join the union of his choice.

And further, that another approach be made to the Mines Department with a view to steps being taken to obtain recognition of the Nottinghamshire Miners' Association and establishing the liberty of the workmen to join such organisation as they desire. (December 30, 1936.)

5. SPECIAL CONFERENCE OF JANUARY 20, 1937

Meantime Ebby Edwards early in January had held interviews with Sir Alfred Faulkner and other officials of the Mines Department. Spencer had made a proposal, which had been reported in the press, that the men should return to work providing the company withdraw the stipulation that the men should join his "non-political union," but that it should be the recognised negotiating body at the colliery. To this the Secretary had replied that he could be "no party to any such terms, and certainly could not advise the return of the men on such terms. The M.F.G.B. by its affiliated body represented the largest number at that colliery, and they must have a voice in any negotiations."

At the Special Conference Ebby Edwards gave the facts already recounted and thanked everyone concerned "right throughout the Federation for the magnificent response to our call for the levy."

Val Coleman of Nottinghamshire told the delegates that since 1926 the Harworth men, as elsewhere in the county, had no means of raising their grievances with the manager except through the non-political union. The difficulties had been formidable; since 1926 no less than four branches had been formed at Harworth and lost, and their members victimised, as he described: "In the manager's own way he has in turn sent into exile every person who has been prepared to accept any official position relating to the Notts Miners' Association." He then went on to tell how a black-legging statement by G. A. Spencer had had the unexpected effect of setting in train a resistance to the non-political union. It had been towards the end of 1935, when the Federation had launched the campaign for the increase in wages.

Press statements had been published that the Nottinghamshire miners were being advised to continue working, despite this.

A meeting was held at Harworth, and a discussion arose resulting in a vote of censure on Mr. Spencer for giving circulation to that statement; and from that moment onwards, owing to the influence of meetings and speeches, and owing to the desire of the Federation to increase wages, things have gone forward, and a Branch was again formed at Harworth, new inspiration was given, membership was increased, and synchronising with that the chains were loosed, the tongues of the men became more free, and they began to discuss with each other such problems as pit inspections, overtime, dirt deductions, welfare representation, choice of family doctors, stoppages for stores, fines for props, intimidation, and the vexed question whether they should not be permitted now to select their own representatives, the colliery company on all occasions still refusing to allow them to communicate their difficulties and grievances except through the medium of the non-political union.

Finally Val Coleman gave a picture of the strike situation and how the police escort for the men who continued to work during the stoppage earned for them the name of "the Chain Gang." Here was Coleman's description:

When the night shift goes to work the men are organised at a certain point for the purpose of going to work, and they are preceded by a police car. The men take the middle of the road, and there are policemen on either side of the road.

Then a few yards behind them there is a line of police directly across the road standing shoulder to shoulder and keeping back the crowd, who are calling out to them "Left right, Left right," and all kinds of other expressions that colliery men and their wives and families make use of.

Then at a certain point the line of police turn round and push back the crowd, and it is at that point where differences of opinion are expressed and objections are made, and as a result we now have six men in prison, and we have had eighteen men fined varying sums from £1 to £5. In addition to that, there is a threat to turn the men and women out of their houses. (January 20, 1937.)

After much discussion the Conference stood adjourned till 2 p.m. to enable the Executive to bring forward a resolution. On its resumption the Chairman called on A. L. Horner of South Wales to move the resolution on behalf of the Executive. Horner said:

. Company Unionism, which is really what Spencerism is, was born in 1926 at a moment when we were engaged in the most serious struggle in the history of the Federation. The owners established it first of all in Nottinghamshire, and later developments of it made their appearance in the South Wales coalfield.

We in South Wales have very great sympathy with our Nottinghamshire comrades in the struggle against this conspiracy. We have very good reason to hate it. There is no experience which has been described here this morning which is strange to us in South Wales. We have seen our men and women batoned down and imprisoned by the hundred in the struggle against this menace. Fines and imprisonments have followed in its path.

After declaring that the Federation could not be satisfied "until this foul thing is swept out of the coalfields altogether," he said that everybody really knew that there could be no successful national struggle whilst it was "on the flanks of the national organisation." They must not, therefore,

regard the Harworth development as something to be sorry about; it is the opportunity that we have been waiting for, to do a job that must be done some day if this Federation is to have its full effect and influence on the miners of this country.

After all, if we have an instrument such as the Spencer Union ready and able to organise an alternative supply of labour for the mineowners, they have at their hand to a certain extent the possibility of destroying our effective bargaining power. (January 20, 1937.)

The Federation, continued Arthur Horner, was trying to reach the position where they could

say to the owners, "You buy from us, for you can buy from no other, and you must pay our price." Scab unionism is an instrument in the hands of the owners to break the "corner" in mining labour which the Federation is trying to establish.

Apart from any personal feelings towards Spencer, or any people of that kind, this Federation cannot do its job, it cannot safeguard or improve sufficiently the wage conditions and working conditions of its members until it does acquire the position of dominant control in the sale of mining labour in every part of this country.

That was why the Executive was not taking a parochial view, merely considering it as a problem for Nottinghamshire. He answered those members who might say why should not the Nottinghamshire miners fight to keep themselves free as others had done:

I want to draw your attention to that which I regard as the greatest miracle of the last decade. Just think of what you were told this morning. There are 36,000 eligible workers in the coalfield, 11,000 of whom are members of our organisation, and yet the representatives tell us that for ten years they have not been able to render even the smallest service to those members in the colliery office.

What are the 11,000 financial members of the organisation paying for? For service? No. For the prospect of service? Yes. They are paying because they really believe in free Trade Unionism, and the future of free Trade Unionism in Nottinghamshire and everywhere else in the British coalfields.

Harworth provided the opportunity for the Federation to become established once more as the recognised force in the county which was the last stronghold of company unionism.

Once the problem is solved in Nottinghamshire we have killed Company Unionism in the British coalfields; but so long as it is there, it may at any moment break out like a fever in adjacent districts, and do damage in other coalfields. We had a bit of trouble the other day with regard to Bedwas, and when we went to the Mines Department for a conference with the owners over the South Wales question, who did we find they were asking to be present at our meeting? Mr. Spencer and Mr. Cooper, of Notts! Any weakness, any struggle, any difficulty in any coalfield, these people will exploit if we allow them to survive in the position they have established for themselves in Nottinghamshire. (January 20, 1937.)

The Executive said that they represented three-quarters of a million men, the miners of Great Britain. The "flame which is the result of the spark at Harworth is going to be spread." If necessary they would use the whole might of the organisation. Horner concluded his speech by "asking the Conference this afternoon for power, without waiting for any further Conference, to take a ballot of the British miners in order that we may start a national strike if necessary to obtain freedom for the Nottinghamshire miners."

J. E. Swan of Durham, where there was a branch of a Spencer union, said it was a question "whether the Mineworkers' Federation shall function, or whether it shall be dictated to by the mineowners and by certain people who may be intimidated and sell their souls through the medium of a man like Mr. Spencer." Joseph Jones wound up the discussion. He said:

Spencerism has been kept alive by the employers in Nottingham, and will continue to be kept alive by them so long as it pays them to keep it alive, and it has paid them.

Comparing the two coalfields of Yorkshire on the one hand, and Notts and Derby on the other, if you take the trouble after this Conference is over to examine the September returns, you will find these three outstanding points. The selling prices were precisely the same to a decimal point in both coalfields. In Yorkshire, the price was 13s. 11·47d., and in Notts and Derby 13s. 11·64d. The wages in Yorkshire were 9s. 2·74d., and in Notts and Derby 8s. 11·38d., or approximately 3¼d. per ton less than in Yorkshire. On the other hand, the profits in Yorkshire were 6·77d., and in Notts and Derby 10·41d., or 3½d. more.

So that what was saved in wages in the Notts and Derby coalfield by Spencerism, went into the owners' pockets. That is the plain and simple deduction from the figures which are available to everybody, and that is the reason why the coalowners in that coalfield and every other coalfield are trying to keep it alive.

Thereafter the resolution was carried unanimously, as follows:

That this Conference of the Mineworkers' Federation of Great Britain having considered the position at Harworth Colliery and the deliberate attempt of the organised employers in that district to prevent the mineworkers joining the organisation of their choice, empowers the Executive Committee to take a ballot vote of the entire coalfields upon the question of enforcing the principle of the freedom of organisation and Trades Union recognition for those so organised.

Further, it requests the Executive Committee to approach the General Council of the Trades Union Congress in order to enlist the support of the whole Trade Union Movement for this principle and in the meantime the Executive Committee to take all necessary steps to deal with questions which have been raised or may arise, and the Conference stands adjourned to be recalled by the Executive Committee. (January 20, 1937.)

6. "HIGH-HANDED ACTION BY THE POLICE"

Early in the struggle public opinion had been aroused by the activities of the police and the local administration of justice. In March 1937, Ronald Kidd, Secretary of the National Council for Civil Liberties, published a pamphlet[1]

---

[1] *The Harworth Colliery Strike: A Report to the Executive Committee of the National Council for Civil Liberties*, N.C.C.L., London, March 1937. Price 1d. 16 pp.

which recorded the results of investigation made on the spot into allegations "of high-handed action by the police." The National Council for Civil Liberties, formed some four years earlier, was not a body whose findings could be lightly brushed aside. Not only did it include Members of Parliament and editors of journals but also outstanding figures in the field of literature, scholarship and science. A non-party body has seldom very much influence on either Government or Opposition in Britain: but in this case not even the Home Office could entirely ignore a protest which had the powerful support of writers of world-wide fame such as H. G. Wells and Havelock Ellis or of special esteem such as E. M. Forster, Henry Nevinson and G. D. H. Cole. Because of the concern felt by this body and on the instructions of its Executive Committee (usually presided over by W. H. Thompson, the trade union solicitor who more than once worsted Sir John Simon in public controversy on points of law about civil rights) Ronald Kidd went to Harworth Colliery and other parts of Nottinghamshire to find the facts about complaints that had been made about "infringements of civil rights in the trade dispute now taking place." In his Report[1] Ronald Kidd stated:

A large number of police (probably between a hundred and a hundred and fifty) have been drafted into the village from every part of the county, and the average extra charge on police funds is estimated at £120 a week. It is not clear whether this heavy charge will fall upon the ratepayers or whether Messrs. Barber, Walker & Co. will be required to pay for it.

He noted that "the village is practically owned by the Company," that the ground on which the church, parish hall and Salvation Army hut were built were owned by it, and stated:

I am satisfied that the Company have used their economic power to deprive the men of their civil right of freedom of assembly.

He also noted that the Chairman of the company, Major Barber, was "also chairman of the Nottinghamshire County

[1] Mention was made of this Report by the Home Secretary, Sir John Simon, in his non-committal way in the House of Commons on April 29, 1937.

Council" and went on to scrutinise police action[1] and the nature of the charges brought against the miners. He observed that the Public Order Act, 1936, which had just been put on the Statute Book following provocative meetings of Sir Oswald Mosley and the British Union of Fascists in the Jewish East End of London, had been used against the miners. It was the first use of the Act, within a month of it becoming law. Ronald Kidd concluded as follows:

It is unfortunate that so much of the public administration of the County is in the hands of those whose economic interests coincide with the interests of the owners rather than with the interests of the men who are dependent on the owners for their livelihood. Whatever the cause, there can be no reasonable doubt, I think, that there have been serious irregularities in the conduct of the police during the dispute and this, coupled with the attitude and composition of the local Bench and with the method of serving summonses and making charges, has led to a feeling throughout the district that the general administration of law and order in the county is being used in a manner which must do infinite harm to a belief in the traditions of public administration and justice.

After the events described in the pamphlet, worse was to come, as we shall see. But the pattern was set.

A particular example of one arrest and trial aroused public interest. Michael Kane, Chairman of the Harworth Branch, was charged at the Nottinghamshire Quarter Sessions at Retford with intimidation in that on November 19, 1936, he had, inside a bus conveying miners brought in to work at Harworth pit, used threats to induce them to abstain from working at the colliery. The evidence was conflicting, some witnesses saying there was only peaceful persuasion. But the seventy-seven-year-old Colonel Sir Albert Whitaker, presiding over a full bench of a dozen magistrates on January 11, 1937,

[1] In the Appendix to this Report Ronald Kidd gives statements he had taken, of which one, with Mrs. G. of Bircotes, may be quoted:

"On Tuesday evening, December 15, 1936, I was standing inside my garden gate arranging with two lady friends about going to Church on Wednesday evening when a policeman told me to 'get inside.' I said, 'I beg your pardon' and he replied, 'Never mind about begging anyone's pardon; get inside.' I then told the policeman that my husband was working in the Pit and he apologised. I replied that I failed to see what my husband's working had got to do with it."

This example of the aggressive attitude of the police to men or women whom they believe to be associated with the strike, and the conciliatory attitude of this officer as soon as he discovered that Mrs. G.'s husband was still working, throws an interesting light on the assurance which was given to me by a highly placed police officer that all the police were entirely impartial. This incident should be compared with the case of Mr. C. (No. 9) where the constable asked "You are not working, are you?"

imposed a sentence of two months' imprisonment. The case went to the Court of Criminal Appeal. On February 8th the Lord Chief Justice and Justices Goddard and Swift[1] dismissed the appeal, though Lord Hewart criticised some of the conduct of the prosecution.

7.   THE DELEGATES INSIST ON A BALLOT

The decision of the January Conference had been communicated to the Secretary for Mines and steps were now taken to publicise issues in the dispute as widely as possible. The General Council of the Trades Union Congress (which had been kept in close touch with the dispute) was also informed of the latest development and of the possibility of widespread action being taken in the coal-fields.[2] Things now began to happen. At the Blackpool Annual Conference of 1937 the Executive Committee, in their account of this dispute, related the course of events and at this point said:

Of course, we had kept in mind the possibility of effecting a solution of the problem by an amalgamation of the two Unions in Nottingham, and we had always felt that if this could be done on anything like reasonable terms it would afford the best solution, for it would not involve the possibility of widespread loss and suffering in the coalfields. Knowing our minds in this matter, our officials had no difficulty, therefore, in accepting an invitation which was received from the Secretary for Mines in the early part of February to meet representatives of the Industrial Union under his chairmanship.

This meeting was held on February 25th, when the representatives of the company union put forward certain proposals for the amalgamation of the two unions in Nottinghamshire.

[1] Michael Kane was unlucky in his judges. For apart from Hewart and Goddard (whose rise to the highest judicial office was never hampered by any reputation for leniency), the third judge was Sir Rigby Swift, who had made his mark first as an advocate for the coal-owners, then as Conservative M.P. for St. Helens from 1910–18. He became more widely known in 1925 when, as the judge at the trial of twelve Communist leaders, he mostly gave sentences of a duration exactly the same as that promised to a meeting of his constituents by the Home Secretary, Sir William Joynson-Hicks. This was bound to cast some doubt on the validity of the well-known constitutional doctrine of the complete separation of the executive and the judiciary. It was, however, unwise to express this doubt publicly. A printer and publisher who did so (referring five years later to Swift as a "bewigged puppet") were sent to prison for periods of nine months and two years respectively, for contempt of court.

[2] The correspondence with the Government and the T.U.C. General Council minutes are given in full in the Report by Ebby Edwards to the Special Conference of April 1st.

These were "certain main principles" which, from their point of view, were essential to the consummation of such an agreement. It was agreed that both sides should report to their respective Executives and meet again on March 4th. On the morning of March 4th, the proposals of the industrial union were fully reported to the Federation Executive which held "a protracted debate" on the whole situation. Should the officials proceed with the discussions with the Spencer union? Or, in view of the nature of those proposals, should discussions be broken off and arrangements made for taking a ballot vote of the coal-fields? Eventually the Executive, "on principle," decided to accept the conditions "subject to any modifications thereof which our officials might be able to obtain." Thereafter discussions with the industrial union were resumed on the same day under the chairmanship of the Secretary for Mines. "Heads" of an agreement were reached and were signed on behalf of the respective organisations, but of course subject to their approval. The Report then says:

Now came a tremendous tussle in regard to the men at Harworth. The terms did not provide for a satisfactory conclusion of the Harworth dispute, and it was never our intention that they should be ratified by the Federation until satisfactory assurance had been given that there should be no victimisation of or discrimination against any of the men at Harworth.

The management would not move. The colliery company reserved itself "complete liberty of action." The Secretary of Mines sent down his people to Nottinghamshire, but when the M.F.G.B. Executive Committee met again on March 24th they found that the position was unchanged, the management having refused to open any discussion on this question until the amalgamation with the Industrial Union had become an accomplished fact. At this meeting, as they afterwards reported:

We also had letters before us from Yorkshire, Lancashire and Northumberland, all of whom requested that a Special Conference of the Federation should be summoned to consider the whole position.

At the Conference, held on April 1st and 2nd, a full report was given on all that had happened since the last Conference.

Immediately there were fierce objections raised to the tentative terms for amalgamation that had been discussed by the Executive Committee following their acceptance of the mediation offered by the Mines Department. "There can can be no such union as is suggested in Notts," said Golightly of Northumberland, who described it as an attempt "to enforce an unholy marriage." S. Sales of Derbyshire said that the terms were "terms dictated by Spencer himself." J. Swan of Durham, claiming that "Nobody would call me a left-wing man," condemned the terms as "obnoxious." On behalf of South Wales Arthur Horner called attention to the truculent speech of Captain Muschamp, the Nottinghamshire coal-owner, with whom Spencer had been hand-in-glove in 1926, and who twelve days earlier had openly advocated Nazi methods of dealing with industrial troubles. Muschamp had said:

We want to adopt the German idea. If the Government is to check future trouble, it must put its foot down and put it down strongly. In this district we have been very much blessed with peace for the last ten years. This district—the Notts district—can take credit to itself for having smashed the national strike, and since then, we have carried on peaceably with the Industrial Union for ten years. The country may thank the Industrial Union for preventing a strike a year last Christmas. (March 20, 1937.)

Captain Muschamp had ended by deploring the policy of the Mines Department which he said was "supporting the Mineworkers' Federation in doing away with the Industrial Union." So, as Horner seemed to suggest by his quotation, there were two sides to the question: but South Wales also was opposed to these particular terms.

Having heard the very strong views expressed by the Districts at the first session, the Executive Committee considered the whole matter again, and in accordance with their duty under the Rules, they submitted to Conference a recommendation in favour of a strike ballot:

That this Conference regards the draft terms for the formation of one Miners' Union for the Nottinghamshire coalfield as unreasonable and unacceptable. It also deplores the absence of any satisfactory assurance regarding the reinstatement of the men at the Harworth Colliery. It resolves, therefore, that a ballot of the coalfields be taken with the object of securing recognition of the

Mineworkers' Federation of Great Britain and adequate assurances to prevent victimisation at Harworth Colliery. (April 2, 1937.)

By a vote of 503 to 32 the resolution was carried.

The ballot was held on April 15th and 16th; the question addressed to the men was in the following terms:

Are you in favour of tendering notice with the object of obtaining recognition of the M.F.G.B. in the Nottinghamshire coalfield and to secure adequate assurances to prevent any victimisation of the workmen at Harworth?

Put your X in the appropriate column according to your desire.

YES	NO

Every effort was made to get a full response in the ballot and to put the issues to the men in plain terms. An explanatory leaflet[1] was sent out in sufficient quantities

[1] A MESSAGE TO THE MINERS OF BRITAIN:

In the dispute in the Nottinghamshire coalfield certain principles are at stake of outstanding importance to every mineworker in the country. The first is the simple, but vital, issue—shall mineworkers who desire to join and be represented by their own Federation be free to do so? The second—shall men be victimised because they have fought for their rights as Trade Unionists? If a definite answer in the affirmative cannot be given to the first question and an equally emphatic "no" to the second, then we are no longer free citizens, and Trade Unionism has lost its meaning.

You will know that in the Nottinghamshire coalfield a satisfactory answer *cannot* be given to these questions. There, large numbers of men have been compelled to join a Union, not of their own choice, but of their employers' choice, and the heroic men of Harworth pit, who, for five months, have fought the battle of free Trade Unionism, are in grave danger of victimisation.

Deeply involved in this dispute is a further and even more vital issue—the future welfare of the whole of the mineworkers of the country. So long as the employers in Nottinghamshire are able to divide our forces, so long shall we have a fatal weakness and be unable to bargain with our full powers, and so achieve peace and justice in the coalfields. Great as are the other issues involved, this overshadows them all; for, in this matter, the whole future of the mineworkers is at stake.

Not wishing to embroil all the coalfields, and desiring, if at all possible, a peaceful solution of the difficulties, the Federation has sought to achieve this by way of merging the two forces in the Nottinghamshire coalfield, and so eventually to create a better and healthier situation. But the present terms of the Industrial Union are not satisfactory; they are not terms which can be accepted by the great free body of mineworkers in this country.

And so you are asked to make a decision. By this ballot vote you are asked to record, not merely your detestation of the violation of the principles of free citizenship and free Trade Unionism in Nottinghamshire, but your determination to fight for those principles if necessary and your Federation unhesitatingly recommends you to do this by recording an emphatic "*YES*" to the question asked you. Armed with your authority in this way, the Federation will then make further efforts to achieve a peaceful and honourable solution of the dispute, but every man must clearly understand that if, after being armed with this authority, the Federation is still met with a stubborn and vindictive attitude on the part of the employers, then it may be necessary to close the ranks and fight bitterly and stubbornly for those rights which are of the very essence of our liberties.

On behalf of the Mineworkers' Federation of Great Britain,

JOSEPH JONES, President.
WILLIAM LAWTHER, Vice-President.
EBBY EDWARDS, Secretary.

April 4, 1937.

for every member to have a copy, and a certain number of posters were also sent to every District.

In Nottinghamshire special efforts were made to obtain as complete a ballot as possible, and two of the Federation's members, W. Pearson and F. Collindridge, were appointed to assist the Nottinghamshire Miners' Association in the organisation of the campaign in that coal-field. Here ballot forms were not confined to the Nottinghamshire miners in the Association: it was made open to all mine-workers in the county, whatever their affiliation. A very high percentage replied, and of these four-fifths were in favour of strike action after more than seven months' struggle. The result of the ballot, received at the meeting of April 20, was:

District	For	Against
Bristol	315	25
Durham	70,337	11,668
Group No. 1	7,170	1,995
Derbyshire	21,309	3,902
Kent	5,025	308
Forest of Dean	2,973	336
Cumberland	3,186	474
Lancashire	34,752	5,166
Leicester	1,622	219
Northumberland	23,244	4,174
North Wales	5,417	517
Nottinghamshire	21,956	4,810
Midlands	25,282	2,320
Scotland	35,463	6,055
South Derbyshire	2,584	536
Somerset	2,104	347
South Wales	81,376	7,945
Power Group	6,271	1,130
Yorkshire	94,160	9,518
TOTALS	444,546	61,445

The number of votes cast was 505,991 in all or 98·9 per cent of the total membership as shown in the returns for the first quarter of 1937. The issue, as it was put, for trade union rights and against victimisation, had roused the coal-fields of Britain.

8. BREACHES OF THE PEACE AT HARWORTH

Following the Special Conference resolution of April 2 and the mid-month ballot, the situation at Harworth became more tense. More and more incidents took place as the police took extreme measures to hamper mass picketing of "the Chain Gang." This culminated in a major disturbance on Friday, April 23, 1937. On Monday in the House of Commons, E. Dunn, of Rother Valley, asked the Home Secretary, Sir John Simon:

Whether in view of the grave breaches of the peace which have occurred at Harworth, and the probability of further outbreaks, he will take immediate steps to institute an inquiry to ascertain how best to restore and maintain public order. (April 26, 1937.)

This was not by any means the first question that had been asked in the House of Commons where, ever since the Communist M.P., William Gallacher, had raised the matter on February 9th and even before that, there had been a series of questions coming up under the heading "Harworth Colliery Dispute." But as the struggle developed the questions and interventions in Parliament had been increasingly taken up by some of the more moderate members of the Labour Party. On this occasion Sir John Simon replied that it was not his responsibility; whereupon Jack Lawson in a supplementary question said that those who "have engaged in strikes have never known anything like the hostility that there is between the public and the police at Harworth." Dunn then at the end of Questions rose in his place to say:

I beg to ask leave to move the Adjournment of the House in order to call attention to a definite matter of urgent public importance, namely: "the refusal of the Home Secretary to take immediate action to prevent further breaches of the peace at Harworth." (April 26, 1937.)

Mr. Speaker having refused to accept, Tom Williams (Don Valley) said that:

On Saturday evening a special midnight court was held and six persons who had been apprehended were brought before the court and, in view of the feeling in the district that those who are working are causing the trouble, and in order to avoid any further riots or misconduct, or breaking of the peace, injuring men, women and children an inquiry should be instituted to find who was responsible for *provoking* the riots.

Three days later, on Thursday, April 29th, under the same heading F. J. Bellenger (Bassetlaw), having been told by Sir John Simon that the matter was now *sub judice* and that he could not comment, then mentioned the bitter resentment "felt in the locality, not confined to any one class, at the callous, one-sided methods adopted by the police in this dispute." Simon, helped by Mr. Speaker, stonewalled: he had "his opinion"; but the Chief Constable of Nottinghamshire had told him that "34 persons have been charged with offences against Section 7 of the Conspiracy and Protection of Property Act of 1875, arising out of the disorder at Harworth on Friday, the 23rd inst." Prime Minister Baldwin, asked by Arthur Greenwood about the possibility of a national stoppage, said: "His Majesty's Government are fully alive to the seriousness of the situation": but hoped there would be no need for debate later. On the same day (April 29th) as these questions came up in Parliament, the Superintendent of Police lodged a complaint against three dozen persons, which followed an indictment, namely:

That you on the twenty-third day of April, 1937, at Harworth in the said County, together with divers other evil disposed persons, unlawfully, riotously did assemble to disturb the public peace and then did make a great riot and disturbance, to the terror and alarm of His Majesty's subjects there being and against the peace of our Sovereign Lord the King his Crown and Dignity.

You are therefore hereby summoned to appear before the Court of Summary Jurisdiction sitting at Worksop, in the said County, on Monday, the Third Day of May, 1937, at the hour of Half Past Ten o'Clock in the Forenoon, to answer the said complaint.

An immediate interest was taken in this by the National Council for Civil Liberties, and at their instance Sir Stafford Cripps (Solicitor-General in the previous Labour Government and very widely respected in the coal-fields for the work he had done at the enquiry into the Gresford disaster) appeared for the prisoners at the Police Court held in Worksop. In his conduct of the case he was able to show that a great many of those in the dock had been apparently indiscriminately arrested by the police without any evidence to show that they were on the scene of the disturbance. More than half of the accused were acquitted, bound over or given very light sentences. The other half, seventeen in all, were sent for trial to the Nottingham Assizes to be held some six weeks later.

9.   REPUGNANCE TO FUSION

The ballot, as can be seen, had given an overwhelming majority (of seven to one—with ten to one in several of the bigger Districts) for a strike in favour of obtaining recognition of the M.F.G.B. in Nottinghamshire and for a guarantee against any victimisations at Harworth. After consideration of these figures, the Executive decided to convene a Special Conference of the Federation in London on April 30th, to consider the question of handing in notices. (April 20, 1937.) The situation was described in the statement we have already quoted, in which the Executive gave an account of its stewardship, as follows:

Opinion in the Federation was now hardening in favour of *direct* recognition of the Nottinghamshire Mineworkers' Association to the exclusion of any other body. The result of the ballot vote seemed to show that the men were alive to the issues at stake, and the question of fusion, while perhaps a practical proposal in the earlier stages of the dispute, was now becoming repugnant to large numbers of our people.

The vote, indeed, had been taken on the question of obtaining *recognition* of the M.F.G.B., and while it had been clearly stated at the Conference of April 1 that recognition might mean either direct recognition or recognition through fusion with the Industrial Union, there was no doubt in our minds that the majority of our men would prefer the former course, and that for the time being, at any rate, the question of fusion must be kept in abeyance.

Four members of the Committee—J. Gilliland of Durham, J. A. Hall of Yorkshire, Arthur Horner of South Wales, and James Bowman of Northumberland—were appointed to act with the officials in carrying on any negotiations. On April 20th they met a representative of the Mines Department.

Then began a series of negotiations in which the owners proved to be very stubborn in their refusal to meet representatives of the Mineworkers' Federation. Even when the Mines Department requested the Nottinghamshire owners to meet the Federation under the chairmanship of the Secretary of Mines, they got the same reply. However, the Secretary for Mines then took the course of inviting the two parties to meet him separately; two only because for negotiating

MICK KANE, CHAIRMAN, HARWORTH BRANCH
On release from imprisonment, greeting his niece

HUNGER MARCH TO LONDON, NOVEMBER 1936
Miners from South Wales pass through Runnymede, where
King John signed Magna Charta

purposes the Nottinghamshire owners and the company union had now formed themselves into one body. So the antagonists met the Secretary for Mines separately at the Mines Department on April 29th, a day before the Special Conference convened for April 30th. Proceedings on the eve of the Special Conference took the form of messages passing between the two sides through the Secretary for Mines. After six hours, all that could be extracted by the sub-committee was this formula:

In deference to a request from the Secretary for Mines, Mr. Spencer will agree to meet representatives of the M.F.G.B. with reference to the signed heads of agreement for amalgamation to hear any comments they care to make thereon on the definite understanding it is without prejudice to his right to adhere to the original signed terms. Before agreeing to this meeting, he requires an assurance that such representatives will be empowered to reach a final and binding settlement. (April 29, 1937.)

The crux of it lay in Spencer's refusal to meet unless the Federation officials were "empowered to reach a final and binding settlement" at it. Were they to break off the talks "which had been so singularly unfruitful" and recommend the Conference to hand in notices? Or should they adjourn the Conference? The Committee decided to continue discussions at the Mines Department and if the stipulations were withdrawn they would continue to negotiate. Accordingly, the Conference was adjourned, and the sub-committee went off to the Mines Department to continue the discussion.

It was now the most critical stage of the dispute. The negotiations went on that day until they reached a point where the Secretary for Mines drew up a memorandum. The proposals in this memorandum were recommended by the Executive to the Conference, as follows:

That this Conference accepts the proposals embodied in the Memorandum drawn up by the Minister of Mines so as to afford an opportunity for the Notts Miners' Association to discuss within their own district, terms for amalgamation. The Conference meantime to stand adjourned and the officials be empowered to recall the Conference if a settlement has not been reached within three weeks. (Executive Committee Meeting, Friday, April 30, 1937.)

But when the Executive made this recommendation to

H   *The Miners*

refer the dispute back for negotiation first in the District, the 129 delegates to the Special Conference rejected it. The delegates, representing 531,000 trade unionists (the number organised had been growing rapidly in 1937), had been waiting till after four o'clock in the afternoon for the resumption of discussion, while the sub-committee on negotiations had been closeted with the officials of the Mines Department. As soon as the recommendation had been moved by President Joseph Jones and seconded by Vice-President Lawther, there were speeches in opposition. "We have come here for one thing, the only way to get rid of Spencer," cried J. Newton of Durham: he asked: "What are we afraid of?" and concluded: "We have decided unanimously in this country for notices to be handed in. Carry out the dictates of the country and dispose of Spencer." Similar speeches followed from Yorkshire, South Wales and Northumberland, the very Districts whose representatives on the Executive Committee made up, together with the three officials, the sub-committee on negotiations. It was clear that feeling in the major coalfields on this issue was reaching boiling-point: and the Chairman adjourned the Conference for an hour to enable the Districts to discuss whether they were or were not in favour of fusion. That evening, when the vote was taken, the recommendation was defeated by 343 votes to 192. The die was cast. Later, the Executive Committee, recounting these events in their Annual Report, decided to criticise the Special Conference for not having accepted their recommendation. That they should do so was perhaps unique in the history of the Federation. They wrote of the treatment of their proposal:

However, the Conference thought that the proposal meant that the dispute would be handed over to the weaker body, forgetting that the power of the Federation is often best exercised, not when it is undertaking negotiations itself, but when it is standing solidly behind one of the districts. It must be remembered that the owners have a district outlook; they claim that disputes can best be settled within the districts, and often they will pay a high price to secure a settlement in a district rather than let the dispute become a matter of national agitation and concern. Because of this, the influence and value of the Federation is by no means diminished simply because negotiations may be carried on in the district.

However, as we have seen, the Conference rejected the proposal, and decided that notices should be handed in to expire simultaneously throughout the Federation on May 22nd. A proclamation to the men to hand in strike notices was then issued under the signatures of the officials.

A CALL TO THE MINEWORKERS OF BRITAIN!

Comrades!

Armed with your authority to fight for the principles of freedom and justice your Federation has now made further efforts to secure an honourable settlement of the troubles in the Nottinghamshire coalfield. Unfortunately, it has failed. *It has failed because the people with whom it has to negotiate do not believe that you are in earnest. They actually think that you do not mean what you say—that you are afraid to fight for justice!*

A mere handful of men are still trying to dictate terms to the overwhelming majority of the mineworkers of the country. They must be taught that your long and honourable efforts to obtain a peaceful settlement were not signs of weakness. They must learn to understand that there are limits to which dictation can go! They must be made to realise that democracy can fight! *Therefore we ask you for another manifestation of your will. We ask you to hand in your notices, and let these men see, beyond the possibility of doubt, that the miners are invincibly determined to fight for justice.*

This may, or may not, mean a National Stoppage. It is hard to forget the cruel persecutions to which so many of our loyal men have been subjected in Nottinghamshire. Nevertheless, we have no feelings of hatred or revenge. We seek only JUSTICE, and there is still time for a just and honourable settlement. But there can be no further dictation. PEACE NOW can be obtained only by a settlement which freely embodies the great principles of *liberty* and *equality* in Trade Union organisation.

Once the notices are put in we shall put the matter to the acid test. We shall see whether mineworkers can obtain justice without having to struggle for it. But again we say to you—let there be no mistake. By putting in your notice, you, IN HONOUR, bind yourself to take part in a National Stoppage if a satisfactory settlement cannot be obtained. With a full sense of our responsibility, and with a clear understanding of what may lie before us all, we urge you to take this action, because we believe that the principles of freedom, justice and democracy, which we are now seeking to establish in Nottingham, are worthy of fighting for to the limits of our strength.

On behalf of the Mineworkers' Federation of Great Britain,

JOSEPH JONES, President.

WILLIAM LAWTHER, Vice-President.

May 3, 1937.   EBBY EDWARDS, Secretary.

10. BALDWIN'S SWAN SONG

The mining delegates, having thus decided on April 30th for strike notices to be handed in, departed for home. On that Friday night in London there began a strike for a 7½-hour day by 26,000 busmen of the metropolitan area, while throughout a dozen counties there were unofficial strikes of men in the bus fleets. These transport disputes, together with the prospect in three weeks' time of a nation-wide miners' strike, could not have come at a more inconvenient time for the National Government. Prime Minister Stanley Baldwin, who had been mainly instrumental in securing the abdication of King Edward VIII the previous December, had hoped to crown his life's work by his arrangements for the Coronation of King George VI. The Coronation of the King and Queen was due on May 12th. Something had to be done and done quickly. Therefore, although even on the Monday (May 3rd) the Prime Minister in response to C. R. Attlee's request appeared to have hopes that the Mines Department would pull off a success in its mediation (and, if never before, the Mines Department was now working overtime), by the next day arrangements "through the usual channels" had been put in hand for a debate in Parliament. As he opened the debate, the leader of the Labour Party, Clement Attlee, said a "critical position" had arisen out of the dispute at the Harworth Colliery: and that a national strike was now imminent, which demanded "the full attention" of the Government. He said:

The strike ballot showed an overwhelming majority in favour of handing in notices: 440,000 for, and 61,000 against. Almost half a million of the men were prepared to face the sacrifices and the hardships that such a strike entails.

What is the reason for that? They are not asking for money; they are not raising a question of hours; they are standing out for a principle.

The issue concerns only a few workers in one village. The great majority of the men who are prepared to come out are not affected in their own lives. People make a great mistake if they think that men will not stand and fight for a principle. (May 5, 1937.)

Attlee, very briefly recalling the facts (now fairly familiar to the members) of Spencerism and of Harworth, the docking of wages to maintain the Spencer union, the victimisation of N.M.A. members, the evictions from colliery company houses, said of Major Barber, the Chairman of the company:

He is chairman of the County Council, and chairman of the Standing Joint Committee which controls the police of the county. In fact the men who work in Harworth are in the control of the company when they are at work and when they are at leisure. The conditions in Harworth are not British conditions.

Attlee, suggesting that the employers' methods "perhaps were imported from continental examples," went on to emphasise that, while the Harworth strike was for "the right of collective bargaining" and for the right of men to be represented "by their own representatives and their own union," behind this lay still deeper issues of democracy and liberty. Earlier he had said "the issue is essentially one of liberty against tyranny," and after appealing to the Prime Minister's own beliefs in these matters of principle, he ended by saying: "I believe that in the House and everywhere there is a desire that men in industry should work as free men and not as serfs."

The Prime Minister rose immediately the Leader of the Opposition had ended: "I do not mind confessing," he said, "that when I was first asked to find time for this discussion, I was apprehensive." He had seen so many occasions when a debate during negotiations could do "irreparable harm; but," he went on, "I welcome the temper in which the right hon. Gentleman has spoken." In what he had to say, he would respond to the challenge about his interest in democracy; he would steer clear of the rights and wrongs of the dispute, for if he expressed a point of view whatever value he might possess ("and I hope it is some value in mediation and suasion") would be lost; and so he would deal with what lay near his heart:

I know that my time is short here now and I felt that I would like once more to say in this House something about things that I have tried to stand for for a great many years and which I would like to finish my career here in discussing.

The Prime Minister went on: "I wanted to say a few words today about democracy and its relation to our industrial conditions": what he had to say was:

Under a democracy, every individual in some degree or another has to do his own thinking, and on whether he thinks rightly or wrongly the whole success or failure of that democracy will rest.

Then coming to the industrial side he said:

I agree very largely with what the Leader of the Opposition said, and absolutely with what he said about collective bargaining.

What is the alternative to collective bargaining? There is none except anarchy, and there are rare elements in the country that would like to see anarchy in the trade unions—in my view the most dangerous thing for the country that could happen.

Another alternative is force, but we may rule out force in this country, and I would lay it down that, so long as the industrial system remains as it is, collective bargaining is the right thing. I have no doubt about that.

And yet we all know in our heart of hearts that it may be a clumsy method of settling disputes, and that the last word has not been spoken.

Some day, when we are all fit for a democracy, we shall not need these aids, but certainly for my part, and as long as I can see ahead, unless there is that change in human nature which we are always hoping for, collective bargaining will be a necessity.

Then reverting to an old theme of his the Prime Minister said:

the one thing we must pray for in this country, not only in our statesmen but in our leaders of trade unions and in the masters, is wisdom. (May 5, 1937.)

By the time the Prime Minister had got to this point in his homily on democracy and its attendant perils and virtues, the members of the House of Commons, according to contemporary witnesses, were visibly affected, partly by the knowledge that it was his swan song and still more by the manner of his utterance. For Baldwin had a conspicuous Adam's apple which when he appeared to be speaking under stress of emotion rose in his throat and produced a slight sobbing effect: and this, as great actors know, induces a melting mood in nearly all listeners—even compels some to an imitative response. This effect became more marked when he referred to the debate on the Gresford disaster and what understanding and sympathy had been shown throughout the House; and then said:

I have always felt that, with regard to the miner's life, we have to remember two things. In an industrial trouble, wherever it may come, never let us think of either of the combatants in abstract terms. All these men and women, on whichever side they are, are human beings just as you and I are, and subject to the same trials, the same difficulties, the same weaknesses and the same temptations.

Rising to the height of his emotional and patriotic appeal, the Prime Minister made reference to the coming ceremony in Westminster Abbey:

In the Abbey on this day week our young King and his Queen, who were called suddenly and unexpectedly to the most tremendous position on earth, will kneel and dedicate themselves to the service of their people, a service which can only be ended by death.

His last sentence seemed, at any rate to some of the press gallery who wrote in the next morning's papers, to come with healing wings as he ended:

I appeal to that handful of men with whom rests peace or war to give the best present to the country that could be given at that moment, to do the one thing which would rejoice the hearts of all the people who love this country, that is, to rend and dissipate this dark cloud which has gathered over us, and show the people of the world that this democracy can still at least practise the arts of peace in a world of strife. (May 5, 1937.)

As he sat down after what was later to be talked about and described as his famous "plea for industrial peace" there were few even among his opponents who remembered vividly at that moment the Baldwin who had broadcast to the American public in 1926 asking them not to send food to the starving miners as it would only prolong the struggle, and who had been responsible for the anti-trade union legislation of 1927. Nor were there any at all in the House who could foresee a time when the name of Stanley Baldwin would become a by-word for sloth and hypocrisy amongst the leading sections of the Conservative Party. These days were far ahead: at the moment the speech (in which the former ironmaster had uttered little beyond a series of platitudes) seemed to them to contribute just what was needed for a settlement of the Harworth dispute.

II.   NEGOTIATIONS FOR FUSION

The next day after Baldwin's utterance the Executive Committee of the M.F.G.B. was meeting at the National Hotel, London. There they received W. H. Mainwaring, M.P., and W. M. Watson, M.P., who both reported upon the activities of the police in regard to the Harworth dispute and on the steps taken to prepare the defence of the men on the charges which had been brought against them, following the events of April 23rd. The Executive also accepted an invitation to discuss the dispute with the Secretary of Mines, who proposed that the question of fusion should be referred to independent arbitration. The case, he said, might be submitted to one or three persons, the object being to get finality. After discussion, the following proposal was carried:

The Executive Committee of the Mineworkers' Federation of Great Britain in response to the Prime Minister's appeal and in the hope of securing a settlement of the dispute honourable to all parties are prepared to suspend for a fortnight from Saturday next, May 8, the handing in of notices to terminate contracts, providing an early conference of the three parties—the Nottinghamshire colliery owners, the Mineworkers' Federation of Great Britain and the Nottinghamshire Industrial Union—can be arranged.

This decision was communicated to the Secretary for Mines, who agreed to issue the invitations immediately to the Nottinghamshire owners and the company union:

to attend without conditions such a conference in London at the earliest possible date under my Chairmanship to discuss conditions in Nottinghamshire. I shall be glad if you will reply not later than noon tomorrow (Friday). I much regret the necessity for such an urgent reply, but if notices are to be suspended action must be taken by the M.F.G.B. by mid-day tomorrow.

I am sure I can rely on your Committee to take into account the Prime Minister's appeal when considering your reply to this invitation.

HARRY CROOKSHANK, Secretary for Mines.

The Prime Minister's eloquence seems to have had less effect on the Nottinghamshire coal-owners than upon the M.F.G.B. Executive Committee who were certainly rather shocked the next day when they saw Captain Crookshank and heard from him the response to their overtures. For though the reply began formally "Having regard to the appeal made by the Prime Minister in the House of Commons," it went on to make a curt stipulation. The owners and Spencer would meet the M.F.G.B. in the way suggested only

if the M.F.G.B. will definitely accept the principle of the fusion of the two Unions in Nottinghamshire and will agree to submit to arbitration any points relative to the fusion left outstanding after discussions. (Friday, May 7, 1937.)

This refusal of the offer of an *unconditional* Conference the miners found "discouraging"; nevertheless "determined to make every effort to secure peace," they made the following further offer:

That we repeat the offer as made to the Secretary for Mines last night, and notwithstanding the refusal of the Nottinghamshire owners and the Industrial Union to meet representatives of the M.F.G.B. unconditionally we are prepared to suspend notices for one week to afford the Minister a further opportunity of arranging such a conference as we suggest. (Friday, May 7, 1937.)

It was also agreed by the Executive Committee that the following wire should be sent to the Districts immediately:

Proceed to collect signed notices, but suspend handing in of notices pending further instructions. (Friday, May 7, 1937.)

The Conference had set a fixed date for the strike of all the coal-fields. It was now unfixed. It was a risk. It was like stopping an army's mobilisation. It went in face of the Conference decision, itself a rejection of the Committee's previous recommendation. It might seem the Committee were, to use a current phrase, "bending over backwards" in their effort to conciliate their opponents. What was the effect on the Spencer-owners group in Nottinghamshire when the Secretary for Mines as intermediary communicated this new M.F.G.B. decision? They seem to have thought that they had got the miners on the run. Spencer was there to tell them that in his experience a strike postponed was a strike abandoned. Whatever their calculations, the response of the Nottinghamshire owners to this was unmistakable. It was received by the Secretary for Mines on May 10th; it was a reiteration of their previous refusal to meet the Federation

H*

unless the Federation agreed in advance to accept the principle of fusion and to submit to arbitration any points left outstanding after the discussions. Accordingly, the Districts were instructed to hand their notices in and a national strike was definitely fixed for Saturday, May 29th.

The Secretary for Mines, or rather the civil servants in his Department, Sir Alfred Faulkner and Mr. W. G. Notts-Bower, now began to be very busy. The sands were running out both of Baldwin's premiership and of the strike notices. Moreover, the Labour movement understood the miners' con-ciliatory gesture much better than Spencer and the owners, and was obviously roused: on May 19th the Co-operative Congress, representing eight or nine million members, pledged its support to the miners in the approaching conflict. Thereafter, in the second half of May there was much to-ing and fro-ing, much pressure exerted by the Mines Department and much casting about in all directions. Under this pressure from the Mines Department, the officials felt that "the principle of fusion" should be accepted. This acceptance was endorsed on May 20th by the Federation Executive Committee, which gave the sub-committee "full powers to negotiate terms of fusion." They also called a Special Conference for Thursday, May 27th, one week ahead. It was to be a busy week. Eventually, under a neutral Chairman the two sides met on Monday, May 24th: and by mid-day on the Wednesday "our negotiating Committee," ran the M.F.G.B. Report, "after a great deal of hard work, were able to present to us provisional terms of settlement. After a thorough examination of these terms we had no difficulty in recommending that the Conference should ratify them."

The provisional terms[1] of May 26, 1937, were for amal-gamation of the two organisations into one body to be called the Nottinghamshire and District Miners' Federated Union, to come into being on September 1st. The new union was to be affiliated to the Mineworkers' Federation of Great Britain, with rules conforming thereto: the officers were to be G. A. Spencer, President; Val Coleman, General Secretary; H. W. Cooper of the Industrial Union, Financial Secretary and Treasurer: of the two agents, one was to be W. Bayliss

[1] See Appendix for full terms.

(of the N.M.A.) and the other a representative of the Industrial Union; G. A. Spencer was to have reserved for him for one year the representation of the new union on the M.F.G.B. Executive Committee: all other posts, delegations and local committees were for two years to be shared half-and-half: a new six-year agreement was to be negotiated with the colliery owners. There were also provisions for the Harworth colliers, alluded to in curiously veiled language as "certain persons referred to in the course of discussions," about whom it was stated in the amalgamation document that "an undertaking has been given by Mr. Spencer that he himself and the officials of the new Union will use their best endeavours to secure employment for such of them as desire it, either at the colliery at which they were last employed, or if this proves impossible, elsewhere in the Nottinghamshire coalfield. The Nottinghamshire owners for their part undertake that they will give favourable con-sideration to any representations so made."

The understanding was that 350 men needed at Harworth Colliery to complete the complement of workers (the total number employed having been much reduced) would be taken on, the order of return to work being settled by drawing lots. On this the M.F.G.B. Executive called off the strike at Harworth Colliery. It had lasted over six months.

On the Thursday Stanley Baldwin, his task in this respect also fulfilled, resigned his premiership and was succeeded by Neville Chamberlain. The same day, by a five to one majority, the Conference passed the following resolution:

That this Conference ratifies the provisional terms negotiated by the Sub-Committee of the M.F.G.B. with the Nottinghamshire coalowners and the Nottingham and District Industrial Union, under the neutral Chairmanship of Mr. John Forster, and resolves that the notices in all districts, whether handed in collectively or by the individual workmen, be withdrawn.

Further, the officials be empowered to render every assistance in the application of the terms and take such steps as are necessary with the Nottinghamshire Miners' Association to give full effect to the amalgamation. (May 27, 1937.)

"So ended one of the most intriguing, difficult, and momentous disputes in which the Federation has ever been engaged. During the course of the dispute hard things were said on both sides, but in the end both parties showed a spirit of accommodation, which should be of the utmost assistance in laying the basis of goodwill and mutual respect in the Nottinghamshire coalfield in the future." (Report of Executive Committee, June 7, 1937.) In these two sentences the Federation leaders briefly summed up the events of the past seven months. Anxious that everything should calm down, they were sparing of words. Plenty of words, however, were being uttered in some of the coal-fields, especially in the area that had been the focus of the whole struggle. There, as events unfolded, the question was raised: was it really a case of "All's well that ends well"?

12.   HARSH PRISON SENTENCES

Work was resumed on May 31st at Harworth. But there was a sequel to Harworth which was to arouse intense feeling not only in the coal-fields but throughout the whole labour movement. Some four weeks later the case of the seventeen headed by Mick Kane, President of the Harworth branch of the Nottinghamshire Miners' Association and J. A. Wilson, Vice-President of the branch, who had been sent for trial on a charge of riot, came up at the Nottingham Assizes. Five of the seventeen were bound over; the remainder, eleven miners and one miner's wife, were sentenced by Mr. Justice Singleton on June 26th to imprisonment and hard labour for the following terms:

> Michael Kane: two years.
> G. A. Chandler ⎱fifteen months.
> J. H. Smith ⎰
> W. Carney: twelve months.
> G. Barker ⎫
> F. Jobson ⎪
> B. Murray ⎬ nine months.
> J. A. Wilson ⎪
> H. E. Risdale ⎪
> Mrs. Margaret Haymer ⎭
> T. Smith: six months.
> T. Richardson: four months.

These sentences caused alarm throughout the whole labour movement. They were amongst the most severe inflicted in this country for cases arising out of trade union activities for many a long year. Moreover, many Labour Members of Parliament had been suggesting in the House of Commons that the conduct of the police had been irregular and that blacklegs had provoked the tension at Harworth. Again, the judicial proceedings were in contrast to the atmosphere which the Prime Minister had appeared to generate in his speech and to the general feeling in connection with the settlement of "let bygones be bygones." There was immediate outspoken criticism. Emanuel Shinwell, M.P., made a speech in Nottingham only a few hours after the sentences describing them as "judicial fascism." The National Council for Civil Liberties in its quarterly journal made the following criticism about the severity of the sentences:

Although it was alleged that in the second part of the riot many people were frightened, there were in fact no cases of injury reported. Damage was done to property belonging to the Colliery Company, but no harm to persons.

Why, then, were the sentences so severe? Was it because of the previous record of the defendants? Of the twelve defendants sentenced to terms of imprisonment, only two had been previously convicted.

Was it, then, due to any particularly prominent part which they played in the riot? Only three out of the twelve defendants were themselves accused of indulging in violence. Michael Kane, who received a sentence of two years' imprisonment was not accused of being armed, of striking anyone, or of throwing anything. (Quarterly Journal, N.C.C.L., October 1937.)

The Annual Conference of the Mineworkers' Federation three weeks later demanded that the sentences be quashed. Tom Cape, M.P., in seconding the resolution of protest expressed his strong feelings that with the dispute "brought to such a happy end any judge in this land could pass sentences as cruel and as harsh as the one passed upon these Harworth people." The resolution was unanimous:

That this Conference of the Mineworkers' Federation of Great Britain protests against the unjust sentences imposed upon our Harworth comrades, and especially one defendant, who was a miner's wife. We call upon the Secretary of State for Home Affairs to remit the sentences passed at the last Notts Assizes. (July 19, 1937.)

The Federation Executive Committee had seen to the lodging of an appeal and had called for a further threepenny levy throughout the coal-fields to meet all the possible costs of the defence and of maintenance and aid to the families of the accused. When, however, the matter came up on July 28th in the Court of Appeal before Lord Chief Justice Hewart, Mr. Justice du Parcq and Mr. Justice Goddard, there was no mitigation of the sentences. D. N. Pritt, K.C., after recounting the facts of the case, argued first that Mr. Justice Singleton "should have severed the incidents at the colliery entrance from those later in the village." Secondly, he said:

The sentences were excessive. All the applicants were persons of good character and it was impossible to believe that they would ever have found themselves within the scope of criminal law if they had not had to pass through many months of acute industrial aggravation. (July 28, 1937.)

Instancing one sentence of nine months, Pritt said that it might be:

greater than that passed on a person guilty of mortal manslaughter or of one who had obtained £10,000 by fraud. Such a sentence must be regarded as completely disproportionate in a case in which there was no threat of civil war or some other serious element.

Counsel for the Crown was not called on to argue: and leave to appeal was not granted.

Thereafter the movement of protest spread not only amongst those most nearly affected but through all sections of the political, industrial and co-operative movement. Deputations of M.P.s went to the Home Secretary; the Miners' Federation as well as the N.M.A. repeatedly brought the matter up. Signatures poured into the offices of the National Council for Civil Liberties for its mass petition against the sentences. Presently these were joined by the General Council of the Trades Union Congress. Indeed a feature of the dispute was the close co-operation with the Miners' Federation by the General Council, which in its report to the 69th Trades Union Congress, held at Norwich,

September 6–10, 1937, recounted the story of the whole dispute and concluded, with a reference to those who had borne the brunt of the struggle:

The friendly atmosphere in which the dispute was finally settled has been marred by the harsh sentences imposed on the miners who were convicted of being implicated in the disturbance at Harworth on April 23rd.

From every section of the Trade Union Movement resentment has been expressed, and the General Council decided that in the event of the appeal which had been lodged being unsuccessful an immediate approach should be made to the Home Secretary.

The feeling roused was voiced by R. A. Bradfield of the Shop Assistants' Union who brought the matter up as the first item in the discussion of the General Council's Report, and proposed that if the General Council failed to get satisfaction when they met the Home Secretary, they should consider organising "a national day of demonstration." He recalled the Sacco and Vanzetti case in the United States ten years earlier, telling how the week before they were executed one of their legal advisers went to them and said, "We have prepared a petition with a million signatures, and we have delegations representing all the leading people in the country to wait upon the Government"; but that Sacco turned round and said, "You have done very well, my friend, but all your efforts are of no avail. There is only one thing that can save us, and that is a million marching feet." Bradfield drew the moral, saying:

I believe if the General Council are turned down when they meet the Home Secretary, they should organise a million marching feet in this country to protest against it. In that way you may well drive from office the Home Secretary whose cynical attitude has disgusted the whole working-class movement, and you may drive from social and public life the luminary of the legal bench who gave the sentences. (September 6, 1937.)

It was not till a year later, however, that the final release from prison took place. In the Report of the General Council to the 70th (Blackpool) Trades Union Congress, September 1938, it was stated that following representations made to the Home Secretary, parts of the sentences imposed on some of the miners implicated in the disturbances at

Harworth had been remitted. In their Report the General Council recorded that the Home Secretary would not see their deputation, asserting that he must maintain the principle that representations in regard to sentences passed by the Courts on individuals "should not be put forward by means of deputations." Consideration, however, had been given to the points put forward in the correspondence from the General Council, and they were one of the factors which influenced his decision to recommend the exercise of a measure of clemency in eight of the cases. The Home Secretary did not think that the time was then ripe (October 27, 1937) for him to give further consideration to the remaining cases, but "would not fail to do so at a later date." Three months after that day the announcement came that one third of the sentences would be remitted in the case of three of the four miners then in prison. On the ground that "it was contrary to practice to consider the remission of sentences until comparatively near their completion," Sir Samuel Hoare had no announcement to make regarding the President of the Harworth Branch, Mick Kane, who had been sentenced to two years. On June 15, 1938, however, it was announced that Kane would be released at the end of August 1938. It was two years after the dispute began, sixteen months after the incident in respect of which he had been charged, and just a year and a quarter after work had been resumed at Harworth.

The freedom of organisation of the miners in Nottinghamshire had been secured. But in the case of Mick Kane, words like those uttered to the Apostle Paul could have been applied: "At a heavy price obtained I this freedom."

TERMS FOR THE AMALGAMATION OF THE NOTTINGHAMSHIRE MINERS' ASSOCIATION AND THE NOTTINGHAMSHIRE AND DISTRICT MINERS' INDUSTRIAL UNION, AS AGREED ON MAY 26, 1937

(1) The two Unions above referred to shall be amalgamated and shall thereafter be known as the Nottinghamshire and District Miners' Federated Union.

(2) The amalgamation shall be effective from September 1, 1937.

(3) The officials of the Nottinghamshire and District Miners' Federated Union shall be:

President	Mr. G. A. SPENCER.
General Secretary	Mr. VAL COLEMAN.
Financial Secretary and Treasurer	Mr. H. W. COOPER.
Agents	Mr. W. BAYLISS, and one other who shall be representative of the Nottinghamshire and District Miners' Industrial Union.

The vacant office of Agent above referred to shall be filled by Mr. Hancock, should he so desire, but should Mr. Hancock decline the appointment, then the vacancy shall be filled by the appointment of another person representative of the Nottinghamshire and District Miners' Industrial Union, elected in accordance with the existing rules of that Union, the election to take place not later than August 1 next.

(4) The appointment of the officials above referred to shall be upon a permanent basis, and they shall be subject to removal only for misconduct in the course of their employment. Such officials shall be entitled to equal remuneration and conditions, upon the basis already mutually agreed between the parties.

Each of such officials will be entitled should he so desire to an individual service agreement embodying *inter alia* the terms above set out, such an agreement to be prepared by Mr. John Forster.

(5) Mr. Spencer shall represent Nottinghamshire on the Executive of the Mineworkers' Federation of Great Britain for a period of one year. Thereafter, such representatives as Nottinghamshire shall be entitled to send to the said Federation shall be elected under the ordinary procedure as fixed by the rules of the Nottinghamshire and District Miners' Federated Union.

(6)   For two years from the date of amalgamation the appointment of representatives of local committees, of delegates, and of other local officials, shall be in equal proportions (that is to say, as to one half to be appointed by the Nottinghamshire Miners' Association, and as to the other half by the Nottinghamshire and District Miners' Industrial Union) from amongst men employed in and about the colliery. Subject nevertheless to certain persons referred to in the course of discussions between the parties being first offered employment.

In the case of the persons to whom reference is made above, an undertaking has been given by Mr. Spencer that he himself and the officials of the new Union will use their best endeavours to secure employment for such of them as desire it, either at the colliery at which they were last employed, or if this proves impossible, elsewhere in the Nottinghamshire coalfield. The Nottinghamshire owners for their part undertake that they will give favourable consideration to any representations so made.

It is suggested that the selection of representatives of local committees of delegates, and of other local officials, should be effected by draw in the branches concerned.

(7)   It is understood that the rules of the Nottinghamshire and District Miners' Federated Union shall conform to the rules and constitution of the Mineworkers' Federation of Great Britain and shall be in strict accordance also with the provisions of the Trade Disputes and Trade Unions Act, 1927.

(8)   The Accountant at present appointed to the Nottinghamshire and District Miners' Industrial Union for the wages ascertainments is to be retained by the Nottinghamshire and District Miners' Federated Union.

(9)   The Nottinghamshire and District Miners' Industrial Union Offices shall be retained until satisfactory office accommodation for the Nottinghamshire and District Miners' Federated Union has been provided.

(10)   Mr. John Forster, the neutral Chairman, who presided over the negotiations from which the above terms have resulted, shall be present with officials of the Mineworkers' Federation of Great Britain, the Nottinghamshire Miners' Association and the Nottinghamshire and District Miners' Industrial Union at the taking over of the Funds of the Nottinghamshire Miners' Association and the Nottinghamshire and District Miners' Industrial Union by the new union, and any question then arising shall be referred to him for determination forthwith, and his decision thereon shall be accepted as final.

Further, should any difference arise as to the application of any of the terms herein contained, such difference shall be referred to Mr. Forster, whose decision shall be final.

(11)   Providing the foregoing terms are ratified, then in so far

as there may be any matters still requiring discussion in connection with the new wages agreement to be effected with the Nottinghamshire Colliery Owners, Nottinghamshire Miners' Association officials shall be competent, together with officials of the Nottinghamshire and District Miners' Industrial Union, to consider and deal with such matters.

Provided, nevertheless, that December 31, 1943, shall be accepted without further question as the date to which such new agreement shall continue.

CHAPTER VI

THE STRUGGLE AGAINST FASCISM AND WAR

1. THE ASTURIAS MINERS OF SPAIN

AMID these happenings at Harworth which in their ramifications had nearly brought a national strike in the coal-fields of Britain, there had been developing outside Britain another struggle in which the Mineworkers' Federation was deeply concerned. The concern had begun years earlier. In 1937 the Spanish Civil War was approaching the climax of its agony, but for years it had been preceded by many strike struggles and revolts amongst the Spaniards, especially amongst the Spanish miners. The record of this begins early in 1935 when the heading "Spanish Miners" appears for the first time in the Executive minutes. The Secretary reported that he had received an appeal for financial assistance, and had sent this to the Districts. "The miners," it was stated, "have borne the brunt of the recent troubles in Spain, and many of them with their families are in sore distress." Money had already been received from Lancashire and North Wales. The action of the Secretary was confirmed and it was agreed:

That the M.F.G.B. advance £250 to meet urgent needs, such sum to be recovered from the district grants made for the same purpose. (February 28, 1935.)

This was the first minute[1] upon a country whose affairs were to be hotly debated in other countries of Europe in the years to follow.

The Spanish monarchy had ended in 1931 with the abdication of Alphonso XIII. He had been the husband of Ena of Battenberg, a granddaughter of Queen Victoria: and since his earliest infancy had been King of Spain. His

[1] Eleven months later a further grant of £250, as a preliminary, is recorded in an Executive Committee minute of January 23, 1936.

country's single century of grandeur from the voyage of Columbus in 1492 to the defeat of the Armada in 1588 had been marked by vast conquests, which brought it all the gold of the Indies, all the wealth of the Caribbean and of North and South America—only to lose it to Bristol adventurers and colonisers and pilgrim fathers from all the lands of Northern Europe in the seventeenth and eighteenth centuries; and then to rebellious colonists under the guns of the British Navy in the early nineteenth century; and finally, four score years later, to the guns of the United States Navy in the Spanish-American war of 1898 which wrenched Cuba and the Philippines from the Spanish grasp.

It was wellnigh a third of a century afterwards that the first effective breach was made in the old bastion of privilege. The downfall of the semi-Fascist minister Primo de Rivera (1923 to 1930) was followed by the concession of municipal elections. These returned an overwhelmingly republican majority on April 14, 1931. King Alphonso XIII abdicated and fled from the country.

The Republic had to plough a heavy furrow. Its opponents were irreconcilable. Within fifteen months on August 10, 1932, there was a monarchist rising. Worse was to come. The successive ministries that followed the General Election of December 1933, being more and more disinclined to allow democracy free play, took a series of repressive measures against the new life that was springing up in the towns and villages of semi-feudal Spain once the incubus of the monarchy had been shifted. Against these repressive measures the miners of the Asturias, the range of mountains in the north-west of Spain fringing the southern sweep of the Bay of Biscay, rose in rebellion in October 1934. It was suppressed with extraordinary brutality by the corps of officers who brought over Moorish mercenaries to hunt down the miners and their leader Gonzalez Peña.[1] It was to this "heroic struggle" (as Ebby Edwards wrote eighteen months

[1] A few months before the Asturias rising, Peña's latest report to the Miners' International Federation ended with these significant words:

"The future of the Spanish miners depends upon the transformation of the capitalistic regime into a new one, which cannot be any other than that of the socialisation of the means of production.

"We must act at the necessary moment if we do not wish to perish."

later in his international Report, adding "No section of workers ever made a braver fight") and to the consequences of its bloody suppression that the British miners had given their support. But it was only to be the prelude to greater events.

2. FASCISM AND SPAIN

The international situation, dominated in the years from 1933 onwards by the rise of Fascism in Germany, began in the course of 1935 to be further troubled by signs of approaching war such as the imposition of conscription by Hitler and his seizure of the demilitarised Rhineland and then by Mussolini's unprovoked assault upon Ethiopia. In Spain, however, the popular forces in 1935 came together in a campaign for democracy called the Popular Front (*Frente Popolar*) which won an overwhelming victory at the General Election of February 16, 1936. Under Manuel Azaña a Government "with a Liberal tone" was formed. When Azaña three months later, on the motion of the moderate Socialist leader Indalecio Prieto, had been elected President, Quiroga on May 13th formed a Government that was "still exclusively Republican (i.e. non-Socialist)," but under which trade unions as well as peasants' associations and workers' political parties could at last begin to function freely.

But the reactionaries would not submit to the verdict of the polls. A conspiracy of Spanish Generals, hatched in Berlin, resulted in widespread and concerted mutiny of the officer caste against the elected Government of their country. A junta of four Generals (of whom General Franco alone survived) in mid-July 1936 plunged Spain into civil war. They had the backing of the monarchists, the absentee landlords and of the Church hierarchy.

From the beginning the Mineworkers' Federation of Great Britain strongly supported the legitimate Government of the Spanish Republic; opposed the Fascists and particularly the sending of aid by Hitler and Mussolini to the rebel Generals in Spain. At the 32nd Miners' International Congress, held in Prague on August 3–6, 1936, Will Lawther on behalf of the British delegation moved a resolution of "most emphatic protest against fascism."

The British miners, he said, "as the largest single industrial organisation in the International" offered their support in every possible way to those "who are battling so strenuously against tremendous odds in combating fascism in their respective countries," and from whom they had heard of the methods adopted in order "to prevent trade unionists having an opportunity of improving the conditions of the workers." Then Lawther turned to Spain, "the latest stage of the development of fascism," on which a brief clause had been hastily added at the end of the resolution, and said:

In Britain it is denied by the Foreign Secretary that any help was given to the fascists in Spain. We know that overtures were made in diplomatic circles by the Ambassador from Germany and an ex-Cabinet Minister who happened to be a wealthy coalowner in Britain. There is an international link between the ruling classes, and we likewise, as a working-class movement, should forge an international link. (August 3, 1936.)

The resolution, supported by delegates from Poland, Czechoslovakia, Roumania and France and supported also by Arthur Horner (who, however, criticised it as being "too defensive in its composition" when a vigorous working-class offensive was needed), ran to some length. It began with a paragraph of protest against Fascism, recorded its sympathy with those thousands "who have fallen victims to fascist brutality," reaffirmed the previous declarations of resistance and renewed pledges to maintain "human freedom." It ended with a further protest against the help the Fascist countries "are rendering against the legal Government of Spain."

3. THE INTERNATIONAL BRIGADE

The Miners' International Conference had discussed the onset of Fascist rebellion in Spain some two weeks after the Generals had led their garrisons and other forces to mutiny. There had been in the Spanish Army of 130,000 some 20,000 officers including no less than 866 Generals or one General to every 150 soldiers. It was indeed a privileged military caste. Out of 120 Generals on active service only nine remained faithful to their oath of allegiance to the Republic. In these circumstances it was only the resistance of the working class organised in their trade unions and hastily given arms by the Government of Giral, a Liberal (whom President Azaña had put at the helm on July 18, 1936), that prevented the concerted mutiny from overthrowing the lawfully elected Parliament and the Government thereto responsible: but prevent it they did.

The effect of this outrage by the militarist and Fascist conspirators was to rouse strong sentiments for support of the Republic in both the east and west of Europe. In Britain it was not only the mine-workers and the other trade unionists but to a remarkable degree the rank and file of political parties who reacted in this way. Young people who would have been expected to become Conservatives or Liberals experienced a revulsion of feeling at the spectacle of the open overthrow of all the canons of political behaviour. They not only sympathised with the legitimate Government of Spain and expressed their detestation of Fascism in words. They sought to uphold their outlook by deeds. They joined the International Brigade, whose first members had helped in the early autumn to stem the onrush of the Fascists to capture Madrid. In the battle of Jarama and at Brunete in 1937, at Teruel and on the Ebro in 1938, and on many another battlefield of Spain, the members of the International Brigade were to play a notable part.

In the ranks of those who made up the British Battalion of the International Brigade there were very many mine-workers. Of these, some died in battle; some mouldered in Franco's prisons; and some came back, having proved themselves worthy in the fight for freedom, to take up again their work in the coal-fields. This extraordinary upsurge of popular feeling was made more poignant and more acute in the discussions within Federation Conferences as it was revealed how many relatives or friends of delegates were facing fearful odds in an armed struggle against Fascism. Right up to the normal age-limit for soldiering and right up to the end of the struggle there were mine-workers volunteering to go and offer up their lives to stop the German and Italian and other Fascists in Spain. As the International Brigade grew in numbers, and included very many who had suffered under a Fascist or semi-Fascist terror in various countries of Europe, the number also grew of volunteers from Britain who eluded the vigilance of the Foreign Office which had taken legal steps (under the Foreign Enlistment Act) to hinder volunteers going to aid the Spanish Republic. Amongst these an overwhelming proportion were working-class lads who for the most part, being members of trade unions, brought their experience of solidarity and discipline. Amongst the mine-workers, some of those who volunteered threw up posts in Britain to which they had been elected as officers of their union. Such men as these included, from one District alone, Will Paynter, an elected member of the South Wales Executive Council and at that time also a full-time officer on special duties at Taff Merthyr; and Jack Jones, then the elected checkweigher at Crosskeys. More was to be heard of them later, Jack Jones becoming Secretary of the Rhondda while Will Paynter was to become President of the South Wales Miners' Federation first, and then Secretary of the national organisation. Paynter had been given the status of a special representative of the South Wales Miners' Federation in Spain and occupied throughout a great part of 1937 a highly responsible post in the British Battalion of the International Brigade.

4. "NON-INTERVENTION"

By the later months of 1936 a grim and terrible civil war was raging within Spain: and, on the international field, a struggle was going on between reactionary and progressive forces over the fate of the Spaniards. The Federation members were deeply concerned in both aspects of the overall struggle. Hitler and Mussolini (in breach of international law) were sending in arms, troops and an air force to aid the rebels, while the request of the legitimate Spanish Government for supplies (in accord with international law) was refused by the British Government.

It was a peculiar situation. The rules of international law in the case of civil war were clear enough—as British Governments know to their cost.[1] Arms if needed could be obtained by legitimate Governments, but not by rebels. Consequently, when the International Federation of Trade Unions and the Labour and Socialist International, meeting in Brussels on July 28th, issued a manifesto for "vital solidarity" towards "our Spanish brethren," they enjoined on their affiliated sections the duty of seeing to it that "in accordance with the existing rules of international law, the legal Government of Spain" be allowed by every democratic State to obtain "the necessary means for its own defence." At this time the Government of the French Republic was headed by the Socialist leader Léon Blum, following on the success of the People's Front (*Front Populaire*) in the General Elections of May 1936. Blum wished to allow arms to go to the Government of the Spanish Republic. Within a fortnight of the officers' mutiny on July 19th, the Neville Chamberlain Cabinet brought pressure to bear on the French not to perform their duty in international law and made it clear that if Fascist Germany on this occasion were to attack France, Britain would not come to the aid of France as stipulated by the ten-year-old Locarno Treaty. To this pressure the French Government capitulated: and presently it initiated proposals for an agreement among the European Powers to withhold munitions of war from Spain. Thereupon on August 18th Foreign Secretary Anthony Eden informed a deputation from the T.U.C. and the Labour Party that he would support "the French Government's proposals."

Thus originated a non-intervention Committee on which there sat with the British the representatives of France, the Soviet Union, Germany and Italy. The U.S.S.R., after two months of intervention by the Fascist Powers, made it clear that the U.S.S.R. would not be bound by decisions of a Committee which were not being carried out.

---

[1] In the American Civil War of 1861–65 the British Government, however sympathetic they might be to the slave-holding Southern States, knew that these must not be allowed supplies of the kind that could be freely purchased by the elected Government of President Abraham Lincoln: and their famous infraction of "the rule of law" (the affair of the armed raider *Alabama*, built and secretly equipped on the Mersey) cost the British taxpayers a very heavy sum in the compensation subsequently adjudicated by international arbitration.

The Soviet government, unwilling to bear any longer the responsibilities for the clearly unjust situation created in regard to the legitimate Spanish government and Spanish people, is compelled now to declare it cannot consider itself bound by the agreement for non-intervention to any greater extent than any of the remaining participants of the agreement. (Note to Lord Plymouth, October 21, 1936.)

The Soviet attitude had been made clear by Stalin's statement that the struggle in Spain "was not the private affair of the Spaniards but the common cause of all advanced and progressive mankind."

The upshot of it all was that a special full Conference of the National Council of Labour (including all Labour Members of Parliament) on August 28th, in full knowledge of "the right of the Spanish Government by rules of international law to obtain arms for its defence," decided nevertheless to fall into line with the Government of France and the Neville Chamberlain Cabinet. But the Conference expressed its regret that it should have been thought expedient, on the ground of the dangers of war inherent in this situation, to conclude agreements among the European Powers laying an embargo upon the supply of arms and munitions of war to Spain, by which the rebel forces and the democratically elected and recognised Government of Spain were placed on the same footing. This was presently to be called "the policy of non-intervention." The British Labour attitude on this was to lead to difficulties within the Labour and Socialist International: and to much fierce criticism at home. The lines of policy thus settled were carried with strongly worded provisos for vigilance to prevent the proposed measures being used "to injure the Spanish Government" through the Trades Union Congress in September 1936 and the Labour Party Conference in October. It was largely the eloquence of Ernest Bevin, Chairman of the Trades Union Congress, who conjured up the picture of European war, that carried the motion on October 5th: and the delegates were unpleasantly shocked when two days later the fraternal delegate of the Spanish Socialist Party denounced Eden's Non-Intervention Pact as "the most powerful of interventions against the Government of Spain." The M.F.G.B. Executive Committee, as we shall see, were in favour of giving the Spanish Republic its full rights in international law. But several of the largest trade unions had subscribed to the Eden policy of an embargo on arms for Spain: and in the T.U.C. General Council the same opinion prevailed. It was expressed at international conferences and elsewhere by the T.U.C. Chairman and Secretary as spokesmen of the General Council on which there sat as M.F.G.B. representatives Joseph Jones and Ebby Edwards. The M.F.G.B. Executive Committee, for their part, uttered no public criticism. But there was a deep division within the Labour movement as a whole on this issue and much questioning over the role of the trade unions.

Trade unions are not political parties. They may have political items in their objects. They may collectively be affiliated to and supply the funds of political parties. And at particular times on great issues they may behave somewhat like political parties. But they have other functions as well; and while their political functions and their other functions may usually run in harness, at times a difference can arise. In fact there is a latent antithesis. The day-to-day needs of their members are met by the trade unions not always through the method of industrial dispute, but most often by national or local agreements involving a large degree of compromise. At the same time as the unions have grown more important, especially with the development of the Welfare State initiated by Lloyd George and Churchill in 1906 to 1914, there has developed more and more an intermingling of trade union functions and State structure. This is shown by over fifty years of legislation. What in the nineteenth century amounted to membership of a Royal Commission or an appointment as Justice of the Peace, has now become an intricate, far-reaching and continuous system of co-operation not only in research but in the preparation of legislation and the problems of administration. This is true of the British unions and is broadly true of most other countries.

This tendency, setting in from the last third of the nineteenth century (for example from the time when Disraeli appointed Alexander McDonald a member of a Royal Commission), was deflected in the twenty-five years from 1885 onwards by the effect of Socialism, of the court-ship and eventual wedding of Socialism and trade unionism in the Labour Party, and by the still later adoption of Socialist aims in the rule-books of many of the trade unions.

The tendency, however, towards closer relations with the employers or with the State remained. Occasionally it became dominant, as in the Mond–Turner agreements of 1927 onwards. On the other hand, it could become entirely dominant as in the American Federation of Labour, which was hostile to Socialism and openly accepted the American capitalist society of "free enterprise" within which it operated. This A.F. of L. tendency, as it may be called, has always been present inside the British trade union movement, and when there has been particularly lengthy domination of the scene by a Liberal or Conservative Government there has been an imperceptible shift towards a *modus vivendi* with the powers that be. It is this and not the standpoint of particular individuals that provides the main explanation for what the Mineworkers' Federation regarded as a disastrous policy.

Eden's policy, then, was not opposed by the National Council of Labour. But the miners were opposed: and in December 1936 the Executive Committee passed the following resolution:

That this Executive Committee call upon the National Council of Labour to consider what effective steps can be taken so as to enforce the National Government to raise the arms embargo and allow the Spanish people who are defending democracy against Fascism to purchase the necessary war material and arms. (December 11, 1936.)

By the end of December they received a reply from the National Council of Labour explaining "the steps it had taken in regard to the Spanish situation." The letter was noted. The miners were not satisfied. Events in Spain and in the rest of Europe were soon to make them still less satisfied. Besides, it was known that various prominent figures inside the Labour movement, including Clement Attlee who a year earlier had succeeded George Lansbury as leader of the Labour Party, were strongly opposed to the Conservative Foreign Office policy.

What would their fellow-miners, who with them had subscribed to the resolution at Prague against Fascism, say to this situation? The answer was to be given the next month in Brussels, where the Executive Committee of the Miners' International Federation passed the following resolution:

This meeting of the Miners' International Committee pays its sincere tribute to the noble courage and heroic sacrifice of the defenders of Madrid.

Along with the Spanish people behind the Government it notes with pride their colleagues of the Spanish Miners' organisation who at this very moment are in the front line of opposition, defending with inadequate means the onrush of Franco and his Moors assisted by the military and air forces of Hitler and Mussolini.

The resolution ended by urging all the miners' unions to give "their maximum support to the workers of Spain until victory is assured over fascism." (January 1937.)

5. "NON-INTERVENTION" DENOUNCED

With the coming of the new year after six months of war, it seemed as though Spain was divided by a line running down the middle from north to south. East of that line were some of the cities with modern industry and developed working class; west were the more feudal portions, and west, too, lay the border of Portugal whose Fascist ruler, Salazar, feared the contagion of liberal or democratic notions not to speak of Socialist or Communist ideas. To this picture there was, however, one main exception: the Asturias on the Bay of Biscay and the adjoining Basque province where the Conservative Nationalists who, from their historic centre in the old town of Guernica, had vainly demanded home rule were now firm supporters of the Republican Front.

It looked as though this state of affairs represented an almost semi-permanent division of Spain, but suddenly, on February 7, 1937, the great city of Malaga, on the Mediterranean side of the south of Spain, was taken by the

Franco forces: and a year later in the book written by Sir Peter Chalmers Mitchell, entitled *My House in Malaga*, British readers were able to get a sensitively written eye-witness account by an honoured British scientist of the Fascist occupation of a great Spanish city. The fall of Malaga was a great shock both to public opinion in this country and in Spain. Its fall was only possible through treachery and lack of vigilance. The result was a complete overhaul of the Republican forces, the institution of conscription, the building of a modern army inside Spain, while it brought to the British miners and other supporters of the cause of the Spaniards a renewed determination to increase the support they were giving in men and materials and to remove the hindrances due to acceptance of "non-intervention."

Consequently the M.F.G.B. Executive Committee on March 24, 1937, sent on a resolution originating from South Wales calling for a special Trades Union Congress. A month later they considered a letter from the T.U.C. General Council informing them of what had been done "to help the Spanish workers and Government" and giving the assurance that "the situation in Spain was receiving constant attention."

The miners, however, had reason to think that the General Council's attitude had not been so greatly altered as to yield the desired practical results. So when it came to the preparation, at their next meeting in May, for the Federation Annual Conference (to be held at Blackpool on Monday, July 19, 1937, and following days) the M.F.G.B. leaders decided for a resolution on Spain.

In the meantime British ships trading with Spain had been sunk, captured or damaged by the Fascist forces. This in international law was undoubtedly piracy. The Neville Chamberlain Government, having abandoned the strict rule of international law, now found itself placing restraints upon the normal duties of the British Navy to pursue and exterminate pirates. The result was that where these outrages took place, some of them by Italian submarines, British war vessels were in the vicinity but did nothing. In Britain where for generations a pride in the Navy had been inculcated, there was now a widespread revulsion of feeling. This found expression in the resolution which, carried unanimously at the Blackpool Annual Conference,[1] ran thus:

This Conference, representing 600,000 British colliery workers, expresses its admiration of the heroic fight now being fought by the Spanish people in defence of democratic government against the attacks of Spanish rebels supported by the Fascist Governments of Italy, Germany and Portugal.

It views with dismay the operation of the policy of non-intervention which, while it binds the democratic peoples of Europe to refuse assistance to the democrats of Spain, is openly flouted by the Fascist States in support of the rebels, and prolongs a war, with all its human suffering, which must ultimately result in the victory of democratic forces.

The Conference views with disgust the failure of the British Navy to protect British seamen and British shipping carrying on legitimate trade with the people of Spain, against the attacks of Spanish pirates, who are allowed with impunity and in the presence of British warships, to capture unarmed British merchant ships in conformity with the policy of the British Government.

We realise that the workers of Spain are fighting the cause of the workers of all countries and we call upon all workers to render every assistance possible to our Spanish comrades until victory has been achieved. (July 22, 1937.)

Meantime, a month before the M.F.G.B. resolution was passed, there had been a significant change in the attitude of the national Labour bodies. This came about following on an appeal from the Spanish Socialist Party, the Spanish Communist Party and the Spanish Trades Union Congress (U.G.T.) (the direct occasion of which was the bombardment of Almeria by Germany) to three Internationals. These were the International Federation of Trade Unions (I.F.T.U.); the Labour and Socialist International (L.S.I.); and the Communist International (C.I.), whose Secretary at this time was George Dimitrov, famous for his defiance of the Nazis in open court when falsely accused of the burning of the Reichstag in 1933. On June 3rd Dimitrov sent a telegram to Louis de Brouckère, Chairman of the Executive Committee of the Labour and Socialist International,

[1] Other resolutions (apart from those given in earlier chapters) were on the subjects of safety in mines, workmen's compensation, condemnation of overtime, unemployment regulations, holidays with pay, increase in old age pensions, oil from coal, shorter hours and "the replacement of the present Government by a Labour Government, whereby the policy of collective security can really defend peace against Fascist war-makers."

proposing that a "joint contact committee" of the three Internationals be set up "to achieve international unity of action against the military intervention of Germany and Italy in Spain."

de Brouckère sent a friendly answer to Dimitrov's telegram, but he found it impossible to set up a joint committee because opposition in the L.S.I. (mainly from the British delegation) was too great. But delegates met, however, at Annemasse on June 21st, de Brouckère and Adler (Secretary, L.S.I.) representing the L.S.I., and it was found that the policies of the two Internationals with regard to Spain were the same, both demanding the lifting of the blockade, the restoration of international law which had been violated, and the application of the Covenant of the League of Nations. It was agreed that a new Conference should take place shortly to consider concrete measures for united action.

On the day before the Annemasse meeting, de Brouckère, Adler and Roosbrock (Treasurer of the L.S.I.) announced their resignations from their posts because of their profound disagreement with the attitude of some sections of their International on the question of a campaign to aid Spain and of international unified co-operation against Fascism. These resignations were dated to take effect after the joint meeting of the L.S.I. and I.F.T.U. to discuss Spanish policy held in Paris on June 24th, but were not actually carried out: for in the meantime the British section of the International had, apparently, come round to the majority view. At any rate on June 23rd the Joint Council of the T.U.C. and the Executives of the Labour Party and the Parliamentary Labour Parties decided to support:

Immediate action by the League of Nations to end acts of aggression against the Spanish Government.
Restoration without delay of the right of the Spanish Government to buy arms.

By the midsummer of 1937, the number of troops and the amount of munitions sent to the rebel Franco from the Fascist Powers far exceeded the help given by the Labour movement and by all other sources to the Government of

I   *The Miners*

the Spanish Republic.[1] The Trades Union Congress met at Norwich in the first week of September, when General Secretary Citrine moved a resolution which had a very different meaning from that passed a year earlier at the Plymouth T.U.C. of 1936. The M.F.G.B. delegation put forward Arthur Horner to speak in support. Horner, who had just returned from the battlefield in Spain, was able to give a harrowing picture of the needs of the Spaniards. He said:

Non-Intervention is a farce. It has always been a farce. It was the cover for intervention to assist Franco, and the instrument to sabotage the granting of assistance to the Spanish Government. It is well that Non-Intervention has gone. The farce has been played out.

The results of this tragic error in our policy have not yet all been counted. Today we stand declaring what we expect the League of Nations to do. We state what we expect our Government to do. Our General Secretary said, and I agree with him, that Italy and Germany are operating a very carefully calculated policy. They are not accidentally being moved by a kind of instinct. The policy is governed by their class interests. They are fighting a class war on the soil of Spain. (Tuesday, September 7, 1937.)

Then Horner concluded with a warning that there would be "another grave error" made in that Trades Union Congress, "unless," he said:

we appreciate that just as Franco is prepared to betray his country in the interests of his class, so there are in this country elements prepared to betray the interests of Britain if the choice is betrayal of their class interests or the interests of their country.

In its resolution, the Congress deplored the fact that the legal Government of Spain was still denied the right to purchase arms necessary for its defence: declared its complete solidarity with the Spanish Government in its appeal to the League of Nations, and also declared that it was the duty of the Council of the League to examine the problem

[1] Nine months later, according to the International Committee of Co-ordination and Information for Aid to Republican Spain (*Information Service* of March 1, 1938), the army of Franco was swollen to 450,000 soldiers of whom 237,000, or over half, were "foreigners," namely 160,000 Italians, 20,000 Germans (mainly airmen and technicians) and 50,000 highly-paid Moors. In the second week of March 1937, there had already been a very considerable number of Italians, who were then put to flight at the battle of Guadalajara. The total numbers of the International Brigade after heavy casualties stood at 10,000 by the late autumn of 1938.

in all its aspects and to propose measures, including the withdrawal of foreign troops from Spain, which would effectively safeguard the peace of nations and enable the Spanish people to recover their political independence.

The Norwich Trades Union Congress had been held in an atmosphere that was tense and brooding. It was only a little over four months since the Basque town of Guernica (April 26th) had been almost razed to the ground by flights of German bombers demonstrating how easily and effectively the developed Nazi weapons could take the lives of men, women and children. The horror of it (to be indelibly recorded for ever in the famous mural by Picasso) was still vividly in the minds of the delegates.

In the latter part of that year 1937 the positions on each side became more clear. Franco, after the sudden death of General Mola, was revealed more clearly than before as a mere instrument of Italian and German Fascism. On the other hand, the reorganised army of the Republic was able with the help of the International Brigade—whose No. 1 company (British) was to be called the Attlee Company—to develop military offensives. Brunete, near Madrid, was re-taken on July 1st, and Belchite, in the province of Aragon, was re-taken by the Republic on September 3rd. On October 1st the elected Spanish Parliament met once more in Valencia. It confirmed the acts and policy of the Government of the Liberal Republican, Dr. Juan Negrin, who had been appointed Premier by President Azaña in May and who was to continue as Premier until his death in exile. The Ministry of Defence remained in the hands of Prieto. At the same time there was a re-election of the Executive Committee of the Spanish Trades Union Congress; these elections brought forward to a leading position Peña, "leader of the Asturias miners in the October 1934 revolt, but who was nevertheless a supporter of the moderate opportunist socialism associated with Don Indalecio Prieto." (*Annual Register*, 1937.)

The renewed strength and spirit of the Republican armies was to be further shown. But the weight of armament came nothing near the amount regularly and copiously furnished by the Fascist Powers to the rebel Generals and their mercenaries. Moreover, the coasts of Spain began to be blockaded. The need of the Spanish people and of their army and of the International Brigade was growing more acute.

6. EXTRAORDINARY MEASURES DEMANDED

The steps taken, outside the arena of Spain, in the struggle against Fascism by the national labour bodies (made up partly of M.F.G.B. representatives) were set out later by Ebby Edwards in summary form in a kind of diary of events. The first step was a joint meeting of the Executive of the International Federation of Trade Unions and the Bureau of the Labour and Socialist International at Paris. This demanded that the League of Nations should, as a first step, take measures to:

(1) Suppress piracy in the Mediterranean, and secure the effective establishment of free navigation for all Flags.
(2) Secure the withdrawal of the Armies sent to Spain by Fascist Powers.
(3) Secure the restoration of the right of the Spanish Government to purchase arms. (September 13–16, 1937.)

Messrs. Citrine and Jouhaux, for the I.F.T.U., and de Brouckère and Longuet, for the L.S.I., were deputed to go to Geneva, where the Council and Assembly of the League were in Session, to communicate the views of the Internationals to the representatives of "the democratic governments" (Great Britain, France and Spain). A deputation on September 24, 1937, to the Foreign Secretary from the National Council of Labour submitted the Paris resolution of September 13th–16th, and urged upon him the restoration of international rights to the Spanish Government, the re-opening of the Spanish frontier, and an intimation by the British Government to the French Government of support in this action.

The Labour Party Conference held at Bournemouth on October 4–9, 1937, instructed the National Executive to launch a nation-wide campaign to compel the Government to abandon "non-intervention" and to restore to the Spanish Government the right to purchase arms.

A fortnight later, the M.F.G.B. Committee had as a

whole volunteered, if necessary, to go to Gijon to see what help they could give. But Gijon was cut off before the Committee had an opportunity to get there. After the fall of Gijon, a joint statement by the I.F.T.U. and the L.S.I. "energetically protested against the participation of fascist powers in the rebel success," and called upon its affiliated organisations to press their Governments for shipping to evacuate the civilian population.

A Spanish Campaign Committee formed on October 27, 1937, by the Labour Party soon set afoot plans for national demonstrations and local meetings in support of the Conference demands. At the beginning of the next month an appeal was issued by the Labour Party for a "Milk for Spain Fund," the Co-operative retail machinery being made available for the sale of tokens; and in this appeal they vigorously asserted the rights of the Spanish Government and emphasised the need for immediate assistance.

After the resignation on February 20th of Foreign Secretary Anthony Eden, and the shift in British Foreign Policy, a joint meeting of the Trades Union Congress General Council, the Labour Party Executive Committee, and the Parliamentary Labour Party Executive Committee adopted (on February 23, 1938) a manifesto. This stated in unequivocal terms the Labour movement's support for international law, as represented by the League of Nations, and for Collective Security, and denounced "the Government's capitulation in the face of the Dictators." No reliance, it stated, could be placed on Italy's verbal promise for the withdrawal of troops from Spain, and by their "sacrifice and betrayal of the Spanish people the British Government had violated the conscience of the nation." It called upon public opinion to make its condemnation of the Government's "weakness and cowardice" felt.

During the winter of 1937-38 the situation both in Spain and internationally grew worse. The M.F.G.B. Executive Committee therefore submitted to the T.U.C. General Council a resolution which declared:

We protest against the proposal that this country shall guarantee financial credits to Italy and Germany which will be used to further the subjugation of Spain and other democratic countries, and we urge upon the General Council of the T.U.C. to call an immediate Special Conference of Trade Unions and Allied Bodies to take such action as may be necessary to prevent this country being subjected to the blackmail of the Dictators as proposed by the present Government. (March 10, 1938.)

The reply of the General Secretary of the Trades Union Congress General Council after this resolution had been considered by them reads:

April 1, 1938.

The General Council fully appreciate the dangers inherent in the present International situation, and the general feeling of anxiety in regard to recent developments which your Union shares. You will be aware that the situation has been constantly under review, both separately and jointly by the General Council, the Labour Party Executive and the Executive of the Parliamentary Labour Party, and the most careful attention has been and will continue to be given to it.

The policy of the whole Labour Movement in respect to the conflict in Spain and the International situation generally has been clearly defined at the Norwich Trades Union Congress and at the Bournemouth Conference of the Labour Party. Since that time the developments which have arisen have been the subject of repeated declarations by the Movement, both nationally and internationally. It is safe to say that no phase of the question has been left out of consideration, and no step open to Labour to further its opposition to Fascist aggression has been left unconsidered.

The General Council are of the opinion that in these circumstances a Special Conference as proposed by your Organisation would not be of any material help to enable the General Council, in co-operation with the Labour Party and the Parliamentary Labour Party, to fulfil its responsibilities to the Movement as a whole.

It is understood that the Labour Party Executive has reached a similar conclusion in respect of the requests which have been made to it for the holding of a National Conference.

Yours sincerely,
WALTER M. CITRINE,
General Secretary.

Entirely unimpressed by this measured answer from the T.U.C. General Council, the M.F.G.B. Executive Committee took the decision to call on April 28th a Special Conference of their constituent unions. When the delegates assembled, they heard from their General Secretary (in much more detail than is given here) a chronicle of activities inside and outside Parliament. After giving this concise summary of "what has been done by the British Labour Movement, the Trades Union Movement, the Political Movement in the House of Commons," Ebby Edwards gave some account of meetings with the Prime Minister and other members of the Government. Of particular interest was the meeting with Lord Halifax on April 6, 1938.

At the meeting Citrine had informed Lord Halifax "that there was a feeling in the whole country that the Prime Minister, and especially Halifax himself, was a believer in the Fascist philosophy," and Lord Halifax had rejected this impeachment and had said of Fascist philosophy that "it would be hell."

On the complaint of the deputation about the terms of a proposed agreement with Fascist Italy, Edwards, listening to Halifax's reply, reported that:

It appeared quite evident, whilst they had not reached the stage of publication of an Italian Agreement, they had initialled the Agreement on the very basis of a fascist victory.

In addition, Lord Halifax left us in no doubt, there was no equivocation about it, on the point of Germany. So far as Germany was concerned, he made it quite clear that the British Government were prepared to negotiate with Hitler as a means of securing appeasement of the present European conflict. That was very, very clear. He also gave no indication at all that there would be any possibility of changing their policy in regard to non-intervention so as to assist the Spanish Government against the invasion of Spain by the Fascist States. (April 28, 1938.)

7. THE RESOLUTION OF THE SPECIAL CONFERENCE

Having received this picture of what had been done, the Conference had to decide what now should be done. The Committee had that morning seriously considered the position, and prepared a resolution to be moved on their behalf by A. L. Horner.

The resolution put to this unprecedented Special Conference was expressed in very strong terms in the opening paragraph:

This National Delegate Conference of the Mineworkers' Federation of Great Britain protests in the strongest terms against the continued denial of the right of the Spanish Government to buy arms for the defence of the freedom and independence of the Spanish nation. Under the pretence of non-intervention, the British Government has made itself a party to the betrayal of the Spanish people in their struggle against the rebel generals and their fascist accomplices.

The resolution referred to the Anglo-Italian agreement which had been signed only twelve days before, on April 16, 1938:

This Conference denounces the infamous bargain of the Government with the Italian Dictator, under which Italian reinforcements and war equipment continue to enter insurgent Spain without protest or hindrance from our own Government, and the withdrawal of foreign forces from Spain is tacitly postponed to await the issue of the struggle.

They were at pains to specify in some detail the consequences of the non-intervention agreement upon which the British Government's policy relied:

Ample evidence has been forthcoming to prove flagrant violations of the so-called Non-Intervention Agreement. The heroic resistance of the Spanish Republican forces has been almost overwhelmed by the superior equipment, heavier armament and larger resources for aerial warfare placed at the disposal of the rebel generals by fascist Italy and Nazi Germany. These resources have been used in the most merciless and inhuman manner to destroy towns and villages in Republic Spain, and the brave fighters for freedom and democracy have been unable to defend the civilian population from mass destruction and slaughter for want of arms.

This Delegate Conference representing the organised mine-workers of Great Britain voices in the name of freedom, democracy and International order, the demand of its members that the British Government shall abandon the contemptible and discredited policy of "non-intervention," and take steps forthwith to restore to the lawful Government of Spain its legal right to buy arms to defend its people against insurrection and invasion.

The resolution, which the Special Conference carried unanimously, ended by demanding that the T.U.C. should call executives of the unions together to get the policy reversed:

Further, we request the Trades Union Congress to convene a meeting of the Executive Committees of the affiliated unions to examine ways and means of giving practical assistance to the Spanish Government and to secure the reversal of the present policy of the National Government. (April 28, 1938.)

Seconding the resolution on behalf of the M.F.G.B. Committee, Sam Watson spoke trenchantly, setting out the needs of the Spaniards: "If we say we will give money, coal, food, and other things, they will appreciate our efforts. It is not chocolates, milk or cigarettes they want, it is machine guns, artillery, aeroplanes and munitions." This at once raised the question of how to get for them the needed armaments: and on this Watson said outright: "We can talk from now until doomsday, but unless we reverse the policy of the National Government we cannot give to the Spanish people the help they so much need. We cannot, in my opinion, reverse the policy of this National Government by a mere political agitation day by day. Unless the whole of the political weight of this country is behind any movement we shall be beating the air, and not get anywhere. We feel that in calling together the National Executives of the several Unions we will be calling together responsible men who have to take responsible decisions."

The standpoint expressed in this resolution of the April 28th Special Conference was also put into effect in the activities of the Executive Committee and the District associations throughout the whole of 1938. Visits were repeatedly made to the battlefield of the civil war in Spain by the officials and members of the Executive Committee and District officials. Moneys were raised in great quantity, at first by donations from funds and by collection and then through a levy. Much also was set aside for the hundreds of children who were brought to Britain, especially from the Basque-speaking area, where the aerial massacre of the inhabitants of the town of Guernica was only one amongst many Fascist atrocities. Finally monetary aid was given to the International Brigade, in whose ranks there were not a few British miners, some of them the kith and kin of members of the Executive Committee.

An example of these activities is afforded by the minutes of the M.F.G.B. Executive Committee of Friday, May 20, 1938. The Secretary reported that the Special Conference resolution of April 28th had been sent to the Trades Union Congress and formally acknowledged; but at the moment "there was no indication that the General Council would

I*

meet the request of the Federation" as contained in the resolution. Members expressed "concern that something more definite had not been received from the Trades Union Congress." It was agreed a further letter should be sent to them indicating this concern.

The President, Joseph Jones, reported fully on his recent visit to Spain, along with Messrs. J. Little (Amalgamated Engineering Union) and W. Squance (Associated Society of Locomotive Engineers and Firemen), and read the following letter, which he had brought back:

The Executive Committee of the Spanish Trades Union Congress (U.G.T.) takes the opportunity of greeting the miners of England and of expressing to them in these few words our gratitude for their solidarity and the support they have given to the Spanish workers. At the same time the Executive Committee assures them that the workers of Spain are determined to continue the struggle until they achieve the total defeat of Fascism, and thus assure the maintenance of peace and democracy in Europe.

On behalf of the Executive Committee,

Barcelona.   RAMON G. PEÑA.

May 16, 1938.

The President pointed out that the feeling in Spain was that British trade unionists were callously looking on, but he felt sure that the delegation had done much to convince the Spanish people otherwise and they were obviously profoundly grateful for the visit. The position in Spain, however, was desperate. Although the Government had the majority of the people behind them—the morale of the army and civil population being marvellous—they were hampered by a shortage of food and war equipment. Franco's successes had only been possible by reason of the fact that he had received so much support—both equipment and men— from Italy and Germany. The three problems in which the Federation and other bodies could render immediate service were:

(1) feeding of the civil population; (2) lack of coal; and (3) the serious position of the orphans of the Asturias Miners, whose fathers had been massacred by the rebel forces.

A full discussion on the President's Report ensued and it was finally agreed:

That the Federation raise a sum of money equivalent to a levy of 2s. 6d. per member. (May 20, 1938.)

Never before had there been such a levy as this in the British coal-fields. Where a levy was called to raise money to support fellow miners in an industrial dispute, it seldom amounted to more than a fraction of a member's normal union contribution. But this unprecedented sum to aid the Spanish people was ten times greater than a normal sized levy called the previous year. It was also agreed to appoint a sub-committee consisting of Messrs. Herbert Smith,[1] Arthur Horner and S. Watson, together with the three officials, to deal with the allocation of the money as it was received. The question of collaborating with other unions engaged in similar work was also urged, and it was decided to discuss the matter with the representatives of the A.S.L.E. & F. and A.E.U. at an early date.

8. AT THE MINERS' INTERNATIONAL

Immediately after May 20, 1938, the Executive Committee went off together with half a hundred other delegates to the 33rd Miners' International Congress[2] held from May 23rd to 26th in Luxemburg. There on Wednesday, May 25th, a discussion on Spain was opened by Ebby Edwards as General Secretary of the Miners' International

[1] The sudden death of Herbert Smith was reported to the next meeting (on June 22, 1938) of the Executive Committee, which appointed J. A. Hall, of Yorkshire, in his place.

[2] The credentials Report gave the following representations:

Country	Delegates	Members Affiliated
Great Britain ..	68	550,000
France	25	200,000
Belgium	26	50,000
Czechoslovakia	9	35,000
Poland	4	18,000
Luxemburg	2	2,000
Roumania	1	8,000
Holland	1	3,500
Sweden	1	7,000
Spain ..	3	—
TOTALS	140	873,500

Federation. He referred to what he had recorded in the Biennial Report before the Congress as follows:

Ever since the Spanish Conflict started your Executive Committee has been unanimous in its desire to render the maximum assistance to the brave Spanish Workers in their fight to maintain democracy. The Asturias Miners who, without arms, in the face of deadly machine-gun and rifle fire, went into action hurling their sticks of dynamite with sizzling fuses in the known certainty of their death, have played a part in the struggle that must make all our members feel the greatest pride in the character and heroism of our class. (March 1, 1938.)

Then after recalling their resolution of January 1937, Edwards concluded his brief speech by quoting with the utmost emphasis the statement "by Comrade Pascual Tomas, assistant secretary of the Spanish T.U.C." made at the Special Conference of the International Federation of Trade Unions and the Labour and Socialist International, held in Paris on September 28, 1936:

The Civil War in Spain concerns everyone. If democracy in Spain is defeated, the reactionaries in other countries will take advantage of it to continue their work of destruction. The T.U.C. and democracy in Spain have received declarations of solidarity; that is not sufficient, they have received assistance, but what they want are arms in order to defend themselves. Is it sufficient to publish declarations, is it sufficient to collect money to help them with ambulances? The democracy of Spain replies that it is not sufficient, and its cry was "we want arms." We feel that the people of the democratic countries want us to receive arms. Germany and Italy have been helping the rebels, and France, Belgium and Great Britain have been adhering to the agreement. The rebels have been receiving active assistance, and we have received none. We want arms, for with arms we can win.

It was clear that Ebby Edwards had a purpose in quoting this passage: the effect of it was to bring to his hearers a reminder of that autumn month of 1936 and of the Labour Party Conference a week later where the eloquence of Ernest Bevin had done so much to tip the scale against the cry of the Spaniards: "we want arms." Since then twenty terrible months had passed.

Next, a miner from Spain told the International Congress that his people were "fighting not simply against its enemies who revolted in 1936 against the legal Government of their own country, but against foreign invasion, against the fascist element who have come from other countries, especially Italy, Germany and Portugal."

If the struggle which is going on in Spain were confined to Spaniards only, we have not the slightest doubt there would be a quick victory for the Republic.

Spain has been the chosen battlefield by international fascists. It is there, that they are carrying on one of the first of the great battles against the democracies of Europe. If fascism is not beaten in Spain today, then it is quite possible that tomorrow fascism will become a menace to the whole of Europe. (May 25, 1938.)

Prophetic words? This the delegates felt as they listened, and felt still more keenly when they recalled them a year and more later.

Joseph Jones testified to the fact that "hostile planes owned by fascist States and manned by fascists themselves are roaring incessantly day and night, raining death and destruction upon the civil population: in forty-eight hours in Barcelona, there were nine separate air bombardments in which 1,000 were killed and 1,700 injured." After recalling the history "of this dreadful holocaust" he concluded:

Spain it is true is fighting for her liberty, but she is also fighting for us as well.

So Pierre Vigne of France from the chair then put the resolution, which was carried unanimously. It began by declaring:

This Congress of the Miners' International Federation expresses its profound and sincere tribute to the noble courage and heroic sacrifice of the Spanish people and especially the Spanish miners, in their struggle in defence of their national liberty and their Democratic Institutions, against the attacks of traitors supported by Fascist Italy and Germany.

It called upon all unions "and the miners' unions in particular," in the various countries which were parties to the non-intervention agreement "to rouse public opinion" to repudiate it. The resolution concluded:

We urge the miners' organisations affiliated to the International Federation, to organise the utmost financial support to provide the much needed medical supplies, food and other requirements, to the suffering Spanish people. (Wednesday, May 25, 1938.)

9. "SPAIN AND OURSELVES"

The situation grew still more serious in Spain and the attitude of the M.F.G.B. leaders became more and more sharply critical of the British Government's foreign policy as favouring the Fascist powers and in particular Franco. Therefore at the Annual Conference[1] they brought forward this resolution:

That this Annual Conference of the Mineworkers' Federation of Great Britain expresses its profound admiration of the magnificent and heroic resistance made so determinedly for the past two years by the Spanish Government and the Spanish workers against the continued attacks of the Spanish rebels aided and abetted by the fascist forces of Germany and Italy.

It protests in the strongest terms against the continued denial of the right of the Spanish Government to buy arms for the defence of the freedom and independence of the Spanish nation.

Under the pretence of non-intervention the British Government has made itself a party to the betrayal of the Spanish people in their struggle against the rebel generals and their fascist accomplices.

After this protest which by its accusation against the Neville Chamberlain Cabinet (repeated from the Special Conference of April 28th) was undoubtedly "in the strongest terms," the M.F.G.B. Annual Conference resolution reiterated its denunciation of the bargain with Mussolini in the Anglo-Italian Agreement of April 16th:

This Conference denounces the infamous bargain of the Government with the Italian Dictator, under which Italian reinforcements and war equipment continue to enter insurgent Spain without protest or hindrance from our own Government, and the withdrawal of foreign forces from Spain is tacitly postponed in the hope that these reactionary forces may win.

The destruction from the air by German bombers of men, women and children in the old Basque capital of Guernica fifteen months earlier had not been an isolated atrocity—although it had temporarily silenced the partisans of Franco

[1] Other resolutions included demands for nationalisation of mines and ancillary undertakings; a new Workmen's Compensation Act; doubling of Welfare Levy to 1d. per ton; and raising of school-leaving age to sixteen years, "with the necessary maintenance grants."

in the British House of Commons. The pattern set in Guernica had continued. Therefore the resolution, using the same terms as in the April Special Conference, concluded:

Ample evidence has been forthcoming to prove flagrant violations of the so-called Non-Intervention Agreement. The resources of fascist Powers have been used in the most merciless and inhuman manner to destroy towns and villages in Republican Spain, and the brave fighters for freedom and democracy have been unable to defend the civilian population from mass destruction and slaughter for want of arms.

We further call upon the T.U.C. to organise immediately the maximum practical assistance for the Spanish people on similar lines to that done by other organisations.

(M.F.G.B. Annual Conference, Whitley Bay, July 20, 1938.)

The resolution was carried unanimously. It had been moved by the President, Joseph Jones, and seconded by Arthur Horner of South Wales. After it was carried G. H. Jones of the Midland Federation suggested that the speeches of the mover and seconder, "in my opinion the best speeches heard in a Miners' Conference for some time" should be printed and circulated to the miners' associations and other unions. The Executive Committee accordingly issued a well-illustrated pamphlet entitled *Spain and Ourselves* which contained not only the speeches at Whitley Bay but also a Report given to the 1938 Blackpool Trades Union Congress by the Vice-President, Will Lawther, on the Federation's activities in the matter of aid for the Spanish people: this Report followed on a resolution on arms for Spain, which had been carried unanimously at the T.U.C. after what Lawther described as a moving speech by Will Paynter.[1]

This pamphlet was such as might well have been issued by a political party carrying on a rousing agitation against its opponents: and indeed, throughout the whole of the Spanish tragedy, the Federation had been acting like a political party and in some ways with greater insight and vigour than the broad political party of which they were an important constituent.

The miners' associations in Britain endeavoured to carry

[1] "A South Wales miners' delegate, who has been a political commissar in the International Brigade, seconded and drew such an eloquent picture of the atrocities of war in Spain that the resolution was carried without opposition from the platform or from the body of the hall." (*Manchester Guardian*, September 9, 1938.)

out to the best of their ability the policy laid down by the May 25th resolution of the Miners' International Federation. The amount of attention given to the struggle of the Spaniards by the M.F.G.B. may be judged by the range and frequency of items in the minutes of the Executive Committee.

Under the heading "Financial Assistance" there are no less than ten Spanish items, beginning with "Asturias Miners and their Families."

Again there was the support increasingly given to the International Brigade Dependants and Wounded Aid Committee. When Dr. Negrin, the Prime Minister of Spain—under much pressure—announced to the Assembly of the League of Nations at Geneva on September 21st that all foreign combatants would be withdrawn from the army of the Republic, the M.F.G.B. Executive Committee made a special grant of £500 "from the Spanish Aid Fund for the purpose of providing food, clothing etc., for the 750 repatriated British members of the International Brigade." (October 20, 1938.)

As the situation worsened in Spain and as the international skies grew darker, the British miners' unions became more and more outspoken in their denunciation of the British Government's policy. Thus at their November session the Executive Committee resolved:

That the Mineworkers' Federation of Great Britain views with grave concern the general concessions made to the Fascist Powers by the Chamberlain Government and, in particular, regards the proposed granting of belligerent rights to Franco as a betrayal of the Democratic Government of Spain. This Executive Committee requests all the peace-loving forces throughout the country to unite in repudiating the Chamberlain policy and urges the combined Labour Movement to oppose the recognition of Franco with all the forces at its disposal. (November 17, 1938.)

A month later a resolution in even stronger terms, passed by the Durham Miners' Association, was adopted and issued to the press as follows:

We view with feelings of horror and indignation the acquiescence of your Government in the schemes now under way to grant belligerent rights to the Spanish adventurer General Franco. . . .

Viewed in the light of recent events every step of your Government seems to be to give way step by step to the bellicose blatant proposals of the fascist Dictators.

To grant belligerent rights to Franco would be in the opinion of the Durham Miners' Association an outrage of British traditions, a calumny on those members of our race who have in the past fought and died for liberty and freedom. (December 15, 1938.)

In Spain the struggle was still going on fiercely and on a very large scale. The battles of the valley of the River Ebro, which ended in mid-November 1938, were estimated to have cost each side more than 40,000 men. By the end of 1938, however, it was clear that men and materials being supplied by Hitler and Mussolini to the Fascist forces were proving too much for the heroic struggling forces of democracy. But the miners still kept up their support and spared no effort to bring aid to the Spanish people.

10.   THE ORPHANS OF THE SPANISH MINERS

From an Executive Committee meeting of the Miners' International Federation, held in Paris on December 20 and 21, 1938, on the question of relief to Spain, Ebby Edwards came back to tell the Executive Committee of the desire of the French miners to set up, jointly with the British miners, a home for miners' orphans in the South of France.

After discussions with the Spanish Ambassador the Federation Committee took a decision on February 16th to give a block grant of £20,000 to the French miners for this purpose, and sent W. Lawther and A. L. Horner to France to meet French and Spanish representatives, and make the necessary arrangements. A "Council of Administration" (Vigne of France, Fernandez and Tomas of Spain, Schevenels of the I.F.T.U. and Ebby Edwards) was set up.

To the fund for dependants of members of the British International Brigade "who had laid down their lives in Spain in the cause of democracy," the Federation Executive allocated £2,000. (February 16, 1939.)

Thereafter there came each month the sombre sequels of

the Fascist overrunning of Spain. At their March meeting the record runs:

That, in the event of any Spanish Miners or their leaders needing assistance, the Secretary be vested with the necessary authority to attend to their needs and the cost be borne from the balance lying at the bank to the credit of the Spanish Aid Fund, which was specially earmarked for this purpose. (March 16, 1939.)

At the April meeting the Secretary informed the members that "Comrade Peña, late President of the Spanish Miners' Federation," needed £50 for his passage to exile in Mexico with his family. The £50 was sent to him.

At the May meeting the plight of the Spaniards came up again in a report from the Secretary that five Spanish refugees who had landed at Cardiff from Valencia without permits had been imprisoned: "unless a guarantee could be given that they would be maintained while in this country they were to be deported to Spain, and this would mean that nothing but death awaited their return. Under these circumstances, and on the understanding that the five refugees were miners, he had given the necessary authority for guaranteeing their maintenance." It turned out that only one of the refugees was a miner. But the quality of mercy was not strained. The Executive Committee "agreed to confirm the situation of guaranteeing the maintenance of the refugees." (May 10, 1939.)

Finally in August there is the following recorded:

Spanish Home of the Miners' International Federation—France. The Secretary read a letter from Comrade Vigne of the French Miners' Federation, intimating that the inauguration of the above-named Home, situated at Commune de Bordères, near Tarbes (Hautes-Pyrénées), was to take place on September 20. The French Miners' Federation was desirous that representatives from the M.F.G.B. should attend and participate in the opening ceremony. Messrs. S. Watson (Durham), J. A. Hall (Yorkshire) and A. L. Horner (South Wales) were deputed to attend along with the Secretary, President and Vice-President. (August 17, 1939.)

The feelings of the miners on these developments, and their attitude towards the Neville Chamberlain administration, were to be expressed again and again that year in Conferences. Meantime in Spain there had been ominous signs that the elected Government was at its last gasp, though bitter fighting was still going on in the old trade union strongholds of Catalonia in the north-east. On February 28, 1939, President Azaña resigned: a week later the Government of the Premier Dr. Negrin in Madrid was overthrown by a so-called "Defence Council." By the end of March Madrid had been surrendered to Franco: and before the summer, though the struggle continued, the fighting was over.

In his Acting President's address at the July Annual Conference, Will Lawther said at the opening:

Twelve months ago we were fired with enthusiasm, with zeal, with high hopes in our endeavour to help our Spanish comrades. No body of men rallied the waning spirits of the British Labour movement more than did our membership to that cause. To-day that bulwark of democracy has gone down in the fight against Fascism; no Government did more to help to kill Spanish democracy than our own National Government.

Others have written of that dark chapter; of how those whom we might have saved have been subjected to every outrage that human fiends could conceive. (July 3, 1939.)

Lawther recalled that "since 1931 reaction in the saddle in Britain has meant reaction intensified abroad," referred scathingly to Sir John Simon's Foreign Secretaryship in 1931 and said:

From the inception of Fascism and terror in Italy, to the enthronement of Hitler and murder in Germany, the Labour Movement has made its protest and urged that a stand should be taken. We know what that means; we realise the terrible consequences. But just as it has been necessary in the evolution of our own movement—the struggle for recognition and to obtain an improvement in the lot of our people—that drastic action and great sacrifices have had to be made, so will we as part of this nation that loveth liberty and cherishes freedom and has placed the right of free speech and assembly as a jewel without price, accept our share in that stand against aggression. (July 3, 1939.)

11. THE MINERS SUPPORT CHINA

The miners' associations were now thoroughly roused against the policy of appeasement, which they regarded as an encouragement to the Fascist powers in their aggressions. The year 1938 seemed to yield proof of what the miners' unions suspected to be the intention of the Chamberlain Government. The resignation of Foreign Secretary Anthony Eden (and Under-Secretary Lord Cranbourne) on February 20th, the persistent criticism by Churchill, showed that inside the Conservative Party there were also misgivings, at any rate on the European scene. But the outlook of the mine-workers was no longer concentrated only on Europe or the danger of Fascism and war in one continent. In every coal-field of Britain the wrath of the workers was growing against all aggressors, in whatever continent. Imperialist and militarist Japan had broken the peace with the invasion of North-East China and when her later aggression had brought a tardy remonstrance from Geneva, Japan, like Mussolini, like Hitler, had left the League of Nations. Then in July 1937 came the full onslaught upon China, the next stage in the career of world conquest envisaged in the famous Tanaka Memorandum (the authenticity of which was to be established in the later claim for domination of all "South-East Asia") and the setting up of the Berlin-Rome–Tokyo Axis.

In the autumn of 1938 there were rumours that Britain, to protect commercial interests in middle and South China, was negotiating behind the scenes with the Japanese aggressor. Such a possibility roused immediate protests. On November 17, 1938, there were resolutions from several Districts before the M.F.G.B. Executive Committee. One from Lancashire asked for an immediate Special Conference of the Labour Party—to which they sent the resolution, together with one from Forest of Dean. This last demanded that sanctions, legally operative against Japan, should be strictly applied by an embargo on trade and "a complete boycott of everything Japanese"; insisted "that we warn Chamberlain" against "a similar betrayal of China" through any "mediation" that would interfere with China's sovereignty or would recognise the results of aggression; and urged a direct loan for China to help "defend her people against a most cruel and barbarous enemy." (November 17, 1938.)

Six months passed. The attitude of the Japanese militarists

became more menacing. Soon it was learned that British subjects in the neighbourhood of Tientsin were being ill-treated by the Japanese who had now in their grasp that part of the mainland of China. The news of repeated ill-treatment was being reported in the early summer[1] of 1939: and that the British Government would soon negotiate about it with the Japanese Government. The miners' delegates were apprehensive that under cover of these negotiations the interests of the Chinese people might be endangered: and at the Swansea Annual Conference an emergency resolution from the Business Committee was moved by Arthur Horner, seconded by William Pearson and carried. It ran as follows:

This Conference of British Mineworkers sends greetings to the Chinese people now struggling to safeguard their freedom in face of the savage onslaught by Japan. It further declares its resentment against the Japanese Government which has not hesitated to interfere with the British people resident in China.

It demands that the National Government shall refuse to recognise any territorial or other advantages secured by Japan in China by the use of Force, and urges that in the Conference about to begin in Tokio, the British Government shall insist upon the sovereign rights of the Chinese people to control their own country without interference from foreign imperialism. (July 6, 1939.)

12. MUNICH

For a long time the miners' unions in their concern with the danger of Fascism and war had been increasingly critical of Government foreign policy. From the spring of 1938 when Hitler forcibly annexed Austria and began his campaign of aggression against Czechoslovakia, things were moving rapidly towards a climax. By the summer and early autumn of 1938 the policy of appeasement of the Fascist powers had developed to the point of endangering the sovereignty and integrity of Czechoslovakia. There was mounting anger at this and when it came to the Trades Union Congress at Blackpool in the first week of September a statement was

[1] Two British subjects were stripped naked and subjected to physical indignities on June 15th; and thirteen more (including one woman) by June 28th—as stated by ministers in reply to persistent parliamentary questions from mid-June onwards. See *Hansard*, vols. 348–50 of 1939.

issued by the executives of the Labour Party, the Parliamentary Labour Party and the T.U.C. General Council:

Every consideration of democracy forbids the dismemberment of the Czechoslovakian State by the subjection of the Sudeten German regions to Nazi government control. British Labour emphatically repudiates the right of the British or any other government, to use diplomatic or other pressure to compel an acceptance of such a humiliation. . . . The time has come for a positive and unmistakable lead for collective defence against aggression and to safeguard peace.

The British Government must leave no doubt in the mind of the German Government that it will unite with the French and Soviet Governments to resist any attack upon Czechoslovakia.

The rest of the story of what happened is well enough known: how Chamberlain flew to Germany to meet Hitler, how he conferred with him again on the Rhine at Godesberg on September 22nd, how it was made to seem that war was an immediate sequel unless agreement was reached with Hitler, and how finally on September 29th at Munich Hitler, Mussolini, the French Premier Daladier and the British Prime Minister Neville Chamberlain, met together and reached an agreement for the dismemberment of Czechoslovakia.

The reaction against this was strong and immediate. One week later the Executive Committee heard a detailed Report of the proceedings of meetings that had been held by the National Council of Labour and the General Council of the Trades Union Congress on the international situation. The Durham Miners' Association had also sent up a resolution on Czechoslovakia. After "lengthy deliberation" covering all the phases of these recent events, the outcome was as follows:

The Executive Committee of the Mineworkers' Federation of Great Britain, representing nearly 600,000 British miners, expresses its deep disgust with the action of the British Government in sacrificing Czechoslovakia to the insatiable appetite of the Dictators.

It regards the foreign policy of the National Government during the last few years, as being that of an accomplice to the murder of the smaller democracies, and as a betrayal of all that is decent in international relations.

The dangerous war situation which prevailed last week was the only possible outcome of this policy, a policy which has disorganised the peace forces and given consistent support to the Fascist war-makers.

We call upon the whole Labour Movement to organise a most vigorous struggle against the present Government, and pledge the full support of the Federation in that struggle.

Further, we request that facilities shall be given to the Trades Union Movement to have its observers in the disputed areas of Czechoslovakia in order to afford some protection to the victims of this act of aggression and to save them from the concentration camp methods of the Nazis.

The Mineworkers' Federation is prepared to appoint representatives to a Commission of this nature that may be formed by the International Trade Union Movement, and also agrees to donate a sum of £1,000 to assist the miner victims in the Czechoslovakia coalfields. (October 4, 1938.)

They had reached decisions before on grave questions and sometimes, though seldom, worded their resolutions in a very sharp and unequivocal way. But now, after much consideration, they were, in carefully measured language, accusing their own Government of being "an accomplice to murder of the smaller democracies" and of being the supporter of the "fascist war-makers." That this was a deliberately thought-out political standpoint was shown by their further decision on the same day.

The Executive Committee of the Mineworkers' Federation calls upon its District Organisations to wage ceaseless educational propaganda amongst their members in order that a proper perspective of the present position arising from the crisis can be placed before them. (October 4, 1938.)

Moreover, copies of the resolutions were to be sent to the District organisations, the Labour Party, the Trades Union Congress, C. R. Attlee, M.P., and the Prime Minister, Neville Chamberlain, "urging their earnest consideration of same." It is unknown what consideration was given to it by Neville Chamberlain who continued that autumn his endeavours to foster closer relations with the Hitler regime on the basis of Munich. Presently there was talk of a friendly visit to Britain by the other prominent Nazi, Hermann Goering. In the second week of November, following on the shooting in Paris of a German diplomat by a Polish Jew, the Nazis and their Government launched a pogrom against the Jews in Germany "as a reprisal." All Jewish newspapers were suppressed, all Jewish cultural and educational societies dissolved, all Jews by decree were excluded from business: hundreds of Jews were arrested. Jewish synagogues and shops were looted, destroyed and burned in an orgy of the *Hitler-Jugend* (Hitler Youth). The United States Ambassador was recalled; and President Roosevelt declared the public of the U.S.A. were deeply shocked by the Nazi persecution of Jews. So were the workers in the British coal-fields. At their mid-November meeting the M.F.G.B. Executive Committee received and endorsed a resolution from the Durham Miners' Association, as follows:

We desire to register a strong protest against the proposed visit of General Goering to this country. We have no prejudice against German people, but we feel that to allow such a creature to come to England without any protest whatever, is to condone the most barbarous and outrageous crimes ever inflicted in the history of the world. He and his gang are seeking to convert the world into a torture chamber. Further it is to admit that the British people are prepared to tolerate the imposition of any form of torture, persecution and injustice on liberty-loving people.

We trust that the British Government and the British people will prevent this blatant bully from polluting the free air of Britain with his objectionable presence. (November 17, 1938.)

By the end of 1938 it was clear that the consequences of the dismemberment of Czechoslovakia would soon be evident. President Beneš had been compelled to resign on October 5th, a week after Munich, and a Government more acceptable to Hitler had been installed. At the meeting of the M.F.G.B. Executive Committee on January 12, 1939, the Secretary read a letter from the British Committee for Refugees from Czechoslovakia about miners in sore straits. He had promised funds sufficient "for the purpose of bringing out of Czechoslovakia the more prominent miners' leaders who were most likely to lose their lives."

At the next meeting, on February 16, 1939, the Secretary reported the difficulties of evacuation of the miner refugees and that there was now "very grave danger of the active leaders in Czechoslovakia being sent back to Sudetenland, which would only end in their extermination." It was decided that Ness Edwards and Dennis Edwards "proceed at once to Prague" to make contact with miner refugees and arrange for their evacuation from Czechoslovakia.

Authority was given Ness Edwards to find accommodation. A home was found at Penarth which the South Wales Miners' Federation was asked to supervise and manage. It was estimated that the liability of the M.F.G.B. for the whole undertaking would be about £3,000, covering some 100 refugees for a period of six months—to be raised by an appeal to the Districts.

But these plans for rescue were interrupted. Early in March Hitler, who had already split off portions of Czecho-slovakia, picked a quarrel with the miserable but not-compliant-enough Hácha (the successor of President Beneš), invaded the now shrunken territory, marched his troops into Prague and occupied the whole country. On March 15th Hitler announced: "Czechoslovakia ceases to exist." Many of the fugitives were trapped: but in the end some fifty-four miners and their families escaped and were lodged in Penarth.

13. SWANSEA ANNUAL CONFERENCE, JULY 3, 1939

Three weeks later Mussolini followed suit to Hitler, suddenly invaded Albania, the small Balkan country across the Adriatic from the heel of Italy, and largely destroyed its chief port of Durazzo. A week later, on the day the King of Italy was being offered the crown of vanquished Albania, the M.F.G.B. Executive Committee were meeting at St. Andrew's Crescent in Cardiff. The Acting President (Will Lawther) referred to the increased tension created in the international situation by the invasion of Albania by Italy. This aggression, it was felt, was due to the lack of a deter-mined foreign policy by the British National Government, and that a protest should be registered by the Federation against "the stagnated policy" still being adopted by the Cabinet. After discussion, it was resolved to send to the British Prime Minister, to Clement Attlee, and to Tom Cape, M.P., a copy of the following resolution, for their information and attention:

That this Executive Committee of the Mineworkers' Federation of Great Britain, registers its emphatic protest against the barbaric invasion of Albania by the Fascist hordes of Mussolini.

It places on record that in our opinion this outrage is the logic of the betrayal of Spain, Abyssinia, China, Sudetenland and Czechoslovakia, and that this destruction of the potential friends of Britain has been connived at by the British National Government.

This Executive insists that working-class support for the defence of Britain must be determined by a foreign policy that has for its object the preservation of peace and justice and the rallying of all peace-loving countries to a common front against aggression, and in this connection regards the close collaboration of Russia in this peace front as a decisive factor.

This Executive Committee, therefore, calls upon all freedom-loving and democratic forces, both in this country and elsewhere, to bring the maximum pressure to obtain a common peace front to end the jungle tactics which have lately tended to rule the world. (April 12, 1939.)

In the Easter of 1939 Hitler's seizure of Czechoslovakia had compelled Neville Chamberlain to repudiate publicly his previous policy of appeasement. Thereafter followed one of the most tortuous periods of British diplomacy, with influential circles still striving to push through the appeasement policy. A system of alliances was announced, particularly with Poland which now began to be threatened by Fascist Germany. But over the working out with the Soviet Union of the detailed application of what was now proclaimed to be the policy of building collective security, there were seemingly inexplicable hesitations. Severe criticisms of this fumbling diplomacy were uttered at the time by Lloyd George and others, who were aware of the activities of the Anglo-German Fellowship. There were in fact very strong influences behind the scenes operating for appeasement with Hitler on the understanding that he would sooner or later attack the Soviet Union. This, as it turned out, came later. At the time the Soviet Government, also aware of all these moves, drew the conclusion that no trust could be placed in the Chamberlain Government, and that it was hoping to make a catspaw of the U.S.S.R. The Government of the U.S.S.R. therefore decided to draw out of these tortuous entanglements and made a pact of non-aggression with Germany in August 1939. Meantime Hitler's preparation for war upon Poland had been going on with growing intensity for over four months. By the end of

August his war preparations were complete: German troops crossed the frontier and marched upon Warsaw.

These facts may serve to explain some of the references made to current happenings in Will Lawther's address to the July Annual Conference. Under the heading "International Affairs," after reference to Spain (already quoted) he said:

Czechoslovakia is another of the outposts of democracy that was sold, sealed and delivered to fascism. Here we have in our midst the living remnants of that outrage, for which, even at this eleventh hour, the Prime Minister admits his guilt. These two betrayals are the major ones; others have followed in logical sequence and others must and will follow unless an immediate change in those in charge of the reins of Government here takes place.

There could be no real advance in social and industrial progress "whilst this menace of fascism hangs over us." They had just returned from the 25th session of the International Labour Office at Geneva, founded in 1919 "to seek to erect a standard of social justice for all toilers." The cardinal feature in all the discussions for a shorter working week had been that a standstill order must operate "until a definite and drastic change takes place" in the political and international situation. It was no use criticising the I.L.O. for this; for "the fault lies nearer home than in Geneva"; and he drew the conclusion that "since 1931 reaction in the saddle in Britain has meant reaction intensified abroad."

It is our duty to our own folk to indicate our profound belief and sincere conviction that there can be no hope of peace, no relief from that anxiety which overwhelms and overshadows all mankind, unless there exist definite alliances with the only Government of the common people in Europe, namely Russia. It is idle, it is stupid, nay it is criminal to delay the signing of that alliance on the flimsy pretexts and pretences that are being put forward in some quarters.

Is there any wonder that Russia doubts our Government's intention and wants clarity? We in this movement are not astonished because we know from bitter experience during the past decade how essential it is to have documents properly signed and sealed when understandings are being effected. Surely it is more necessary for heads of our Government to meet the heads of the U.S.S.R. than it was to fly to Munich to sign the betrayal of a brave nation.

That action would be in the nature of atonement for past errors.
(July 3, 1939.)

This address had been given by Will Lawther as Acting
President. In the elections he became President for the next
twelve months, receiving on the second count 320 votes
against 274 votes for Harry Hicken of Derbyshire. For the
Vice-Presidency there were five nominations. James Bowman
of Northumberland was successful on the first count, receiving 455 votes, and for the remainder of the years of his
Vice-Presidency he was re-elected each time unchallenged.
He was the youngest ever to occupy the post. Born on
March 8, 1898, James Bowman had returned after war
service to Ashington, where in his early twenties he was on
the Branch Committee and the Welfare Committee as well
as becoming pit inspector, and soon was chosen as the first
full-time Secretary of Ashington. Five pits with some three
thousand pitmen under the Ashington Coal Company were
linked together in the Ashington Mineworkers' Federation
of which Ebby Edwards was the first Secretary: Bowman
was one of his successors. He also sat on the county executive.
In 1935, when William Straker retired at a great age, James
Bowman was elected by ballot vote as Secretary of the
Northumberland Miners' Mutual Confident Association, and
within four years was elected M.F.G.B. Vice-President.

The resolutions passed at the Annual Conference (listed on
page 286) covered a wider range and were more numerous than
usual. Delegates were also able to note in the period under
review a vigorous preparation of pamphlets disseminating
useful information to Federation members. The last of these
(in July 1939) was *Workmen's Compensation*—to which Ebby
Edwards wrote a foreword concluding: "I desire to recognise
and express my great appreciation of Mr. Sidney Ford, a
member of my staff, who, with great diligence and unremitting work, collaborated to make this achievement possible."

When the 149 delegates assembled in the Brangwyn Hall,
Swansea, on that summer day of 1939 there was no delegate
present whose personal memory could call attention to the
significance of the time and place of the meeting. But there
were some alive, notably William Brace, who could recall
that fifty years earlier the Miners' Federation of Great Britain

had been founded in Newport at the eastern end of the coal-field. Now they were meeting in the town of Swansea, at the western end of the same coal-field. The national organisation, now in its jubilee year, was older than the South Wales Miners' Federation in whose territory it was meeting and whose membership it had embraced for over forty years. But though it was the jubilee year, there was no jubilation. Despite the wholehearted service given to the cause of democracy in Spain, the Fascist forces from Germany and Italy with the "connivance" of the Chamberlain Government had crushed democracy. These they recognised as the forces that had defeated all the efforts of the people and of the working class of Britain in which amongst the trade union bodies the Mineworkers' Federation had been one of the foremost champions of Spain. With the success of Fascism in Spain, with the destruction of the independence of Austria and Czechoslovakia by Hitler, of Ethiopia and Albania by Mussolini, and the further inroads of Japanese Fascism by the continuing war of aggression upon the people of China the danger of war was visibly coming closer.

Nevertheless, in spite of the imminent danger from war and Fascism, there was a hopeful spirit, greater than there had been half a dozen years earlier, in that Mineworkers' Federation Annual Conference. The resistance to Fascism, the good fight they had fought, had built up the morale of the Federation as a trade union body. In all the utterances the feeling was clear that the miners had helped to maintain the honour of the British people that was being "dragged in the dust" by the Neville Chamberlain Government, a Government to which they were more and more bitterly opposed.

But whatever their feelings, anticipations, analyses or resolves, there was none could see the immediate future, or know that in sixty days they would all be engulfed by the war danger which they had striven so hard to avert. In the twenty-fifth year of its existence, the Miners' Federation had been plunged into the First World War; in the fiftieth year of its existence it was plunged into the Second World War.

LIST OF RESOLUTIONS PASSED AT THE SWANSEA ANNUAL CONFERENCE 1939

Old Age Pensions—demand for £1 a week.

Unemployment—urges control of location of industry.

Safety in Mines—welcomes recommendations of Royal Commission "although not fully meeting the demands of the Mineworkers' Federation" and urges immediate legislation together with other safety demands.

Welfare Fund—to meet the cost of laundry services for provision, cleaning and maintenance of pit clothes.

Hours of Work—demand for seven-hour day underground (forty-six hours per week on surface) without wages reduction.

Transit Underground—facilities for workmen to ride "where the coal face is more than one mile from the pit bottom" to be obligatory on mine-owners.

Mine-workers' Holidays—call for legal one week annual holiday without loss of wages "and also payment of wages for all statutory holidays."

Organisation--"This Conference declares that all workers in and around the coal mines must be members of the Mineworkers' Federation of Great Britain."

Nationalisation—"This Conference of British Mineworkers calls upon the Government to nationalise the mines and ancillary undertakings."

Coal Mines Act, 1930, Selling Agencies—"This Conference demands that provision be made in the scheme of Selling Agencies for representatives of the workers."

Overtime—"demands that all overtime be abolished."

National Health, Unemployment and Compensation Acts—Waiting Period— for abolishing of period of three waiting days.

Emergency Resolution on China (quoted in full in Chapter VI, page 277).

CHAPTER VII

THIRTY MONTHS OF WAR

1. THE FIRST EFFECTS OF THE WAR

BRITAIN declared war on Germany on September 3, 1939. That evening the Atlantic liner *Athenia* was sunk by a German submarine off the north coast of Ireland with great loss of life. Schoolchildren were evacuated from the main industrial centres. Gas masks were distributed to the population. The whole apparatus of government, national and local, was switched on to a war basis. Within a few days the Secretary for Mines had talks with the miners' representatives. This he followed up with a letter on the need for a greatly increased production of coal to meet war requirements. He estimated the need at from 260 to 270 million tons a year or between 30 and 40 million tons more than the total of 1938. He wrote similarly to the Mining Association of Great Britain and suggested the two bodies should meet.

In the consequent Joint Standing Consultative Committee meeting of September 21st, the nine Federation representatives (three officials and six of the twenty-four Executive members) pointed out that other questions than the need for higher output were bound to arise in wartime and that it would be difficult for the Joint Standing Consultative Committee to cope with these questions so long as it was limited by the formula[1] under which it had been set up in 1936. They therefore suggested that there should be a new joint body between the two sides of the industry with authority to take decisions. Sir Evan Williams, Chairman of the owners' organisation, would not immediately agree to this: he said that while the employers were willing to be flexible in their attitude there were certain questions that would have to

[1] "The consideration of all questions of common interest and of general application in industry, not excluding general principles applicable to the determination of wages by district agreements."

be referred back to the District mine-owners' associations. No conclusion therefore was reached at this stage. But at the next meeting a week later Sir Evan Williams was able to say that the owners would agree that the J.S.C.C. should be the body to deal not only with increase of coal production but with questions of a general character likely to arise from the war, with power and authority to reach decision wherever possible. From the standpoint of war needs this was a real extension of functions while from the M.F.G.B. standpoint it gave much of what they had demanded over a period of years.

Meanwhile it had become clear that any raising of production depended first on satisfactory conditions in the coal-fields. On this a problem within the scope of the joint committee had already cropped up. This was the need for an addition to wages to meet the sudden leap in the cost of living.[1] The nine Federation representatives having discussed this rapid rise "in spite of the promises of the Government to take action against profiteering," took on themselves at the September 28th J.S.C.C. meeting to make claim for a wage advance outside the slow-moving machinery of the District boards, based on regular ascertainments. Not only was the claim put forward nationally but it was for a flat rate advance of one shilling a shift for adults (sixpence for non-adults) instead of any percentage arrangement. The owners at once recognised that something must be done but were divided in opinion as to what was the best method.

By the next meeting on October 12th the owners said that a responsibility lay on the Government, which had earlier got from them "an undertaking that there would be no wholesale increase in the price of coal" but which had not prevented other price rises both in consumer goods and in the colliery supplies of various materials. It was in their opinion a national responsibility. They would make representations to the Government "with regard to the price of coal as they could not bear the additional cost" of materials and

---

[1] The cost of living index of the Ministry of Labour, on the basis of July 1914, was up by 40 per cent in 1933, by 55 per cent in 1937 and was still at 55 per cent in August 1939. It jumped ten points in September 1939: and within a twelvemonth was up by 34 points.

OLD-STYLE MINERS' HOUSES
Hartford Colliery, Northumberland

CLIPSTONE, NOTTS.   MINERS' NEW HOUSES

until that was done, they could not deal with wages. The Federation representatives "expressed keen disappointment" and resented the implication that "merchants had to be paid what they requested, but labour power had to be placed last in the category of the obligations of the employers": but finally they agreed to wait the outcome of discussions with the Government. It turned out to be unfavourable.

At the J.S.C.C. meeting of October 19th Sir Evan Williams reported that the Government, seriously concerned about the financial position, "viewed with some alarm the suggestion that wages should vary automatically with the cost of living": and would only allow that the depressed export prices of coal be brought up to the level of inland prices. The Federation representatives heard this report with some dismay. Were Neville Chamberlain and his Chancellor of the Exchequer going on the path trodden in 1914? The owners might be obdurate, but the Government it would seem were obtuse. Had they no realisation of the coal problem? Nevertheless the owners, having given a promise to consider an advance, were prepared then and there "to discuss the quantum of the increase." It was to be a long discussion. The owners offered sixpence a day, being half the Federation's claim. After a prolonged session, with many retirements on each side, the Federation said they would settle at eightpence for adults and fourpence for non-adults. To this the owners agreed. The term "adult" was to be interpreted (the M.F.G.B. had asked for all over eighteen years of age to be paid the adult advance) in accordance with the custom of each particular District. It was to be paid in November and December. The final clause in this arrangement ran:

For ascertainment purposes, the advances shall be termed a war bonus and shall be merged in any rise of wages that may hereafter be accorded by the district ascertainments owing to increased proceeds. Such districts whose wages paying capacity reaches a point beyond that of the award shall then secure their advances as per the ascertained percentage of their district ascertainment.

Would all this be accepted by the M.F.G.B. Special Conference, called for Friday, October 27th? The Districts, now after a dozen years of autonomy (and sometimes of cross-purposes) were to some extent uneasy about it. It was a peculiar situation. The nine men of the workmen's side of the Joint Standing Consultative Committee had applied for a national advance without the usual democratic District and Conference discussions and, finally, instructions. They had done it off their own bat. They had asked for a flat rate. This bore on the old question of the differential rate of the skilled man, whose advance would be less than if it had been on a percentage variation. Moreover, they had secured, and the Executive were recommending, only two-thirds of what they had claimed, while the cost of living was going up each month.

All these points were raised in questions or debate, though many said that after having heard the opening speech by Edwards they would not persist with their objections. Indeed, what other course could they pursue than that of acceptance? Rejection, besides depriving the men of an advance secured for two months, was only likely to have an effect if they were willing to pursue it to the bitter end, namely to a strike ballot and national stoppage: and this it was generally agreed was out of the question. These arguments, skilfully driven home by Edwards and following him by the new Vice-Chairman James Bowman and by Arthur Horner ("I am speaking as one of the negotiating committee responsible for bringing about this offer, and I do it with a full appreciation that the district of which I am President has turned down the offer by nine votes to one: that does not make me feel that what we have done has been a mistake"), won over the majority of the 178 delegates for their Committee's recommendation. It was carried on a card vote by 342,000 to 253,000, with Yorkshire, South Wales, Scotland and Forest of Dean making up the large minority vote. The decision was:

This Conference having received the report of the Executive Committee on the negotiations with the Mining Association in relation to advances in wages, agrees to accept the offer made by the Mining Association to apply to the whole of the coalfield.

Further, the Conference authorises the Executive Committee to continue the negotiations with a view to securing wage advances which shall, at the minimum, compensate for the increased cost of living. (October 27, 1939.)

Meanwhile in these first two months of the war the M.F.G.B. Executive Committee had been busy on many other problems arising from the new circumstances as well as dealing with matters that had first come up in the earlier part of the year. These last ranged from how to apply the recommendations of the Royal Commission on Safety in Coal Mines (given additional urgency by the explosion in October at the Valleyfield Colliery in Fife[1]) to parliamentary matters such as the personal position of Aneurin Bevan, M.P. The Labour Party officials and Executive Committee had earlier in 1939 expelled some of the most prominent M.P.s, such as Sir Stafford Cripps, for their support of the Popular Front campaign. When Aneurin Bevan, who was one of those thus expelled, applied in the autumn for membership, it was demanded that he first sign an apology. The Federation Executive could not tolerate this attitude of the Labour Party officials, with whom the matter was discussed. It was "intimated to the Party officials" (October 26th) that the Federation Executive could not accept the modified proposal of the "special undertaking required" of Bevan who ought to receive the same treatment as anyone else applying for membership: and the Federation officials, if there were further difficulty, should meet the Labour Party Executive Committee. By December 14th, however, the Secretary reported that the dispute had been "amicably settled."

2. A COST OF LIVING FORMULA

Negotiations with the coal-owners on the Joint Standing Consultative Committee were resumed on November 23rd and then on December 13th and December 20th. The negotiating Committee took up first the special question of the bonus being made available to men disabled and under the Workmen's Compensation Act, who were suffering from the rise in the cost of living. On this Sir Evan Williams said that

[1] See *A History of the Scottish Miners*, Chapter XI.

workmen's compensation was a legal liability quite different from the contractual relations between employer and employee and that the hardship, which he admitted, applied to every industry and must be dealt with by an alteration of the law. The rate of accidents in mining put the industry in a class by itself and, as Edwards said later, no other subject secured such unanimous support and attention, not only of the Executive and negotiating Committee, and not only of Conferences, but of the men in the coal-field, as the question of workmen's compensation. Consequently when it came to the next Special Conference the decision was unanimous:

> This Conference views with grave concern the serious plight of the injured workmen who have to exist on rates of compensation which have always been regarded by the Mineworkers' Federation as being totally inadequate, and whose condition is now much worsened in consequence of the increase in the cost of living. This Conference therefore calls upon the Government to take action without delay to substantially increase the rates of compensation both to men totally and partially incapacitated. (December 29, 1939.)

On the question of advances from January 1, 1940, to meet the still rising cost of living (the January rise was twenty-four points above August 1939) the negotiators did not find it easy. The M.F.G.B. Executive Committee had adopted the following as the basis for a formula:

> The average wage per man-shift worked for Great Britain is taken for the twelve months ended June 1939, viz., 11s. 4¾d., and is set against the cost of living figure for the same period (100 for 1914 plus the per cent increase at that period). 100 per cent of the average wage is then ascertained to represent "Standard," 7s. 4d. Therefore for every 1 point rise in the cost of living the wage advance would be one-hundreth of the "Standard," viz., 0/0·88d.

The employers were not as yet ready for a formula and were in addition under some pressure from the Government which did not agree that wages should rise step by step with the cost of living. Finally on December 20th they made an offer of an additional 4d. a shift. The Federation representatives would not accept this and the M.F.G.B. Executive decided to raise the matter with the Government. To the

Secretary for Mines on December 28th they stated that "The Mineworkers' Federation would under no circumstances agree to any policy which meant that our members' hard-earned pre-war standard of living should be reduced during the war." From this interview they got little change except the general statement that "the Government had no desire to interfere in ordinary industrial negotiations": and consequently at the second Special Conference on "Wages and the Cost of Living" the decision was carried as follows:

This Special Conference of the Mineworkers' Federation, representing 600,000 members employed throughout the coalfields of Britain, rejects the offer of the Mining Association of a wage increase of 4d. for adults and 2d. for youths, as being insufficient to meet the increased cost of living.

It therefore requests that the District Associations affiliated to the Federation should empower the Executive Committee to negotiate an advance in wages to operate as and from January 1, 1940, which shall, at the minimum, compensate for the increased cost of living.

In the event of the negotiations being unsuccessful, a further Conference of the Federation be called to consider what action should be taken to enforce this demand. (December 29, 1939.)

In the new year 1940 at the resumed negotiations on January 4th and 18th the employers set out their views in a fully argued memorandum. They saw objections to "any rigid formula" but appreciated the argument "from the workers' side" that it would "conduce to the smoother operation" of the machinery of negotiation: and so they would agree in principle provided each side had the opportunity of amending or ending the arrangement. They improved their offer to an additional 5d. a shift for the first quarter of 1940. But on the formula itself they proposed ·62d. as equivalent for a lower-paid man to each one point of the cost of living index. Between this and the Federation figure of ·88d. the collective bargaining went on for hours. Eventually a compromise nearer the owners' figure was agreed upon and recommended to the M.F.G.B. Special Conference, which had been convened to consider the "formula for automatic adjustments of wages related to the cost of living": this would operate as from the beginning of 1940. The Conference accepted the Mining Association's amended offer as follows:

That 0·70d. per shift be the variation in the flat rate war additions to the shift wage of the adult worker corresponding to a variation of one point in the cost of living index number, subject to three-monthly reviews, and that there should be no change in the flat rates unless the index figure varies by not less than 5 points. (January 25, 1940.)

The majority on a card vote was 524,000 to 70,000, the minority being made up of Scotland, Kent, Cumberland and Forest of Dean. But, since the Federation Executive Committee had asked to be "empowered" by the mining unions to conduct these negotiations, the matter had to be ratified or otherwise by a vote of each of the constituent bodies. Within ten days the decision was ratified but by a lesser majority than in the Delegate Conference. The District voting returns showed the South Wales miners also in opposition, while Forest of Dean were now in support. Thus the ratifying vote was:

For Acceptance ..	..	..	421,721
Against Acceptance	..	..	166,600
		Majority ..	255,121

The way was now clear for a national agreement on these lines. But this was held up by internal differences within the Federation, due to discrepant interpretations of the terms made with the employers. Three of the largest Districts treated the terms as having an application quite other than that reached by their chief negotiators, the President and Secretary, with the result that "the owners knew of this conflict of opinion within the Federation" and, as Edwards commented bitterly enough, the owners' Secretary with whom he was negotiating, "never failed to remind me of this." The fact was that although the miners' associations had empowered their Federation to conduct these wage negotiations, they were now, after a dozen years of separate wage boards, as reluctant to yield some of their powers to a federal body as the former New England colonies were a hundred and fifty years earlier to delegate authority to the new United States. This at least was the opinion of the M.F.G.B. Secretary, who felt that the ground had been cut from under his feet: "Unfortunately," he wrote, "we have ended in a divided and disorderly council when unity of policy was most essential"; and added "It is my most tragic experience in thirty-five years of negotiations." Ebby Edwards was indeed angered. He wrote a very lengthy letter of personal explanation and also of reproach, beginning "My dear Colleague," to each member of the M.F.G.B. Executive Committee—which they afterwards meekly embodied in their Annual Report. The relative weakness and lack of cohesion within the Federation in these early months of the war is indicated by the closing paragraph of his letter:

Negotiations of any kind when your own side is weak are most difficult; to enter negotiations when your opponents know your weakness is to court disaster. As a result of these difficulties an outstanding thought comes uppermost in my mind; is it possible to negotiate national settlements while districts operate under local autonomy and your national negotiators of necessity have a district mentality? (February 29, 1940.)

The Executive Committee, discussing this on February 29th, contented themselves with unanimously expressing "our complete confidence in both the Secretary and the President." Three weeks later the agreement between the Mining Association of Great Britain and the Mineworkers' Federation on war additions to wages was signed. The first clause laid down the principle:

The district wage arrangements shall continue to operate during the war, subject to mutually agreed alterations, but increases of wages necessary to take account of the special conditions arising out of the war, and particularly the increased cost of living, shall be dealt with on a national basis by means of uniform flat rate additions. (March 20, 1940.)

The remainder of the agreement[1] set forth how the war additions, payable for a maximum of six shifts in each week, would be related to the cost of living index, on a quarterly reckoning; and how related to the District ascertainments; and other details. Then in the last clause, to be of much significance later, it was laid down that the agreement,

[1] See Appendix to this chapter.

while open to proposals for variation "by reason of change of circumstances," was to last until six months after notice had been given by either side "after the cessation of hostilities." No one could foresee that it was to last for many a year ahead; while the clause stipulating that the "district wage arrangements" would otherwise continue was bound to cause difficulties in the future, especially for those Districts where the wage was extremely low as a result of the difficult conditions of the previous twelve years.

Averaged out over the whole of the coal-fields the weekly cash earnings had been low. During the last full year before the war they were £2 15s. 9d. This figure of average miners' earnings[1] placed the miners in the 81st rank in an official list of nearly a hundred trades. The Minister of Labour had gone one better than the poet Dante in whose Inferno the lowest circle was the ninth: in Britain it was in the second lowest circle that the miners existed. Subsequent additions under the March 20, 1940, agreement brought a few additional pence per shift from April 1st onwards, and another small addition from October 1st onwards. Thus in the year 1940 as a whole average weekly cash earnings stood at £3 8s. 8d.

The months while these war additions to wages were being negotiated coincided with the period described as "the phoney war"—because although the Navy was active against Germany, the land and air forces of Britain and France seemed to be passive; while in mid-winter munitions of war and volunteers were being hurriedly gathered for Finland[2]—for use against the Soviet Union. Hugh Dalton in his memoirs tells how at a time when the Air Force was doing nothing but dropping leaflets on German soil, he urged the responsible minister, Kingsley Wood, to set fire with incendiary bombs to the Black Forest and was told it would be contrary to the Hague Convention.[3]

---

[1] *Hansard*, House of Commons, October 17, 1944.

[2] In the war between Finland and the U.S.S.R. (November 1939 to March 1940) the Finns were sent by Britain and France several hundreds of aeroplanes—the lack of which was to be felt later when the Finns were fighting on the side of the Nazis.

[3] Kingsley Wood spoke more frankly to two Conservatives who had urged the same thing: to General Spears he said, "You can't do that. That's private property": to Leo Amery (soon to be Secretary of State for India) he replied that there was no question of bombing "even the munitions works at Essen, which were private property" (from *Prelude to Dunkirk*, p. 31, and *My Political Life*, Vol. III, p. 350, respectively, as cited by Dalton in *The Fateful Years*, p. 276).

Leaders of the Mineworkers' Federation could not but be aware, through their representatives in the Labour Party Executive Committee and their Members of Parliament, of a certain growing dissatisfaction at the "phoney war" in that winter of 1939–40. It was a hard winter. Complaints were also reaching them from the embodied troops then in camps (some under canvas only) throughout Britain, complaints which showed that they, too, were "browned off." But apart from such representations as could be made individually there was no general discussion in the Federation or any steps contemplated. Neville Chamberlain for his part professed himself well pleased with the conduct of the war in these first seven months; and in a famous phrase uttered on April 4, 1940, said of Hitler that he had "missed the bus." There was to be a rude awakening not only for that Prime Minister but for all who had put their trust in him.

3. OUTPUT AND MAN-POWER

When in September 1939 the Secretary for Mines had put the need for coal at up to 270 million tons a year, the Mineworkers' Federation were willing to do all they could and the owners had the same attitude. But a willingness on the part of all concerned was not enough without drastic and far-reaching changes in everything connected with the industry. The past years weighed too heavily.

The M.F.G.B. Executive, however, after the Joint Standing Consultative Committee meeting on September 21, 1939, sent out to its Districts a questionnaire. This asked how many unemployed ex-miners would be willing to return to the pits; the number of days that could be worked; whether any closed pits could be reopened; and a series of other pertinent questions, the answers to which might show how to gain greater output. But the Federation Executive knew that this would not be enough to supply an amount equivalent to that produced fifteen years earlier, when the output had been 267 million tons. By 1930 it had fallen to 244 million, by 1938 to 227 million. Manpower in the collieries had fallen still more rapidly. There

K*

were 1,214,000 employed in 1924. By 1930 there were 931,000 employed. By 1938 there were 781,000; and even so at the end of that year, out of some two million registered unemployed workers, 124,000 were miners.

Moreover, boys were not entering the industry. A whole generation had been taught by experience of unemployment (and the Means Test) that there was "no future in mining" and were paying heed to their mothers' saying "Don't go down the mine, son." In the coal-fields of Britain the fathers had eaten the sour grape of idleness and the children's teeth were set on edge. The reduced man-power was thus to a greater extent than ever before made up of ageing men, who would soon fall out of the industry. This annual "wastage" was mounting. So not only was there a shortage of man-power to meet war needs but, unless special measures were taken, there was bound to be an increasing shortage. Moreover, by the first two weeks of the war some 27,000 men had left the industry to join military and civil defence services.

Aware of all this, the miners' leaders had a twofold concern. First they had to help find the best solution of this formidable problem: second, they had to be vigilant against wrong methods of solving it. The older leaders remembered how in the 1914–18 war they had to resist Government proposals for longer hours, for the recruitment of the cheap labour of women and children and for the introduction of foreign labour, especially Chinese. Ebby Edwards had forebodings of what might happen. Therefore together with the questionnaire on means to gain more output he wrote a letter warning the Districts not to agree to a longer working day; nor to lowering of the school leaving age which "should be strenuously opposed"; nor to any extension in the employment of women, nor in the employment of boys on the night-shift. (September 23, 1939.)

During the later months of 1939 and throughout the winter, though man-power and output increased, there were difficulties in the distribution of coal. Exceptionally severe weather, coupled with delays in transport both by land and sea, brought a bad situation. Hundreds of thousands of people, not only in the smaller townships but also in the largest cities, were unable to procure supplies of fuel while at the same time many pits were working two and three days a week. Reporting to the July 1940 Annual Conference the M.F.G.B. Executive Committee said that the position then "could only be described as one of utter chaos" and that it had become "increasingly obvious" that even to maintain production man-power would have to be augmented.

The Government, in some alarm at the worsening situation, set up a Coal Production Council on April 9, 1940. Its purpose was to promote the greater production of coal "with a view to increasing coal exports while maintaining supplies for essential home consumption." Lord Portal was appointed Chairman: with him were nine others, three of them the officials representative of the mine-workers, three civil servants (from the Mines Department and from the Ministries of Transport and of Shipping) and three representatives of the mine-owners headed by Sir Evan Williams, Bart. The Council got to work rapidly. In that month of April Lord Portal visited and investigated fourteen different Districts. By April 30, 1940, the Council made its first Report to the Secretary for Mines. It was not optimistic and, indeed, could not be. Though the recruitment of some 60,000, mainly unemployed, miners had nearly made good the loss of 65,000 who had left the industry since the previous August, Lord Portal wrote "in terms of quality the loss of labour sustained is greater than is suggested by the figures." The rate of output pre-war was not high enough and man-power must be increased.

Our first concern is that the existing man-power shall not be further depleted; and as a first step we have already recommended that no more men employed in or about collieries shall be recruited for the Services, whether from underground or from surface.

But an even more serious factor was the continuing loss of men from collieries to firms engaged on Government work. In some Districts the loss from this cause was already as high as 10 per cent, rising at some large colliery undertakings to 15 per cent. This question, they considered, was "one which must be solved by His Majesty's Government." The Report also asked for the return to the mines of experienced colliery workmen engaged in civil defence or in such home defence units as the searchlight and anti-aircraft services. The Report of the Coal Production Council was put to the Economic Policy Committee of the War Cabinet. The decision was taken to keep the miners in the pits. On June 4, 1940, the Undertakings (Restriction on Engagement) Order[1] was applied to coal-mining. By the time this step was taken it was rather late and meantime the whole scene was altered.

4. BLACKPOOL ANNUAL CONFERENCE, 1940

A dramatic and dreadful change had occurred in the war situation. In January and February the French and British Governments had been busily despatching large quantities of arms and other munitions of war to Finland, then engaged in hostilities with the U.S.S.R., and the Prime Minister had been contemptuous of the German war effort. Suddenly in the second week of April 1940 the Germans overran and occupied Norway and Denmark and the subsequent British efforts to dislodge them suffered total defeat. In the second week of May the Germans invaded Holland and Belgium and soon penetrated deeply into France. The result was the resignation of Neville Chamberlain and the formation of a new Coalition Government under Winston Churchill as Prime Minister. The Labour Party joined the new Government with Clement Attlee as Deputy Premier. The Mineworkers' Federation supported this step. The new Government had to face a situation which worsened every day, with little immediate prospect of a way out. "I have nothing to offer but blood, toil, tears and sweat," said Churchill in the House of Commons on May 13th. By May 28th Leopold, King of the Belgians, surrendered to the Germans, while Holland was fully occupied. By May 31st British troops were being evacuated from Dunkirk with the loss of nearly all their armament. The next month saw the declaration of war by Italy upon Britain and France on June 10th and by mid-June Marshal Pétain had become the new Premier of the French Republic and was asking Hitler for terms of peace.

[1] S.R. & O., 1940, No. 877.

On May 13th the Labour Party Conference had given full support to the new Government by 2,413,000 votes to 170,000. Ernest Bevin, the new Minister of Labour and National Service, on the same day issued a call for maximum production to which the whole working force of the country responded. The output per man employed in the mines in the first quarter of 1940 had been 73·61 tons; in the second quarter from April to June it had jumped up to 81·09 tons. This was only accomplished by a prodigious effort which in the nature of things could not be sustained for more than a very short period. It was the highest figure reached during the war.

When the 182 delegates of the Mineworkers' Federation of Great Britain, together with the Executive Committee of 24 and the 3 officials, assembled in Blackpool on July 15, 1940, for their Annual Conference, they had to review the whole situation created by the outbreak of war and particularly the acute problems created by the Nazis' overrunning of so much of Europe, and finally the consequent changes in the political situation at home. On the question of the war itself there was no visible difference of opinion: but on the question of the new Coalition Government there was revealed a big division. Actually there were three resolutions before the Conference: one from Yorkshire, one from South Wales and one from Durham; and the Business Committee had been unable to obtain agreement from these three Districts on a composite resolution. The first resolution on the prosecution of the war was moved by W. E. Jones on behalf of the Yorkshire Miners' Association. It ran as follows:

The Conference of the Mineworkers' Federation of Great Britain expresses its fullest confidence in the British Prime Minister, and pledges its energetic support in the continued prosecution of the war.

It calls upon the Government to deal stringently with every influence which impedes in any way the prosecution of the war to a successful conclusion.

It further emphasises its determination to continue the struggle until the forces of freedom, now held in fetters in Europe, are released. (July 16, 1940.)

Ernest Jones in his opening speech stressed the resolution's three aspects, and then recalled how since the Nazi seizure of power in 1933 there had been "the destruction of the trade unions" in Germany and the other dreadful consequences, so that "we have seen comrades who have been associated with us in the fellowship of our miners' international movement murdered in concentration camps." All through the successive aggressions "by the Nazi hordes" there had been voices warning the former (Chamberlain) Government "that their policy of appeasement was strengthening the aggressor," voices not only from the British Labour movement—which was one reason why in the resolution "we make reference to the British Prime Minister." Ernest Jones, anticipating some opposition to the first aspect of the resolution, explained that the Yorkshire District had been "particularly anxious not to express its fullest confidence in the Government as it was constituted at this moment," and hence the expression of confidence "in the leader of the nation under whose guidance and leadership the trades unions and political movement at the beginning of May agreed to serve."

The resolution, formally seconded by E. Jones of North Wales, was then thrown open to discussion. Immediately J. W. Besford of Northumberland said the Yorkshire resolution was "both unnecessary and undesirable." He asked them to look at the record "of the present Prime Minister between wars" which "has been one of unswerving opposition to Labour and Trade Union policy": and ended by saying: "Any peace terms that are settled by a Government with Mr. Winston Churchill at the head will be peace terms with the object of continuing the exploitation of the workers on behalf of that privileged class."

Old Peter Chambers of Scotland, saying the resolution "has brought me out of my retirement," described Winston Churchill as "one of the cutest, cunningest and most unscrupulous politicians living in Britain today," and asked the delegates "Do you think that Winston Churchill will make any bones about crushing the Mineworkers' Federation whenever it suits him?" The rest of his speech was an out-and-out diatribe against Churchill in the course of which he recalled the 1926 struggle, saying that "anybody who knows Winston Churchill, or his father before him, knows perfectly well they have one of the blackest records in British history as far as politics are concerned." Peter Chambers, recalling his own I.L.P. propaganda of "thirty years ago," ended by warning the delegates that the Prime Minister "is going to turn another somersault":

He is looking ahead to Winston Churchill lasting all the time, and capitalism. My friends, I want to say to you that if this Conference passes a vote of confidence in Winston Churchill, then God help you.

After these two angry speeches it was obvious that a very heated discussion was likely to develop. So at this point Ebby Edwards intervened to suggest that all three resolutions should be taken together in discussion with separate votes at the end of the debate. This suggestion found favour with the Chairman. His ruling on procedure went to a vote and was carried by 356,000 to 135,000, the minority being made up of Scotland, Lancashire, Derbyshire, North Wales and the Forest of Dean. South Wales did not vote.

After the Durham resolution[1] had been moved by E. Moore and formally seconded, it came to the resolution of South Wales, which proved to be very contentious. It ran:

This Conference of the Mineworkers' Federation of Great Britain deplores the situation in which the British people find themselves largely in consequence of the policy pursued by the Chamberlain Government; a policy which has resulted in strengthening the potential enemies of Britain whilst weakening the forces who had common interests with us in preventing aggression.

The Conference pledges itself to do everything within its power to assist in maintaining the freedom of the British people and to ensure that neither occupation of British territory nor capitulation to the forces of aggression shall take place.

It considers it fundamental and essential to success in this effort that all those who, led by Chamberlain, pursued the policy which has created this situation shall now be retired from all offices in the Government so that a Government more representative of the people of this country shall be installed forthwith. (July 16, 1940.)

The resolution had been prepared as a result of prolonged discussion between the members of the Executive Council in South Wales and between them and the Welsh miners' Members of Parliament. Arthur Horner, moving the

[1] Given at the end of this section.

resolution, also went through the development of Chamberlain's policy, which had "strengthened the very forces which now menace this country."

Then, since no page in history had ever recorded "a ruling class forfeiting its power to save its country," Horner said bluntly:

Every time they have betrayed it, and betray it they will again. They will gag us. They will seek to smother us. They will endeavour to suppress criticism, and they will call it patriotic restriction. It is the preparation of the betrayal that it may be they are even now preparing. In this Government I am told Chamberlain is a hostage. You cannot get rid of him because he has got two or three or more Tory Members of Parliament who have declared that they will not support Churchill if Chamberlain is not retained in the Government. The thing is rotten—rotten with treachery. History will write what happened in France, after all the calumny and lies. But there is no record in the pages of the recent history of France where a member of the working class betrayed his country —never one case where a worker has been found guilty of treachery and rendering his country in the position of being lacking in defence.

Finally he ended by making it clear that it was not a matter of personalities but in his opinion of class interests, saying:

Why, the very submarines that have been sinking British boats came into existence as a result of a treaty entered into by Chamberlain with Hitler, behind the back of his ally, France, and in defiance of the terms of the Versailles Treaty. The very guns which come from the Skoda works, the money which has produced armaments, the ships which are sinking British ships, never would have existed had the British capitalist class hated Hitler. No, they hated working-class power.

We therefore declare that the time is coming when the slogan throughout the country, if the country is to be saved, must be: The old order has failed; the working class must begin to think of taking power. The time is rapidly approaching when we can no longer afford the luxury, or the risk, and no longer afford the danger of association with class interests which demand the termination of the war and the destruction of the best interests of the working class. (July 16, 1940.)

Horner was seconded by J. Williams of the Forest of Dean, who in his closing remarks also asserted it was not a question of personalities but of policies. He said that

Chamberlain's appeasement policy was "the policy of the City," and then he concluded:

I want Mr. Chamberlain removed so that his past policy can be buried for ever, and never resurrected. His policy has largely been responsible for our present position. He treated Russia as though it were a leper. He fraternised with Hitler and Mussolini at Munich. He ignored and despised Russia. Russia was excluded, with calculation, from the Munich negotiations. I submit that that treatment was responsible for the Russian and German non-aggression pact. We have paid dearly for that policy. For that folly we are paying dearly now. We shall pay dearly for it in the future.

Jack Williams wanted improved relations with the Soviet Union which was "a nightmare to Hitler" and which "in the last round of this scrap," he predicted, would be together with Britain against Germany: but "so long as Chamberlain remains in the Government, Russia will be suspicious." The South Wales resolution was immediately assailed by a speaker from Northumberland, W. Hogg, followed by J. E. Swan of Durham, who urged strongly that South Wales should withdraw its resolution. H. Cooper of Nottingham supported the Yorkshire resolution as "the simplest and the most straightforward."

At this point Ebby Edwards intervened and suggested that both Yorkshire and South Wales resolutions should be withdrawn. In particular against South Wales he quoted statements from the Secretary of the Labour Party (James Middleton) and from a broadcast by Attlee directed against any change in the Government at this time. He ended by saying:

I think we should leave the situation to those men who are in the Cabinet. There are more ways and means of testing the honour and integrity of Chamberlain and others than merely passing resolutions. I do not want to go into ways and means, but I hope Yorkshire and Wales will withdraw their resolutions. With sufficient success and the ability to negotiate at the right time we should be able to lay the foundations of what will be a permanent peace the world over. (July 16, 1940.)

After W. Pearson of Scotland had spoken in favour of South Wales the Chairman took up the Secretary's suggestion and asked if Yorkshire and South Wales were prepared to withdraw. W. E. Jones said that they were prepared to amend their resolution, but South Wales would not move. The Chairman then said:

I say emphatically that if the Welsh resolution was carried in this conference, the honourable thing for this Federation to do is to say that in the event of that not being carried out, then every member we have got in the Government—and it is not only Dai Grenfell; there are Tom Williams, George Hall, Wilfred Paling, and Whiteley—to say that every one of them shall clear out of the Government, because you cannot be linked with a Government that has someone in it with whom you do not agree.

After the Chairman's statement W. E. Jones said: "I have to indicate on behalf of Yorkshire that they withdraw their resolution, and decide to give full support to the Durham resolution." The Chairman thereupon called for a vote on the Durham resolution which ran as follows:

This Conference of the Mineworkers' Federation of Great Britain firmly endorses the Statement of Policy as declared by the Labour Party and the Trades Union Congress, on Labour, The War and The Peace.

We further endorse the declaration of Mr. C. R. Attlee, M.P., Leader of the Labour Party, in defining Labour's Peace Aims in his speech on November 8, 1939, which was further implemented on February 9, 1940, by the statement issued by the National Executive of the British Labour Party, stating clearly the policy of the Party on Labour, The War and The Peace.

We assure our loyal support to the Labour Party and the Trades Union Congress in the stand they have taken against aggression and for the restoration of freedom and liberty and the building up of a new Social Order amongst the nations of the world, believing that this is the only sound basis for peace and progress, amongst the peoples of all nations. (July 16, 1940.)

This resolution, which did not raise any of the contentious issues, had the wholehearted support of the Conference and was carried unanimously. Thereafter the South Wales resolution went to a vote and was defeated by 430,000 to 161,000, the minority being made up of South Wales, Scotland, Cumberland and the Forest of Dean. Thus ended a debate which had brought out very clearly the different opinions subsisting inside the Mineworkers' Federation on the outlook towards the Coalition Government, though all seemed to agree in their main attitude towards the war.

5. THE GROWTH OF A COAL CRISIS

At Blackpool the delegates to the Annual Conference were only too well aware how war now affected the mining industry. A resolution[1] on coal trade policy (finally remitted to the Executive Committee) began as follows:

This Conference of the Mineworkers' Federation of Great Britain having examined the enormous changes which have taken place in the coal trade perspective of Great Britain in consequence of the recent occupation of Holland and Belgium, the declaration of war by Italy and the cessation of hostilities between France and Germany, including the interference with the coal export trade of this country, declares:

(1) That we consider it necessary that every possible step should be taken to maintain the maximum coal production during the present crisis, that export markets may be maintained and extended wherever it is possible to export coal, and that provision be made to carry on the industries of the country in all circumstances while maintaining a reasonable supply of fuel to the inhabitants.

(2) That we are of the opinion that existing units should be kept in production even though short time working might be necessary for the time being, and that the man-power allocated to the industry should be maintained.

But it was another matter to carry out these proposals. The catastrophic change, not only in exports, but in all the conditions of inland transport together with the new strain caused during that summer of 1940 through the bombing of airfields and railways by Luftwaffe aeroplanes from Germany or from occupied France, Belgium and Holland, made it impossible to maintain maximum coal production. Many pits were stopped for days at a time. Thousands of miners could get no work. The number unemployed in the coal-mining industry had been 124,000 in December 1939: so slowly had the slack been taken in. But by June 1940 this number had been reduced to 32,000, many of whom were more in need of sick care than of

[1] Other resolutions dealt with workmen's compensation; a weekly minimum wage of £3; scientific treatment of coal; air raid precautions (A.R.P.); and new rules stipulating that the District associations keep the Federation officials informed of any important negotiations and that "each district association shall send to the Secretary of the Federation copies of all documents, literature and balance sheets as issued to its membership."

employment. Two months later the number of unemployed miners leaped up to 56,000 and was increasing week by week. By the autumn the number of wage earners on the colliery books had fallen steeply, but these unemployed miners were not allowed by the Undertakings (Restriction on Engagement) Order of June 4th to enter any other industry or any of the Services that were crying out for men. One of the other resolutions adopted at the Annual Conference, instructing the Executive Committee "to negotiate a demand for a weekly minimum wage of not less than £3 per week for all adult workers," indicated clearly the sort of step which could have retained man-power in the first five months of 1940 and would have attracted man-power when this sudden unemployment came to an end.

By the beginning of September 1940 the "Battle of Britain" began with enemy bombing of London and other towns and centres of industry by day and by night. These raids continued with full intensity till mid-May 1941. This brought all the problems connected with air-raid precautions and civil defence, while there were other problems arising from the additional taxation and from food rationing. The supplies of food in mining villages had been at a comparatively low level in the years preceding the war. The new Ministry of Food rigidly based its distribution schemes (and later the famous "Points" scheme) on pre-war consumption statistics. The miners' consumption of food, because of unemployment and low wages, had been lower than elsewhere: yet on this low standard, due to their poverty, their war-time allocations were based. This had inevitable inequalities. More goods than were necessary were for a time going to seaside towns on the southern coast, many of whose inhabitants were evacuated, while on the other hand, supplies to the mining villages were seldom really satisfactory.

By the late autumn and early winter of 1940, amid the preoccupation of miners' officials and of union committees with these additional problems, the plight of the newly unemployed miners became urgent. On September 5th, it was the subject of a debate in the House of Commons. The matter was much discussed with Dai Grenfell who had been appointed Secretary for Mines in the new Churchill Coalition Government and who himself was one of the best known of the miners' M.P.s from South Wales.

It was Grenfell's business to retain as large a man-power as possible. He worked out various expedients to meet the case of the unemployed miners, but with the pressure of demand from the Services and from the munitions industries, he was forced to yield. For on September 20th, Ernest Bevin as Minister of Labour announced that young miners would be called up, and that some older men would be released for other work. The next day Dai Grenfell had to tell the Executive Committee that after other schemes for absorption of unemployed miners had been tried "there still remained a large number of miners who would not be able to be absorbed, and the only course left open for them was to join the Armed Forces. This was to be made effective by the Minister of Labour by raising the age of reservation in the mining industry." Finally at a meeting of the Coal Production Council on October 15th the following proposal was made and accepted the next day by the M.F.G.B. Executive Committee:

The only men who can be spared from the Coal Mining Industry without serious interference with supply of essential requirements are those registered by the Ministry of Labour as wholly unemployed. Such men, being no longer employed in the industry, should cease to be reserved from Military Service for that reason, and if above the age required for such service should be available for other industries. (October 16, 1940.)

The result was a loss of mining man-power to the Armed Forces and to the new munitions industries. The figure of the average number of wage-earners fell quarter by quarter throughout 1940 and up to the middle of 1941, with a corresponding fall in output. Here are the figures:

Quarter	Average No. of Wage-earners	Output of Saleable Coal (tons)
April–June 1940	764,307	61,974,100
July–Sept. 1940	755,257	55,168,100
Oct.–Dec. 1940	716,659	51,179,000
Jan.–Mar. 1941	695,433	50,249,600
April–June 1941	690,404	51,064,600

The Government was later to come in for severe criticism for having conscripted miners and encouraged them to drift out of the industry in 1940 despite warnings given; the Select Committee on Expenditure of the House of Commons considered that:

The consequent psychological effect on the miners of the absence of any measures to meet this sudden change in demand was deplorable, as at one moment they were urged to produce as much as possible and the next they found themselves without work.

Amid that winter blitz of 1940–41 the warnings of the Secretary for Mines had not come home to the Government. Week by week and month by month man-power and output were falling. The crisis was growing, but it was not until the spring of 1941 that the Government realised the development of a coal crisis.[1] Thereafter it was never absent from the minds of the Cabinet Economic Committee. But this did not mean that they found an immediate solution. Months and years had to pass before the necessary drastic steps were taken and even that was too little and too late. In the spring of 1941 the immediate step they took was to apply the Essential Work Order under the Emergency Powers Act.[2]

6. M.F.G.B. PLANS FOR THE COAL CRISIS

Meantime, during the growth of a coal crisis, the Federation leaders were working towards a solution of the problems that beset the industry. For some considerable time they had retained a hope that the Government would make full use of the remarkable provisions of the Emergency Powers (Defence) Act of May 22, 1940. A year later the Executive Committee in its May 31st Report

[1] Opening a parliamentary debate the President of the Board of Trade (Oliver Lyttelton) frankly admitted the crisis ("due to unemployment and this disparity in wages") and said: "If those 75,000 were in the industry there would be a production greatly exceeding the target." (*Hansard*, May 28, 1941.) But the Government's proposed solution for the coal crisis (as well as their responsibility for its emergence) came under criticism from the mining Members of Parliament.

[2] S.R. & O., 1941, No. 707. Emergency Powers (Defence) Essential Work (Coalmining Industry) Order, 1941, May 15th.

was still calling particular attention to it, and to "the enormous, nearly unlimited power the Government secured":

CLAUSE 1. The powers conferred on His Majesty by the Emergency Powers (Defence) Act, 1939, shall, notwithstanding anything in that Act, include power by Order in Council to make such *Defence Regulations making provision for requiring persons to place themselves, their services, and their property, at the disposal of His Majesty*, as appear to him to be necessary or expedient for securing the public safety, the Defence of the Realm, the maintenance of public order, or the efficient prosecution of any war in which His Majesty may be engaged, or for maintaining supplies or services essential to the life of the community. (Italics by E.C. of M.F.G.B.)

They added the comment that "these are great powers for a democratic government." Indeed, they were such powers as no Government, democratic or despotic, modern or feudal, had ever possessed in this country. There began to be keen disappointment that these powers were not used. Five months after the Act the Federation Executive sent on to the Trades Union Congress and to the Labour Party the following resolution from the Scottish District:

That we ask the Government to put into operation (The Emergency Powers Act of May 22nd, 1940, which gives the Government power to conscript persons and property) that part which up till now, has not been operated, viz., "The Conscription of Wealth." (October 16, 1940.)

They learned on January 17, 1941, that the Labour Party Executive would consider it at its next meeting.

At its September 1940 meeting the M.F.G.B. Executive Committee took up the resolutions referred to it from the Annual Conference on coal trade policy and national control. They were told at that meeting that the Government had decided to compensate the coal-owners for maintaining in a state of productivity collieries affected directly or indirectly by enemy action by means of a levy on all disposable coal produced: and the Secretary for Mines at a later stage of the meeting attended and explained this scheme for compensating coal-owners. The Executive then decided that a sub-committee should formulate a policy on the basis of the resolutions of the Annual Conference.

By their meeting of November 21, 1940, the sub-committee recommended the step to be taken, namely, that the Trades Union Congress and Labour Party should be invited to implement *Labour's Plan for the Coal Industry*, the policy of nationalisation adopted in 1936–37; and a week later it was learned that these two bodies had decided to set up a joint committee to examine the problem.

When this joint committee of the two national bodies gave their Report it was accepted at the National Council of Labour (composed of representatives from the same two national bodies, together with representatives of the Co-operative Union) on December 17, 1940. When on the next day it came up to be ratified by the T.U.C. General Council, Ebby Edwards moved its reference back—which was carried. Thereafter there was considerable correspondence and further meetings. The whole matter was fully reported to the January 31, 1941, meeting of the M.F.G.B. Executive Committee by Edwards, with the recommendation of the National Council of Labour that "the promotion of legislation to implement the Labour Plan for the Mining Industry is not feasible in present circumstances": he stated that "the General Movement is not prepared to go forward to seek by legislation to embody their own plan for the mining industry as passed by National Conferences in 1936" but that it requested the Federation to consider the possibilities of securing a scheme of national control and national pooling as a war emergency measure.

The miners' leaders were not pleased (and six months later their Annual Conference showed itself very displeased) at the way their proposals for saving the industry had been treated. But they took up the task to see how far arrangements could be made for the unification of the industry. At successive executives and sub-committees, under the heading of Coal Trade Policy, they worked out the plan for a National Board to cover the mining industry, to be composed of an equal number of representatives of employers and workmen, and to deal with all matters. But when the first formulation of this policy (March 24, 1941) came up before the Executive, it had to be held in abeyance as they found themselves faced with new Government proposals to solve the crisis. Thus it was not until some months later that the final formulation of this policy was reached and put forward, together with what they regarded and reaffirmed as the better policy, namely nationalisation.

7. COMPULSION OVER MINE-WORKERS

While the Federation, concerned with the developing coal crisis, had been engaged on its two alternative solutions each of which applied to the industry as a whole, the Ministry of Labour and National Service had been concentrating mainly on one facet of the problem, the shortage of mine-workers. For one reason and another the coal crisis had not been foreseen: and when in the early spring of 1941 the insatiable demand of the war brought it forcibly to the attention of the Government, a rapid solution was sought in piecemeal measures. Neither of the M.F.G.B. plans for a thoroughgoing solution were considered by the Government to be at all necessary. Apart from other lesser measures, their proposed solution was the use of compulsory powers under the Essential Work Order. The essence of this was that each colliery became a "scheduled undertaking" from which a worker could neither go nor be dismissed and in which therefore he must have his regular wage guaranteed. Any question of leaving or dismissal came before a National Service Officer into whose hands was committed also the disciplinary power in cases of misconduct or absenteeism. Other industries had come under the scope of this Order from March onwards: but its application to coal-mining, a low-wage industry (which for over six months had also been subjected to sudden and severe unemployment) was bound to have peculiar effects. Contractors in other industries, often under the "cost plus" system, had been eagerly recruiting labour at relatively high rates of remuneration. But since in the coal-fields there was no general increase in wage-rates, coal-mining seemed to be singled out as an occupation where men would be tied to the pits under specially onerous conditions. Thus one change effected by the Essential Work Order, as the official historian of the Second World War candidly points out,[1] was that in the name of the national interest the colliers were bound to the industry more closely than had happened at any time since the old days of "the yearly bond" on the north-east coast or of the "statutory slavery" of the Scottish miners in the eighteenth century.[2] Under these circumstances, the Essential Work Order, whether or not it would be efficacious to solve the coal production problem in 1941, was certainly likely to be productive of trouble in the months ahead.

The miners' leaders got an inkling at the Coal Production Council on April 1st of proposals arising for compulsion of labour. The Executive Committee discussed it the next day and resolved:

That this Federation declares its opposition to the principle of compulsion as applied to the retention in, or return to the industry of mineworkers, unless satisfactory wage standards can be negotiated and some effective measure of control of the industry be extended to the workmen's representatives. (April 2, 1941.)

On April 8th they heard by letter from the Mines Department that the Government wished to apply the Essential Work (General Provisions) Order[3] of March 5th to coal-mining and asked for joint deliberation on it by owners and men. The M.F.G.B. Executive Committee drew up a series of eight propositions, most of which on the next morning the owners accepted: and Sir Evan Williams acted as spokesman for the agreed proposals at the meeting with the Secretary for Mines. But to three of the M.F.G.B. propositions (a joint national board to cover all problems affecting the industry, a satisfactory guaranteed weekly wage, abolition of non-unionism) the owners did not agree: and, as it turned out, neither did the Mines Department. So a day later the whole Executive Committee argued these three points with the Secretary for Mines. David Grenfell, it turned out, was personally in favour of a National Board, saying, "I would have no objection to endorsing the question of a National Board as stated by you." He was willing to

[1] *Coal* by W. H. B. Court, Chapter VII (iii), p. 140.
[2] See *The Miners*, Chapter I, and *A History of the Scottish Miners*.
[3] S.R. & O., 1941, No. 302.

make a recommendation to the owners that they should meet the miners on these points; and asked:

If we say that we will endeavour to get this meeting to consider those points, would that satisfy you? (April 10, 1941.)

After this interview the Executive Committee had a lengthy discussion. They decided to "note" the decision of the Government to introduce the Essential Work Order and "to inform the Minister that the Federation calls for the collaboration of the Mines Department towards the establishment of a National Board with power to consider wages or other matters affecting the industry." (April 10, 1941.)

In subsequent meetings with not only the Secretary for Mines but also with his superior, the President of the Board of Trade, Oliver Lyttelton, it became clear that the desired collaboration would not be forthcoming nor would the Government countenance the inclusion in the Order of the three stipulations put forward by the Federation. This brought a sharp difference of opinion within the Executive Committee at its meeting on May 1st. Some were for accepting the Order. Some wanted to reject the Order. Both these motions were defeated; and it was agreed simply to call a Special Conference which should decide the matter.

At this two-day Special Conference there was keen discussion. Joe Hall of Yorkshire bluntly asked: "What is the cause of this Order?" He gave as the reason for it "the continued complaints through the Press" and the "prosecutions of our men for absenteeism, with no defence in court." This continued ridicule, which he found "astounding," was also "untruthful":

Under the contract system in the mines a man must be perfectly fit when going into the pit. He cannot go like an ordinary workman to the factory or the man who goes to his office, saying he is going whether he is fit or not. He has to be fit. Ours is an industry where Nature has never been kind to us, and never will be. (May 8, 1941.)

Vice-Chairman James Bowman, who considered that the guaranteed week was "the only single advantage which accrues from the application of this Order," criticised the provisions in detail, especially the powers of the National

Service Officer. He recalled what had happened a year earlier, when, following the visits of Lord Portal to the Districts, the miners' unions "threw themselves into the spirit then evinced by the whole of the people in the coal-field to spur on and meet the needs of production." At that time they had set up Pit Committees. But, he went on:

What did we find? We found that at the collieries, instead of the whole issue of production being discussed, the colliery manager was simply shelving everything and making Pit Production Committees, at least in my district, a medium for discussing absenteeism and absenteeism only, and it is because of that that Pit Committees fell out of use in my district. Some districts had even arranged to impose penalties by way of fines. (May 8, 1941.)

But the Essential Work Order went much further than the practice of earlier months in which the function of the Pit Committees for increasing production had been largely misused.

Under this Order it will not be a question of Pit Committees imposing penalties on men for absenteeism. It is provided that men may be fined to the extent of £100 or imprisoned for three months if convicted of a breach of this Order, which can include continued absenteeism after the National Service Officer has given his decision.

The Chancellor of the Exchequer had a policy "of holding wage levels, of holding price levels, in order to avoid inflation": but, said Bowman, they had learned that morning that "the Colliery Owners by the use of those powers which they are so able to use amongst the circle of their friends within and without the Government, have been able to get past that policy of the Chancellor of the Exchequer, and have been able to arrange for price increases to cover the cost to them of the guaranteed week." He claimed that in certain Districts the owners had gone one better, and had got price increases apart from the guaranteed week. Bowman concluded that "unless we get a National Board and a wages advance, and unless the non-union position is assured, we are not prepared to be associated with the operation of the order."

The South Wales standpoint was then put by Arthur Horner, who gave a warning that, unless necessary steps were taken, "next winter will see the most serious coal famine this country has ever experienced." The chief factor for reduced production was neither absenteeism nor slackening effort but reduced man-power. The number of men employed had been contracting ever since June 1940.

"In South Wales we were 140,000: now we are not 109,000." Men had been leaving because mining was less attractive, and could not "compete in wages or conditions" with other industries.

"We were putting forward proposals before the Essential Work Order was thought of," said Horner, recalling their plan at Gloucester in November 1940 for "the solution of the problem by taking the industry out of its present archaic situation, and unifying the control of it so that the workmen have a say in the operation." But the National Council of Labour had not accepted this "due to their commitments to the Government" but would support plans for greater control: "national control short of national ownership, and we accepted that position with regret."

If you want coal production increased you get the men and keep the men, and in order to do so, and attract others, you must increase the wages, and guarantee the men six days' pay when they are available for work. There are thousands of skilled miners in Government jobs, some sweeping floors, for higher wages than they can get as skilled colliers. And these men, many of whom would return to the mines, are prevented from returning even if they want to do so. (May 8, 1941.)

They must have the men back. He had had scores of letters from men in the Territorials who had done nothing since the war began but clean officers' boots. Horner ended by urging that they should go to the National Council of Labour, "and ask them if they will keep their second promise, their own suggested course of action."

The next delegate, William Pearson from Scotland, asked the delegates to bear in mind that "just at the time when this country was suffering from a coal shortage during the winter, Mr. Bevin was demanding more and more men from the mining industry into the armed forces, and that policy of the Government is responsible for the present position of the mining industry." He said that the great

powers assumed by the Government had been operated
"against the working class, but when it comes to dealing
with the owners of property, then the Government is not
prepared to put into operation any powers at all."

In this animated and critical manner the debate went
on, with increasing demand for the Executive Committee
to put proposals. On the morning of the second day the
Executive Committee proposed that the Conference adjourn,
to enable the Executive Committee "to impress upon the
Government the necessity of their consent to our request
on the three points—the National Board, increased wages,
and non-unionism—if needs be in or outside the Order."
This was carried by 464,000 to the 100,000 of the South
Wales Miners' Federation which alone voted "against the
Essential Work Order on principle." The Executive Com-
mittee a few hours later returned from their interview bearing
the following message from the hands of Oliver Lyttelton,
President of the Board of Trade.

(1) The Government regard it as a matter of vital national
importance that the miners' representatives should today
recommend the acceptance of the Essential Work Order.
(2) The Government regard the subject of rates of wages as a
matter for negotiation under the existing machinery and
could therefore not agree to introduce legislation which
would compel the establishment of a National Board.
(3) The Government understands that if so requested the
owners are prepared to enter at once into these negotiations,
and the Government undertakes to do all possible to ensure
that they are carried through speedily.

After this was read and explained to the resumed Special
Conference, the Executive Committee made the following
recommendation:

That the Conference strongly protests against the owners and
the Government failing to appreciate the need for increased wages
in the operation of the Essential Work Order, but in view of the
serious war situation the Conference recommends the Consultative
Committee be given power to examine, seek to amend and apply
the Order in terms applicable to the mining industry.

Further, the Conference recommends the Executive Committee
to press for fundamental changes in the industry having regard
to the wages position. (May 9, 1941.)

This resolution was then carried by 370,000 to 194,000, the minority being made up of South Wales, Scotland, Northumberland, Kent and Cumberland. The terms of the acceptance, as well as the higher minority vote, showed how uneasy the miners felt about this measure. Aware of this, the Executive Committee at its May 14th meeting decided to press for a weekly minimum wage of not less than four pounds for every adult mine-worker.

8. THE ATTENDANCE BONUS

At the National Joint Standing Consultative Committee on May 21st the request for a satisfactory guaranteed weekly wage in the shape of £4 a week minimum was put forward: and was argued by Ebby Edwards with his usual skill. But Sir Evan Williams, Chairman of the Mining Association since 1921, was also very skilled. He recalled the special war additions agreement of March 1940, that wages generally must be dealt with District by District and not on a national basis, saying "we know of nothing of a national character that applies to this industry as a whole or other industries as a whole, which has changed the question in a way that would warrant any application from you for a departure, even of a small nature, from the basis on which we made that agreement." Sir Evan professed himself at a loss to understand why this demand had been made, saying that the fact that higher wages were paid in other industries did not make the miners' position any worse; and that the demand, if granted, "would be a most deleterious thing for the industry as a whole; a lot of people having the same wage quite regardless of the work."

Sir Evan Williams then made an offer of a weekly bonus to be given "for the man that puts in full time," remarking in his most sympathetic manner that "it is very difficult for you when you have made a demand authorised by a Conference like you had, to go back and say that you have got nothing." Normally the owners would have faced that, but at this time they doubted if they should "allow an atmosphere of friction to be created." He concluded:

Now it is purely in the interest of what is called atmosphere that we make this suggestion, not that we think that circumstances justify it.

Ebby Edwards protested. He argued that the circumstances in the industry were really changed since the fall of France, including also "the tremendous difference in the wages paid in other industries." He gave an example, "here you have men working in this industry where their daughters are working on the other side of the road and taking £2 a week more than their fathers home in wages." Just before the miners retired to take counsel together the following exchange took place:

Mr. W. Lawther: You make the offer of a principle?

Sir Evan Williams: Well, we would quote a figure in addition to the 4d. cost of living increase you will be due to receive in July. We are prepared to put another 6d. a day on that to cover all regular workers.

Mr. Ebby Edwards: I take it now, Sir Evan, before we retire, that you have really considered the offer that you are making? In concrete form it is 6d. a day conditionally on a man attending at his work for a complete working week?

Sir Evan Williams: Yes, but I say that we must insist upon the Government giving us a corresponding increase in the price of coal from the day on which we have to pay this sum. If the Government cannot give us a corresponding increase in the price of coal, we cannot even do what we have offered. (May 21, 1941.)

The Federation representatives on the Consultative Committee had information that a number of the Districts were in favour of flat rate increases and opposed to the minimum wage proposal of £4 per week. Sir Evan Williams, it appeared, also knew this.[1] So they went back with a counter request

---

[1] In their report to the Annual Conference the Executive Committee commented on this as follows:

"The decision of your Committee to request a £4 weekly minimum wage was taken by the only means available; that of a majority vote on May 14, 1941. The meeting with the owners to consider our request was fixed for May 21, 1941. Between these two dates a number of districts, covering a substantial proportion of the Federation membership, had already made it known they were opposed to the application of a a minimum weekly wage of £4. They desired a general advance in wages as distinct and in opposition to the suggested minimum. This procedure reduces national negotiations to a farce.

"Further, it is a common feature that between the negotiation of your Consultative Committee with the owners and the time elapsing to report to the Executive Committee, districts arrive at decisions and determine policy. The National Executive members thus become merely mandated district delegates and are prohibited from viewing the facts in the interests of the membership as a whole. To say the least, it is unsatisfactory." (June 9, 1941.)

EBBY EDWARDS
At the 78th Trades Union Congress, Brighton

YORKSHIRE MINERS' GALA AT BARNSLEY

for 1s. a day for adults and 6d. a day for others. To this Sir Evan Williams replied:

Well, you have put a very difficult problem to us. We find it exceedingly sticky. We believe quite definitely that there is a responsibility attached to the Government for this position. They have come into these discussions and said certain things to you and quite frankly they have said to us that something must be given because of the situation that has arisen. They say, "here is a position where a demand has been made; if you refuse it, it will have a bad effect on the atmosphere of the war situation. Now you are asking us to meet an increased cost of 1s. and 6d." You are putting us into a position of having to ask the Government for practically double the needs we believed would be necessary. (May 21, 1941.)

Then the mine-owners conferred together. By the next day they concluded that "if we can get the mines department to finance the thing, we would put no obstacle in the way of accepting the request for 1s. and 6d. respectively." The Government did agree; and it put up the price of coal by 10d. a ton from June 1st. The M.F.G.B. Executive Committee, however, were not yet satisfied with the conditions under which the bonus would be payable: further negotiations brought agreement on June 6th.

Five weeks later the Annual Conference opened at Ayr. The conditions attached to the bonus had roused a storm in the coal-fields; in practice they were found to work out with great unfairness, and any 1s. not paid accrued to the benefit of the coal-owners. After a long and in parts very stormy debate on the reference back of the Executive Report on this matter, the outcome was unanimous:

That this Conference, in the light of their experience of the working conditions attached to the attendance bonus, instructs the Executive Committee through the National Consultative Committee to approach the Owners with a view to the withdrawal of the conditions attached to the attendance bonus. (July 15, 1941.)

Three weeks later the M.F.G.B. Executive Committee, dealing with the attendance bonus and being "convinced that its operation is not helping but hindering the production of coal" resolved to demand "the withdrawal of the conditions attached to the bonus as being against the national interests and the well-being of the miners."

The owners in the course of the summer had also found out how much trouble the bonus had caused. So on September 4th it was agreed "that the conditions as to full attendance attached to the bonus are dispensed with," while the District Coal Production Committees were now to see to it "that machinery be set up at each pit to ensure that effective measures shall be taken at the pit to deal with any persons whose conduct militates against the maximum possible production of coal."

Thus by the last quarter of 1941 the miners were getting cost of living war additions of 2s. 8d. a shift to which there was now added unconditionally the bonus of 1s. The cost of living additions according to the Executive Committee's reckoning should have been ·88d. for each point rise in the Index. But the March 1940 agreement had settled it at ·7d. for each point. Therefore the Executive Committee Report to the Annual Conference could only make the rueful comment "the cost of living has gone up (by February 1941) 42 points since the war, so that the difference between our request of ·88d. and the settlement of ·7d. means a difference to a disadvantage of 6·7d. per shift, or 3/4d. per week of six shifts." (May 31, 1941.)

After these arduous negotiations with the Government and with the coal-owners in May and the first part of June, negotiations which involved a great deal of detail and left the miners' representatives (and to an even greater extent the men in the coal-fields) not at all satisfied, there came an unexpected development in the war situation. This was to have a profound effect on every section of the British people and not least on the miners.

9. CLIMACTERIC OF THE WAR

It was, as Churchill put it, a climacteric of the war when Nazi Germany suddenly attacked the Union of Soviet Socialist Republics on June 22, 1941. Three weeks later at the Annual Conference the delegates passed unanimously the following resolution moved by H. Tunney of Durham and seconded by Abe Moffat of Scotland:

This Conference of the Mineworkers' Federation of Great Britain places on record its warm appreciation and support for the speech made by the Prime Minister, Mr. Winston Churchill, on behalf of the British Government, Sunday, June 22, 1941, when he promised to support the Soviet Union in the struggle against the unwarranted and unprovoked aggression of the Nazis.

Further, we pledge ourselves to do all in our power to assist the Russian workers in their fight against fascism by giving economic and military support to them in the struggle.

We urge that the workers in Europe will not support their military leaders in making war on the Soviet Union and call upon them to use every means in their power to prevent this being done.

We send our warmest greetings to all the Peoples of the Soviet Union, and trust that in the great struggle against fascism, which is the common task of all the workers of the world, the British and Russian peoples shall work together for the purpose of eliminating fascism from Europe, so that the peoples of the oppressed countries can once more enjoy national independence and economic security in a world free from oppression and Nazi brutality.

Further we pledge ourselves to loyally support the Government in every effort they make to supplement military and economic support to the Russian people. (July 15, 1941.)

It was unusual in unopposed resolutions that were likely to be carried unanimously for there to be additional speakers beyond the mover and seconder. But on this occasion supporting speeches were made by rank and file speakers. I. Evans of South Wales, with his eye on the Chairman, recalled heated discussions of a year and a half before, claiming (but in a mild enough manner) that "South Wales does seem to have been right in their opinion as regards the Soviet's getting new frontiers in Finland. Leading the people of Finland at that time was the famous butcher[1] Mannerheim. He is in his proper place at the present time along with his fascist allies.

"We cannot forget also that in 1926 our Soviet comrades came to our aid so magnificently, and I am hoping that this M.F.G.B. Conference will pledge itself just as the South Wales coalfield has already done, to see to it that full aid is given to the Soviet Union despite any pro-Fascism that may exist in the country or in the Government."

[1] Ianto Evans amplified his epithet in an explanatory passage:

"We cannot forget the time when that man led out three thousand of our best trade unionists and told them to dig their own graves on that famous field in Finland, and mowed them down with machine guns, buried them in those very graves, and called that field afterwards the 'Field of Liberty.' "

The Executive Committee elected at the Annual Conference set up at its first meeting a fund "to demonstrate in a practical way the bonds of friendship and solidarity between the Russian miners and the Mineworkers' Federation of Great Britain." They asked the Districts to endorse a payment of 2s. 6d. per affiliated member towards this end. A week later Ebby Edwards was able to send a telegram to I. M. Maisky, Ambassador of the U.S.S.R. in Great Britain, informing him of "a gift of over £70,000 to the Russian workers in their struggle against Nazi aggression" and adding:

Please convey to all the peoples of the U.S.S.R. our deep-felt gratitude and appreciation at the fight your heroic Red Army men, sailors and Air Force men are waging with immeasurable gallantry. My Federation invites a visit to Great Britain of representatives of the Russian miners. The workers of our two countries must be brought closer together if such a titanic struggle is to end speedily and successfully with the complete freedom of the toilers of all lands. (August 15, 1941.)

In reply Maisky conveyed the Soviet Government's "warmest gratitude" together with the poignant suggestion that the best form this aid could take would be "surgical instruments and medical supplies." These were purchased and sent, several Labour Members of Parliament having gladly helped in the choice and inspection. Meantime things had gone badly on the Eastern Front where the Nazi drive had behind it an enormous weight of armour, concentration of the Luftwaffe and a man-power of some 300 divisions. Most of the experts had assumed that the U.S.S.R. would collapse—some said in six weeks, and the more optimistic, in the same number of months. But at the opening of the winter of 1941–42 the Nazi onrush was held before they could reach Moscow. On December 3rd Ebby Edwards received a further letter of thanks from Ivan Maisky to the Federation for their "very generous help towards my country, and more particularly towards the Red Army so heroically fighting, not only for their own Fatherland, but also for the freedom and liberty of all nations." Maisky pointed out that:

The Miners' Federation of Great Britain was the first of the public bodies to take the initiative in helping the Soviet Union

in its hard and difficult struggle. It was also the first to fulfil the
list of requirements forwarded by my Government, and the first
in sending substantial medical supplies from that list to the
U.S.S.R.

This appreciative letter the Secretary circulated to all
Districts so that it could be brought to the attention "of
the individual members of the Mineworkers' Federation." A
fortnight later the Executive passed the following resolution:

The British Peoples and the British Mineworkers in particular,
are following with profound pride and appreciation the heroic
and determined resistance of the Russian Peoples against their
cruel and dastardly aggressors.

With acclamation we congratulate the Red Army on its magnificent successes now being evinced by its glorious offensive against
the Nazi hordes, and pray that with the assistance of its Allies,
the U.S.S.R. will soon have purged its beloved soil of the impious
and execrable Nazi hordes. (December 19, 1941.)

10. NATIONALISATION AND/OR CONTROL

Eight months had passed since the M.F.G.B. Committee
had put forward their plans for making the coal-mining
industry fit to do all that was needed in the war emergency,
six months since their proposals had been rejected by the
leaders of the Labour Party. Now, reviewing the much
more acute stage of the coal crisis at their Ayr Annual
Conference, they took a twofold decision. The first was as
follows:

This Conference of the Mineworkers' Federation of Great
Britain regrets the action of the Labour Party and Trades Union
Congress General Council in failing to implement the resolutions
relating to the nationalisation of the mining industry and reiterates
its demands for the nationalisation of the coal mining and ancillary
industries, with effective workers' control.

Having regard to the international situation, the precarious
state of the country, the importance of producing a considerably
increased output of coal in the present emergency and the need
for an increased rate of wages for the workpeople employed in the
industry, it instructs the National Executive Committee to make
an early approach to the Government in connection with this
matter. (July 16, 1941.)

What the miners regarded as a second best solution of the coal crisis was remitted by the Annual Conference to the Executive and its responsible sub-committee to be re-examined and restated in final form. This was put with a preamble in shorter compass as follows:

The Mineworkers' Federation of Great Britain regards the control of the Mining Industry by the Nation as one of urgency, with a view to obtaining the maximum efficiency in production by which the needs of the nation can be safeguarded. Such control shall provide for National and District Boards, upon which representatives of the workers shall be appointed to deal with all questions connected with the industry, and, towards that end, demand:

(1) That we seek to have established a National Board to cover the Mining Industry. The Board to be composed of an equal number of representatives from the Mining Association of Great Britain and the Mineworkers' Federation of Great Britain.

(2) The National Board shall have power to consider and decide either by agreement or in the event of failure to agree, by recourse to an Independent Chairman, or Board of Arbitrators, all matters which directly or indirectly affect the mining industry, namely, coal production, distribution, prices, profits, wages, mining conditions, safety, pensions and welfare.

(3) The National Board shall have power to set up District Boards to act under the accepted principles and direction of the National Board. (August 20, 1941.)

The colliers bore ill with the new conditions under the Essential Work Order imposed on May 15, 1941. Nor did their leaders think that this Order or later measures taken by the Ministry of Labour and National Service were likely to be efficacious in solving the coal crisis. The E.W.O. had tied the colliers to the mines: but it did not bring back the skilled men. The need for this, urged both by the Federation and by the owners, was not fully realised by the Government till nearly twelve weeks after the Essential Work Order had first been mooted. Even then the first steps taken were largely ineffective. Ernest Bevin, as Minister of Labour and National Service and member of the War Cabinet, made a special broadcast on June 23rd appealing for ex-mine-workers to go back to the mines. But it misfired.

Instead of the 50,000 that he hoped for, a mere driblet came in. Not until then did they stop recruiting miners for the Armed Forces. Moreover when, under the new Registration of Miners Scheme, all under sixty with mining experience in the previous five years had to register on July 17th and 18th, the final results in the end were to be much less than the figures disclosed of those apparently available for re-entry into the industry. For one thing, the other Government Department concerned with munitions of war sought and obtained power to block the transfer back of ex-miners, and to include the condition that a substitute must first be found for any man they decided could be so released.

The coal industry was now under two separate Departments at Whitehall, one of which had had little to do beforehand with the problems of the industry. The Federation Executive Committee, accustomed to the Mines Department, took very ill some of the conduct of affairs by Ernest Bevin or the officials of his ministry: and they passed some very sharply worded resolutions about it.[1]

By the autumn it was clear that the measures the Government had adopted in preference to the policies put forward by the Federation had been entirely insufficient.[2] The coal crisis had not been surmounted. As a consequence all sorts of desperate remedies were proposed to the Federation Committee by the Department of Mines. One was that Hungarians who were prisoners of war should be brought into the mines—and Chinese. This proposal for what was then notoriously cheap labour had been brought up more than once in the history of the mining industry,

[1] e.g.: "That Mr. Bevin, Minister of Labour and National Service, be asked that all documents in relation to man-power and other matters of mining issues be sent direct to the Mineworkers' Federation of Great Britain, and he also be informed that district organisations will refuse to act on any intimation they may receive from the Ministry of Labour or any Government Department unless they receive intimation through the Federation itself." (July 13, 1941.)

[2] In an August parliamentary debate, a soothing speech by the new President of the Board of Trade (Sir Andrew Duncan) did not blunt but if anything sharpened the criticism from mining Members, amongst them Aneurin Bevan who said that the Minister of Labour (Ernest Bevin) had applied the Essential Work Order to the mining industry "not as part of, but in substitution for, a sane wage policy for the country as a whole" and that "all it did was to make the men sullen, disappointed and even angry." Bevan went on to say: "Some of the Press and certain other people began this attack on the miners for absenteeism. It is my opinion that this attack has soured the miners more than anything else." George Griffiths (Member for Hemsworth) gave chapter and verse for his warning that "There is greater unrest today in the mining industry than there has been for fifty years." (*Hansard*, August 5, 1941.)

particularly in the 1914–18 war, and met the inflexible opposition of the mining trade unions. They rejected it this time also, resolving briefly:

The Mines Department be informed that we will be no party to the employment of foreign labour in British coal mines. (August 8, 1941.)

Another proposal was to lengthen the working day: and this too met with total rejection, as once before in 1914–18. On this last, Secretary of Mines Grenfell sought an interview with the Federation leaders. To a specially summoned Executive Committee on September 11th Grenfell explained that so far from the coal crisis being solved by the Government measures, the situation was little better than in the previous spring. He gave the figures. Some 104,000 ex-miners had been registered. Of these about 55,000 were exempted or obviously unfit, leaving as apparently available 45,000: but out of this number only 16,000 were back in the mines. Against this there was, of course, the high rate of "wastage" in man-power which would nearly cut in half the last of these figures. For, with the extremely long working week through the greatest possible number of shifts being crowded in, the strain on the ageing labour force was growing greater. So Grenfell, in view of the ill-success of the Government's measures, now pleaded for a longer working day.

Earlier that year, on April 1st, when Sir William Beveridge made the proposal that the working day in mines should be lengthened, the Federation Executive Committee strongly resented this, which appeared to them more like an April Fool joke than a serious proposition. Now they listened to Grenfell making a similar proposition, for "a temporary increase." They had great sympathy with him as one of their own M.P.s, whom they believed to be placed in a difficult position by the officials of his Department and by the ministers in the War Cabinet: but they most definitely rejected any such possibility and resolved:

That in the light of the knowledge of every district representative upon the Executive Committee, they do not believe that increased production can be secured by increased hours.

And further, in view of the Government's refusal to expedite the increased manpower required for the industry, which we are confident would make the most effective contribution to increased coal production, we cannot agree to proceed along the lines of an increased working day beyond present statutory limits. (September 11, 1941.)

What was this "knowledge of the district representatives"? What they knew (better than the men in Whitehall) was that the miners were now working more shifts than ever before, that their exhausting labour was stretched to the maximum and that any increase in the working day would only result in accident, sickness, and other causes of absenteeism, both "avoidable" and "unavoidable."

II. NON-UNIONISM

It took a good many months before a solution could be found for the problem of non-unionism. At a meeting of the Joint Standing Consultative Committee (to which the President of the Board of Trade had suggested the matter should be referred instead of to the Coal Production Council) the M.F.G.B representatives asked that non-unionists should not receive the direct benefit of negotiated wage advances and further that the owners should exert pressure upon workmen to join their appropriate unions as follows:

That a provision be added to the National War Wage Agreement and Bonus Agreement to provide that these payments shall only be made to workmen who are members of their appropriate Trade Unions. (October 23, 1941.)

Sir Evan Williams remarked at this meeting that he did not think there was any difference of opinion between the two sides. There was less reason, he thought, than at any other time for men not being members of the bodies with whom arrangements were made and to whom the owners looked for carrying out the arrangements. It was no use looking to anybody except responsible organisations to see that the arrangements were carried out, so that there was "not only no desire on the part of the owners to stand in the way of the miners' unions but every desire to see that

L*

there was no sort of disturbance at the collieries that would interfere with the desire of the men to do their best or with disciplinary action taken by the organisation." He thought the owners' side were bound to admit at once that "if action that the miners' side might take at the colliery on absenteeism was distasteful to a large number of people and reduced their enthusiasm for trade unions, it would militate against the influence of the Committee." The owners could not ignore that aspect of the matter. The greater the number of the men "who left the unions on that account the worse the position would be" as regards increasing coal output.

The mine-workers' representatives suppressed their astonishment at the utterance of Sir Evan Williams and refrained from exclaiming "Is Saul also amongst the prophets?" But when it came to the next meeting of the Joint Standing Consultative Committee two months later the Central Council of the Mining Association stated that "they were unable to accede to our request to refuse to pay national negotiated advances to non-unionists, as they were under legal obligation to pay all wage additions and bonus payments to all men under contract with them." It turned out, however, that they would put no bar on any District organisation which cared to make any arrangement with the county associations (meeting of J.S.C.C., December 18, 1941). The Executive Committee then agreed that the District organisations make the best arrangements possible to meet the position either by the retention of the 1s. attendance bonus from non-unionists, the deduction of contributions by colliery managements at the colliery office "or any other suitable method that may be devised to deal satisfactorily with the position." By the next meeting of the Executive Committee on January 8, 1942, negotiations were still going on in various Districts with considerable hope of success.

Apart from the three main objections put by the M.F.G.B. when the Essential Work Order was introduced, the terms of the Order itself bore hard, as it turned out, on the mine-workers in ways that were considered unfair: and by the end of the year the original Order No. 707 and its Amending Order No. 2008 were superseded by the Essential Work (Coal-mining Industry) Order No. 2096 of December 18, 1941.

It was now nearly thirty months since the beginning of the war. The situation was grim. Each day of that winter brought hard and heavy tidings. Though the danger of invasion of Britain had receded, her armed forces were hard put to it in North Africa and South-East Asia. This military situation had its effect on the miners' leaders. In wartime not only are the laws silenced (or at any rate superseded by emergency Orders and Regulations) but the legislators too. Not only in the parliamentary but in the industrial democracy of Britain the normal processes of public discussion, pressure and voting were muffled. But though the miners' leaders, anxious about the outcome of it all, were willing to subordinate their own standpoint to that of the authorities, they could not feel happy about the way things had developed in the coal industry. The attitude of the Cabinet of the first nine months of the war (e.g. the reluctance to allow that miners' wages should keep pace with the cost of living) seemed to them to have lingered on beyond the demise of the Chamberlain Government. The coal crisis that had emerged in its stark reality in the course of the second nine months of war had not yet been surmounted: while their own main solution for it had been placed on one side. The need for man-power was unsatisfied: but it was not the only need. The need to organise the coal industry for total war, now in the third year of hostilities, was so urgent that, even if satisfied, the damage done by delay could never be wholly made good: nor could the best of measures now make the promise: "I will restore to you the years that the locust hath eaten." Thus, themselves dissatisfied but anxious above all about the issue of the war, the leaders of the miners tried to keep everything going in the pits: but they were not without forebodings.

WAR ADDITIONS AGREEMENT, MARCH 1940

AGREEMENT between the MINING ASSOCIATION OF GREAT BRITAIN and the MINEWORKERS' FEDERATION OF GREAT BRITAIN for the purpose of regulating War Additions to Wages related to the Cost of Living Index Figure as published by the Ministry of Labour.

(1) The district wage arrangements shall continue to operate during the war, subject to mutually agreed alterations, but increases of wages necessary to take account of the special conditions arising out of the war, and particularly the increased cost of living, shall be dealt with on a national basis by means of uniform flat rate additions.

(2) The flat rate additions from November 1 to December 31, 1939, having been paid at the rate of 8d. per shift for adult workers and 4d. per shift for others; and as from January 1, 1940, to March 31, 1940, at the rate of 1s. 1d. per shift for adult workers and 6½d. per shift for others, the amount of the rates payable as from April 1, 1940, shall be determined by the formula set out in sub-paragraphs (a) to (f) below provided that it shall be open to either side at any time to propose a variation in the formula or in the conditions of its application by reason of changes in circumstances:

(a) There shall be ascertained quarterly the amount by which the index number of the cost of living published by the Ministry of Labour exceeds the figure of 155 at which it stood immediately before the outbreak of war.

(b) The flat rate war addition to adult workers during the next three months shall be the amount, to the nearest penny, found by multiplying 0·7d. by the number of points by which the cost of living index figure last published exceeds 155.

(c) The calculation shall be based on the cost of living index figure for March 1940, to determine the war wage additions for the months of April to June 1940; the procedure to continue for the future by quarterly calculations as herein set out.

(d) The war addition payment for workers other than adults shall be one-half the amount payable to adults. The term "adults" to be interpreted in each district in accordance with the custom of the district.

(e) The cost of living index figure for March 1940, having been 179, or 24 points in excess of the index figure immediately prior to the outbreak of war, the amount of the war addition as per sub-paragraph (*b*) for April to June is 1s. 5d. for adults per shift and 8½d. for others per shift.

(*f*) There shall be no alteration of the amount of the uniform flat rate war addition determined at any time in accordance with sub-paragraph (*b*) of this paragraph unless and until the cost of living index number, which forms the basis for a subsequent determination of the war addition, shows a variation of 5 points or more from the index number on the basis of which an alteration of the war addition last took place.

(3) In the calculation under the district wages ascertainments for determining in respect of any period after March 31, 1940, the amount available to be expressed in the form of the percentage on basis rates, account shall be taken of the cost of war additions actually paid during the period of ascertainment (including amounts paid in the form of percentage in lieu of flat rates prior to the commencement of the amounts of the 5d. war addition) which shall be treated as a charge against the wages balance.

(4) The flat rate war addition is payable in respect of ordinary shifts worked subject to payment for a maximum of six shifts worked in any one week.

(5) This agreement shall continue in operation until terminated by six months' notice on either side, which notice may be given at any time after, but not before, the cessation of hostilities whether the war and the state of emergency have been officially terminated or not.

For and on behalf of the Mining Association of Great Britain:

(*Signed*) EVAN WILLIAMS, President.

W. A. LEE, Director.

For and on behalf of the Mineworkers' Federation of Great Britain:

(*Signed*) WILL LAWTHER, President.

EBBY EDWARDS, Secretary.

March 20, 1940.

CHAPTER VIII

THE GREENE BOARD

1. SET-BACKS AT HOME AND ABROAD

IN the first half of 1942 things went from bad to worse with Britain and her Allies. Without warning Japan had attacked the U.S. naval base at Pearl Harbor in Hawaii on December 7, 1941, and invaded the colonies of the British and Dutch Empires. Her speedy conquest of all South-East Asia brought her armies through Burma to the borders of India and her fleets to within striking distance of Ceylon. At the same time the Nazi armies were advancing both on the Eastern Front, to penetrate deeply into the territory of the Soviet Union, and also in North Africa. There (under the strategic direction of General Wavell) General O'Connor's conquest of Cyrenaica in January 1941 with the capture of 200,000 Italian troops had first been halted by the withdrawal of forces for the Greek adventure of Spring 1941: and then had been more than cancelled by the advance of Rommel's Afrika-Korps.

In Malaya, the British fleet suffered a serious reverse, and on land the whole peninsula was rapidly overrun by the Japanese. Newspaper accounts of "whisky-swilling planters" and ineffective British defences were followed by an angry debate in the House of Commons at the end of January. The fall of Singapore on February 15, 1942, and the surrender of the tens of thousands of its garrison, described by Churchill as "the greatest disaster to British arms which our history affords," cast a deeper gloom in a week of humiliation caused by the passage up the English Channel, unharmed, of the German battle-cruisers *Gneisenau* and *Scharnhorst*.

At home, too, there were not a few set-backs amid the growing organisation of the war effort. Of these set-backs the situation of coal became increasingly serious during the winter of 1941–42. Consumption was growing and there was a widening gap ahead between estimated consumption and estimated production. There was not enough man-power in the mines, despite the Essential Work Order, the bringing back of men from industry and in the spring of 1942 the release of a few thousand from inessential jobs in the army. Moreover the man-power was made up largely of the older men with an enormous wastage through death, retirement, disablement, silicosis and war strain. With this complex of problems the Departments and Government Committees and finally the War Cabinet itself began to be more and more concerned.

The miners' leaders had been aware of the need for drastic changes at an earlier date as we have seen, and at their July 1941 Conference had reaffirmed the plan for nationalisation as well as the alternative lesser plan for a national board. Negotiations went on throughout the autumn of 1941 with the Labour Party and Trades Union Congress. A memorandum on the Federation demand of immediate nationalisation of the coal-mining industry prepared by Ebby Edwards was endorsed on November 20, 1941, and the Consultative Sub-Committee was instructed to prepare further the case for nationalisation for presentation to the Labour members in the Cabinet.

But on December 4, 1941, Ernest Bevin, speaking in the House of Commons, laid down a formula for control and requisition of private property. This, as the Executive Committee pointed out in its Report to the M.F.G.B. Annual Conference six months later, was found unsatisfactory: "the formula presented to the House of Commons restricted in its application that which the miners desired." By January 6, 1942, they secured the presence of Messrs. Ernest Bevin, Arthur Greenwood and D. R. Grenfell at a further discussion. Ernest Bevin pointed out that he was limited by the Cabinet decision. But he agreed that "if it could be proved that the implementation of *Labour's Plan for the Coal Industry* would assist the war effort, such plan would not be precluded by the government."

It was obvious to the miners that drastic changes in the industry must be undertaken if crisis (which even the non-miner could see was looming ahead) were to be avoided or mitigated. To them, nationalisation was clearly the best, and finally the inevitable solution. But the fact that they had advocated this a score of years earlier and that it had been a storm centre of political controversy was now held to be a proof not of their prescience but of some kind of obsession with peace-time proposals that were unsuited to war-time. Consequently there was a resistance, not only from coal-owning interests but from many in the Government and still more in the two chambers of Parliament to proposals that might otherwise have been judged solely on their merits. Moreover, the steps taken so far, after thirty months of war, to control the industry were on a much smaller scale than had been carried through in a corresponding period of the 1914–18 war. In the years between the wars a Mines Department had been built up with a personnel inured to the dominance within the industry of the coal-owning interests. How all these matters were discussed within the War Cabinet and what was the standpoint of each Labour member of the Coalition Government has not been disclosed. An inkling of these inner controversies, however, may be discerned in the frequent and animated parliamentary debates that bore on the coal crisis in the first half of 1942. It is significant that Arthur Greenwood, who after some twenty months was to be dropped from the War Cabinet by Churchill in February 1942, seems to have represented a view that accorded with that of the Mineworkers' Federation. In the Commons debate of May 19, 1942—six months after the Edwards memorandum had been endorsed on November 20, 1941— Greenwood said:

the palsied hand of vested interests and the old-fashioned methods which so many people in the mining industry still cling to so very tenaciously must be moved if the men in and about the mines are to be enabled to put the whole of their weight into and to pull all their strength for the national cause.

New drafts of proposals were being worked on both by the Federation and by the National Council of Labour in January and February 1942. Finally the National Council of Labour on February 24th agreed to put the matter first before the Labour representatives of the Cabinet and then to the Government itself.

At this point the Prime Minister had made alterations in the Government and Sir Andrew Duncan was succeeded by Hugh Dalton as President of the Board of Trade. Hugh Dalton immediately pushed ahead with proposals to solve the coal problem. The first proposals tackled the excessive consumption: a rationing scheme prepared by Sir William Beveridge was announced by Dalton in Parliament before it was put into force. All the vested interests rallied against it and it was agreed that its operation should be postponed. But the crisis remained. And after anxious weeks a plan for production emerged. It was a compromise.

2. THE WHITE PAPER OF JUNE 1942

From March 1st, as we have seen, when Hugh Dalton became President of the Board of Trade, a complicated struggle was going on that involved both sides of the industry, the national Labour bodies, the different Departments of Government, the Cabinet Committees and, finally, not only the War Cabinet but the House of Commons. During these months precious time was lost. In the coal-fields the miners, whose position was worsening in comparison with other industries, became more and more impatient. In several coal-fields there were big strikes.[1]

The factional struggle against rationing was focused in the 1922 Committee of the Conservative Party which represented various interests. As for the coal-owners, their attitude was unyielding. When Dalton had an interview on March 19th with the coal-owners Sir Evan Williams made a speech of nearly two hours' duration in which he went through the whole history of the industry to prove his argument that all would be well in coal-mining if it were not for political interference.[2] Sir Evan was an adept at this speech which in one form or another he had often enough delivered before. It seems to have been on very similar lines to the speech he made in Autumn 1926 to Winston Churchill who, as Chancellor of the Exchequer,

[1] In the first three weeks of May there were eighty-six short strikes lasting two to three days on the average and involving 58,000 men. (*Hansard*, June 2, 1942.)

[2] Dalton: *Memoirs 1931–45*, p. 390.

was then the Government spokesman. Amid all this welter of contending interests and alternative plans the Government at last reached a decision. On May 13, 1942, Sir Stafford Cripps informed the House of Commons that the Government had decided to submit to the House after Whitsun their coal proposals as a whole, covering both production and consumption and the organisation of the industry. Three weeks later the Government published its White Paper.[1]

The main changes were as follows: (1) the Government was to take full control over the operation of the mines but the ownership and finance were to remain in the hands of the private owners. For the purpose of control there would be a responsible Minister assisted by a Controller-General with four chief officers. (2) In each coal-producing Region there was to be a Controller to whom would be delegated the powers of the Minister to control colliery undertakings and give directions to managements. The Controller would be assisted by three directors. (3) Parallel with this there would be a National Coal Board and Regional Coal Boards. The function of all these boards was advisory, and covered the need for increased production and all other questions—except wages. (4) Wages and conditions were to be dealt with after discussion with both sides of the industry by new procedures and by a permanent machinery to be set up. (5) Pit Production Committees were relieved of all responsibility for dealing with individual cases of absenteeism but remained to assist pit managers to secure maximum output. (6) A scheme of rationing of fuel (attached as an Annexe to the White Paper) was not to be imposed immediately. As it turned out later it never was imposed.

There were a number of other proposals such as that coal-mining would be added to the list of priority industries which might be chosen in preference to military service; that steps would be taken to improve conditions for the recruitment of juveniles; that a Medical Consultative Service would be set up for mines; that coal would be allocated to industry on an organised system and with improved methods of coal consumption.

On the day that this White Paper was published Sir

---

[1] *Coal.* Cmd. 6364, June 3, 1942.

John Anderson, Lord President of the Council and Chairman of the Cabinet Coal Sub-Committee, had asked the miners' representatives to attend that Cabinet sub-committee, to hear from their own lips the proposals of the White Paper. Miners' representatives who were on the Consultative Sub-Committee felt it was imperative to have an immediate meeting of the Executive Committee on Friday, June 5th. There the White Paper was examined and after a prolonged discussion the following decision was reached:

This Executive Committee of the Mineworkers' Federation of Great Britain, having considered the Government's White Paper on Coal Mines, reaffirms its view that ownership and control of the Mines is essential to efficient organisation.

Whilst acknowledging that the Government's Plan will give an increased measure of control and organisation in the Coal Mining Industry, the Federation is of the opinion that such Plan does not provide for a complete solution of the coal production problem.

The Federation declares, however, that having regard to the urgency of the question of coal production, it will, as hitherto, do all that lies in its power to meet the needs of the Government in relation to increased production, and having regard to the decision of the Government to implement the Plan, urge upon the Government the necessity of amending and strengthening its Plan in respect to the following:

(a) Ownership;
(b) Managerial control;
(c) Financial structure;
(d) Absenteeism;
(e) Pit Production Committees;
(f) Direct representation of Federation on the National Board;
(g) Nomination of single persons;
(h) Determination of Regions.

After certain ideas had been advanced by the members of the Committee in considering the Government's White Paper, it was then agreed that the matter should be relegated to the N.J.C.C. Sub-Committee to prepare amendments to the White Paper.

Five days later the amendments were ready and had been given to the mining Members of Parliament—and through Arthur Greenwood to the Parliamentary Labour Party, etc. The Executive Committee decided the amendments should be submitted to a Special Conference and that Arthur

Horner should explain them to the delegates. At the same time the Executive put on record its appreciation of the services of the National Joint Consultative Committee Sub-Committee[1] for the "part played in formulating the amendments to the White Paper, especially does this appreciation apply to the Secretary and Mr. A. L. Horner."

The next day at a Special Conference A. L. Horner explained the situation to the delegates on behalf of the Executive Committee. He began by saying they had known since the beginning of the year that coal output was nearly a million tons per week below the essential requirements. There had been a tremendous expansion of war industries, and many more new units of production would be coming into operation. If the tendency of coal consumption to exceed production continued, very many essential units already in production would have to stop.

This situation caused the Miners' Federation a long time ago to urge the Labour movement to take cognisance of the facts. We were informed by the Labour movement that the Ministers within the Government were prohibited from contending for complete nationalisation and we were informed by Mr. Bevin's declaration that the Government would adopt any plan, irrespective of pre-war prejudice or post-war interests, which could be shown to be capable of bringing about an improvement in production. Because of the situation we were able to win the support of the Labour movement for what is known as the Coal Plan of the National Consultative Committee.

Whilst we were debating about this plan, the Government was compelled to awake to the difficulties of the situation, and to face the fact that some drastic changes must be made if the mining industry was to meet the needs of the country. (June 11, 1942.)

Horner described how the Government had set up a Special Committee; and whilst it was sitting, the Coal Plan had been adopted by the Labour Party Conference. He continued:

We were called before this Committee and asked our opinions as to what we thought ought to be undertaken to obtain an improvement in the industry. We said that there are three things wrong

[1] This National Joint Consultative Committee Sub-Committee of the M.F.G.B. Executive Committee (usually called simply the Joint Consultative Committee) was appointed each year at the first Executive Committee meeting after the Annual Conference. As this was a matter where skill and experience in negotiating with the owners counted heavily, the tendency was for most of the Committee to be re-appointed from year to year. The members of the Committee at this time were the three officers and A. L. Horner, H. Hicken, S. Blackledge, J. Barbour, H. Booth, J. A. Hall, and G. H. Jones.

with the industry. First, the men in it are dissatisfied with the treatment they are receiving in relation to other workers in war industries. Secondly, we said that we have not enough men. And, thirdly, that we never will be able to improve the mood of the men so long as their efforts can be connected to profits to mine owners, whom they hate and detest over a long period of years. In short, we put forward before the Anderson Committee arguments in favour of the Coal Plan adopted by the National Consultative Committee. (June 11, 1942.)

He concluded by declaring that they considered the Government's scheme for production most unsatisfactory:

It is what all compromise schemes are—it is an attempt to reconcile irreconcilable factors. (June 11, 1942.)

The M.F.G.B. Special Conference approved the Report on the White Paper, together with the proposed amendments. But before these amendments could be sent to the Mines Department there had been a change in personnel as well as in the structure of governmental administration. A new Ministry, the Ministry of Fuel and Power, into which were absorbed the Mines and Petroleum Departments of the Board of Trade and its Gas and Electricity divisions, had been set up following the White Paper. David Grenfell had not been in agreement with his colleagues in the Government on the latest steps and dropped out. The new Minister was Gwilym Lloyd George who, with his sister Megan, made up a large part of the fragment of the once powerful Liberal Party that was headed by his father, the ex-Prime Minister. Gwilym had spent nearly eighteen years in or around Downing Street and had been early apprenticed to politics becoming a Member of Parliament in 1922. Thus more than many of the Peers he might be considered an almost hereditary legislator. But though, like his father, he had a keen eye to the main chance and had a very similar sense of scruple he fell far short of the famous David Lloyd George in his general abilities. While his sister gradually came to be more and more sympathetic to the Labour Party, Gwilym moved on the whole in an anti-Labour Party direction. He was, however, brisk enough and even a shade brusque as was shown by the tone of his first formal letter in reply to the letter enclosing the M.F.G.B. proposed

amendments.[1] Most of them he treated like a cautious
cricketer playing himself in and giving his first exhibition
of stone-walling on July 1, 1942. So the miners had to be
content with an organisation of the industry which was
neither the thoroughgoing nationalisation which they considered the best method for meeting the needs of Britain
at war, nor the lesser scheme which they had elaborated
in 1940 and 1941 and had been adopted by the national
Labour bodies and put forward within the Government by
Labour ministers. They naturally had their doubts about
it, but they were prepared to work it to the best of their
ability.

3.   A WAGES DEMAND

While all the discussions had been going on in the first
five months of 1942, the position of the workers in the
coal-fields had been worsening. There had already been
several strikes. The M.F.G.B. Executive Committee, which
had been so largely preoccupied with working out a total
remedy for the crisis of the coal industry as a whole, had
now to take steps to meet the pressing needs of the miners'
income. At their meeting on May 22nd they heard their
President, Will Lawther, telling of his statement to the
press that the "unrest in the coalfields" was chiefly due to
the "poor rate of wages" as compared with other workers.
Letters, too, had been received from the Districts, Lancashire,
Northumberland, Yorkshire and South Wales, demanding
that an immediate increase in wages for mine-workers be
sought. They decided to claim at the next meeting on the
N.J.C.C. a minimum weekly wage of £4 5s. od. for all
adults; and an immediate flat rate advance of 4s. per shift
for adults and 2s. for others. When this request for 4s. a
shift together with the overriding demand for a minimum
wage of 85s. was brought to the coal-owners, it met with a
refusal. As Ebby Edwards said reporting to the Special
Conference of June 11th, "Our claim was rejected. The

---

[1] The M.F.G.B. suggested amendments in the following respects: Government
ownership; mine-workers' and mine-owners' representation on the National Coal Board;
its function; regions and regional machinery, including appeals against the Controller's
decisions, payment of managers by the State; Pit Committees, and wages machinery.

owners made no bones about it. They recognised the discontent in the coalfield on the disparity of wages, but they
were not prepared to give us an advance." But though there
was this "breakdown with the employers" it seemed that
the latter would consider some form of incentive payment.
The matter, however, was soon mixed up with the discussions
with the Cabinet Coal Committee about the White Paper
proposals. Part of these proposals were for new machinery
of wages negotiations. Sir John Anderson, President of the
Council, suggested that this machinery should take the form
of a Board of Investigation. Its purpose in the first instance
would be to consider and report on the immediate wage
issue with the understanding that whatever was decided
should date from June 1st. This the miners' representatives
accepted, and decided to present to this body a statement
of their case.

They settled on a number of points to make. These
included a decision to press that workers of eighteen should be
classed as adults, and that Districts should supply information
on current wages paid to youths. An effort should be made
to get facts on wages paid in Government factories. They
would make it clear that they were opposed to wage
advances being conditional on output. Finally they decided
to co-opt W. S. Hall on to the N.J.C.C. Sub-Committee,
which was entrusted with preparing the evidence.

The result of the Federation's decision to accept the
Government's proposals for this new wages inquiry, and
to put their case before it, was momentous. It was set up as
a Board of Investigation; its terms of reference were twofold.[1] It was to report on "the immediate wage." But it
was also to inquire into the existing machinery and methods
of determining wages and conditions, and to make "recommendations for the establishment of a procedure and
permanent machinery" for dealing with them.

The Board of Investigation (called afterwards the Lord
Greene Board after its Chairman, the Master of the Rolls)
got to work very quickly. Indeed, in record time. It was
appointed on June 5th, held its first meeting on June 9th and
made its award on June 18th. The Federation got to work

[1] See Appendix to this chapter.

with comparable or even greater speed. They secured the assistance of the Labour Research Department in the preparation of their case. By the opening day of the inquiry they presented a first statement on their wages claim, and four days later, in the middle of the inquiry, a second statement: a big array of facts, figures and appendices, on which there must have been much overtime put in by the staff of the Labour Research Department. In his foreword to the reprint of these documents and of the verbatim Report of the investigation, Ebby Edwards wrote: "appreciation of the assistance rendered to the Secretary by Mr. W. H. Williams of the Labour Research Department and Mr. Arthur L. Horner must be recorded here." And he went on to say: "The award granting the wage increases was made on June 18, 1942. The Minister of Fuel and Power, Mr. G. Lloyd George, intimated to the Mineworkers' Federation on June 19, 1942, that the Government accepted the recommendations of the Board made in paragraphs 7 to 16 of their Report."

So speedily had the work been done that on the morning of the opening of the inquiry after the Master of the Rolls had said that it would be held in private, Ebby Edwards was able to supply the court with the documents and to give a hundred copies to the employers. The Chairman naturally asked Sir Evan Williams, representing the mine-owners, to "let us have a similar document at the very earliest opportunity." The following dialogue followed:

Sir EVAN WILLIAMS: We have nothing in the way of a text. We have prepared some figures and they are really very few; I do not suppose they will be more than about half a dozen sets of figures altogether, but we have nothing prepared in the way of an argument or even of a statement in writing of our case.

THE CHAIRMAN: You will let us have what you can as soon as you possibly can?

Sir EVAN WILLIAMS: Certainly.

THE CHAIRMAN: Until we have heard Mr. Edwards today we shall not be in a position to know the exact day on which we shall wish to hear you, Sir Evan Williams, but in the meanwhile do let us have any information on which you are going to reply which you have ready.

Sir EVAN WILLIAMS: Certainly.

THE CHAIRMAN: Any statistics, figures, or anything of that kind which you think we ought to have before us, do let us have them at the earliest possible moment because it is quite impossible to absorb them by word of mouth. You see what I mean?

Sir EVAN WILLIAMS: Clearly, my Lord; we will certainly have copies made for the Committee.

THE CHAIRMAN: Do not let us have them just at the last moment if you can do it, but send them in to the Secretaries and then they will be distributed to us.

Sir EVAN WILLIAMS: Do I understand, my Lord, that you suggest that we should be better utilising our time by preparing that document this afternoon rather than by remaining here?

THE CHAIRMAN: I should naturally want you to be present while Mr. Edwards is opening his case. I do not know whether that will take us all today or part of tomorrow, or how long it will take; I cannot tell at the moment.

Sir EVAN WILLIAMS: We will prepare what you suggest. It will not be a full argument in writing. (June 9, 1942.)

This peremptory manner and somewhat summary treatment of the owners' Chairman by Lord Greene reflected the extreme anxiety[1] of the Cabinet to cut through the usual tangle of lengthy procedures and get the matter settled.

Ebby Edwards, dealing only with the wages claim, showed the cause of the difficulties in the coal industry in the shortage of man-power, the dissatisfaction due to low wages and technical shortcomings arising out of war conditions. He dealt with age distribution and the possibilities of recruiting man-power. He quoted a reply of Ernest Bevin, Minister of Labour, in the House of Commons five days earlier who had been asked why more miners at present in the Royal Ordnance factories had not been transferred back and who had replied:

In the last six months I have transferred, *at a great loss of wages to themselves*, over 36,000 men from munitions factories to the mines. (June 4, 1942.)

Ebby Edwards, speaking of the danger and the physical strain involved in coal-mining, said that to emphasise that answer of Mr. Bevin, he would put in a pay-check as part of his evidence. This was the case of a Somerset coal-miner who "was not good enough for the mine at one time and

---

[1] Ebby Edwards, in an interview with the author (November 28, 1959), recalled that the Government, after delays of so very many months, had suddenly got into a kind of panic about the possibility of a "social upheaval" in the coal-fields.

so he went into a government establishment." As a miner his total wage was £3 7s. od. for a full week's work. In the factory his pay-check showed that he got £6 1s. 7d. plus 12s. 6d. bonus. Ebby Edwards handed in the two pay-checks, saying that this was a concrete case "of a man who had passed the stage where he can be classed as an efficient worker in our industry going into a factory and getting £6 14s. od. a week. Can you understand the failure of men to come back into this industry in those circumstances?" The statement of the Federation on this ran as follows:

When they come back, what do they find? An arduous and dangerous occupation. They are called upon to expend greater physical energy than in the job which they left. They have to take greater risks. In 1937 miners had a compensation rate of 23·23 compared with quarries 10·45, railways 4·65, factories 3·97, docks 11·27, constructional work 4·50 and shipping 5·93.

When they are killed or maimed or pensioned off with a certifiable disease their families face life with an income reduced to about a third or a half. Their wages go and they may get compensation of £2 1s. od. a week with a small family.

Accidents, at a rate four or five times more than in other industries, with their effect on the men's income, were important in considering the actual level of miners' wages, they emphasised.

These men who have gone into the other industries are reluctant to come back. They have, to put it bluntly, seen something better. It is notorious that thousands of men escape by all devices being taken back under the Emergency Powers Order. The industry must offer them as good terms as they are getting now.

The re-entrants come from an industry where nowadays they receive facilities as Government employees. For instance, in the matter of transport, fares over 3s. a week are paid by the Government in scheduled jobs, outside mining. In mining, fares may run up to 10s. or 12s. a week, and the miners have to pay. The proposal to impose a trifling levy on coal to form a "transport pool" was rejected recently.

A further section of the Federation statement showed that the miners were "not asking for exceptional treatment" but that, on the contrary, they were working in an underpaid industry. Miners were "doing probably the most exhausting and dangerous work in industry," and yet their average earnings were 8s. 6d. less than in industry as a whole.

When compared with industries of similar importance in the war effort, the contrast was startling; for the miner's pay-packet was £1 1s. 10d. less than the worker in shipbuilding, £1 3s. 3d. below general engineering and £2 8s. 7d. below the worker in motor and aircraft production. In the Government's own industrial establishments £1 4s. 7d. more was paid to men and 5s. 9d. more to boys.

Other sections of the Federation statement dealt with food needs.

The miner's exacting job requires more food and rest than the ordinary worker if his output is to be maintained. Today miners are working an average of 5½ shifts—the largest number of shifts in the history of the industry—and using proportionately more of their energy and strength.

Figures show that a great effort is being made by the workers. The White Paper dispels the absenteeism canard. But effort needs food.

Fifteen months earlier the clamour about absenteeism (which indeed was traditional in the newspaper press, due partly to the fact that most journalists were at the mercy of over-simplified and badly served-up statistics) had concentrated public attention, and to a degree the War Cabinet's attention, largely upon what was only one aspect of a complex problem. Now, over a year later, the same Government were concerned to undo the mischief: "the White Paper dispels the absenteeism canard."

Again, the statement that "effort needs food" was backed up by facts and figures about the lack of canteens and provision of food:

In the whole country only 59 pithead canteens serve whole meals. Even in South Yorkshire, by far the most advanced coalfield in this respect, only ten out of seventy large collieries as yet have canteens serving a full hot meal. For the rest, what canteens exist provide only tea, cold pies, etc. (June 8, 1942.)

In this connection, too, the ageing nature of the labour force, which was due partly to the earlier recruitment, now so widely condemned, of the younger men for the forces and for other industries, was brought out clearly enough:

Moreover, 40 per cent of the workers today are over 40, 20 per cent of them over 50; and the health of many of these has been adversely affected by years of unemployment. If they are to

maintain anything like the present output per man-shift, they must
have a standard of living which provides for the especially exhausting
nature of their work. (June 8, 1942.)

Summed up, the argument was that the miner was not
being fairly treated, either absolutely in obtaining proper
remuneration or relatively to the rest of the community.
Because of the low wages of the miner, they had reached
"the present stage of crisis, with widespread dissatisfaction."
Nor were they going to get production out of this feeling
of dissatisfaction, "nor win the war by slave driving."
Measures to get more coal could not be successful "without
a satisfied labour force."

After Ebby Edwards had put the case for the miners'
claim on the first day (Tuesday, June 9, 1942) to the
Board of Investigation, Sir Evan Williams made some
general observations of the coal-owners' point of view and
commented on what had been put on behalf of the miners.
His opening statement was partly historical and partly
to put the viewpoint that any increase in wages must be
linked with increased effort on the part of men while at
work. He proposed that the District should be taken as the
unit and that increases in wages should be dependent
upon increases in the output per person employed for the
District as a whole. On Friday, June 12, 1942, the Board of
Investigation had received and read a memorandum from
the coal-owners on which Sir Evan Williams gave explanations in reply to questions. Ebby Edwards then dealt with
the Mining Association's document which he described as
"a case presented as a negative reply to our positive
application." This immediate answer was supplemented by
a second statement prepared by the Mineworkers' Federation
that same day.

It noted that the Mining Association had agreed that
wages would have to be increased, and then hit hard at
their detailed proposals:

We suggest that the owners' parsimonious niggardly way of
going about this serious object of securing greater production is
futile, and even disastrous in present circumstances. We submit
that this is the effect of the attendance and output bonus proposals
of the Mining Association. (June 12, 1942.)

Apart from the attendance and output bonus the owners' points covered: absenteeism and fall in output per man-shift; "unavoidable absenteeism"; fall in output at coal-face; minimum wage; the health standard; allowances; transport. The Federation statement replied to these in detail, and concluded by striking "a note of advice" to the employers:

The owners in this great basic industry have available for service in the interests of their industry and the country a fine body of men seething with a *real genuine grievance* that negatives the spirit of goodwill to coal production. The proposals the Mining Association put to this Board of Investigation as a remedy, if adopted, would have precisely the opposite effect to what they desire. The grievances will not only remain, but would be intensified if their proposals were accepted.

We would like to strike a note of advice to the owners—who, with us, whatever the form of control or ownership, will have mutually to endeavour to serve this great industry in the present crisis, and in its future possibilities. We would say to them, withdraw your narrow approach to this vital issue. Look away from your prejudices and have vision for the future.

Present wages would not maintain production nor attract man-power to fill the wastage. In "this great crisis" they asked that their "simple, straightforward demand be awarded": that was, the wage claim, and the establishment of the long-sought National Board to settle wages, hours and conditions. The miners' Secretary ended the Federation statement with an eloquent appeal:

The granting of our claim would go far to raise that status and the dignity of the men in relation to those employed in other industries; it will get rid of the atmosphere of unfairness that pervades the coalfields and overcome the sense of inferiority that dominates the mineworkers, especially the lower paid men and boys. (June 12, 1942.)

4. THE AWARD OF JUNE 18, 1942

At the end of the proceedings for the third day (Monday, June 15, 1942), Lord Greene asked for the two sides to let him have a preliminary outline of ideas about conciliation machinery together with the record of the past and existing

agreements from the different Districts. This was a matter
on which the mine-owners and to some extent the mineworkers had assumed there would be speedy progress. The
matter, however, turned out to be so complicated that it
was not weeks but many months before the second Greene
Award could be reached.

On the immediate claim, however, it was only a matter of
three days before the award was made, on June 18, 1942.
The Report stated "after careful and prolonged examination
of all relevant facts and the arguments presented to us by
the parties we submit our unanimous recommendations as
being a just solution of the questions with which we are
asked to deal." They estimated the cost of their proposals
that would come into force immediately as £23,500,000 a
year. The proposals included:

(a) An unconditional flat rate addition of 2s. 6d. per shift to
wages of all workers over the age of 21.

(b) A like addition to the wages of all underground workers
between the ages of 18 and 21.

(c) Graduated additions to the wages of all underground
workers under the age of 18 and of all surface workers under
the age of 21.

(d) The foregoing additions to be stable increases and not to
be liable to diminution through the operation of the percentage system.

(e) A national minimum wage for all workers over the age of
21 at the rate of 83s. a week for underground workers and
at the rate of 78s. a week for surface workers—these figures
to be reduced to terms of shifts worked.

(f) An addition to the wages of all workers in accordance with
sliding scale for increases of output beyond a variable
standard figure fixed for each pit.

Here we must consider the effect of the main recommendations which came into force as from June 1, 1942.
The effect of the flat rate addition of 2s. 6d. per shift was
very considerable. It is true that the claim had been for
4s. per shift, but nevertheless the miners had reason to be
pleased with a general improvement in their wages as
against mere war additions to keep pace with the cost of
living. It had the effect that wages in the mining industry
were at a stroke raised from their lowly position of 59th
place on the Labour Ministry's list of trades to 23rd place.

This new position of 23rd place might not be commensurate with the importance of coal-mining in the national
economy, especially in relation to the war effort, but it was
a step in the right direction. Would it suffice to make the
industry attractive? This remained to be seen. The answer
to the question also depended on whether the position were to
improve or to deteriorate. As we shall see, in the course of the
next eighteen months the mine-workers were to find themselves
in an inferior position in contrast with some other trades.

But the most important change was the establishment
of a National Minimum Wage of 83s. a week (78s. for
surface workers). It was not the figure (which was 2s. less
than the miners claimed) but the guarantee of a basic weekly
wage which made the difference. For as far back as living
memory could go the mine-worker had been paid for each
daily shift. In the old days, or even during the war period
due to any disorganisation in the pit, the number of shifts
available might only be two or three in a week; but the
budget of the miner's household had to be reckoned on a
weekly basis as there was no day in the week when he and
his family did not require to have food, shelter and clothing.
Of course, wages continued to be reckoned by the shift—
as they were reckoned by the hour in the building trades
and many other industries. But over a large range of
occupations there was amongst the manual workers, not to
speak of the salaried staffs, a regular weekly guaranteed
wage, while notice for termination of employment as for
letting of rooms was normally on a weekly basis. Many
other contracts might be for a longer period; a newspaper
editor, for example, is entitled to six months' notice. In the
coal industry, too, the period of notice had usually run from
one pay day to the next—which might be either a week or
a fortnight. But the remuneration had always been tied to a
shift. The Greene Award in meeting the miners' claim for a
minimum wage weekly made a very big difference. In 1912
the miners had struck work throughout Britain for the individual minimum wage for each shift; 30 years later the
principle was extended for each week worked.

It will be seen that clause (f) in the summary of recommendations referred to a scheme for payment for increased

output. On this the Report said the Federation had assured the Board that the removal of grievances would have a beneficial result on output. The Board therefore recommended, to take effect at the earliest possible date, an addition on a sliding scale for output beyond a standard figure, fixed for each pit; and provision should be made for adjusting it to meet "changes affecting output, whether upwards or downwards, over which the workers have no control." Since the scheme was experimental, it should be reviewed after it had been working for some time. Ten weeks later on August 28, 1942, the Greene Board issued a Supplemental Report on the scheme for output bonus. This was put into operation a week later by the Minister of Fuel and Power. The story of this output bonus, however, and the difficulties that arose under it as a District scheme falls mainly within the year 1943.

Five days after the Greene Award an M.F.G.B. Special Conference attended by 204 delegates representing a union membership of 596,701, received a Report from the General Secretary who then moved the following resolution:

This Conference having received the report of the Recommendations of the Investigation Board on Wage Increases and the establishment of National Minimum Wage Rates for Underground and Surface Workers respectively, notes that they have now been accepted by the Government.

The Executive Committee whilst reaffirming the miners' claim to equality with workers in other War industries recommends acceptance of the findings.

The Conference further notes the proposals to introduce a Bonus Output Scheme, and instructs the Executive Committee to examine this proposal or alternative proposals calculated to improve coal production. (June 23, 1942.)

Ebby Edwards put forward this Executive resolution in a speech explanatory of the clauses of the award. Seconding the resolution on behalf of the Executive Committee, A. L. Horner gave a broad survey of the arguments which had been in the minds of the Executive and which it was thought should be accepted by the Special Conference:

The results represented by these recommendations of the Board of Investigation which we are now considering are not equal to those for which we asked. We asked for 4s. and we have got 2s. 6d.

ARTHUR HORNER AND WILL LAWTHER

Before the meeting with owners and the Ministry, March 8, 1944

JAMES BOWMAN, VICE-PRESIDENT M.F.G.B., 1939-44

We asked for a single national minimum wage, and we have got two minimum wages. But having said that—having deplored the fact that we have not secured what we asked for, we must recognise that we have secured, in defiance of all our war-time agreements, the greatest single increase in the history of the Miners' Federation, and we have after long years at last established the principle and the fact of a national minimum wage for the mineworkers of this country. These are not mean results.

Later, looking back over the long, vexed period, it became clear in the coal-fields that, whatever difficulties were to flow from the Supplementary Award and however much it fell short of their claim, the basic findings of the Greene Board were to mark an important turning-point.

5. THE DUAL CONTROL OF THE INDUSTRY

With the acceptance of their White Paper of June 3rd by Parliament and by the Mineworkers' Federation, the Government set about to carry out its decision to assume full control over the operation of the mines and to organise the industry on the basis of National Service. National and regional machinery was set up. Provision was made for the establishment of a National Coal Board and the industry was divided into eight regions of coal-producing Districts each with its board. On the National Board, the General Secretary represented the Federation and the following workmen's representatives were appointed on the Regional Boards:

Regional Boards	Workmen's Representatives
Scotland	A. Moffat
Northumberland and Cumberland	H. McKay
Durham	S. Watson
Lancashire, Cheshire and North Wales	J. McGurk
South and West Yorkshire	J. A. Hall
Nottingham, North Derbyshire, South Derbyshire and Leicestershire	G. A. Spencer
North Staffs, South Staffs, Warwickshire, Cannock Chase and Shropshire	G. H. Jones
South Wales, Forest of Dean, Somerset and Bristol	A. L. Horner

It was some months before these Boards were established. The first meetings of the Regional Boards were held in the autumn of 1942, but it was December before the National Board could be called together for its first meeting. But, of course, the operation of the new machinery under the Regional Controllers and under the Controller-General, Lord Hyndley, had begun much earlier. The operation of the Pit Committees with their newly defined functions began earlier in some places and later in others. All concerned had to accustom themselves to the new state of affairs where the Government controlled the operation of the mines, but the ownership and finance remained in the hands of the colliery companies. This was the system of dual control.

When the M.F.G.B. Annual Conference assembled at Blackpool, July 20–22, 1942, they heard their President Will Lawther say in his opening address: "Miners prefer these practical steps in cash to the tap-dancing of the intellectuals on ideological staircases. A National Minimum Weekly Wage is also established for which we have fought many battles." And then he said, "We have not only been living through the period of seeing historical changes being enacted, we ourselves have been making them: National Control, increase of wages, a national minimum and a National Board bringing to us definite rights, but they also bring new duties and responsibilities." Will Lawther, anticipating the debate which was to take place that afternoon, foreshadowed the outlook of a resolution saying: "These changes in the economic structure of the industry mean that there must be organisational changes in the Federation. The Bow-and-Arrow Trade Union cannot function with a dive bomber economic coal organisation."

6. THE ORGANISATION OF THE MINING UNIONS

With the achievement of the National Weekly Minimum Wage and the prospect of the National Conciliation machinery, the Executive Committee had been quick to draw conclusions. They saw an immediate need to have a

corresponding new shape of trade unionism in coal-mining.
So they put forward at the Blackpool Annual Conference
this resolution:

This Conference empowers the Executive Committee to draft
proposals for a change in the form of our Miners' organisation to
meet the changed circumstances and conditions which must arise
in the industry out of the Coal Trade proposals as presented by the
Movement, and to report their findings to a Special M.F.G.B.
Conference. (July 20, 1942.)

The resolution had been purposely put in this somewhat
general form in order that the delegates should have an
opportunity to bring out all that was in their minds, both
about the new situation in the industry and about their
experiences of the past. For the subject if viewed only in
the light of the past was not a new one. The formation of a
single trade union body had been advocated for well over
30 years. But after the coal-owners in 1926–27 had imposed
wages agreements which accentuated the difference between
one coal-field and another, the situation altered. The slogan
of "One Union for all Miners" now seemed to be held aloft
simply as the "banner of the ideal," while the utmost that
could be decided upon at any Federation Conference was
that there should be a reorganisation within the Federation.
So in the past ten years there had been resolutions passed,
Committees appointed, much detailed work done—on paper:
but, in the end, no substantial change. All these fair vessels
of reorganisation had been wrecked on the rocks of District
differences.

Midsummer 1942 had brought a really new situation.
So the reorganisation sub-committee at its meeting on
July 11th, in preparation for the Annual Conference, had it
clearly in mind that the object of the resolution was "to
merge all the individual district and sectional miners' unions
into one national organisation covering all mine-workers
employed in or around the collieries of Great Britain."
But at the same time they understood clearly that "the
terms of the amalgamation shall be agreed to after full
consideration with the district unions." The delegates from
the county associations also understood these considerations
and that the resolution, if carried, would commit them this

time to a process, however long and elaborate in its Committee work, that would end in the predetermined goal of a single union. The discussion, therefore, corresponded to the second reading of a Bill in Parliament; the principle only was to be discussed. The Vice-President, James Bowman, proposed the resolution. He dealt, first of all, with their experience of a score of unions in the industry; he said:

I want this Conference to remember its bitter history of splendid district isolation. I can remember Lancashire coming to the rostrum at a recent Conference in this hall when John McGurk complained against Scotland and the North-Eastern coalfields selling their coal in the markets of Lancashire at a cheaper rate than the collieries of Lancashire could sell it—a position only made possible by the vicious and savage reductions forced on the miners in the North-East. Let us acknowledge, favourable and unfavourable districts alike, the interdependence of one district upon another, because no district can be driven down and have its standards lowered without the repercussions of that reduction being felt throughout the entire British Federation. (July 20, 1942.)

Jim Bowman recalled that when speaking on past occasions in this fashion he and others had been "accused by the opponents of one National Union of speaking in a vacuum": he admitted that there might have been some truth in that imputation when they were faced with varying District arrangements and with the absence of national machinery through which to put forward national demands; but "it is not so today."

As soon as Bowman had ended, the delegates found themselves in the midst of a hot debate. George Spencer of Nottingham at once came forward to "take this opportunity of rising to state the opposition of my district to this proposal," and ended by saying:

The district interests can best be served by the men who know the districts. By the men who know a district's peculiarities, by the men who can approach the district problems from their own particular standpoint. To turn those things over to the Federation in the loose way which is being suggested, in my opinion, will be making one of the greatest and gravest mistakes that has ever been made by the districts.

Arthur Horner from South Wales rose at once to answer. After stating bluntly that it was "no surprise to the advocates of greater unification of the Federation to find that under all circumstances and in any conditions Mr. Spencer would be opposed to it," Horner urged delegates not to let the discussion become an argument between rich and poor in the Federation. He answered Spencer on detailed figures about the financial position in different Districts and ended by saying:

No, Mr. Spencer, the pre-war world will not be the post-war world. Many of the values of the old world have been blown sky high and exploded as fictitious. We have worshipped them too long. The thing that is going to count in the future, if we exist in a form in which we can express our will, is that there must be a reasonable return for the labour of every man, and we must have an organisation strong and powerful enough to force that right out of those who will at that time be seeking to refuse us that right.

The next speaker was Sam Watson of Durham, who rose to say:

I think Mr. Horner touched the crux of this debate when he suggested we should not enter into a quarrel between the richer and poorer districts.

Watson said Spencer's argument presupposed that the structure of the mining industry would remain unchanged:

It is an argument against the nationalisation of the coal industry. If we accept the position that the coal industry will be one day nationalised, we must also accept the logical conclusion that the mineworkers inside that industry will one day belong to a national organisation.

Sam Watson then dealt with several other points which Spencer had raised, particularly the suggestion that this was an old resolution, proved unsuccessful, dressed up in new clothes:

The last resolution we had was that it should be as district amalgamations and we opposed that, quite frankly, for this reason, that there was no sincerity in it. The district leaders did not intend to come together in that type of amalgamation. (July 20, 1942.)

After James Barbour of Scotland had given his support to the Executive Committee's resolution, G. H. Jones of the Midland Miners' Federation rose. He had been a miners' agent well before the 1914–18 war and even then had had a special knowledge of schism in Warwickshire. With his ripe experience he said:

From the Midlands we have heard the voice of dissent against this resolution sponsored by the Executive Committee, and I have no doubt that Mr. Spencer's speech rallied every conservative and reactionary element in this Conference. This proposal to some extent cuts into the vested interests of many men in this Conference. It bumps into the vested interests of myself and most of the Miners' Agents and Officials in the Conference. But we must be big enough to view it from the standpoint of the men in the pits.

After two speakers from the smaller Districts, Fred Swift from Somerset and J. Elks from Kent, the resolution was voted upon. There were two dissentients. The principle of a single union for the coal-fields had once more been carried.

7. THE SECOND FRONT—AND INDIA

In mid-July of 1942, after the successive defeats of the opening months of that year in nearly every theatre of war, the position was very grave indeed. It had seemed to many that it was important to have a Second Front in Europe in addition to the Eastern Front where the Red Army of the Soviet Union was being compelled to yield ground to the enemy between the Baltic and the Caspian Sea, while elsewhere in Europe there was no other fighting front. Hopes were stimulated further by the conclusion on June 10, 1942, of a Treaty of Alliance between the Government of the United Kingdom and the Government of the U.S.S.R. The terms of this Treaty were accompanied by a statement that the Governments of the Allies had decided to open a Second Front in Europe that year, 1942. The extent to which this was a hard and fast decision was afterwards questioned, but the Federation delegates assumed, in their resolution on the subject, that it was so. But there were, at the same time, fears that powerful forces in Britain were opposed to a Second Front. Thus in moving the emergency resolution on the war situation and the Second Front, Will Paynter of South Wales voiced this viewpoint:

I think we have to accept the conclusion that there are those in this country who for political considerations seek by argument and

propaganda to embarrass those in the Government who are for
the launching of a second front. It is noticeable that these elements
were conspicuous in the advocacy of non-intervention in Spain,
and in their support for the betrayal of Munich, and they are still
openly putting forward propaganda that can only be accepted as
designed to weaken the confidence and the enthusiasm of the people
of this country in the power and the strength represented by the
alliance between Great Britain and the Soviet Union and the
other United Nations. (July 21, 1942.)

Will Paynter then went on to say that: "The pro-fascist
and anti-socialist record of some of these people and the
type of propaganda that they are now pursuing has to be
faced up to and met by declarations from working class
conferences such as this"; and in pressing for unanimous
acceptance he stressed that it would indicate the attitude
of the miners to issues that were "issues of life and death."
The resolution ran:

This Annual Conference of the Mineworkers' Federation of
Great Britain expresses its appreciation of the services rendered
to the cause of Progress and Democracy by the Armed Forces and
Merchant Seamen of the United Nations, and welcomes the
growing opposition of the peoples of the countries enslaved by
Fascism.

This Conference welcomes the decision of the Governments of
the United Nations to open a second front in Europe this year and
expresses the conviction that the gravity and urgency of the military
situation in Egypt, the U.S.S.R. and the Far East necessitates the
immediate organisation of such a front as the only means whereby
Britain may be saved from the dangers of invasion and the Nazi
war machine decisively defeated.

It pledges the mineworkers of Great Britain to give full support
to every measure necessary to create and sustain such a second
front and to share in the sacrifices that the victory over Hitlerite
Germany will demand. (July 20, 1942.)

The resolution was seconded by Sam Watson of Durham
who, in drawing attention to the three component parts of
the resolution, said, on the Second Front, that it was Labour
Party policy: "The Party policy is that of support to the
Government in relation to the Tripartite Agreement reached
by America, the U.S.S.R. and Britain on the necessity of a
second front this year." As civilians they could not "as
Mr. Paynter says lay down the date, the time or the place
where the second front shall be"; but they had the right

and responsibility to let the Government know that the Second Front principle had the full and whole-hearted support of the Mineworkers' Federation of Great Britain. The resolution was supported by Will Pearson of Scotland, who said that "stoppages of work at the present time are a blow against a second front," and that the whole power of the Federation must be used against "whatever elements are responsible for such stoppages." George Griffiths, M.P., of Yorkshire, and then W. Betty of South Wales, the latter of whom criticised strikes that had occurred in his coal-field, made further speeches in support. The resolution was carried by acclamation.

It is perhaps necessary to explain that the decision that morning on the Business Committee's Report to have an emergency resolution on the Second Front, together with the suspicions expressed in the debate, had their origins partly in a debate in the Trades Union Congress the previous autumn. Sir Walter Citrine, as General Secretary, had moved a resolution which not only gave special support to the peoples of the U.S.S.R. but proposed the setting up of an Anglo-Soviet Trade Union Committee. It was in the course of the debate on this that Jack Tanner, a representative of the Amalgamated Engineering Union (and afterwards for several years its President), had revealed to the delegates statements made by a member of the Government which shocked the Congress—which might have been more shocked still had it known of a somewhat similar statement made that summer by the U.S.A. Vice-President Truman. Tanner said that the Minister of Aircraft Production had expressed "the hope that the Russian and German armies will exterminate each other" and that Britain would then be "the dominant power in Europe": and he had the support of the Congress delegates in denouncing such an attitude as "a terrible danger."

Meantime, a crucial situation had been reached in India, where the Indian National Congress, under the leadership of Mahatma Gandhi and Jawaharlal Nehru, had maintained an attitude of some aloofness since the beginning of the war; they were opposed to Fascism, but they were also opposed to British rule in India. In the spring of 1942, when the Japanese armies not only rapidly overran Burma but approached the frontiers of India, the Cabinet felt it necessary to break new ground. Churchill in February 1942 had taken Sir Stafford Cripps into the War Cabinet. From his record it seemed that Cripps would be more acceptable to the Indian National Congress than any of the Conservatives or even than Attlee, who had incurred a measure of distrust as a signatory to the Simon Commission Report of 1930 which had met with violent opposition in India. Therefore Cripps was sent to India. His mission, however, was unsuccessful in healing the breach. It was shortly after his return and after an Indian debate in the House of Commons that the Annual Conference debated an emergency resolution on India. The resolution recognised "the grave situation" arising from "the failure to settle the question of Indian relations"; believed it absolutely necessary to secure their "whole-hearted co-operation in the common struggle against Fascism"; called upon the British Government to reopen negotiations to settle immediate problems now, "with a view to the ultimate granting of complete independence"; and urged both Governments to approach their difficulties "in a realistic manner" taking the war situation into account.

The mover of the resolution was Alexander Sloan, M.P., one of the few M.P.s who sat on an Executive Committee of a District Association, in his case Scotland. The speech made by Sloan in moving the resolution was extremely critical of the Government and went considerably beyond the terms of the resolution. He criticised Cripps as well and he fiercely attacked the Conservatives who were unwilling to give self-determination to India with its 400,000,000 population.

The resolution was formally seconded by James Barbour, President of the Scottish mine-workers. Then after a short interchange between the Chairman and Alexander Sloan, M.P., the Chairman suggesting that Sloan had gone beyond the terms of the resolution in his speech, the resolution was put to the vote and carried. Nothing, however, came of the resolution; for less than three weeks after its adoption Gandhi, Nehru and all other Congress leaders were put in prison and kept there for the duration of the war.

M*

After these two discussions, on the war situation and on India, one other political question, this time on home affairs, was discussed. This was the suppression of the *Daily Worker* in the spring of 1941. The matter had been raised at the M.F.G.B. Annual Conference at Ayr in 1941 and had been referred to the Executive Committee which was satisfied that "if the *Daily Worker* were published it would be used as an organ to develop the struggle in this war and to forward the efforts to increase production of coal and everything else in the country." With this view of the M.F.G.B. Executive Committee there was no need for long speeches. The following resolution was moved by Arthur Horner of South Wales and seconded by J. McKendrick of Scotland:

This Conference of the Mineworkers' Federation of Great Britain agrees the following resolution be submitted to both the Labour Party and the Trades Union Congress, for inclusion on the Agenda of their Annual Conference:
"This Conference of the Mineworkers' Federation of Great Britain declares its support of the demand for the removal of the ban on the *Daily Worker*. It considers that the publication of a newspaper with its long anti-Fascist record would serve as an organiser of production so essential in the National interest." (July 20, 1942.)

The resolution was carried unanimously. But before this resolution[1] could come up at the Trades Union Congress in September, with similar resolutions from other unions, the Government had reckoned the odds and on August 26th removed the ban.

8. FURTHER WORK OF THE GREENE BOARD

Throughout the autumn and winter of 1942 discussions went on in the M.F.G.B. Executive Committee and between them and the Mining Association of Great Britain, and between both of them and the Greene Board of Investigation, on the future machinery for the regulation of wages and conditions of work. By August 7th the Mining Association and the Mineworkers' Federation had reached an agreement on

[1] Other resolutions dealt with pensions, appliances for injured workmen, workmen's compensation, improvement in the conditions of boy labour, safety in mines.

the main features of this future machinery. When these were put to the Board of Investigation on August 13th, members of that Board raised several points; these again were considered by owners and men at the August 27th meeting of the Joint Standing Consultative Committee. So it went on, month after month. Certain differences remained between owners and men. But the bigger differences were between the standpoint of the Greene Board and that of both owners and men. In Lord Greene, the Master of the Rolls, the two sides of the industry encountered a personality who, with his colleagues, was not content to pick and choose between the views of the two sides of the industry, but had positive conceptions of the sort of conciliation machinery that was necessary. Lord Greene had shown in the first few days of June that he and his colleagues could work with speed, but on this most vexed question of future machinery he was determined that nothing should be botched by hasty or ill-considered decisions. He was working fast, but he was not working to a time-table.

By November the M.F.G.B. Executive found themselves considering the Greene Board's draft scheme. By January 22, 1943, an M.F.G.B. Special Conference was held "to consider a report and the recommendation of the Executive Committee, in respect of the negotiations in connection with the establishment of National Wages Machinery for the coal-mining industry, with a view to arriving at a decision." The owners, however, had objected in November to the action of the Greene Board in submitting its own draft. They thought that the intrusion of its own views about machinery by the Board at the end of October was not only unnecessary, but very unwise. In spite of pressure from the M.F.G.B. representatives the owners would not agree to consider the "Greene Document": in their opinion the matter should be solved "within the industry and without outside interference." As Ebby Edwards put it in his document of January 11, 1943, preparatory to the M.F.G.B. Special Conference, the owners "stressed the fact that they desired that any arrangement made with the Federation should be entirely free from political atmosphere." The matter had been further considered at the Joint Standing

Consultative Committee meeting on November 26 and 30, 1942; and finally when the Committee met the Board of Investigation on December 1st, Lord Greene intimated that he would re-draft the document. The revised draft scheme was presented by him to the officials of both sides on December 17th, and then by the Joint Standing Consultative Committee on December 30th when, subject to one or two points, the scheme as a whole was accepted by both sides of the industry. It was this scheme which came before the January 22nd Special Conference and which the Executive Committee recommended should be accepted.

In moving the Executive recommendation, Ebby Edwards explained the draft conciliation scheme. There would be a National Conciliation Board for the coal-mining industry (to be called "the National Board") consisting of (a) a Joint National Negotiating Committee (to be called "the Negotiating Committee"); (b) a National Reference Tribunal (to be called "the National Tribunal"). The Negotiating Committee was to consist of twenty-two members, half nominated by the Mining Association of Great Britain and called "the Employers' side" and half nominated by the Mineworkers' Federation of Great Britain and called "the Workers' side." The National Tribunal would consist of three permanent members, none engaged in the coal-mining industry, nor a member of either House of Parliament (save in the case of a member of the House of Lords who had held high judicial office): these three would be appointed, after consultation with the two national bodies, by the Master of the Rolls (or by a Lord Justice of Appeal nominated by him). National questions would be discussed by the Negotiating Committee with a view to settlement; failing such settlement they would be referred to the National Tribunal for final decision. Settlements, awards and decisions would be binding upon the two national associations. Ebby Edwards, in explaining all this, drew particular attention to the stipulated "Uniformity of District Conciliation Agreements" and said: "If there was one thing that Lord Greene impressed, and repeatedly impressed upon us, it was that he wants to present to the government a water-tight Scheme that will keep this industry running."

In seconding the recommendation on behalf of the Executive Committee, Arthur Horner recalled that some twelve months earlier they had been told a different story by Oliver Lyttelton:

We were told by him that our demand for the establishment of a National Board could not be conceded by the Government. I remember the question being put to him at the time: "Is this Cabinet policy?" And Oliver Lyttelton replied: "I would not speak with such definiteness unless I were sure that I was expressing the mind of the Cabinet." (January 22, 1943.)

Why had there been this change in the Government attitude? asked Horner. It was because the Government had realised that if things were allowed to go on as before in the mining industry, there was a danger of a stoppage of work that might seriously impede the war effort; and because they had realised the fundamental importance of coal without which the country could not function or wage effective war. For this reason the Government intended the scheme to be effective after the termination of the war. Many would question the sincerity of this intention, many would wonder "whether we are being provided with a sop now to get us through the war, and whether there is the subterranean intention to take this away from us after the war is ended." To this Arthur Horner answered: "My view is that this country can never again afford to allow the kind of anarchy to exist in the mining industry which has been existing up to now." He dealt with some of the difficulties. There were eleven members delegated to act as the workers' side, but there were some twenty different Districts "with their District Agreements, jealous of their autonomy, anxious to preserve their rights" and they had somehow merged District questions into national questions without disturbing the very much valued District autonomy. In answer to a question as to whether the scheme was intended "to dock the demand for the nationalisation of the mines," Horner replied:

We asked for nationalisation. The Labour Movement said we could not have it because of their commitments to the National Government which debarred them from pressing for nationalisation. Then we went forward with our Coal Control Plan, which the Labour Movement adopted. The Labour Party Conference carried that Plan. After that we were offered the White Paper. Now the

White Paper provided two things: (i) control of the operations of the industry, and (ii) the provision that machinery would be set up to deal with questions of remuneration and the conditions of labour.

In accepting the White Paper they had accepted existing control and the establishment of a National Board. But "this has nothing to do one way or the other with our right or our determination to work for nationalisation."

After many questions the Executive recommendation for acceptance of the scheme and for a District vote upon it was carried unanimously. By February 22nd the returns of District voting had been received and at the Joint Standing Consultative Committee of February 25th the Federation representatives reported their unanimous decision to accept the proposed conciliation scheme. There was, however, a series of other meetings between the two sides and meetings with Lord Greene before it could be considered that the agreement was water-tight.

But now there came a snag. At their meeting on March 11th the M.F.G.B. Executive Committee became aware of it: a letter was read from Northumberland in which that District referred to a recent decision of the National Arbitration Tribunal. The decision arose from an application by the Northumberland Miners' Association for increased overtime rates. The Northumberland Mineowners' Association, having refused the application in the District, argued before the Tribunal that that body had no power to alter the existing Overtime and Week-end Agreement, because Clause 1 of the National War Wage Additions Agreement stated that ". . . the district wage arrangements shall continue to operate during the war, subject to mutually agreed alterations." Therefore, as there was no mutual agreement to do this, it could not be altered by arbitration. The Tribunal accepted the view that any variation except by mutual agreement was "precluded by the terms" of the Agreement of March 20, 1940.

But Northumberland pointed out to the miners' Executive that their District Overtime Agreement was quite separate and distinct from the ordinary Wages Agreement for the District, and it was submitted, therefore, that the decision could only mean that no Agreement could be altered unless there was agreement between the parties; any question of arbitration either by a Referee or by a Board would therefore seem to be ruled out during the existence of the National War Wage Agreement.

It was the contention of the Northumberland represent-ative that such a decision would bring about a complete nullification of the new conciliation machinery (which had just been accepted by both sides of the industry) so long as the National War Wage Agreement endured. After discussion it was agreed that the Secretary be instructed to place the facts before Lord Greene with a view to obtaining his observations.

A somewhat similar question came up from Cumberland at the M.F.G.B. Executive Committee of April 8th. But Lord Greene was too skilled a lawyer to be caught by chaff. Not only did he use the authority of his experience but also got an opinion formulated by the Greene Board which had the same force as an award. Moreover, he made provisions for all the old District negotiation arrangements being brought fully into order with the new conciliation machinery. Finally, on May 1, 1943, the new machinery, the "two-handed engine" of conciliation, came into existence. Behind it stood another engine, which for the coal-mining industry was un-precedented and in the past always rejected by the Miners' Federation—the compulsory arbitration power vested in the National Reference Tribunal.

9. FIFTY YEARS OF CONCILIATION

If was fifty years since, under the chairmanship of Foreign Secretary Lord Rosebery, the two sides of the industry had agreed on a scheme of conciliation. That scheme, in which the M.F.G.B. Committee constituted the workers' side, had been limited to the federated area, that is, Yorkshire, Lancashire and the Midlands (in the broader sense: including Derbyshire and Nottinghamshire as well as the area of the Midland Miners' Federation). There was no such machinery then existing either in Scotland or South Wales; and the conciliation schemes of Durham and Northumberland, though established earlier, were at that time quite separate. It was the aim of Ben Pickard and the other founding fathers to have the whole of the British coal-fields included in one single scheme of conciliation machinery—hence the title Miners' Federation of Great Britain. While the federated area came to comprise one or two other coal-fields in addition to the original number and while the decisions reached by the conciliation board of the federated area came to govern the decisions reached in such smaller coal-fields as Cumberland and Somerset, the aim set by Pickard was never reached. Neither the coal-owners of South Wales nor Scotland, when they finally agreed to Conciliation Boards, would, for a moment, consider becoming part of the Board of the federated area. Thus by 1910, when Durham and Northumberland had become constituents of the Miners' Federation so that all the mining unions were federated in one body, their wage negotiations were carried on through five major Conciliation Boards together with a number of smaller ones, amounting to seven or eight in all.

The war of 1914–18 had compelled war advances to be negotiated nationally and it had been hoped that a continuation of these war conditions would result in more or less unified negotiations. The owners, however, had always been opposed to this and, after the defeat of the miners in the 1921 lock-out, the District machinery of negotiation had been reinforced by the establishment of the system of ascertainments which, on their quarterly basis, yielded what would be paid to the men in each District. After the defeat of the miners in the 1926 seven months' lock-out, this process was carried a stage further. The number of separate District agreements was increased and the Miners' Federation of Great Britain as such was excluded, to all intents and purposes, from wages negotiations. Not only were there now some twenty different Districts negotiating with full autonomy on wages questions, but the agreements concluded in 1927 had increased the differences between one District and another as regards wages, conditions of work and even hours of labour. This had an inevitable result. The interests of one District could, and several times did, come into conflict with the interests of another District or of a number of other Districts. Thus the Federation, once so powerful and united, had been seriously weakened and made subject to internal dissensions. It had been able, nevertheless, to continue: partly because there was room for a body which could represent the interests of the miners on matters of legislation in the same way as the old Miners' National Union under Alexander McDonald and Tom Burt had done in the 'seventies and 'eighties, before the formation of the Miners' Federation of Great Britain; and partly because any attempt to break away from it would have extinguished the hope that burned in the mind of every active trade unionist that one day the full unity of all mining interests would be restored to what it had once been, and even carried beyond that. A very small step had been taken when the Joint Standing Consultative Committee was set up in 1936; this meant that after ten years, during which the Mining Association would not recognise the Miners' Federation and steadily refused to meet them, there was now the possibility, at any rate, of such a meeting. It was a token: and only a token. The onset of war had changed all that; now at last, after fifty years, full national machinery with District machinery subordinate to it had been established. The half-century-old aim of Ben Pickard, Robert Smillie and other founders had at last been reached.

While the negotiations for this devoutly desired consummation had been going on, the whole war situation was altering, while at the same time the social atmosphere of Britain was undergoing a striking change. The grave and perilous situation for all the Allies of the first months of 1942, and indeed right up till the mid-autumn, had been transformed by the victory of the Red Army in the defence of Stalingrad and the capture of over a quarter of a million German troops, while at El Alamein the victory of the Eighth Army had driven Rommel to retreat along the coast of North Africa. At home, in December 1942, there had been published the Beveridge Report on Social Insurance and Allied Services[1] which stated that its proposals had as their goal "freedom from want" in the future.

[1] The Report, drafted by Sir William Beveridge as Chairman of the Committee in charge of the problem, suggested far-reaching changes in the schemes of social insurance that had grown up piecemeal, and proposed measures (some of which were to be carried into effect after the war) for comprehensive health and rehabilitation services, many other kinds of benefits and allowances and the avoidance of mass unemployment after the war emergency had come to an end. (Cmd. 6404.)

APPOINTMENT OF BOARD OF INVESTIGATION

WAGES AND WAGES MACHINERY IN THE COAL-MINING INDUSTRY

Whereas a claim for an increase of wages and a guaranteed minimum wage has been submitted by the Mine Workers' Federation of Great Britain;

And whereas the Mining Association of Great Britain take the view that any increase should be in the form of a bonus on output;

And whereas the following statement as to His Majesty's Government's views and intentions is contained in the White Paper (paragraph 20, Command Paper 6364):

> "The Government take the view that the success of the proposed National Coal Board as a body for promoting increased production would be gravely prejudiced if it were associated in any way with wages questions. It is, however, desirable that a system should be developed by which questions of wages and conditions in the mining industry would be dealt with on a national basis and by a properly constituted national body.
>
> "The Government therefore propose to discuss with both sides of the industry the question of establishing a procedure and permanent machinery for dealing, against the background of a continuous review, both nationally and locally, with questions of wages and conditions."

Now therefore We, the Minister of Labour and National Service and the President of the Board of Trade, appoint the following to constitute a Board of Investigation:

> The Right Honourable Lord Greene, O.B.E. (Chairman),
> Colonel Ernest Briggs, D.S.O., B.Sc.,
> George Chester, Esq.,
> Sir John Forster,
> Dr. Arnold Duncan McNair, C.B.E., F.B.A., LL.D.

And we direct that the terms of reference of the Board shall be as follows:

1. To consider and to report in the first instance upon the immediate wages issue; and further,
2. To enquire into the present machinery and methods of determining wages and conditions of employment in the industry, and to submit recommendations for the establishment of a procedure and permanent machinery for dealing

with questions of wages and conditions of employment in
the industry.

We further appoint Mr. D. T. Jack and Mr. J. H. Wilson to be
joint secretaries to the Board.

(Signed) ERNEST BEVIN,
Minister of Labour and National Service.

(Signed) HUGH DALTON,

June 5, 1942.   President of the Board of Trade.

CHAPTER IX

THE DILEMMA OF DUAL CONTROL

1. THE FIRST AWARD—BOYS' WAGES

AFTER the new conciliation machinery had come into being on May 1, 1943, the Master of the Rolls nominated a Law Lord, Lord Porter, as Chairman of the National Reference Tribunal, and two other members, drawn from the universities. The first case came before them in mid-August; their first award was given on September 3, 1943. It was a great disappointment to the miners. It was concerned with juvenile wages, to which there had been a dark and difficult background.

The Sir John Forster Committee had been set up at the same time as the appointment of the Greene Board of Investigation in June 1942, of which Board Sir John Forster was a member. This special Committee on juveniles had submitted to it very full evidence and issued a very weighty and important series of recommendations.

The actual fixing of a figure for wages to remedy the state of affairs disclosed by the Report of the Sir John Forster Committee had to await discussions between the owners' side and the workers' side of the new conciliation machinery. In the discussions the Federation representatives put forward the national scale on a weekly basis. The owners, however, found it difficult to present an alternative scale and gave their view, on July 8, 1943, that the minimum should be fixed on a daily basis and further that a difference should be made between those working on the surface and those underground. The Federation representatives stressed the urgency of the matter which they felt should be referred, since agreement was unlikely, to the Tribunal: and the M.F.G.B. Executive Committee accepted this proposal of its Joint National Negotiating Committee representatives. This was on July 18th. On the next day the Annual Conference began. On Tuesday, July 20th, after the delegates had heard an address by Ernest Bevin, Minister of Labour and National Service, they spent the afternoon on the question of recruitment of juveniles. The following resolution was put forward:

This Conference calls upon the Government to implement the "Forster Report" for young miners by immediate legislation in relation to health, safety, training and general welfare of youths in the mining industry and demands an adequate guaranteed minimum weekly wage for all young miners, similar to the principle already established for adult miners. It regards such measures as imperative to safeguard the interests of young miners and to attract youth to the mining industry. (July 20, 1943.)

William Pearson, Secretary of the National Union of Scottish Mineworkers, said that the Minister of Labour had cast "a gloom on many of the sunshine stories" about the coal situation which they had had from the Minister of Fuel and Power in the past year.

The Government will require to stop tinkering with the man-power problem within the mining industry. They appointed the Forster Committee. That committee met each of the districts. They heard our views. They gave a considered viewpoint. The question which this Conference is entitled to ask the Government is: why appoint a committee to enquire into the recruitment of juveniles if you have no intention of operating that Report?

Pearson said that the youth of Britain was not afraid to enter the mining industry, and recalled that one of his earliest memories, when he was seven, was of his father's being brought home after being killed in the pit:

I remember my mother saying that none of her boys would ever go into the mining industry. But I well remember that poverty drove us into that industry. The poverty and the conditions that existed then do not exist today. The power of this Federation is such that they will never be allowed to exist again in the future.

Every lad entering the industry must be guaranteed efficient training, that his health would be looked after, and that he would receive wages comparable with the work asked of him. Properly treated, the youths would enter the mining industry as readily as any other; and it was the Federation's job to create conditions which would encourage them to do so.

There is not one of us ashamed to proclaim anywhere that we are miners. We have a pride in the fact that we are miners. Why not give our youth the same pride? They belong to a class of men who are prepared to struggle within the industry in order that the conditions of the youth now entering can be improved as compared with the conditions met with by the youth of yesterday.

This is the reply, I think, that this Conference must give to any appeal to the youth of this country—that they are going to enter into just as honourable an occupation as the lads flying over the skies and dropping bombs on the fascists in Sicily and on Germany.

The resolution was seconded by Fred Swift of Somerset, who said that the minister had recently visited Somerset where they had a Conference of all pit production committees. He described what had happened:

I put a question to that conference. I said, "Every man in this meeting, managers, officials and miners' representatives, who has a boy working in the pits put up his hand." Only one solitary hand went up, and I believe his boy was over 30 years of age. That indicates the reason we have this man-power problem, and whatever inducements we hold out to the youth to enter the industry, unless their manhood is made secure it will have no vital results. (July 20, 1943.)

The resolution was carried; the speeches had given a vivid picture of what lay behind the whole question of juveniles and their needs.

With this background in mind the workers' side submitted to the National Reference Tribunal on August 11, 1943, a claim for a National Minimum Wage Scale on a weekly basis. This claim was buttressed by arguments, together with tables showing the total shift wages paid to boys during May 1943 in each of twenty Districts and distinguishing underground from surface workers. The owners also put in a statement with a corresponding array of tables. The Tribunal sat on August 17th, 18th and 19th, considered the case, heard statements and discussion from the two sides and considered their findings. Their award, issued September 4, 1943, fixed the minimum wage at the various ages for each half-year after fourteen. Following are set out four typical years, together with the M.F.G.B. claim in brackets.

MINIMUM WAGE

Age	Underground		Surface	
14	32s.	(42s.)	27s. 6d.	(40s.)
16	40s.	(51s.)	35s. 6d.	(48s.)
18	52s.	(53s.)	44s.	(60s.)
20	60s.	(76s.)	53s.	(72s.)

In the Report afterwards issued by the Miners' Federation[1] Ebby Edwards in an introduction said of this first case and first award that it was "unfavourable inasmuch as the owners had offered a wage during negotiations in excess of the award of the tribunal" and he divulged the fact that "the government itself, anxious to have some grounds for directing youth into the mines, would have been glad if the award had approximated the figures of the application of the Miners' Federation." The miners' side had claimed 42s. a week at the age of fourteen rising to 76s. at the age of twenty (for six shifts). They were awarded 32s. at the age of fourteen and 60s. at the age of twenty. Ebby Edwards in the introduction quoted above, after referring to the Government's anxiety to encourage the entry of youths into the mines—all the more in that they had "rejected the request that skilled miners should return from the Armed Forces"— wrote:

The progress and attention given to the miners during the last four years is economic and not psychological or moral. The appointment of the Lord Greene Board of Investigation; the wage advances; the interest of the Board in watertight arbitration machinery to prevent strikes in the industry; the setting up of the Sir John Forster Committee to consider the reluctance of juvenile workers to enter the Coal Mining Industry, etc., etc.; all the investigations made, and all the measures taken related to the coal mining industry arise out of the economic importance of coal as part of the war effort and not out of propaganda or any change in the application of moral principles applied to the mineworkers as such. (November 1943.)

If the General Secretary could pass such strictures on this "unfavourable award," then it can be understood how it was greeted with indignation in the coal-fields by the miners

[1] Private and Confidential. M.F.G.B. The National Reference Tribunal under the Conciliation Scheme in the Coalmining Industry. Chairman: Lord Porter. National Minimum Wage Scale for Juveniles Employed within the Coalmining Industry.

and by the boys themselves. For as far as the vast majority
of the pits were concerned, no boy was a penny better off
as a result of the award; his wages for the six-day week in
the case of the underground workers were already higher
than the minimum given by the tribunal. Indeed, they were
higher in many coal-fields than the M.F.G.B. claim. For
example, at the age of fourteen the wages paid for six shifts
varied from 36s. in Northumberland to 50s. 6d. in South
Derby for work underground, as against the award of 32s.
Similarly, at the age of twenty there was no case in May
1943 where the wages paid came anywhere near as low as
the £3 that was all the tribunal had offered as a minimum.
The nearest were South Wales with 68s. 11d., Cannock Chase
with 68s. and North Staffs with 68s. 2d.: on the other hand
the Cumberland wage for twenty-year-olds was 88s. 10d. or
approaching half as much again as the award figure of 60s.

The brand-new machinery of the National Conciliation
Board, fashioned in so many negotiations over so many
months of 1942 and 1943 by the Greene Board, had thus
got off to a bad start. Was it a case of good machinery in
the hands of unskilled operators, lawyers and professors new
to the job? Time would show. But in this first award the
miners' leaders saw trouble being laid up for the future.

2. THE FALL IN MAN-POWER AND OUTPUT

By the summer of 1943, despite the measures taken, the
production of coal was falling and the need for man-power
in the industry was growing desperate. The matter was
debated in the House of Commons on June 23rd on a Report
from its Select Committee on National Expenditure. This
Report mainly stressed the need for measures against
absenteeism. To those more deeply versed in the problems
of the industry within the Ministry of Fuel and Power this
seemed an amateurish, if not superficial, treatment. Other
factors were brought out in the June House of Commons
debate and the Minister of Fuel and Power indicated various
measures that would be taken including extra rations for
miners, provision of canteens at the pits, better transport

arrangements, improvements in mechanisation, etc. The question of absenteeism was put in its proper perspective. The minister pointed out in the debate of June 23rd that the total man-shifts lost were a little over 11 per cent of which 6·98 per cent was due to unavoidable causes and only 4·47 per cent was avoidable. In any week there were 50,000 men not working through injury or sickness. In a given week the men actually employed averaged 5¾ shifts. He said the high average attendance must be borne in mind "whenever accusations are made against miners as a body," and that the searchlight directed on miners' attendance or absence was "such as exists in no other industry." He referred, finally, to an "irresponsible minority, mainly composed of young men, who absent themselves particularly at weekends." Persistent absenteeism was dealt with by a Regional Investigation Officer and in serious cases this was followed by prosecution. This was one side of the debate.

Now to summarise the serious nature of the problem: firstly, man-power was still falling, nor could the call-back of miners from other war work be repeated; secondly, output per man-shift had fallen 3 per cent since 1938 and, though this fall was not as great as the 11 per cent of the 1914–18 war, it was extremely serious; thirdly, the absence of coal rationing proposed in the early months of 1942, then postponed in its operation and, because of the resistance of various interests, never brought into force, made consumption higher than it need be. The figures given to the House of Commons in that month of June show the following picture:

MAN-POWER AND OUTPUT

Year	Output in million tons	Average No. of Wage-Earners	Tons per Wage-earner per week
1939	231	766,000	5·81
1940	224	745,000	5·72
1941	206	697,000	6·67
1942	203	709,000	5·50

To meet the man-power situation Ernest Bevin, the Minister of Labour and National Service, was driven to take two successive steps. In the first place those called up to join the

Army were given an option to enter the mines instead. There was some response from each successive age-group of those conscripted, but it was not sufficient. By mid-summer about 3,000 had gone in. Therefore in his address to the Annual Conference of the Mineworkers' Federation, Ernest Bevin announced the second step. He said "at the end of this coal year there will be not enough men and boys in the industry to carry it on. It is a serious position for us. It is the one great difficulty in this war effort. You will be down as I understand it by the normal wastage and shortage of recruitment to about 690,000 people at the end of this coal year, together with the fact that obviously your average age is going up. That intensifies the difficulty." (July 20th.) He drew the conclusion that he would have to "resort to some desperate remedies" and then stated "I shall have to direct young men to you, and I have got to ask the Miners' Federation to help me with it." This was the announcement of conscription for the mines. As it worked out, conscripts were balloted and every tenth person on whom the lot fell was directed into the coal-mining industry. In the same address, Ernest Bevin stated:

I took 47,000 of your men back from the factories to the pits; and let me take this opportunity of publicly thanking those men for going back so smoothly, because all of them had been driven out ruthlessly before I had to send them back. I know of nothing in this war that stands out more magnificently than the way those men gave up good jobs, after being badly treated before they went into them, and went back to the pits. The country is indebted to them, and must be.

We have also given those joining up in the Army an option, and they in turn to the number of about 3,000 have gone in. But it has to go further. As far as I can calculate it with Major Gwilym Lloyd George—and we have been into it very carefully—to meet the increased demands being made upon us, for the coming years we must get up to round about from 720,000 to 750,000 people to the industry, and make good wastage. And wastage, as I say, is getting heavy. (July 20, 1943.)

Four months later in an M.F.G.B. Special Conference (November 26, 1943) it was recalled by Alex. Sloan, M.P., that the cost of advertising to secure these 3,000 optants, as revealed by the Minister of Information, was no less than

£24,000. The attempt to get volunteers for mining was a
failure. Compulsion had been applied to keep skilled miners
in the industry: compulsion would now be applied to gather
the raw recruits—then called "the Bevin boys."

3. DIFFICULTIES OF DUAL CONTROL

By the summer of 1943 the dual control had been in
operation for a year. It became clear to everyone concerned
that it was not working well. To take one example, there
was a division of responsibility in the case of the pit managers.
Operational orders came from the Controller-General of
the Ministry or the Regional Director. But the manager
was the paid servant of the colliery company; if the interests
of the colliery company conflicted with the policy of the
Ministry the manager was in a cleft stick. For their part the
colliery owners made no secret of their dislike of State control.
The Ministry, on the other hand, felt that the control should
be strengthened. But its plans for this purpose in the summer
and autumn of 1943 came up against opposition in the
Cabinet and also in Parliament, where the coal-owners were
well represented.

One section, however, of the Cabinet was concerned to
work out a plan for greater control following on the Labour
Party proposals of the spring of 1942. Accordingly, by the
beginning of 1943 and throughout the early part of the
year the Federation Committee were in discussion together
with the Labour Party on the future organisation of the
coal-mining industry. Documents had been drafted by the
Coal and Power Sub-Committee of the Labour Party which
provided for a Ministry that would supervise the coal, gas,
electricity and by-product industries while each industry
would have its own Board. The Federation Executive
Committee agreed that the general principles of the scheme
should be adopted as an alternative policy on the expiration
of the present form of control. (March 10, 1943.)

A fortnight later at the Joint Standing Consultative
Committee (March 25th) the owners raised the question of
post-war policy, which brought about a long discussion.

In the course of it, the Federation representatives pointed out that the industry was at present under a certain form of control; they were well aware of the owners' apprehension in this connection, and there was a suspicion among the workmen's representatives that the owners had not done all that had been possible to make a success of the present scheme. In addition, the Federation were involved in discussions within the Labour movement, around proposals for dealing with the industry when the present control ceased. Any such proposals would naturally be based on nationalisation, and it seemed, therefore, that the J.S.C.C. would have to decide how far it was possible to proceed in the light of the Federation's views.

The owners' representatives stated that they had no desire to lay down any conditions in connection with the proposed discussions. They would not expect the Federation representatives to change their political views as a preliminary to these discussions. In their opinion the most sanguine supporter of nationalisation could not look upon the present position of control with satisfaction. The industry had to be made as efficient as it was possible to make it and in future the men would have to get a fair wage for the work they performed. It was because of this that they desired these joint discussions. To counter a suspicion that seemed to be in the minds of the miners' representatives concerning the attitude of the owners towards the present form of control, the owners had "recognised from the commencement" that the proposals of the White Paper could bring about certain advantages under war conditions and they had made a public announcement to the effect that they would do everything within their power to assist the Ministry; they had never departed from that attitude.

After a very full discussion it was agreed that a sub-committee, consisting of six representatives from either side[1] should be established to examine the whole question of post-war policy, and that the Government should be requested not to commit itself in this connection until there had been an opportunity of consulting the industry.

[1] It was decided by the Federation side to appoint A. Horner, J. A. Hall, G. A. Spencer and the three officials as members of the sub-committee. (March 25, 1943.)

Not only for the future of the industry after the war, but for its present troubles, the miners had two remedies. The one was nationalisation, consistently put forward by them from the first beginnings of the coal crisis of 1940, but not pushed or promoted by the Labour Party in view of the political complications that might ensue. This demand again found emphatic expression at the 1943 Blackpool Conference[1] in a resolution which instructed the Executive Committee "to take immediate steps with a view to the nationalisation of the mines forthwith."

The other was the provision of a lesser remedy, lesser in its scope and effectiveness but—in their opinion—an improvement on the dual control. Thus at the Annual Conference in Blackpool another resolution urged "the need for strengthening Government Control" by the following measures:

(a) More administrative power to Coal Boards and Pit Production Committees.

(b) Colliery managers to receive directions from the Controller and to be servants and paid by the State.

(c) Consultations between the Control and the Miners' Union before prosecution takes place under Order 1305.

(d) At all inspections carried out for reorganisation or concentration, a workmen's representative should accompany inspector without loss of wages.

(e) All persons responsible for undertakings should have a first-class manager's Certificate under the Coal Mines Act.

(f) Steps should be taken to have most efficient persons in charge of Control. (July 20, 1943.)

The resolution on nationalisation of mines was moved on behalf of the Yorkshire Miners' Association by E. Hough and seconded by J. A. Hall. The Control of Industry resolution was moved on behalf of Scotland by Abe Moffat and seconded by Alf Davies of South Wales and spoken to by James Bowman, the Vice-President, Sam Watson of Durham, G. H. Jones of the Midlands, W. Arthur of South Wales and J. McKendrick of Scotland.

The difficulties of the dual control grew greater, while

[1] Other resolutions apart from those dealt with in this chapter were on workmen's compensation; wages; pensions; social and allied services; post-war policy; post-war hours reduction (to 6½ per day); Labour Research Department; service pay and dependants' allowances; disabled servicemen's pensions.

the situation of man-power and output grew worse. On September 23rd, following on discussions between the officials and the Ministry, representatives of the Ministry attended a meeting of the Federation Executive Committee. Lord Hyndley, Controller-General, in view of the shortage suggested the following means to secure an immediate increase in output.

(a) The working of a 12-day fortnight by pits at present working only 11 days a fortnight (except where the Regional Controller is satisfied that for technical reasons or the physical conditions at the pits this course is impossible);

(b) The clearing of the faces each day;

(c) In certain contingencies the working of one Sunday in four.

Lord Hyndley expressed the hope that if these proposals were not acceptable to the Federation, the Federation itself would submit proposals as to any steps that should be taken to improve the position.

The Secretary circularised the Districts asking their opinion of the Ministry's production proposals, and on September 30th the Executive examined the returns. These showed that no difficulty arose on two of the proposals: the twelve-day fortnight could be left to the few Districts which it affected; whilst clearing the faces daily in general had support and was being carried out. But the Districts were opposed to the proposal for Sunday work.

It was a long discussion, in which it was noted that satisfactory overtime rates were very closely bound up with the Government's three proposals. The owners were still arguing that as overtime rates were already covered by District Agreements, the subject could not be considered nationally. Moreover, the owners did not seem to regard overtime rates as a pressing question. They argued that overtime, in the main, arose from the delinquencies of the workmen during the normal working hours and absenteeism on the part of others. They held that any increase in overtime rates might increase such delinquencies and absenteeism.

Executive members argued that the proposals of the Government were utterly inadequate to deal with the present serious position: a sub-committee were to draft a reply. (September 30, 1943.)

The Executive, aware that the situation of the industry had become a matter of acute difference within the Government and, to some extent, throughout the country, cast their reply in a form that would give a general picture and a full solution to the emergency that had developed in output and man-power. The statement[1] began by a consideration of the Ministry's proposals, which they examined in some detail and rejected as inadequate.

After pointing out that the Ministry of Labour and National Service had met with very limited success in its attempts to transfer men back to mining, the statement declared:

These men resist every effort that is made to bring about their transference to the coal-mining industry. Their objection to returning to the mining industry arises from the very simple fact that wages and conditions as experienced in their present employment are far more favourable than those in the coal-mining industry, in which work is far more arduous and dangerous.

They believed results from letting men due for call-up to opt for mining would be "infinitesimal," nor would direction (i.e. conscription) provide the solution:

Such men as might be directed will not only be unfitted for work in the mines for a considerable period, but they will be unwilling to train for employment which they intend to leave as soon as the opportunity presents itself.

In our view, therefore, the main burden of coal production during the war must remain on the shoulders of the present man-power together with those ex-mineworkers who ought to be returned from the Services and other industries. They could, of course, be supported by such additional workers as it may be possible to obtain through option or direction. (October 7, 1943.)

The statement then put forward for the consideration of the Government a series of proposals based partly on the views of the Districts on the causes that were impeding production, under the following headings: (1) Control of the Mining Industry; (2) Future of the Industry; (3) Wages; (4) Workmen's Compensation; (5) Food Supplies; (6) Transport; (7) Holidays With Pay; (8) Output Bonus Scheme.

They had from the first, the statement recalled, grave

---

[1] Statement of the Mineworkers' Federation in respect of the proposals of the Ministry of Fuel and Power for increasing coal production and the counter-proposals of the Federation. (October 7, 1943.)

doubts of dual control and the confusion it would lead to, and these had been justified. But since to restore pre-war conditions of ownership would be disastrous, there was, therefore, no alternative other than for the Government to take over full financial and operational control.

Under such a system of control, we attach considerable importance to colliery managers and supervisory technicians becoming the direct servants of the State.

In the White Paper, the Pit Production Committee is envisaged as a committee ". . . to assist pit managers to secure maximum output," but unfortunately in a great number of instances these committees have merely been representative of the two sides of the industry—the manager owing allegiance to his employers and the workmen's representatives responsible to the workmen.

Many Pit Committees had consequently ceased to function. The Federation considered that committees should be strengthened, with effective liaison with the regional authorities. Moreover, they should be representative of workmen and technicians, "unhampered by any loyalty to individual colliery concerns, some of which are far too often concerned with the post-war reactions of the present effort to produce coal."

On the "future of the industry," after setting out the problems, the statement said:

In this respect it is necessary to determine *now*:

(a) Immediate legislation governing hours of work after the war.

(b) The provision of guarantees for Government control of the disposal and price of coal, both inland and export. An international arrangement will be required in this connection; such an arrangement should be provided for in the Peace Treaty.

(c) The continuation of the guaranteed week and national minima, below which earnings should not be allowed to fall.

(d) The erection of pit-head baths and canteens or snack bars at all collieries; a programme to be completed within 10 years of the termination of the War.

(e) A comprehensive Workmen's Compensation Scheme on the lines of that presented to the Royal Commission on Workmen's Compensation by the Federation.

(f) New Safety measures based on the Recommendations of the Safety Commission and to include Special provisions in respect of Dust Suppression.

(g) Extension of scientific research on coal utilisation under Government Control. (October 7, 1943.)

On wages the statement proposed a minimum of £6 a week, with corresponding increases for surface and juvenile workers and that the "Porter Award" for youths should be reviewed in the light of these higher adult rates.

Piece rates should be adjusted to take into account any new minimum that might be granted.

They saw no reason why wages should not compare favourably with any other industry. Although wages had been increased during the war the point was put that:

Workmen fear that the war advances will be taken away from them following the cessation of hostilities, hence their concern as to the standard of the operating minimum.

Unless there is a substantial improvement, the present discontent is certain to continue and it will express itself in sporadic stoppages with increasing frequency, arising from frustration, and this situation will not be helped by the fact that men directed back to the industry will tend to draw comparisons between their earnings in those industries and the earnings of workmen employed in the mining industry.

The statement concluded with these words:

In conclusion, the Federation submits that the industry is suffering from a number of accumulating factors that cannot be wholly solved so long as the ownership of the industry remains in private hands. The responses that are required by the Nation from the men cannot be forthcoming unless the workmen can be assured that the benefits of these responses do not accrue to the colliery companies.

October 7, 1943.   EBBY EDWARDS, Secretary.

Clearly the statement was not only a reply. It was also a manifesto in preparation for the parliamentary debate on the coal-mining situation due to open on Tuesday, October 12th, in the House of Commons.

4. A CRITICAL DEBATE IN PARLIAMENT (OCTOBER 12–13, 1943)

The coal-mining situation came up for debate in the House of Commons for the fourth time since the White Paper of

June 1942. Dual control had aroused such dissatisfaction that some drastic change was awaited. But the carefully balanced and non-committal speech of Gwilym Lloyd George found no favour with the Labour members, who realised also that the Minister of Fuel and Power was in the hands of higher authorities. The voice was Gwilym's but the hands were the hands of Esau: and Esau was in the War Cabinet. As the Minister sat down, Aneurin Bevan rose on a point of procedure:

> It is not good enough for the House that the Minister, for whom the House has great affection and respect, should be called upon to defend a policy for which the War Cabinet itself was responsible. (October 12, 1943.)

Emanual Shinwell emphasised this point, saying that the Minister who was "in a hopeless position," had stated "a case that is really no case at all" and asked the Deputy Prime Minister whether they could have the views of the War Cabinet: to which Attlee suavely replied from the Front Bench that members of the War Cabinet would be present during the debate "and if there should be occasion for one of them to intervene, no doubt he will do so."

Thereafter the debate began in earnest with a forceful speech by Jack Lawson (of Chester-le-Street) who supported strongly the proposals of the M.F.G.B. memorandum and quoted from it largely. Next Lieutenant-Colonel Lancaster (of Fylde), a coal-owner, spoke of the need for discipline but also criticised the Ministry for failing to bring in power-loading machines and the Government for failing to give a pledge of a guaranteed wage and guaranteed employment for five years after the war. Such a miners' charter, he said, "would go a long way towards allaying the frightful spectre of insecurity for the miner when the war is over."

F. S. Cocks (of Broxtowe) at once rejected the Minister's appeal "for a placid debate," saying:

> The state of feeling among the miners at the moment is not placid; it is developing into a raging maelstrom, a foaming Niagara of discontent, and the House should be informed quite clearly as to what the position is among the men in the industry at the moment and what grave events are possible. Unless the causes of discontent are removed grave events are possible; unless they

are removed I think it is the duty of Labour Ministers to leave the Government. (October 12, 1943.)

Cocks gave example after example from his own constituency of the way things were going wrong: and in answer to the demand for "Discipline" said with some intensity of expression:

> You talk of the Essential Work Order, and say that discipline cannot be maintained until managers recover the power of dismissal. Discipline is not maintained today by the power of the sack. That would be an order of release from slavery. If you abolished the Essential Work Order, half the men in the pit would leave the industry tomorrow of their own voluntary accord.
>
> Discipline, certainly in Nottinghamshire, if you call it discipline, is maintained by a system of organised and authorised bullying in an atmosphere of noise, dust, heat, sweat and blasphemy. (October 12, 1943.)

Thereafter, though the next speaker, Major Braithwaite, with some knowledge of the industry, maintained some placidity in his criticism (for he too criticised Government policy) the debate "hotted up." Two speeches from back-bench Conservatives, who put the main blame for the situation upon the mine-workers, must have set the teeth on edge of those Ministers who had hoped for a placid debate. That night there seemed a fair likelihood that at the end of the next day's debate, as Aneurin Bevan had intimated, a division would be called with at least the Labour members, and quite possibly a number of Conservatives and Liberals, going against the Coalition Government's policy. It was high time for one of the War Cabinet "to intervene." Which of the seven[1] was it to be? When the course of the debate was reported to the Prime Minister, it became clear that he

---

[1] Actually there were eight, but the eighth, an Australian who was entitled "Minister of State Resident in the Middle East," was by the very definition of his functions unable to play any part in coal policy. The others were:

Prime Minister, First Lord of the Treasury and Minister of Defence—Rt. Hon. WINSTON SPENCER CHURCHILL, C.H., M.P.

Lord President of the Council and Deputy Prime Minister—Rt. Hon. CLEMENT RICHARD ATTLEE, M.P.

Secretary of State for Foreign Affairs and Leader of the House of Commons—Rt. Hon. ROBERT ANTHONY EDEN, M.C., M.P.

Chancellor of the Exchequer—Rt. Hon. Sir JOHN ANDERSON, G.C.B., G.C.S.I., G.C.I.E., M.P.

Minister of Labour and National Service—Rt. Hon. ERNEST BEVIN, M.P.

Minister of Production—Rt. Hon. OLIVER LYTTELTON, D.S.O., M.C., M.P.

Secretary of State for Home Affairs and Home Security—Rt. Hon. HERBERT MORRISON, M.P.

himself would have to intervene, if the policy announced by Gwilym Lloyd George was to go through without a division. The debate the next day, therefore, began with Winston Churchill apologising "for intervening in the Debate," having been absent the day before. But, he said, he had read both the newspaper reports and much of Hansard and had spent since then a good deal of time "discussing the position with various friends and colleagues."

Churchill then said it might help if he "reminded the House" of "the general foundations upon which we stand," saying:

> We have a National Coalition Government, which came together to try to pull the nation out of the forlorn and sombre plight into which the action, or inaction, of all political parties over a long period of years had landed it.
>
> Hon. Members: The Tory Party.
>
> It all depends where you draw the datum line. I stand very well placed in that matter, having been out for 11 years. (October 13, 1943.)

Then the Prime Minister put the question: "What is it that holds us together?" and answered it in these words:

> We are held together by something outside which rivets all our attention. The principle that we work on is: "Everything for the war, whether controversial or not, and nothing controversial that is not *bona fide* needed for the war." That is our position. (October 13, 1943.)

In his view nationalisation of coal-mines was not *bona fide* necessary: and "we should not be justified in embarking upon it without a General Election" which he held would at that moment "be very difficult." Therefore, he said:

> I could not be responsible, as at present advised, for undertaking any further great change, and certainly not a permanent great change in the mining industry during the war, because that I think would require to be ratified or preceded by a national mandate. Therefore, we must resist all such proposals, and we must ask for the support of the House in so doing. (October 13, 1943.)

Churchill sweetened this outright rejection of what had seemed to many to be necessary as a war-time measure to meet the coal crisis, by the rest of his speech, in which he said many kind things about the miners, referred feelingly to "those unhappy periods when cruel unemployment racked the mining industry" and then implicitly rebuked the Tory "wild men" when he said:

. . . almost everything stands on coal. It is vital to our war-making capacity. All our refined manufactures of civilisation in time of peace go down to the footing of this intense labour underground by a comparatively small section of our people, the miners.

We must not underrate the strain upon the miners. Their average age has increased. Their food is less stimulating and their diet is less varied. They do not get the holidays or leisure for which their exceptionally arduous calling has called in the past during the summertime when coal consumption was small. They are now pressed to work just as hard, or harder, in the summertime in order to pile up for the winter and to make good the needs of the war.

These are very considerable factors, and no one should underrate them or make them the basis of an indictment against the mining population. (October 13, 1943.)

It was a superb performance by a master of rhetoric and of the special art of parliamentary debate. After Churchill sat down it was clear that no bell would ring for the division lobbies. The House of Commons, faced by the alternative he had presented, had to accept his policy, or, rather, the policy of the War Cabinet. But acceptance did not in all cases mean conviction. This was abundantly clear when the next speaker arose, who as former Minister of Mines was perhaps the most formidable critic possible on the subject of debate. This was D. R. Grenfell, member for Gower, who began by saying:

I am sure the House will desire me to express its appreciation of the eloquence, the consideration and the good feeling displayed by the Prime Minister. I am sure that the House will also share the disappointment that I feel with the contents of the right hon. Gentleman's speech. (October 13, 1943.)

Dai Grenfell, on whom there had fallen the heavy burden of keeping chaos at bay in the coal industry during the first two years of the Churchill administration and whose sound policies for this purpose had been more than once rejected, went thoroughly into the main aspects of the coal-mining situation. Finally, in stressing the absolute bedrock importance of getting more man-power (and getting back more

skilled miners from the Forces) he criticised the Minister of
Labour who had been responsible for "the dispersal of the
manpower in 1940." Rather brusquely treated at this point
by the Minister for Labour and National Service who
interjected "I do not care what the hon. Member does,"
Dai Grenfell then gave chapter and verse for his criticism,
and was able to cite the names of five highly respected
mining members who had also been concerned in the
proposals for maintaining the needed man-power in coal,
proposals which Bevin turned down on the ground "that
the mining industry was holding too many men and that
it must make its contribution." Stung by another intervention from Ernest Bevin who, never very good at taking
criticism, exclaimed "I cannot sit here and allow these
statements to be made," Dai Grenfell, quoting from documents, revealed to the House of Commons how Bevin's
behaviour at that time had contributed to the growth of the
coal crisis:

> The right hon. Gentleman did not have one word of consultation
> with me, but was talking to Members of the House and telling
> them to go and persuade me that I was wrong—not one word of a
> consultation that should have taken place. He insisted, and here
> are the proposals. There are more that I can read to him if he
> likes.
> The right hon. Gentleman must admit that he is responsible
> for the weakening of the man-power position of the mining industry.
> I asked that the figure of 720,000 should be maintained.
> At the time, the right hon. Gentleman was putting every pressure
> possible to break up the personnel of the mining industry. I failed
> to get a single word of consultation with him. Now does he want to
> intervene? He can do so if he likes. (October 13, 1943.)

Bevin did intervene but not with sufficient effect to shake
Dai Grenfell, who repeated without further challenge his
earlier assertion that:

> Proposals were made to me then which would have ruined South
> Wales and Durham. If I had accepted the proposals of the Minister,
> which I can read, this industry would have been 20,000,000 tons
> down in 1941, and our war effort would have broken down for
> want of coal. (October 13, 1943.)

When later in the debate Alexander Sloan, of South
Ayrshire, got up to speak, it became obvious that mining

trade union opinion in the House was against the policy they were being compelled to accept. Alexander Sloan said in the course of his speech:

We ask that the statement issued by the Miners' Federation should be closely examined. It may be true that great constitutional changes cannot be made during the war: there is talk of the need to face the electorate and to do a lot of other things. In the day of Dunkirk many more drastic changes could have taken place without any consultation with the electorate.

The Prime Minister today was very amiable. He emphasised what the Minister of Fuel and Power told us yesterday. The control will remain until Parliament decides otherwise. Of course, Parliament can decide anything, but is the mining industry to be left in the position where a Tory majority can at any time end control, as they ended it in 1921? I do not forget what happened then. I do not forget that miners received their pay one week on the basic rate of £1 os. 6d. a day and the next week received their pay on the basic rate of 8s. 4d. a day. (October 13, 1943.)

Then, speaking with some bitterness and with an ironic parody of some of the Churchillian phrases Sloan showed how little he had been moved by the Prime Minister's eloquence:

The Prime Minister was always a great war leader. He was the leader of the vested interests in 1926 when they were fighting the miners. Nobody has any time for him as a peace time leader; nobody believes in him as a peace time leader; he has always been a great war leader. He was a great war leader during the period of Dunkirk, when his speeches roused the nation.

Great reliance was placed upon him then and great reliance was placed upon him in 1926. We were at war; they declared so, nakedly and unashamed. We did not feed the Germans during the war and so why feed the miners? The vested interests were led by a great war leader and the fight was fought out to the bitter end. The miners were defeated, but not without a struggle. They fought on the hills of Scotland and on the beaches of the North-East coast, the valleys of South Wales and in the streets of the Midlands, but it was all of no avail. They were defeated. I am not distressed. (October 13, 1943.)

When Arthur Greenwood, who had been for nearly two years a member of the War Cabinet, also weighed in with severe criticisms of the lack of policy for the future, it meant that although the War Cabinet had staved off a parliamentary crisis, they had not overcome the abiding and intensifying crisis in coal. This was soon to be demonstrated by events in the coal-fields.

5. THE PORTER AWARD

The proposals of the Federation for increasing coal production, as outlined in the statement submitted to the Minister of Fuel and Power and the further developments thereon were brought before an M.F.G.B. Special Conference in Conway Hall on Thursday, November 25, 1943, and succeeding days. The submission of the statement had been followed first by the two-day debate on coal in the House of Commons where Prime Minister Churchill had made a decisive intervention; and, second, by a letter on November 2nd from the minister. The letter, an interim reply, dealt with the seven headings of the proposals put forward by the Federation; indicated on some things that the Ministry would do what it could to meet the proposals and on other points it suggested further meetings or stated that there could be no change from previous decisions. To this the Federation on November 4th replied in an argumentative but diplomatically worded letter. This correspondence, together with the statement, was laid before the Special Conference. The executive resolution moved by James Bowman, and seconded by Arthur Horner, ran:

This Conference having considered the report of the Executive Committee in regard to the negotiations that have been proceeding with the Government in connection with the situation in the coal-mining industry, endorses the action of the Executive Committee in pressing upon the Government the urgent need to implement the proposals of the Mineworkers' Federation.

The Conference expresses its profound regret that the negotiations have not yet reached a stage approaching finality and instructs the Executive Committee to continue the negotiations with a view to a speedy solution to the present difficulties and for the purpose of receiving a further report a Conference shall be called by not later than January 14, 1944.[1]

Meanwhile the Conference, fully appreciative of the urgent requirements of the country for Coal, calls upon the workmen in

[1] Postponed by mid-December E.C. to January 27, 1944.

the coalfields to assist in maintaining the highest possible level of production. (November 25, 1943.)

It was a stormy Conference, reflecting "the dissatisfaction of our men throughout every District" who were asking, as was said by Vice-Chairman Bowman, "what are the Federation doing?" Unless this dissatisfaction (now beginning to be felt also towards the M.F.G.B. leaders) were met in a big way, then, the Government had been told, "men will continue to correct their grievance by guerrilla tactics at pit after pit and District after District." Bowman then said:

We have passed the phase in this war when slogans and appeals are of any use. The speech of the Prime Minister in the House of Commons in the recent Coal Debate was one of the greatest disservice to the mining industry. . . . Men in the coalfield have seen as a result of the statement by the Prime Minister, that anything which involves major political changes cannot be done during this war, and the capitalists are now crawling out of their funk holes and claiming their position for the post-war world. (November 26, 1943.)

The Conference, attended by 212 delegates representing 602,112 members, divided on the resolution. It was carried (each vote representing a thousand) by 467 votes to 141, the minority being made up of South Wales and Lancashire. But the feeling of frustration in all the coal-fields, shown in this Conference[1] by the negative vote of two large Districts, was soon to be manifest on a bigger scale. The claim for minimum wages, put forward on December 15, 1943, and rejected by the employers, was argued by Ebby Edwards on January 5, 1944, before the National Reference Tribunal. Expeditiously enough there followed the Porter Award: and then the trouble began.

The National Reference Tribunal, made up of the Right Honourable Lord Porter, Principal J. S. Rees and Professor T. M. Knox, having issued its first award on September 4, 1943, and its second and third on paid annual holidays and on overtime by the end of November, had now to deal with the claim for an increase of the minimum wage. The claim

[1] The M.F.G.B. Executive on November 24th had protested "in the strongest possible terms" against the decision of Herbert Morrison, the Home Secretary, to release Sir Oswald Mosley, and called for his "immediate re-internment." A resolution of the Conference, moved by William Pearson and carried unanimously, ran: "That this Conference endorses the action of the Executive in objecting to the release of Mosley and that Mosley should be taken from the place he now is back to where he came from."

N*

was for a National Minimum Wage of £6 per week for men underground and £5 10s. on the surface with corresponding increases for juveniles. The claim was strongly supported in the M.F.G.B. Special Conference of November 25th. During the 18 months up to December 1943 while wages in other industries had been rising, in coal-mining they had remained on a constant level with the result that the position of the miners in the list of industries had fallen back from 29th place to 40th or 41st place.

The Tribunal made its award on January 23, 1944: a minimum of £5 underground and £4 10s. on the surface, an increase of 17s. and 12s. respectively on the rates as settled by the Greene Award in June 1942. The rates for boys were raised so that at twenty years of age those underground were to get 80s. and 70s. on the surface. At the same time, the award rejected the claim for an increase in piece-work rates to take account of the new minimum rates. This decision was to be productive of great trouble, not only in its effect on piece-workers, but also on craftsmen and other sections. However, to begin with, the miners' delegates, at an M.F.G.B. Special Conference held on January 27 and 28, 1944, decided to accept the award as giving an advance in lower paid Districts and as a step forward to a minimum on which they could build. But at the same time they warned the Government of the problems and serious anomalies created by this award.

The National Reference Tribunal, in rejecting the piece-rates claim, gave the ground that "it is not consistent with the granting of what is merely a minimum wage." They said also that "the consideration of so great an alteration must await the general overhaul of the wages structure which is long overdue" and that their award was to be considered as "merely a temporary expedient which will afford an opportunity for the wage structure throughout the industry to be reconsidered and thoroughly reviewed." The M.F.G.B. Executive Committee were of course ready to enter into immediate discussion with the owners and with the Government on the "overhaul of the wages structure," but the assumption of the Tribunal that they need not make even a temporary award in respect to piecework rates turned out to be a false reckoning. No man can tether time or tide, especially in the matter of wage anomalies.

What were these anomalies? First, the earnings of the productive workers at the coal-face, engaged in the most hazardous and arduous work, were restricted; secondly, the skilled day-wage workers previously paid higher than the District minimum were now down on the minimum rate of £5 in the lower paid Districts. This was the same as their assistants or as trainees new to the mines. In other Districts the gap between the grades or, as it is now called, the differential, was considerably reduced.

At the Special Conference of January 27th and 28th the M.F.G.B. Executive Committee were instructed to take up these matters. After discussion with the owners on February 3rd (this with the full knowledge of the Government) it was agreed that negotiations be opened in the various Districts with the owners in order to settle the anomalies. The owners in the various coal-fields reached agreement with the county and District miners' associations on increases that would get rid of the anomalies created by the Porter Award. The miners' unions, and apparently the coal-owners also, believed that these would be met by the Government out of the Coal Charges Fund. Since 1942 there had been this Coal Charges Account, a financial instrument designed to keep up the industry's output during the emergency. Rises in production costs had been reflected in price increases, but these in themselves did not mean solvency for the less profitable undertakings which, without special assistance, would have gone out of production.

All colliery companies were required to pay into the Account a flat rate levy on each ton of coal produced. They drew varying sums to recover what they paid out on wage additions, guaranteed wage payments, etc. By this means, the burden of increased costs resulting from the war was spread. In addition, colliery companies drew sums which varied from District to District in order to make up a "standard credit balance" laid down for each District. In short, the low-cost Districts had to subsidise the high-cost Districts. Payments were also made out of the Account to keep solvent "necessitous undertakings"—companies for which the

ordinary drawings on the Account were insufficient. There
was also a subsidy from the Exchequer to the Coal Charges
Account—which subsidy in the five years from 1942 mounted
up to nearly thirty million pounds.

Suddenly, when a number of such agreements had already
been negotiated and announced to the miners, the Government issued a statement on February 11th that the cost of
adjusting anomalies would not be met from the Coal Charges
Fund. The settlements were thus invalidated.

It appears that the coal-using industries had urged that
there should be no further increase in coal prices. The
Government, in its talks and in House of Commons statements, put it that it did not wish to raise the price to the
public. The impression created in the coal-fields was that the
Government was not prepared to operate the award and
face its full implications.

The result was an outbreak of unofficial strikes in various
coal-fields on such a scale as had not been known since
the beginning of the war. The Government's action had
put the fat in the fire. It was the development of a new sort
of coal crisis brought on, it must be said, by the Government's
own decision. The total figures were not immediately disclosed. But in the whole year 1944 the number involved in
mining disputes were no less than 568,000. The duration in
working days of all disputes that year was 2,480,000, a figure
that had only once been exceeded in the previous seventeen
years. But a still more significant figure is the number of
disputes, big and small. There were no less than 1,253 disputes in 1944, half as many again as in the preceding year,
1943, which year had the highest total of disputes since the
beginning of the century. Within the short space of two-and-
a-half months principal disputes are recorded as follows:

Coal-field	No. of workpeople affected	Date when dispute Began	Ended	Aggregate duration in working days
Lancashire	19,000	Jan. 24	Feb. 5	
Staffordshire	17,000	Jan. 28	Feb. 5	
Yorkshire	15,500	Jan. 31	Feb. 14	300,000
Durham	7,400	Feb. 24–29	Feb. 25–29	
Scotland	15,000	Mar. 8	Mar. 20	
South Wales and Mon.	100,000	Mar. 6	Mar. 18	550,000
Yorkshire	120,000	Mar. 16	Apr. 11	1,000,000

As the Government came to realise the enormity of the blunder which had caused men who were whole-hearted supporters of the war effort to come out on strike in large numbers and for several weeks at a time when they knew the launching of the Second Front was imminent, they made an effort from the second week of March onwards to remedy the damage caused. In the first place on March 9th they announced advances to piece-workers; this left out the day-wage men whose skilled rates had been telescoped in many cases with those of less skilled grades. This was pointed out by the miners' representatives; so on March 24th the Government announced increases to certain grades of craftsmen, mainly on the surface.

6. THE FOUR-YEAR AGREEMENT OF APRIL 1944

The Government had been appalled by the consequences of their own blunder of mid-February, itself a sequel to the imperfections of the Porter Award of January 1944. They realised that they had been gazing down into an abyss of industrial problems—which indeed could have been foreseen had anyone possessed the requisite knowledge and vision— in which the whole war effort could be engulfed or at the least seriously crippled. The War Cabinet knew, though the country did not, that D-Day of the Second Front was only some ten weeks ahead. By rapid concessions from the second week of March onwards they had bridged that abyss. But how long would the structure of the bridge endure? It was clearly necessary to institute some fundamental changes in industrial relations, even if the Cabinet's decision of October 1943 had ruled out both the requisitioning of the mines and the nationalisation of the industry. So after much anxious discussion, the step was taken. On March 24th, the Government put forward a far-reaching series of new proposals which would affect both sides of the industry and involve undertakings by the Government itself. The effect of these proposals, once they had been accepted, was as follows:

(1) The existing ascertainment agreements in the various districts were suspended for the duration of the new National

Agreement which was to last for four years, that is, beyond the expected duration of the war.

(2) A new National Minimum Wage Rate was set up higher than the minimum in any other industry.

(3) The percentage additions payable under the old ascertainment system was merged in the minimum basic wage; the flat increases in wages (other than the 16/– a week War Addition to meet the cost of living) right back from 1936 were also merged in the District Wage rate.

(4) The District Output Bonus operating under the Greene Awards from the latter part of 1942 was discontinued.

(5) A satisfactory increase was given to pieceworkers on a rather complicated formula related to the district Wage Rate.

(6) No further general change in the rates as settled by the conciliation machinery or on a district basis was to be sought by either side of the industry during the currency of the new agreement.

These proposals, given only in summary form, were as regards their general terms acceptable to the Federation. But details in some cases were unsatisfactory to some important Districts. Consequently, there were several weeks of negotiations to remove some of the remaining anomalies created by the Porter Award. Finally, an M.F.G.B. Special Conference on April 12th heard a Report of Ernest Bevin's offer of another £1,750,000 to meet these anomalies. After the Delegate Conference there were further negotiations with the Government and the owners. Finally, on April 20, 1944, the new agreement was signed.

It was a landmark in the history of wages negotiations only second, if that, in importance to the work of the Greene Board in June 1942 and thereafter. It gave an increased incentive to piece-workers; it consolidated wages to an extent that had never occurred before and against the whole tendency of splitting up and endless complications; it stabilised the National Minimum Rate for a period of four years in advance; it obliged the Government to maintain for at least four years the Coal Charges Fund or other form of the national pool, out of which wages payment would be available. Finally, for the same period it put into cold storage the ascertainment system,[1] which had caused

---

[1] See *The Miners: Years of Struggle.*

so much suspicion in the minds of the colliers for over twenty years.

The ascertainment system, set up after the lock-out of 1921, had taken the place of the old Conciliation Board methods of settling wages that had been in operation earlier in the century and back into the 'nineties, just as these in turn had taken the place of the still older sliding scale agreements by which wages varied in relation to the pit-head price of coal. The ascertainment systems were on a basis of "profit sharing," District by District. After the lock-out of 1926 there were great differences between the separate District Agreements. But in every District there had been a suspicion that the ascertainments, though correctly worked upon by firms of accountants, left out of account profits made by the owners in enterprises that were closely connected with coal-mining, but by the terms of the agreements, ruled to be outside the industry.

Then in cases where in bad times the miner's wage was made up to "subsistence level" there was provision made for "recoupment" to the coal-owners of the sums thus expended before there could be, in a more prosperous market, any increase of wage-rates. "Recoupment" was regarded in many parts of the coal-fields as a source of profit to the owners and a loss to the mine-workers.

All in all, the agreement of April 20, 1944, marked a very big and important advance. This revision of wage structure had been reached under governmental pressure and the owners up to the morning of their signature had remained sceptical as to its outcome. But for the remainder of 1944 the National Conciliation Board functioned smoothly. Within six months of the April 20th agreement the collier's average earnings (as stated by the Minister of Fuel and Power on October 17, 1944) had brought him up to 14th place in a list of nearly a hundred trades. A new pattern had been set.

Appendix A

HEADS OF AGREEMENT
between the Mining Association of Great Britain
and the Mineworkers' Federation of Great Britain.

1. The Mining Association of Great Britain and the Mineworkers' Federation of Great Britain having considered the suggestions for the overhaul of the wage structure of the coal-mining industry submitted to them by the Minister of Fuel and Power on 8th March, 1944, agree to operate the proposals set out in paragraph 2 hereof.

2. (i) The existing ascertainment agreements shall be suspended for the duration of this Agreement, such percentage additions as are at present payable thereunder being merged in the day-wages or piece-rates payable as provided herein.

(ii) Flat-rate additions to wages, other than the cost-of-living advance, shall, subject to the approval of the Minister of Fuel and Power, in each district or wage area be incorporated in wages as follows:—

(a) In each District the day-wage basis rates shall include the District ascertainment percentage existing at the date thereof and the District flat-rate advances.

The day-wages of skilled craftsmen as defined in the schedule hereto and of the day-wage workers in a district set out in the schedule hereto applicable to that District shall be further increased by 1s. per shift provided that if such wages are at or below the minimum wage awarded for that class of work by the National Reference Tribunal for the Coal-mining Industry on 22nd January, 1944, such 1s. per shift shall be paid in addition to such minimum wage.

(b) In each District or wage area the piece-rates shall be increased by the percentage set out for each district or wage area in the attached Schedule approved by the Minister of Fuel and Power; which percentages have been arrived at by ascertaining the percentage which the flat rate allowances, other than the cost-of-living allowance, bear to the effective district minimum shift rate for the particular district or wage area.

(c) The District Output Bonus Scheme which came into operation in September, 1942, shall be discontinued at the end of the first output bonus period following the date hereof, but payments falling due in respect of that period shall be made. Special consideration will be given to wages in districts which have regularly earned District Output Bonus.

3. This agreement shall operate as from the beginning of the first pay-week next after the date hereof and shall continue until notice in writing shall be given by either party hereto to amend or terminate this agreement at the expiration of six months from the date of serving such notice, provided that such notice shall not be given before the 31st December, 1947.

4. The parties hereto agree that during the currency of this Agreement no variation will be sought in the rates awarded in the existing operative awards of the National Reference Tribunal or District Conciliation Machinery for the Coal-mining Industry or in district rates as modified by this Agreement. Further, no application for alterations in wages rates at a pit shall be made other than those normally made in respect of changed methods or conditions of working in accordance with custom or Agreement existing in the district.

5. The parties hereto re-affirm their view that in war-time and in the transitional period from war to peace the smooth working of the coal-mining industry is essential to the social and economic life of the Nation and for the well-being of the industry itself. Realising that the purpose of this Agreement for a term of years is to secure industrial peace and stability, the parties pledge themselves to use their full authority to ensure observance of this Agreement by their members, and to ensure that no support, financial or otherwise, is given by the parties hereto or by any of their constituent Associations to any member acting in breach of this Agreement. They further undertake to continue to use every endeavour to ensure maximum output, efficiency and regularity of attendance and the speedy determination of any disputes by the machinery established nationally or in the districts for that purpose.

As duly accredited representatives for and on behalf of the Mining Association of Great Britain; and for and on behalf of its Constituents and affiliated Associations.

(signed) { AND. K. McCosh
          { W. Benton Jones
          { W. A. Lee

As duly accredited representatives for and on behalf of the Mineworkers' Federation of Great Britain; and for and on behalf of its constituent and affiliated Federations and Associations.

(signed) { Ebby Edwards
          { Will Lawther
          { James Bowman

(signed) G. Lloyd George
Presiding Chairman

20th *April*, 1944.

The table that follows is combined from two separate tables attached to the
Heads of Agreement.[1]

NATIONAL WAGES AGREEMENT—20th APRIL, 1944

District	Percentage additions to Basis Rates in the various districts at April 20, 1944, which became merged in the consolidated wage.	SCHEDULE I. Percentage applicable to piece-rates in each district, or wage area, as approved by the Minister of Fuel and Power, in accordance with paragraph 2 (ii) (b) of the Heads of Agreement
	Percentage	Percentage
Northumberland	45	49
Durham	70	49
Cumberland	30	48
Lancashire and Cheshire ..	6	45
Yorkshire: South	38	42
West ⎰ Eastern area	38 (except Surface—36·34)	43
⎱ Western area	38 (except Surface—33)	47
Nottinghamshire	87	32
North Derbyshire	4·61	38
South Derbyshire	74·63	42
North Staffordshire	44	48
Cannock Chase	43·77	48
South Staffordshire	40	52
Leicester	85·37	42
Warwick	95 less 2	34
Shropshire	32	52
Forest of Dean	30 ⎰ on standard rates (equals 75·5 on basis rates)	53
Somerset	41·26	57
Bristol	25 (piece-workers), 27 (others)	57
Kent	32 (37 for lower paid workers)	38
South Wales and Monmouth ..	30	42
North Wales	22	58
Scotland	12·5	50

[1] The preceding part of this Appendix is an exact copy of the official document as reprinted in Part I (1940–46) of the National Coal Board Memorandum of Agreements, etc., with all its typographical inconsistencies of capital letters and small letters.

Appendix B

NATIONAL REFERENCE TRIBUNAL AWARDS

Eleven meetings (8th to 18th) of the National Joint Negotiating Committee under the Conciliation Scheme were held in 1944. From the date of the inception of the machinery on May 25, 1943, the following twelve Awards were made by the National Reference Tribunal.

1st. National Minimum Wage scale for Juveniles (September 4, 1943).

2nd. Holidays with Pay (November 29, 1943).

3rd. Payments for overtime and week-end work (November 18, 1943).

4th. Increase in the National Minimum Wage Scale (January 22, 1944).

5th. Payments for overtime and week-end work (January 22, 1944).

6th. Interpretation of "ruling rate" as provided for in paragraph 8 of the first report of the Board of Investigation, 1942 (January 22, 1944).

7th. Scottish submission *re* "Pay-as-you-Earn" (March 24, 1944).

8th. Interpretation of Clause 4 of the 5th Award (May 22, 1944).

9th. Interpretation of the 4th Award in respect of men working seven and five shifts in alternate weeks (May 22, 1944).

10th. Interpretation of the 4th Award in respect of continuous shiftmen (May 22, 1944).

11th. Interpretation of the 5th Award in respect of certain workmen working short week-end shift (December 19, 1944).

12th. Inconsistency of District Referee's Award with a National Award (December 19, 1944).

CHAPTER X

A SINGLE UNION

I. THE REORGANISATION SUB-COMMITTEE AT WORK

It was away back in the spring of 1942 that the M.F.G.B. Executive Committee had agreed to submit to the Annual Conference a resolution for "a change in the form of our Miners' Organisation" (April 16, 1942). It was ten weeks before it was decided that the Federation's Reorganisation Sub-Committee should be charged with preparing a scheme. Certain principles were quickly formulated to be put to the Conference. They were not to be voted upon; they were "vital and fundamental factors" which would be presented for the purpose of debate, consideration and guidance. But it was hoped that Districts would make their attitude clear before the sub-committee started detailed work: for, failing this, it would be of no use for any Committee to spend time and money in considering detailed schemes. These were the main principles:

(1) To merge all the individual district and sectional miners' unions into one national organisation covering all mine-workers employed in or around the collieries of Great Britain.

(2) For the purpose of union administration the areas shall be the same as the districts covered by the separate district organisations at present affiliated to the Mineworkers' Federation of Great Britain, always providing that this shall not prevent any two or more adjoining districts voluntarily agreeing to become one area.

(3) The terms of the amalgamation shall be agreed to after full consideration with the district unions, it being understood procedure will be adopted in order to reach finality and practical application within a specific period to be determined.

(4) Each individual union shall on a date to be decided transfer to the National Union a proportion (to be later determined) of its assets and liabilities.

(5) A uniform amount of contributions shall be paid for every full member (half-members to pay half such amount) to the National Miners' Organisation. (July 11, 1942.)

The subsequent proceedings at the 1942 Annual Conference in July (recorded in Chapter VIII) made the members of the Reorganisation Sub-Committee very wary and very careful about the way they were to do their job: they needed first to collect information from the Districts; and it was also thought necessary to ask that three representatives from each District should come to London to discuss their views of the principles. This proposal (on October 15, 1942) was endorsed by the M.F.G.B. Executive Committee. Armed with this decision, the sub-committee set out on what proved to be a lengthy task. It was over seven months before (on May 20, 1943) they could ask the Executive Committee to hold a special meeting to consider their recommendations and proposed changes of rule. Three weeks later the Executive considered the sub-committee's Report which proposed centralising industrial work and that Districts with special benefit funds should keep complete control of them. Some forty-five draft Rules were put forward.

The Executive decided to submit a Report and draft Rules to the Districts, and discussed whether, at the forthcoming Annual Conference, members should be allowed to put forward their District's views if contrary to the Executive's viewpoint. On this it was agreed:

That there should be no change from the present procedure, viz. that no member of the Executive Committee be allowed to oppose a majority decision of the Executive Committee when such is being discussed at a conference. (June 10, 1943.)

This rule of procedure has remained in force up to the present day.

2. THE EXECUTIVE'S 1943 REPORT

The Executive proposals were in the form of a draft of new rules preceded by a brief explanation of how the 1942 Annual Conference resolution had been interpreted. That resolution had instructed the Executive Committee "to draft proposals for a change in the form of our Miners' Organisation"; but had made no reference to what form would be required "to meet the changed circumstances and conditions which must arise in the industry." But the change, it was generally recognised, would be based on the principle of "one union for all mineworkers."

So far, so good. But now came the crux, the obstacle to all earlier schemes, the formidable question of how the county associations and District bodies would fit into the plan for a single national union. The Executive Committee, taught by experience, explained how they proposed to get round this awkward corner, as follows:

In view of all the difficulties involved, difficulties which at this stage it is considered are insurmountable, any possibility of the complete dissolution of the present district organisations has been ruled out. The proposals of the sub-committee which have since been endorsed by ourselves are based on the conception:

(i) that the whole of the industrial activities of the several district associations could well be centralised immediately, and

(ii) in view of the very substantial divergence of practice and custom as between the different districts in respect of contributions and benefits (apart from normal industrial benefits) there should be as little interference as possible with this particular aspect of the work already performed by the district associations. (June 1943.)

How were the industrial activities of the associations affiliated to the Mineworkers' Federation to be centralised and to become the responsibility of a central authority, the proposed National Union of Mineworkers? "We recommend," wrote the Executive, "that 5d. per member per week[1] should be remitted to the centre."

In return the national union would assume responsibility for the present liabilities of the district associations in respect of industrial activities, viz., salaries of full-time Officials and Staffs,

---

[1] The 5d. a week may seem an unusually small contribution, even for 1943; but the lowest existing rate of contribution set this limit. In the Executive Report it was stated:

"In their discussions with district representatives the Officials had to meet complaints from certain districts as to the difficulties which would arise particularly in those districts where there was a weekly contribution of 6d. and out of which benevolent benefits had been paid in the past, and it is to meet the misgivings of these districts that we have proposed that the industrial contribution to the national union should be only 5d. per week."

expenses of Council and Committee members and delegates attending authorised meetings of the area or national organisation, legal and other charges in respect of workmen's compensation, negotiations, etc., and allowances to branches to meet authorised branch expenditure.

Further, we recommend that the collection of any contributions by the areas or branches in excess of the industrial contribution of 5d. for the purpose of meeting what might be termed benevolent benefits should remain the responsibility of the area or branch concerned. (June 1943.)

What would be the responsibilities of the District Associations or representatives under this scheme? The Executive Committee was concerned to make it clear that it would not try to deal with every question arising in Districts; it would delegate powers, "it always being understood that in the ultimate the activities of area representatives must be subject to the overriding authority of the national organisation." (June 1943.)

The two-score existing unions in the industry differed considerably in their structure and rules, procedure and customs. How were these to be brought into some conformity with one another and with the new national body? Here was a problem which offered the prospect of endless debate and jealous retention of county traditions. The Executive Committee got round this corner by the simple proposition to postpone consideration of it till after the new national body had been established and to tackle it in the succeeding twelve-month: they wrote:

It is proposed that during the first twelve months from the establishment of the new organisation, present procedure shall continue and that during that period model Rules providing for committees and representation thereon, Officials, election of representatives on committees, tenure of office, and certain other questions dealing with detailed administration of the union shall be drafted and submitted to a conference for endorsement. (June 1943.)

Lastly came the thorny question "What is to become of me?"; the question of how to square personal outlooks and prospects with the best interests of the organisation. In their books on trade union history and theory the Webbs laid particular stress on just this difficulty. They knew the traditional reluctance of trade union members ever to unseat an existing official, in their knowledge that employers fought shy of taking on an active trade union leader in the workshop, at any rate in the nineteenth century. Besides, in those days there was not even any scheme for superannuation. A similar sort of difficulty occurred again and again in this century when schemes of amalgamation were brought to the test of personal loyalties of trade unionists to their own elected officials who might be demoted in a new and enlarged trade union. This obstacle, too, was got round by the Federation Executive Committee in the following way:

We are of the opinion that no schemes could be regarded as satisfactory unless it provided that the existing full-time Officials and Staffs will be maintained.

We therefore propose that during the first twelve months from the date of the inception of the new organisation, the present rates of salaries, emoluments and allowances will be maintained and that during this period the whole question will be considered with a view to the establishment of a general scale to operate throughout the national organisation.

We are also of the opinion that having provided for an age limit in respect of Officials and Staffs there should be established a superannuation scheme covering all employees. (June 1943.)

The N.E.C. was authorised to make grants to those who were too old to be brought into superannuation schemes. To give effect to all these proposals, it was recommended finally that the existing rules of the Federation should be rescinded and a new set of rules adopted in place thereof.

It was a comprehensive and carefully worked out Report. Too many schemes for too many years past had been wrecked early or late in the course of their elaboration for the Executive Committee to be other than very careful. But just because of this they knew the shoals and the reefs: and steered their course accordingly.

3. AT THE 1943 ANNUAL CONFERENCE

On the afternoon of Wednesday, July 21, 1943, the delegates from the miners' associations began their discussion on reorganisation of the Federation and continued it all through the next day. They had before them the twenty-page section of the Annual Report of the Executive Committee containing draft rules of a proposed national union, together with the explanatory paragraphs set out above. In the first session (and for part of the second session) they listened to their General Secretary and then plied him with questions. Ebby Edwards opened by saying, very bluntly:

The Executive are very anxious that we shall have a very frank, and, I might add as equally important, an honest expression of opinion of the representatives of the districts on this matter, so that we may know whether there is a desire, even if you secure the alterations you want, to have one organisation functioning for this great industry.

He hammered this point home by adding these words:

I specially say that because on a number of occasions when this question has been up we have passed resolutions in principle, we have drafted constitutions, and immediately we got up to the exact position as to whether we will apply them, then we have had excuses; and nothing has been done. Furthermore, we have wasted a considerable amount of money and a considerable amount of time; whereas if we had been told honestly and straightforwardly at the outset that you had no intention of going in for one organisation, it would have been much better, because then we should have understood exactly what the position was, and perhaps there would have been considerably more concentration as to what we could do with the organisation as it exists. I think it was necessary to make that remark, and I make it clearly as an observation on behalf of the Executive. (July 21, 1943.)

Telling how after "a heart-to-heart talk" with the Districts and many days spent they had at last reached the draft, he made it clear that no decision was wanted "for or against at this Conference," but only an expression of opinion: after that the proposals would go to the Districts for discussion and amendment, and thereafter to a Special Conference. Edwards then went in summary fashion through the proposed new union's draft Rules, calling special attention to several novelties. First of these was a rule "to give to the centre a power to organise within breakaway districts": and the delegates who listened were well aware that this had been put in because of past experiences going right back to the early 'nineties.

On finance ("In the past we have never been much troubled with finance in this organisation, because we have never had any" was his sardonic remark) he said that in order to have a fair amount of money to start the new organisation there would be paid to it from each constituent once and for all a capitation fee of £1 a head (women and boys under 18, 10s.), apart from the regular weekly 5d.—and apart, of course, from the power to call special levies.

Another novelty was a rule fixing the age limit for officials at sixty-five and giving power to make grants. Ebby Edwards said:

I was appointed by ballot vote under conditions that there was no age limit. Then the intelligence of the Federation said: "They are not so good now when they get old; we had better fix it at 70." Peter Lee had to go. Now they say "Even at 70 they are not so good as they were, and, therefore, we had better fix it at 65."

The debate turned upon acceptance or rejection of the plan as a whole. Against it Will Arthur of South Wales, speaking for himself and not as a member of the national Executive, argued passionately. He said that the time was not opportune: they were putting the cart before the horse. Old stalwarts had argued for a national organisation based on the need for national ascertainment of the proceeds of the industry so that there could be uniformity and security. The fundamental difficulty, he said, had been "that internecine competition as between District and District, and again selfishness within Districts, has prevented national unity." But they were not discussing one mine-workers' organisation on the basis of destroying District ascertainments (which he would have supported). It would probably be argued that the next step after setting up a national organisation would be to start to destroy District ascertainments. It was not his belief: it would retard progress towards a national ascertainment.

This speech brought three powerful rejoinders from District leaders who were also members of the Executive Committee: first from Abe Moffat of Scotland, second from Sam Watson of Durham, and third from A. L. Horner of South Wales who conceded part of his fellow-Welshman's argument in order to undermine and explode it. Beginning with the appeal "I urge this conference not to throw away the breathing-space we have been given to reorganise our forces between now and the end of the war" Horner said:

> If I have a complaint against this scheme, it is because it is such an emasculated scheme. Why is it emasculated? It is emasculated because we have to take into account not only the general interests of the men, which would drive me to one all-out Mineworkers' Union involving the liquidation of the District Unions. But we have to be realists and take into account the vested interests of the Districts, and the state of the emasculated form of that scheme represents what we believe to be is the maximum of concession that we can give in order to get even this step forward in the march towards one Mineworkers' Union.

He then dealt with W. Arthur's argument about prior need for a national ascertainment, saying:

> In my opinion, a National Ascertainment will never be realised by the miners of this country so long as we remain twenty separate autonomous District Unions. It is impossible.

The question was: which should come first? He answered:

> To get one National Ascertainment we have to secure the agreement of our enemies, but to get one Mineworkers' Union we have only to get agreement amongst ourselves. Let us do what we can to establish this stage of development towards one Mineworkers' Union. (July 21, 1943.)

Twenty-five years ago he had written a pamphlet, with diagrams, for one union. He had believed he had "a nice flat floor on which to build a lovely union." Experience had taught him that it was not a flat floor: there were different District interests, conceptions and degrees of development.

> But this we are now proposing is an attempt to make a superstructure over what already exists, and we cannot do it independently of what exists.

Horner concluded by making it clear that he was speaking at "the unanimous wish of the Welsh miners, who have never on any occasion been divided on the question of the necessity to establish one Mineworkers' Union." After this and after a supporting speech by Jim Hammond of Lancashire there was no question but that the Conference were in favour of the suggested scheme. Against this tide of opinion George Spencer of Nottinghamshire forbore to put his arguments and only put in a procedural plea, in a few sentences, for a further "discussion of this great question. I disagree on fundamental principles, but I am not going to speak about that now."

The 1943 Annual Conference decided not to prolong the discussion and agreed on the scheme which would go to the Districts for amendment and then to a Special Conference. In parliamentary phrase, the Bill had gone through the Committee stage.

4.   UNAVOIDABLE POSTPONEMENTS

Well before the end of the year 1943 the Districts had discussed the draft Rules and had sent in their amendments. By mid-December the Reorganisation Sub-Committee had been instructed to submit their views on these amendments. By mid-February 1944 the sub-committee's Report was presented to the Executive Committee; this was endorsed and circulated to the Districts in preparation for a Special Conference in April. By April the situation in mining and particularly the aftermath of the Porter Award was such that all else had to give way: the Special Conference had to be postponed. On May 11th the Executive Committee decided not to lump together the postponed Special Conference and the approaching Annual Conference, in July, but to take it a month later on August 16th and the following days. But now there came a greater cause for postponement. Six months earlier at the Teheran Conference President Roosevelt, Prime Minister Churchill and Premier Stalin had set down their accord in historic words:

We have concerted our plans for the destruction of the German forces. We have reached complete agreement as to the scope and timing of the operations which will be undertaken from the east, west and south. The common understanding which we have here reached guarantees that victory will be ours.

And as to peace, we are sure that our concord will make it an enduring peace. (December 7, 1943.)

By the early summer, the Anglo-American forces were advancing in Italy, the Soviet armies had freed the soil of the U.S.S.R. of its invaders and were advancing to the Vistula, while the D-day of the Second Front in the west was daily drawing nearer. The first postponement had been on May 8th.

A month later the landing in Normandy of British and U.S. armies had begun, with increased strain on the transport services. Both from the General Council of the Trades Union Congress and from the Minister of Labour and National Service letters had been received on the curtailment of railway travel. The Government was of the opinion that no Conferences involving long-distance travel by considerable numbers of persons should be held during the next few months unless directly concerned with important and urgent business related to the war effort which could not be postponed. So on June 8th the Annual Conference, convened for July 17th, was postponed by the Executive Committee, though the Reorganisation Conference on August 16th went ahead. On the same day Minute No. 14 runs:

Reference was made to the opening of the "Second Front" and it was *agreed*:

That we congratulate all concerned in the military operations now proceeding on the Continent and on behalf of all employed in the Coal-mining Industry undertake to render the fullest and most effective assistance in this supreme effort to rid Europe of Nazism. (June 8, 1944.)

Both in the original draft as submitted to the Annual Conference of 1943 and in the same draft (with half a dozen amendments made to meet the wishes of the Registrar of Friendly Societies) as submitted by the Executive Committee in February 1944 the membership Rule had begun with the following words:

4.—(a) All members for the time being of the associated trade unions specified in the first column of the Schedule hereto shall be members of the Union. . . .

What were the associated trade unions specified in the Schedule? In the main these were the county associations built up in the latter half of the nineteenth century by and for the underground workers. It was not until nearly the end of the century that the Miners' Federation of Great

SCHEDULE

Constituent Associations	Area	1944 Membership
Bristol Miners' Association	Bristol	400
National Union of Cokemen and By-product Workers	Cokemen	3,000
Cumberland Miners' Association	Cumberland	7,500
Derbyshire Miners' Association	Derbyshire	25,000
Durham Miners' Association	Durham	106,472
Kent Mineworkers' Association	Kent	5,100
Lancashire and Cheshire Miners' Federation	Lancashire and Cheshire	40,000
Leicester Miners' Association	Leicester	4,000
Pelsall Miners' Association Cannock Chase Miners, Enginemen and Surfacemen's Association North Staffordshire Miners' Federation South Staffordshire and East Worcestershire Amalgamated Association of Miners Warwickshire Miners' Association Shropshire Miners' Federation Highley and District Miners' Association	Midlands	30,000
Northumberland Miners' Mutual Confident Association	Northumberland	28,561
North Wales and Border Counties Mineworkers' Association	North Wales	7,526
Nottinghamshire and District Miners' Federated Union	Nottingham	30,000
National Union of Scottish Mineworkers: Ayrshire Miners' Union Fife, Clackmannan and Kinross Miners' Union West Lothian Mineworkers' Union Stirlingshire Miners' County Union Lanarkshire Mine Workers' Union Mid. and East Lothian Miners' Association	Scotland	51,000
Somerset Miners' Association	Somerset	2,600
South Derbyshire Miners' Association	South Derbyshire	5,743
South Wales Miners' Federation	South Wales	100,000
Yorkshire Mine Workers' Association	Yorkshire	115,000
Durham Colliery Mechanics' Association Durham County Colliery Enginemen's, Boiler Minders' and Firemen's Association Northumberland Colliery Mechanics' Association Northumberland Colliery Winders, Enginemen and Firemen's Association Yorkshire Colliery Enginemen, Fireman and Allied Trades' Association Yorkshire Winding Enginemen's Association	Group No. 1 (Craftsmen)	15,200
Lancashire and Cheshire Colliery Tradesmen and Kindred Workers Lancashire, Cheshire and North Wales Colliery Enginemen's, Boilermen's and Brakesmen's Fedn. Derbyshire, Notts and Midland Counties Colliery Enginemen, Firemen, Motormen and Electricians' Union Scottish Colliery Enginemen, Boilermen and Tradesmen's Association	Group No. 2 (Craftsmen)	12,200
National Union of Enginemen, Firemen, Mechanics and Electrical Workers (Colliery membership) Cumberland Colliery Enginemen, Boilermen and Electrical Workers Transport and General Workers' Union (Colliery membership)	Power Group	13,561
		602,863

Britain had claimed to speak on behalf of the then almost wholly unorganised workers on the surface: thereafter, the surface workers (and in some coal-fields, such as South Wales, other grades as well) came to be organised along with those underground. Though we speak of county associations it must be borne in mind that some of the constituents of the Mineworkers' Federation were themselves described as Federations: and this not only for the obvious reason that in South Wales, as also in Lancashire and Cheshire, more than one county was covered. In both these cases the original Federation was made up of a number of local or valley associations, with an autonomy that went beyond that of a miners' lodge. The same was true, though in a lesser degree, of North Staffordshire and Shropshire. In the case of Scotland there was a Federation of the six Scottish counties: for thirty years this had gone under the title of "National Union" which only turned from an aspiration into a reality shortly after the schedule was published. Somewhat similar to Scotland, up to 1944 at any rate, was the organisation of the Midland counties in the Midland Miners' Federation.

Secondly, there were the associations of colliery mechanics and enginemen, also of similar long standing and also mainly growing up in county coal-fields in England; these were not brought into the Federation until the end of the First World War, and in representation at Conferences or on the Executive Committee were set in three groups, two under the heading of "craftsmen" (one of these sometimes called the National Federation of Enginemen), and a third called the "power group." Two of the three "power group" unions were affiliated to the Miners' Federation only on their colliery membership: and, of these two, one was the Transport and General Workers' Union, then the largest union in the United Kingdom, in whose ranks were some ten thousand of the labourers on the surface. Thirdly, there was the National Union of Cokemen and By-product Workers.

With these explanations it is possible to turn to the schedule of forty-one constituent associations, and twenty areas, to which a column has been added giving the August 1944 membership of each area.

It should be noted that the six separate Scottish county unions in this schedule, having fused into a single Scottish Union by March 1, 1944, had disappeared by the time the postponed Special Conference was held, and indeed were in process of dissolution since their amalgamation ballot of November 1943.[1]

5. THE OBJECTS OF THE UNION

By the time the delegates to the Special Conference on "The Re-organisation of the Federation" had assembled on August 16, 1944, they had possessed for nearly six months the draft Rules, the numerous amendments submitted in the latter half of 1943 by the Districts and the February 1944 memorandum of the Executive Committee on all the amendments. The memorandum examined the amendments, opposed most of them, accepted some and on a few was neutral. The most voluminous amendments came from the Yorkshire Miners' Association: with their traditions of having done so much over half a century earlier to found the Federation, they had devoted much time and study to the structure of the Federation's successor. This Yorkshire body of amendments, however, as the Executive Committee memorandum pointed out, as a whole contained a thorough-going theory of how a national trade union should be constructed. It was not consistent with the cautious step-by-step policy hitherto followed: it meant a clean break with the past: and, while some of it might be taken as a pattern for future further reorganisation of the union it was mostly rejected at this Conference. The South Wales Federation, with amendments on a more limited scale, were more successful with several of their proposals: where Durham and South Wales agreed the majority of the delegates tended to accept. Other Districts played their part on rather specialised amendments: and, as is usual in trade union Conferences, some delegates were more often vocal than others. Partly through luck and partly through good guidance this final M.F.G.B. Conference, as it turned out to be, was held in

---

[1] See *A History of the Scottish Miners* (1955), Chapter XI.

Nottingham, where there had been hitherto the most strongly expressed opposition to any such merger. (It recalled the choice of Newport, Monmouth, fifty years earlier as the scene in a neutral area for founding the Miners' Federation.) It meant that the welcome was given by the Nottinghamshire Federated Union through the voice of George Spencer, who at first as host ("We are delighted to see you all") and thereafter as delegate was seldom silent for long during the three-day Conference.

Seven objects and a score of consequential rules had sufficed for the new-born Federation in 1889. The scope of the Federation had widened with the years, but the total number of rules had altered but little. In these fifty-five years, however, not only legislation (especially the Trade Union Acts of 1906, 1913 and 1927) but a host of legal decisions had complicated the relatively simple position of trade unions as it had been left by the Acts of 1871 and 1876. Taught by this and their other experiences, the Executive Committee, on the advice of their lawyers, had enumerated in their draft no less than seventeen objects. Many additional objects were proposed in sundry amendments: most of these were opposed by the Executive Committee, through its spokesman Vice-President James Bowman, chiefly on the ground that they were not objects but matters of policy under the objects. Nevertheless, three additional objects[1] were added to the Rules by the Special Conference, as well as amendments to the objects. To the first object,

(*a*) To secure the complete organisation in the Union of all workers employed in or connected with the coal mining industry of Great Britain

there was added, by a South Wales amendment, the words

and membership of the organisation shall be a condition of employment in the industry.

A new object, proposed by the Durham Miners' Association with the support of Yorkshire and not opposed by the Executive Committee was:

(*g*) To seek the establishment of Public Ownership and Control of the mining industry.

[1] The whole of the objects are under Rule 3 in the set of Rules of the National Union of Mineworkers (with subsequent alterations) to be printed hereafter.

O   *The Miners*

Another new object combined an immediate legislative target with far-reaching social aims: it ran:

(i) To promote and secure the passing of legislation for improving the condition of the members and ensuring them a guaranteed week's wage with protective clauses for the miners even when they cease work, when cessation is due to causes beyond the immediate control of the members and to join in with other organisations for the purpose of and with the view to the complete abolition of Capitalism. (South Wales.)

It was opposed by the Executive Committee spokesman and by the Chairman who said that this was "already covered by the Durham proposition which Yorkshire have accepted."

"A. Horner: We cannot accept that nationalisation of certain industries is the abolition of capitalism."

After debate this object was carried.

The third new object: "(j) To negotiate a National Wages Agreement with the national ascertainment covering the whole of the British Coalfield," at this point was proposed by Will Arthur of South Wales, who at the Annual Conference of 1943 had been against the whole scheme because he thought a national union without a single national wages agreement would be a step backwards.

He was vigorously opposed by George Spencer, who said: "Unless you get a uniform basis of wages and a uniform percentage you could not attain the desires of my friend. I am naturally opposed to one ascertainment which means uniformity of wages."

He was also opposed by Alexander Sloan, M.P., of Scotland who said that while they too thought that wages should be on a uniform basis hoping for uniform wages, they did not agree that it should be arrived at by "the antediluvian method" of the ascertainment.

In another speech in opposition to the proposal the important question of the piece-workers was brought up by G. H. Jones of the Midlands who said the object ("to give for the work done equal pay to the worker wherever he may be and in whatever district he may be in") could not be achieved in their case:

The Government came down and said they would give a consolidated wage, and did it in a hurry, and in a hotch-potch sort of way, while we were thinking of a scientific investigation of the whole of the wages and conditions under which men are working in the various districts, with a view to uniformity throughout the British coalfield. (August 16, 1944.)

But this was not the way to achieve it, and would create discontent amongst piece-workers getting higher rates in one District than another. At this point in the Conference proceedings it looked as though Will Arthur's cherished proposal would not be accepted as a new object. But now two speeches tipped the balance of opinion. Arthur Horner asked:

How can you negotiate a National Agreement unless you know the national resources of the industry, and how are you to know them except by ascertaining them? That is the only way. Is it to be regarded in this Conference as something outrageous that we ask for a National Agreement? There is nothing in this about uniformity. (August 16, 1944.)

These remarks made the proposal seem somewhat less of an edged tool than had been feared: while Sam Watson of Durham argued in support even if the fears of earlier speakers had been justified.

I would like to support Mr. Horner on this. The outcome of the National Wages Agreement and the National Ascertainment would be to create discontent and would tend towards lessening percentages in certain districts and levelling them up in other districts. But surely if we are to have one Union, then as far as practicable and possible within the ideals in which we believe one miner in one district is entitled to the same treatment as other miners in other districts, and this resolution moved by South Wales meets the basic principle involved in the one Union, and because it will create discontent is no reason why it should be rejected by this Conference.

Indeed, it is the danger light which this Conference can see, because if the one Union is not to follow the line of National Wages Agreements and National Ascertainments, we will have one Union in name only and district organisations in practice.

The amendment to have this additional object was carried. But the debate revealed what big differences, the product of historical conditions, would have to be reconciled within the framework of the new organisation. Over twelve years later the problem of the piece-workers, though by no means so intractable, was still far from finding a generally acceptable solution.

o*

6. THE RULES: MEMBERSHIP

Rule 4, which dealt with membership (the opening sentence of clause (*a*) was quoted in the section dealing with the schedule of "the associated trade unions") had two other sub-clauses. The first, sub-clause (*b*), was to give the N.E.C. power, if an associated trade union had to be expelled, to re-admit to membership of the union all those whom they considered had opposed or were not responsible for what had led to the expulsion. The next, sub-clause (*c*), provided for the N.E.C. making regulations to enable such members as had been re-admitted in this way to appoint representatives and delegates, or vote on proxy or by ballot.

There was an amendment by the Lancashire and Cheshire Miners' Federation to "delete the whole of both clauses," and another amendment by the Yorkshire Mineworkers' Association to delete the whole rule. On this the Executive Committee had expressed themselves very strongly in their February Report "in respect of amendments to draft rules." It had been clear to them that the essence of their draft, which was to centralise industrial activities only, left wide possibilities of a breakaway, or secession. This they were as determined to prevent as was Abraham Lincoln to prevent the secession of the Southern States of the U.S.A. Hence the exceptionally firm and almost ultimatory wording of draft Rule 4: hence too the comment in this Report, which declared that in the interests of the Scheme it was essential that the:

Union shall have the fullest authority to intervene in the affairs of any area on the question of organisation. We cannot disregard the fact that an Area may at some time or the other decide to thwart a majority decision of the Union with the result that the mineworkers in that Area must subsequently disassociate themselves from the affairs of the Union.

The Executive Committee could not contemplate allowing such a position to continue indefinitely; the Union must obviously have the authority to speak on behalf of mineworkers employed in all coalfields and therefore it is proposed that in the event of such a position ever arising the Union itself could undertake the organisation of mineworkers in any Area who were prepared to accept the policy of the Union.

The Report went on to point out that if the amendments to Rule 4 were accepted it would mean that an area

failing in its obligations could simply disassociate itself from the Union and the mineworkers in that Area could not be organised by the Union and would simply, therefore, have to maintain membership with an Association not connected with the larger body.

The Executive Committee is strongly opposed to both amendments.

This argument was effective; both were withdrawn. But it should be noted that Yorkshire's motive had been, not to weaken the union towards its constituent parts, but to strengthen it by a greater degree of centralisation and a merging of the existing associations. For on the next membership Rule (No. 5) giving power to alter the schedule in the event of any amalgamation (as had taken place that spring in the case of the Scottish counties) Yorkshire had down an amendment (subsequently withdrawn) to delete all and substitute:

Membership shall consist of all persons working in or about a mine being direct members of the National Union of Mineworkers.

Vice-President James Bowman, who was now piloting the bill of Rules through the Special Conference with his usual coolness and circumspection, made the following statement:

The difficulty here is that so far as the Executive Committee is concerned in the Constitution they are presenting, they are seeking at this early stage to prevent any rupture in the formation of the National Union of Mineworkers. (August 16, 1944.)

Opposing an amendment by Yorkshire which proposed rearrangement and amalgamation of Districts, he argued:

Our position is that we leave the Areas as at present, and district associations and groups affiliated with each other. They simply remain as at present and become areas of the one National Union. Yorkshire proposes to reduce by these amalgamations, which I suggest we have no power to force on the districts at this stage.

This brought to his feet George Griffiths, M.P., of Yorkshire.

Already afflicted by the illness which ended fatally, sixteen months later, Griffiths spoke vehemently:

The Vice-President says we cannot do this and the other, but I understand you have been able to do certain things up to now. Why is it that you cannot adopt this suggestion? South Wales have been pouring some stuff out here about the wages ascertainments and a national wage. If you have a national wage, why cannot you have a national organisation? (August 16, 1944.)

He received a mild reply from Bowman who said:

We have to creep before we walk. Visualising we may have to walk some day, we have deliberately put Rule 7 in, and that gives us power to review the districts, and that review will probably take place. All we are saying is that at this stage this morning we cannot go as far as Yorkshire seeks to take us.

The amendment was lost. But the debate was now "hotting-up" and the discussion on the next amendment led to a card vote. Draft Rule 7 read as follows:

It shall be the duty of the National Executive Committee to review the organisation of the Union in the various Areas, and if they consider it advisable after discussions with the Areas concerned, the National Executive Committee may recommend to Conference that Areas adjoining one another shall be combined to form one Area. (August 16, 1944.)

Lancashire had proposed an amendment to add the words "and agreement" after "discussion." This seemed to the Executive Committee to be going too far in the opposite direction to Yorkshire's standpoint. For the Lancashire amendment would in their opinion have left them just where they had been in all the years that scheme after scheme of District amalgamation had been tried and tried in vain: for "so long as it was left optional and by agreement" no progress was made. They believed that the central union must wield some authority: if there were a decision of the union recommending amalgamation of Districts, it would be a decision by a majority of the membership. It was essential to have that kind of authority.

Finally, the amendment went to a card vote, where it was lost by a narrow margin (South Wales abstaining) of 243,000 votes for and 266,000 against. After two further other card votes had been taken, one on an amendment to have area elections by ballot vote (which was carried) and the other to make the area elections triennial instead of biennial (which was lost), the first morning's work of the Conference came to an end.

Thereafter in the next two sessions there was no prolonged debate, except on the age limit Rule where strong feelings of compassion at the plight of some of the older officials was shown: and by midday of Thursday, August 17th, they were two-thirds through their agenda. But now came the snag, the Rule on contributions: to which the whole of one session was devoted. To this we must now turn as it brings out very clearly the type of difficulty that had to be overcome in forming a single union.

7. HOW MUCH MONEY?

One pound a head capitation fee from each area, due three months after "these Rules" came into force, was the means proposed to get the new union started, after which the question of the model Rules for the areas could be examined at more leisure. It might take a few months, it might take many months: but meantime the national Rules would be in operation and the union would be a going concern. When the first amendment from South Wales was moved by W. H. Crews and seconded by W. Llewellyn that the capitation fee should not be given until after the model Rules for the areas had come into force, there was a blaze-up. The fat was in the fire. For the first time in the Conference, the Vice-President, Jim Bowman, argued with passion, as he denounced the amendment saying: Were they to assume that if the model Rules were not strictly in accordance with South Wales' views, the District would oppose payment of a capitation fee?

Are we to have the question of the capitation fee depending on whether or not the model Rules suit this Area or that Area? The payment of the capitation fee is a principle of the establishment of the one Mineworkers' Union. (August 17, 1944.)

There had to be the transference of the financial strength of the M.F.G.B. from the areas into the central fund, "in order that the new organisation can have life."

T. Oakey of Yorkshire supported the Executive but then George Spencer of Nottinghamshire jumped in on the side of South Wales with such weight of emphasis that some delegates began to think he was "rocking the boat." He said that "we shall not pay until we see the model Rules." He went on to discuss the rates of pay of officials, comparing them with those paid in Nottinghamshire where they were "higher paid than any officials in the Federation, including the Secretary of this Federation—far higher paid, and they are not going to pay a capitation fee until they are sure that their officials are protected under the model Rules."

He had enquired into the pay of trade union officials generally, and stated there was not a single union of any standing "which has paid such miserable standards of remuneration to its officials as has this Federation, including the Secretary."

This speech with its implications of possible refusal to accept majority decisions brought to their feet successively Abe Moffat of Scotland, Sam Watson of Durham and Willie Allan of Northumberland, each of whom directly or implicitly rebuked George Spencer and in persuasive speeches urged South Wales to withdraw their amendment. In response Will Arthur said that South Wales "will be one of the first to send forward the fee if the majority decide that the fee is to be paid immediately."

The South Wales amendment received the support only of Lancashire, the Midlands (with Leicester) and Nottingham and was defeated by 405 votes to 204.

The Scottish amendment (to halve the capitation fee) was the next and this was defeated. Then came the tussle over the second clause of the Rule, namely "a weekly contribution for industrial purposes of the Union of 5d. per member" with half for women and those under eighteen years and with the understanding that out of this 5d. per head there would be returned to each area 1d. to cover the costs of industrial work. The argument of the Executive Committee in its February Report was that "the areas industrially will have no financial responsibilities whatever," since their industrial expenditure would be met by the centre, while each branch of an area would retain 20 per cent of the proposed 5d. a head. Thus the areas would be responsible only for "Benevolent Benefits"; but in those areas where no such benefits or funds to maintain them existed the effect would be different. In some such areas with small obligations great reserve funds would be built up. For example, South Wales, it was argued, actually received contributions at the rate of 6d. per member per week; and, "inasmuch as the Area will have no special benefits of any kind to meet, the whole of its expenditure will be met by the Union" so that if 1½d. of every 6d. were retained a very substantial area fund would be built up. (April 18–20, 1944.)

South Wales proposed 4½d., Durham 4d., Yorkshire 1s. for all purposes: Lancashire was for 4½d. to be paid as 1s. 6d. per lunar month, with 3d. per month for sick, injured and out of work members. Northumberland was for forty-eight weeks' payment, omitting the four weeks in each year when the quarterly political fund payments were due: this was accepted by the Executive Committee. It was agreed to have all these amendments argued out in one discussion and then to vote on them separately. The South Wales amendment for 4½d. was moved by W. J. Saddler who said:

In South Wales we are not a Friendly Society. We are purely an industrial organisation, and the one penny left to us in the draft Constitution does not give us sufficient revenue to carry on the Branch work. At the moment we return to our Branches 25 per cent of the present contribution—1½d. out of 6d.—for Lodge administration. (August 17, 1944.)

Sam Watson argued that in the case of Durham, which proposed 4d., there were benefits being paid out which would be endangered by a payment to the centre of 5d. At this George Spencer rose immediately and said:

The whole proposals are a hybrid conglomeration of nonsense, with no uniformity of contributions and no uniformity of benefit. Anything short of those things is not one organisation at all.

You are leaving under the present circumstances a variety of organisations which are different in their functions, different in their intentions, different in the amounts that they are receiving, different in the amounts of benefits they are going to pay.

He was followed by L. Plover who protested that Spencer was really trying "to wreck the principle of the one Mine-workers' Union"; and while supporting the principle of the Durham amendment, he withdrew that of Lancashire.

The next was a maiden speech ("This is the first conference I have attended") by J. R. A. Machen of Yorkshire who urged one shilling as the contribution and, referring to George Spencer, said:

When I listened to that blackmailing speech—and I say this not in a laughable manner, but I say it because I feel it—I felt it was a blackmailing speech, and as I listened my mind went back seven years—(Cries of "No, no"). Well, I will leave it there. But it was quite a nice allusion; nothing to be afraid of.

He asked delegates to realise that "this grumbling about the odd farthing" degraded "this most historic moment" and concluded:

I feel that having regard to the high plane on which we have carried this Conference up to now, we should continue to face our obligations like men. If we want one organisation, let us pay for it.

H. Leese of the Midlands, pleading that they should "leave the local autonomy as it has been hitherto," supported Durham's 4d. proposal in a speech somewhat charged with emotion. This brought up George Griffiths, M.P., who with equal fervour put Yorkshire's historic standpoint as follows:

I have been bitterly disappointed during the last hour-and-a-half. The crux of the matter about this finance is that you people up to now have not had the pluck to face your men and tell them they have to pay more. The miners have had increases of wage of over 100 per cent during the last four years. That is what the Federation has done for the men. And if you cannot get an increase in contributions now, tell me when you ever will? You have got to face up to it. Fancy a paltry cheap-jack sixpenny Union with a minimum wage of £5 a week. (August 17, 1944.)

They should take advantage of the golden opportunity the present time gave them:

Go back to your districts and say, "Yes, we have decided on the one Union now for the mineworkers, and we will pay for the one Union." I beg of you to stand by the Executive on the figure of 5d. and not the Durham 4d.

The Chairman, Will Lawther, wound up the discussion, saying:

There is a tremendous lot of real shrewd commonsense in what was said by George Griffiths, because everyone here in their propaganda days lamented the fact that we had to carry that burden put upon us in the original conception of trade unions when they came across from the Friendly Societies' side, but they believed that we would ultimately reach a stage when the Friendly Society side would not be the responsibility of the trade union.

The craft unions have carried that to a greater extent than we have done, and some of them have what seem to us to be enormous contributions. (August 17, 1944.)

The first card vote was on the South Wales amendment for 4½d. instead of 5d. Durham, which with Lancashire and the Midlands—and Nottinghamshire—stood for 4d., was forced to vote for South Wales (half a loaf is better than no bread): but South Wales, having carried its amendment by the extremely narrow margin of 308,000 to 297,000, had no need to consider voting for Durham's amendment which was lost by 207,000 to 402,000. So the new national organisation was to start with a weekly contribution of 4½d.: but, as events turned out this was to prove insufficient, and twelve years later the contributions had been raised, in three stages, to 7½d. a head. The contribution of 4½d. a week compared with a minimum wage of £5 a week underground as settled in January 1944 by the Porter awards amounted to a little over a third of one per cent.; but the notion of the union contribution becoming a regular percentage of wage-rates, as was common enough in some continental countries, seems never to have become an effective proposal in any British miner's organisation.

When all the other amendments had been dealt with, when all the draft rules up to the thirty-year-old provision for a two-thirds majority in a ballot vote for a national strike and the brand-new provision for a four-fifths majority of the members in a ballot vote for dissolution of the union had been passed, the Chairman proposed three Executive Committee resolutions, which put the change in the desirable legal form.

(1) That the name of the trade union heretofore known as THE MINEWORKERS' FEDERATION OF GREAT BRITAIN be changed to THE NATIONAL UNION OF MINEWORKERS.

O**

(2) That the existing Rules be and they are hereby rescinded and that the Rules in the form submitted to this Special Conference and signed for the purposes of identification by the President be and they are hereby adopted as the Rules of the Union in substitution therefor.

(3) That any seven members of the National Executive Committee be and they are hereby authorised to make application to the Registrar of Friendly Societies for the Union to be registered under the Trade Union Acts, 1871 to 1927. (August 18, 1944.)

These three resolutions, seconded by A. Horner on behalf of South Wales, were carried. The old organisation was ending, giving place to the organisation of the future. It was a tribute to the present and an augury of the future that the delegates dispersed after carrying with acclamation the following resolution:

This Conference of Miners' representatives, meeting in Nottingham, applauds the gallant and successful efforts of the Allied armed forces on land, sea and in the air, and assures them of the fullest possible support with a view to bringing the struggle against Fascism to a successful conclusion. (August 18, 1944.)

The struggle was not to be over as soon as they hoped—nor as soon as hoped for by Field-Marshal Sir Alan Brooke (who was certain that August that the Germans would not last another winter): and, after many casualties by land and sea and air, it was another August before the war came to "a successful conclusion."

8. THE BALLOT VOTE

A month after the Special Conference arrangements were well in hand for the ballot of the membership which would be necessary to endorse the Nottingham Conference vote. Copies of the Rules as adopted by the Special Conference had been circulated to the Districts: the Ballot Paper, drafted after consultation with the Federation solicitors, had been printed; posters urging the membership to endorse the Special Conference decisions were available for distribution throughout the Districts; and two documents—one a statement on behalf of the Executive Committee (which was carrying on until everything was through) to be issued to

District and branch officials and Committees, and the other a leaflet giving a summary of the new Rules for the use of the membership—were now submitted to the Committee for its approval. These last were endorsed on September 15th. The M.F.G.B. Executive Committee, having been "blasted out" of their old premises in Russell Square by a V1 bomb, had to meet at Barnsley (while subsequent meetings that year were held at Blackpool, Derby and Newcastle upon Tyne), and there they also agreed (i) That the ballot take place from Monday, October 23, to Saturday, October 28, 1944, (ii) That half as well as full members should participate therein, (iii) That ballot papers be counted in the Districts in accordance with normal procedure, but "the result of the ballot within a given area be not publicly declared but returned to the Federation Office by not later than November 1, 1944." (September 15, 1944.)

From the Executive Committee statement, sent out by Ebby Edwards from 8, Selwyn Gardens, Cambridge (whither the intensive bombing of London in Autumn 1944 had compelled the removal of the union offices), on September 15, 1944, it is clear that anxiety was felt about the possible outcome of the ballot vote: there was much argument in it and rebuttal of possible objections or misconception. This anxiety grew greater when at their mid-October meeting the Executive Committee learned about what had happened in Nottinghamshire and in Yorkshire, the two counties which had in some respects been at opposite poles in the arguments for a single national union but in each of which there had cropped up difficulties about the carrying out of the agreed decisions. The Committee were relieved to think that meetings and discussions would smooth over various mis-apprehensions that had arisen.

In the midst of all these anxieties the ballot took place as arranged. However, all's well that ends well. And no doubt the pessimists were agreeably surprised at the result. When the Executive Committee met on November 16th, the Secretary reported on the result of the voting of the different Districts. The aggregate voting was 430,630 against 39,666, a majority of 390,964 in favour of endorsing the decisions of the Conference.

It was a ten to one majority. Moreover the members of every District Association had overwhelmingly decided to support the proposed change. And so it was immediately agreed that the National Union of Mineworkers, a new powerful form of miners' organisation, would have the day of its birth on January 1, 1945. The last day of the old year was the last of the fifty-five-year-old Mineworkers' Federation of Great Britain. It had deserved well not only of the miners but of the nation and leaves a proud record in history. Great changes were still to come to the coal-mining industry and to the life of the miners. But the new generation as a whole were never to undergo such sudden reversals of fortune as befell their fathers in the years between the wars. A man who in January to March 1921 was earning an average of a pound a shift was down by October of that year to nearly half that income and by the next January to less than half. Ten years later when this volume begins in January 1931, the memory of what had been made it all the worse, as Chaucer wrote a good five hundred years before their time:

> For of fortunes sharp adversité
> The worste kinde of infortune is this,
> A man to have ben in prosperité
> And it remembren, whan it passed is.

Again, what a reversal of fortune it was for the workers who had come thronging into the pits that out of 1,044,830 insured coal-miners in August 1932 there was no work for a man-power of 435,000. Nor enough work for long thereafter until the whirligig of war-time brought in his revenges and there was not enough man-power for the work. Small wonder then that a last act of the old Federation was to bequeath to its successor a new object that went beyond nationalisation and sought for a new social order where its members would no longer be the sport of this outrageous fortune.

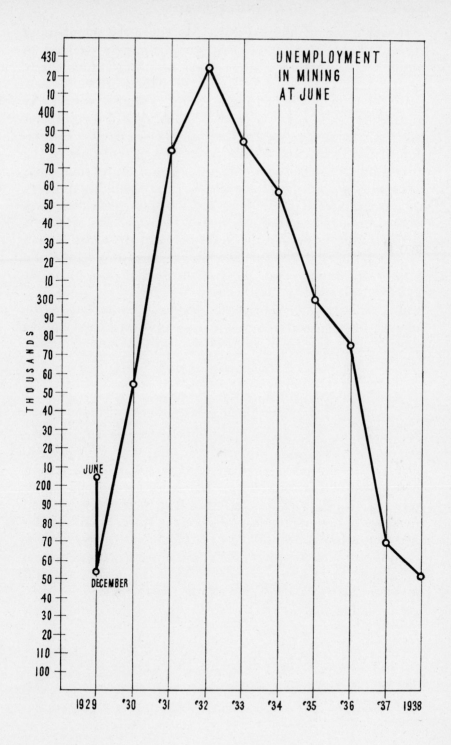

GENERAL APPENDICES

(i) NOTE ON "ABSENTEEISM"

The question of "absenteeism," the figures assembled under this heading and controversy aroused in Parliament and the press were often based on misconceptions of the nature of the industry as well as of the more important causes of the coal crisis. It should therefore be noted that these figures of non-attendance were not supplied in the same way from any other industry or occupation.[1] Yet coal-mining was never carried on with a regularity comparable to engineering or textiles and this for a variety of reasons. Examples may be seen from the table given below.

AVERAGE NUMBER OF DAYS WORKED AND LOST AT COAL-MINES IN EACH QUARTER.

Quarter ended	No. of Days on which the Pits Wound Coal	Number of Coal-winding Days Lost through						Total No. of Coal-Winding Days ‡
		Holidays	Disputes	Want of Trade *	Accidents to Men and Machinery	Other Causes †	Total No. Lost	
				Mine	Days			
1932								
March	59·92	2·61	0·01	12·23	0·27	0·05	15·17	75·09
June	55·63	2·18	0·06	16·92	0·23	0·12	19·51	75·14
Sept.	51·32	2·78	0·07	20·77	0·22	0·01	23·85	75·17
Dec.	59·76	1·67	0·23	13·22	0·27	0·08	15·47	75·23
1938								
March	69·97	0·25	0·30	3·73	0·39	0·46	5·13	75·10
June	58·94	4·22	0·40	10·73	0·35	0·30	16·00	74·94
Sept.	57·63	4·72	0·20	11·80	0·43	0·19	17·34	74·97
Dec.	63·78	1·79	0·14	8·35	0·42	0·58	11·28	75·06

* Time lost through transport difficulties, largely the effect of bad trade, was included prior to 1932.

† Including time lost through pit meetings, weather, etc., and transport difficulties since 1932.

‡ The time accounted for represents the total possible working time, amounting on the average to 5¾ to 5⅘ days per week throughout the year. The remaining ¼ day (⅕ day from 1927) is accounted for by ordinary stop or idle days, including the Saturday afternoon shift. It is not necessarily implied that all the persons employed worked every day the mines were open.

Tables similar to this were not published for the war years: but it is known that transport difficulties, included before 1932 under "want of trade" and after 1932 under "other causes," were greatly

[1] Not even for attendance or non-attendance at the sessions of Parliament by the paid representatives of the people—as was more than once mentioned in House of Commons debates.

accentuated, so that for the export fields conditions became more than irregular and were sometimes described as chaotic.

When the figures in question began to be much used, the category "absenteeism" was found to include sickness and accident: and though divided into "avoidable" and "unavoidable," the assumed loss in production was usually related to the total undivided figure. Moreover, it is clear that a subjective factor, of considerable variability, was bound to enter into the reckoning of what was "avoidable" or "unavoidable."

As the Minister made clear in the Commons debate of June 23, 1943, more shifts were then being worked than before the war. The effective, though not the statutory, working week was lengthened: so that the miners were working harder than in any year before the war, with consequent greater (and cumulative) fatigue from their arduous labour. There were more and more shifts offered and accepted: but the tendency to raise the number to the maximum soon entered into a vicious circle. To cope with lessened output from all causes, including "absenteeism," the number of shifts were increased to a point where more absenteeism was bound to result: until it was realised that the aim should be not the maximum but the optimum number of shifts. Yet "absenteeism," blamed upon a small minority and much publicised, was never of the importance ascribed to it. The causes of fall in output lay much deeper. The loss of skilled man-power, especially of workers at the face, was a chief factor throughout. The fall in the output per man-shift in the later years of the war had a variety of causes, including the rise in the rate of accidents and, above all, the general conditions of the industry and of the miner's life as dealt with in Chapters VII to IX.

There is a certain degree of fallacy in all figures of "tonnage lost." Statistics of production may contain errors in their account of what did happen, but statistics of "non-production" are hypothetical, they are exercises of the imagination, as no one can tell what would have happened—except on paper. Little regard was paid to these considerations in the war-time controversies and for a while "absenteeism" became a kind of "social myth" that opened out an escape from reality.

(ii) TABLE OF MEMBERSHIP

From the General Fund Table showing the number of members returned to the Federation for each quarter of the year upon whom 1½d. per member was paid: with average number of wage-earners from Ministry of Fuel and Power Statistical Digest.

Year	Average No. of Wage-earners (in thousands)	M.F.G.B. Membership (end of year)	
1930	917	529,958	
1931	850	526,502	(1)
1932	803	498,487	
1933	772	496,799	(2)
1934	774	499,269	(3)
1935	759	501,711	
1936	756	531,059	(4)
1937	778	546,240	
1938	782	587,125	(5)
1939	766	588,321	(6)
1940	749	588,402	(7)
1941	698	581,496	(8)
1942	709	599,141	(9)
1943	708	n.a.	(10)
1944	710	602,331	(11)

N.B.—No percentage rate of trade unionism can be shown, as many thousand wage-earners were in unions other than those comprising the Miners' Federation.

NOTES:
  (1) South Derbyshire and Power Group outstanding, July/September Quarter figures taken.
  (2) South Derbyshire, July/September Quarter. Midlands, April/June Quarter figures.
  (3) Midlands, April/June. Somerset, July/September figures.
  (4) Forest of Dean, July/September Quarter figures.
  (5) Kent ditto.
  (6) Kent ditto.
  (7) Kent and Forest of Dean ditto.
  (8) Cumberland, Kent and Leicestershire ditto.
  (9) Bristol, Cumberland, Derbyshire, Kent, Midlands, North Wales and Somerset ditto.
 (10) No figures available.
 (11) Kent, January/March, Midlands and Somerset, July/September figures.

From 1930–1937 inclusive Cokemen are outstanding and not included.
From 1938 onwards the Cokemen are included in the figures.

(iii) MINERS' FEDERATION[1] OF GREAT BRITAIN EXECUTIVE COMMITTEE[2]
1931–1944

OFFICIALS

President:	TOM RICHARDS 1931
	EBBY EDWARDS, M.P. 1931
	PETER LEE 1932–1933
	JOSEPH JONES 1934–1938
	WILL LAWTHER 1939–1944
Vice-President:	EBBY EDWARDS, M.P. 1931
	PETER LEE 1931
	JOSEPH JONES 1932–1933
	WILL LAWTHER 1934–1938
	J. BOWMAN 1939–1944
Secretary:	A. J. COOK 1931
	EBBY EDWARDS 1932–1944

MEMBERS OF THE EXECUTIVE COMMITTEE
(in the order of their first election and arranged according to counties and groups[3])

LANCASHIRE

H. Twist	1931	T. J. Brown	1937
G. Rowson	1932	S. Blackledge	1938, 1941
H. Smith	1933	B. Ball	1938
W. Foster	1934, 1939	J. E. Hughes	1939
H. Howarth	1935	W. Nicholson	1940
J. McGurk	1936, 1940, 1943	P. Potts	1942
		W. Cross	1944

YORKSHIRE

J. Jones	1931	W. E. Jones	1938–1942
J. A. Hall	1931–1944	G. H. Farrow	1939–1941
E. Dunn	1931–1935	T. W. Illsley	1942–1943
H. Smith	1934–1937	E. Hough	1943–1944
F. Collindridge	1936–1937	J. R. A. Machen	1944
A. Smith	1938		

[1] Mineworkers' Federation of Great Britain after 1933.

[2] On some occasions there are additional E.C. members for certain Districts who were not elected at the Annual Conference.

[3] Due to variations in composition of groups, a few names appear under different headings at different times.

MIDLAND FEDERATION

H. Whitehouse	..	1931	W. Johnson ..	1934, 1938
J. Blakemore	..	1932, 1939	W. Bagnall.. ..	1935
H. Leese	.. ..	1933, 1937, 1940	A. Hoggins.. ..	1936
			G. H. Jones ..	1941–1944

SCOTLAND

J. Barbour ..	..	1931, 1941	J. Armstrong ..	1939
A. Clarke ..	..	1932, 1936, 1939	W. Pearson.. ..	1940
			J. Potter	1940
W. Adamson	..	1933	J. McKendrick ..	1941
J. Hunter ..	..	1934	J. Colthart	1942
J. Brown ..	..	1935	J. Rutherford ..	1943
J. Cook ..	..	1937, 1942	P. Henderson ..	1943
A. Sloan ..	..	1938	A. Moffat	1944
W. B. Small	..	1938	A. Cameron ..	1944

SOUTH WALES

T. Richards	..	1931	N. Edwards ..	1938–1939
S. O. Davies	..	1931–1933	E. Williams ..	1942
O. Harris ..	..	1932–1940	W. Arthur	1943–1944
J. Griffiths ..	..	1934–1935	W. J. Saddler ..	1940–1944
A. L. Horner	..	1936–1944		

NORTHUMBERLAND

J. Carr	.. ..	1932–1934	W. Golightly ..	1939–1940
J. Bowman ..	..	1935–1938	H. McKay	1941–1944

DURHAM

T. Trotter ..	..	1931	W. Pearson.. ..	1935–1938
J. Gilliland..	..	1931–1934, 1936, 1939	J. Kelly	1937, 1939, 1942
J. E. Swan ..	..	1932–1933	G. Harvey	1938
P. Lee.. ..	..	1934	J. D. Murray ..	1936, 1940[1]
E. Moore ..	..	1935, 1938, 1940–1944	J. Pearson	1941
			J. Carruthers ..	1943
S. Watson ..	..	1935–1937, 1939–1944	W. Todd	1944

[1] Present at E.C. meeting August 27, 1936, but not elected at Annual Conference. His name has been included, however, as it is given at end of Annual Report 1936–1937 in list of E.C. members.

NOTTINGHAMSHIRE

V. Coleman	..	1938	H. W. Booth	..	1941
H. Cooper ..	..	1939, 1943	G. A. Spencer	..	1942
W. Bayliss ..	..	1940, 1944			

DERBYSHIRE

| H. Hicken .. | .. | 1931–1941 | J. Kitts | .. .. | 1944 |
| J. Lynch | .. .. | 1942–1943 | | | |

CUMBERLAND

T. Cape, M.P. ..   1938, 1940   T. Stephenson ..   1939, 1941–
1944

NORTH WALES

E. Jones   1938–1944

KENT

J. Elks..   1938–1940

NATIONAL FEDERATION OF COLLIERY ENGINEMEN AND BOILERMEN

R. Shirkie 1942   W. Williams .. 1943–1944

POWER GROUP

S. Hall   1931–1937   I. J. Hayward ..   1938–1941,
1943–1944

GROUP NO. 1

W. S. Hall ..	..	1931, 1935, 1939, 1942–1944	J. H. Harrison	..	1933, 1937, 1941
			G. Peart	.. ..	1934, 1938
J. M. Gillians	..	1932	W. D. Lockey	..	1936, 1940

GROUP NO. 2

F. Swift	.. ..	1931, 1935	W. Rowell ..	..	1938, 1940, 1943
J. Williams..	..	1932, 1936			
C. Gill..	.. ..	1933, 1937, 1942	H. Buck	.. ..	1939, 1941, 1944
J. Elks..	.. ..	1934			

GROUP NO. 3

T. Gowdridge	..	1931	F. Swift	1938, 1941
J. R. Barker	..	1932, 1934, 1936	C. Thompson ..	1939, 1943
			J. Williams.. ..	1940
T. Jones	.. ..	1933	J. Elks..	1942, 1944
E. Jones	.. ..	1935, 1937		

GROUP NO. 4

H. Hughes ..	..	1931	T. Gowdridge ..	1935
V. Coleman	..	1932	Wm. Bayliss ..	1937
H. Buck	.. ..	1933, 1936[1]	G. Spencer.. ..	1937[2]
H. W. Booth	..	1934		

GROUP NO. 5

H. Buck 1931

[1] Although H. W. Booth was elected, H. Buck attended E.C. as representative for Group No. 4. H. Buck is therefore given as representative, and not H. W. Booth.

[2] W. Bayliss elected, but G. Spencer also present at September 23rd E.C. meeting. His name is therefore also included.

BIBLIOGRAPHY

SOURCES

The main sources are the printed proceedings of the miners' trade unions and federations of unions together with the proceedings of Parliament and the Reports of the Trades Union Congress. To these should be added the records of the Labour Research Department, the smaller pamphlets of which contain information not readily available elsewhere. Occasional use has been made of N.U.M. office files.

There are book lists in Volumes I and II of this history, and for wider reference use has always to be made of the bibliographies to the works on trade union history and theory by Beatrice and Sidney Webb, and later by G. D. H. Cole. Below is added a further short list of books consulted.

LIST OF BOOKS

ATTLEE, C. R., *The Labour Party in Perspective*, Gollancz, 1937.
BASSETT, R., *1931 Political Crisis*, Macmillan, 1958.
BRADY, R. A., *Crisis in Britain*. Cambridge University Press, 1950.
COLE, G. D. H., *The People's Front*, Gollancz, 1937.
COURT, W. H. B., *Coal*. H.M.S.O. and Longmans, 1951.
DALTON, H., *The Fateful Years*, Frederick Muller, 1957.
GOLLAN, John, *Youth in British Industry*, Gollancz, 1937.
HANNINGTON, Wal, *Ten Lean Years*, Gollancz, 1940.
HEINEMANN, Margot, *Britain's Coal*, Gollancz, 1944.
HORNER, A. L., *Incorrigible Rebel*, MacGibbon & Kee, 1960.
JONES, Joseph, C.B.E., J.P., *The Coal Scuttle*, Faber & Faber, 1936.
LABOUR RESEARCH DEPARTMENT PUBLICATIONS
   The National Wages Board—And After, 1933.
   South Wales, 1934.
   Coal Combines in Yorkshire, 1935.
   Who's Who in Anthracite? 1935.
   Coal Combines in Northumberland, 1937.
   Coal Combines in Lancashire and Cheshire, 1938.
   Coal Combines in Durham, 1939.
   Pageant of South Wales, 1939.
   The Factory Acts in Danger, 1940.
   The Keynes Plan, 1940.
   Wartime Profits, 1940.
   Workmen's Compensation, by W. H. Thompson, 1940.
   Workmen's Compensation Up to Date, 1944.
   Canteens in Industry, 1941.

LABOUR RESEARCH DEPARTMENT PUBLICATIONS—*continued*

Essential Work Orders, 1941.
E.W.O. Questions and Answers, 1944.
The Threat to Wages, 1941.
What's Holding up Production? 1941.
Health of the War Worker, 1942.
Income Tax and the War Worker, 1942.
Wages in 1942, 1942.
Coal in 1943: Practical Problems, 1943.
Industrial Assurance, 1943.
New Weapons Against T.B., 1943.
The Beveridge Report: What it Means, 1943.
Accidents at Work, 1944.
National Health Service, 1944.
Reinstatement and Disablement, 1944.
Social Insurance, 1944.
Wages During the War, 1944.

LEE, W. A., *Thirty Years in Coal 1917–47,* Mining Association of Great Britain, 1954.

MERRETT, H. H., *I Fight for Coal,* Spottiswoode, Ballantyne & Co., 1932.

ROTHSTEIN, A. F., *The Munich Conspiracy,* Lawrence & Wishart, 1958.

SCHUMAN, Frederick L., *Night Over Europe,* Robert Hale, 1941.

SHINWELL, Emanuel, *Conflict Without Malice,* Odhams, 1955.

WEBB, Beatrice, *Diaries 1924–32,* ed. Margaret Cole, Longmans, Green, 1956.

WHITELOCK, G. C. H., *250 Years in Coal.*

WILLIAMS, W. H. (Ed.), *The Miner's Two Bob,* Martin Lawrence, 1936.

WILSON, Harold, *New Deal for Coal,* Contact, 1945.

GOVERNMENT PUBLICATIONS

Committee on National Expenditure Report, 1931, Cmd. 3920.

Reports on the Causes of and Circumstances attending the Explosion which occurred at Gresford Colliery, Denbigh, on September 22, 1934, Cmd. 5358. January 1937.

Royal Commission on Safety in Coal Mines Report, Cmd. 5890. 1938.

Coal (White Paper), Cmd. 6364. 1942.

Ministry of Fuel and Power Statistical Digest, 1944, Cmd. 6639.

Coal Mining: Report of the Technical Advisory Committee (The Reid Report), March 1945. Cmd. 6610.

INDEX OF NAMES

GENERAL INDEX

GEORGE ALLEN & UNWIN LTD

London: 40 Museum Street, W.C.1

Auckland: 24 Wyndham Street
Sydney, N.S.W.: Bradbury House, 55 York Street
Cape Town: 109 Long Street
Bombay: 15 Graham Road, Ballard Estate, Bombay 1
Calcutta: 17 Chittaranjan Avenue, Calcutta 13
New Delhi: 13–14 Ajmeri Gate Extension, New Delhi 1
Karachi: Karachi Chambers, McLeod Road
Mexico: Villalongin 32–10, Piso, Mexico 5, D.F.
Toronto: 91 Wellington Street West
São Paulo: Avenida 9 de Julho 1138-Ap. 51
Buenos Aires: Escritorio 454–459, Florida 165
Singapore: 36c Princep Street, Singapore 7
Hong Kong: 1/12 Mirador Mansions, Kowloon